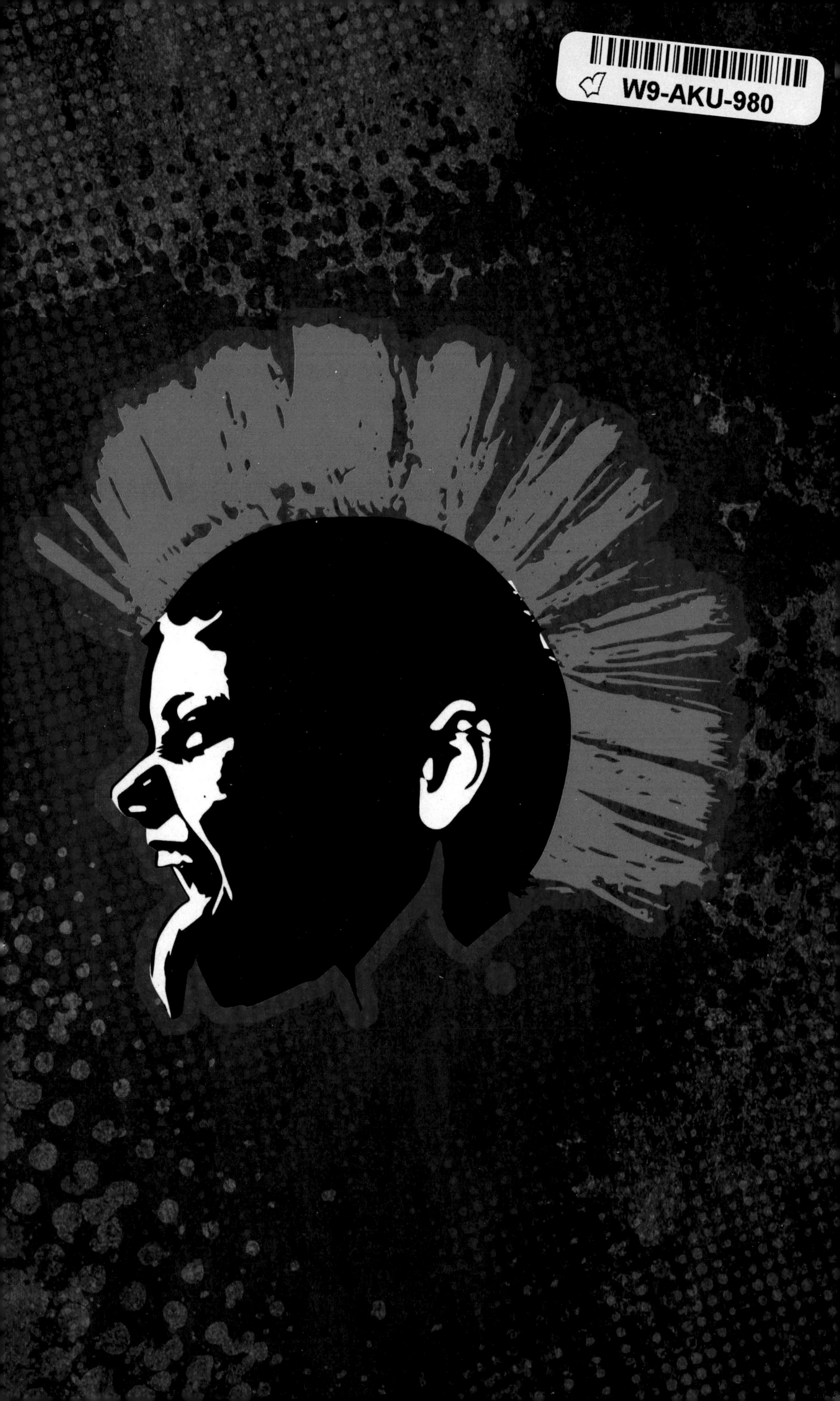

PUNK MAMBO™

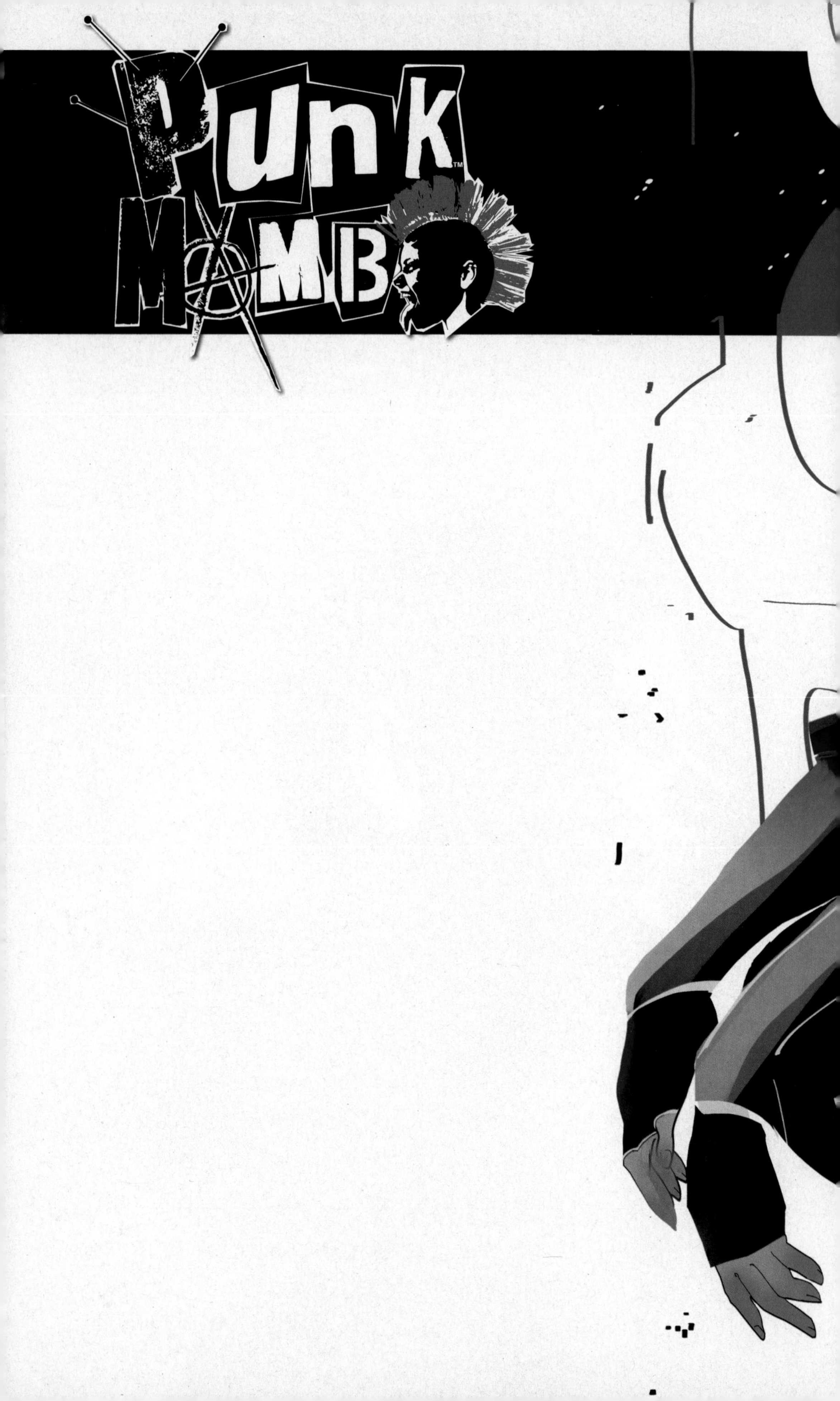

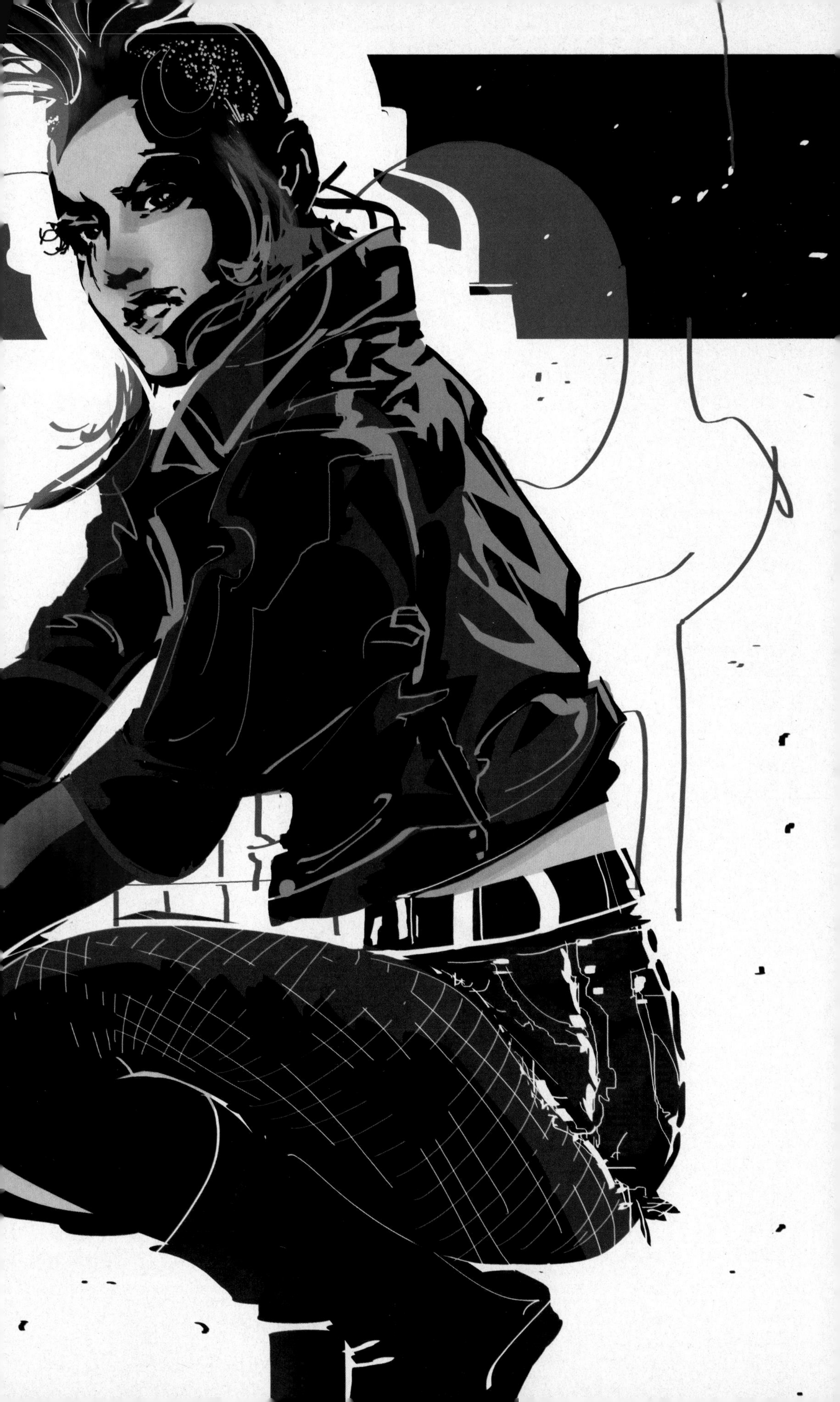

PUNK MAMBO™

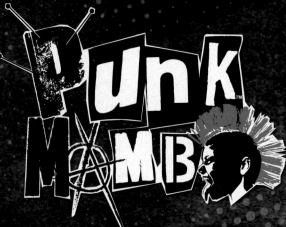

WRITERS
CULLEN BUNN
PETER MILLIGAN

ARTISTS
ADAM GORHAM
ROBERT GILL

COLORISTS
JOSÉ VILLARRUBIA

LETTERERS
DAVE SHARPE
DAVE LANPHEAR

COVERS BY
DAN BRERETON
RUSSELL DAUTERMAN
MATTHEW WILSON

ASSOCIATE EDITOR
DAVID MENCHEL

EDITORS
LYSA HAWKINS
ALEJANDRO ARBONA

GALLERY
DAN BRERETON
CRIS DELARA
ROBERTO DE LA TORRE
MICHAEL GARLAND
ADAM GORHAM
TRAV HART
RIAN HUGHES
JESSE KEEN
DAVID MACK
ZU ORZU
NINA OSEGUEDA
JOSH SCHWARTZ

COLLECTION COVER ART
DAN BRERETON

COLLECTION BACK COVER ART:
ADAM GORHAM WITH MICHAEL GARLAND

COLLECTION FRONT ART:
CRIS DELARA

COLLECTION EDITOR
IVAN COHEN

COLLECTION DESIGNER
STEVE BLACKWELL

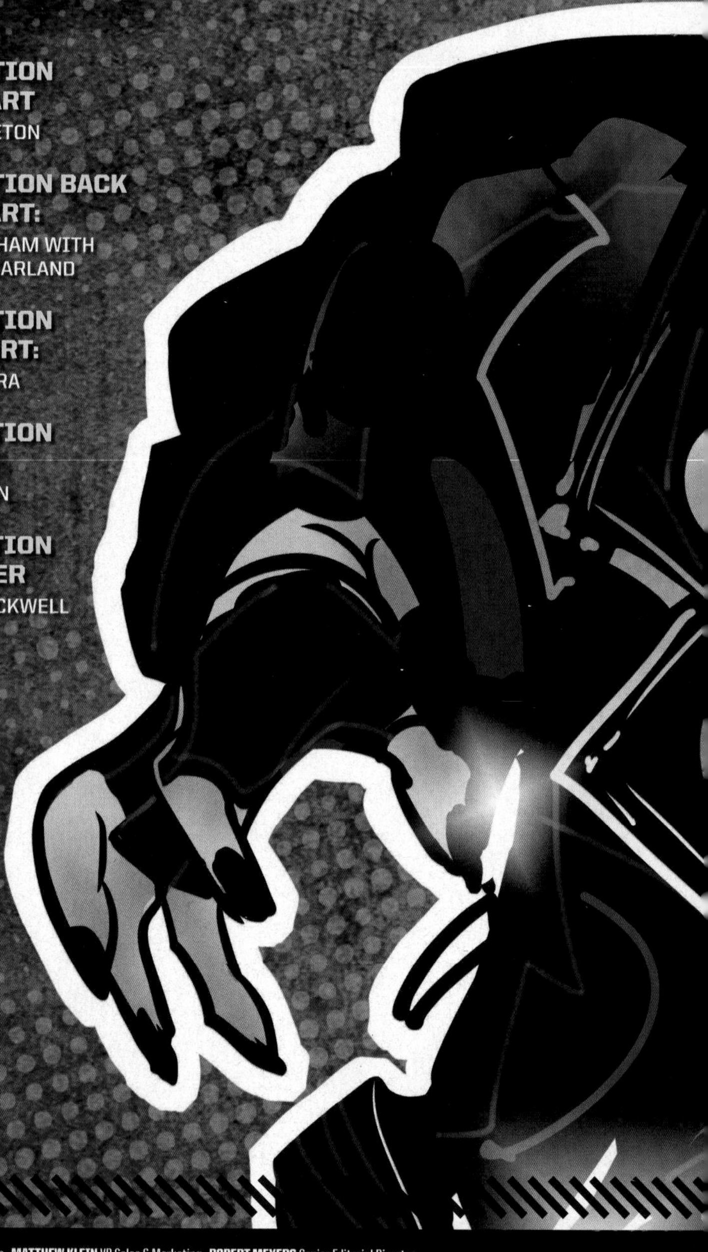

VALIANT

DAN MINTZ Chairman **FRED PIERCE** Publisher **WALTER BLACK** VP Operations **MATTHEW KLEIN** VP Sales & Marketing **ROBERT MEYERS** Senior Editorial Director
TRAVIS ESCARFULLERY Director of Design & Production **PETER STERN** Director of International Publishing & Merchandising **LYSA HAWKINS, HEATHER ANTOS & GREG TUMBARELLO** Editors
DAVID MENCHEL Associate Editor **DREW BAUMGARTNER** Assistant Editor **JEFF WALKER** Production & Design Manager **JULIA WALCHUK** Sales & Live Events Manager
EMILY HECHT Digital Marketing Manager **CONNOR HILL** Sales Operations Coordinator **DANIELLE WARD** Sales Manager **GREGG KATZMAN** Marketing Coordinator

RUSS BROWN President, Consumer Products, Promotions & Ad Sales **OLIVER TAYLOR** International Licensing Coordinator

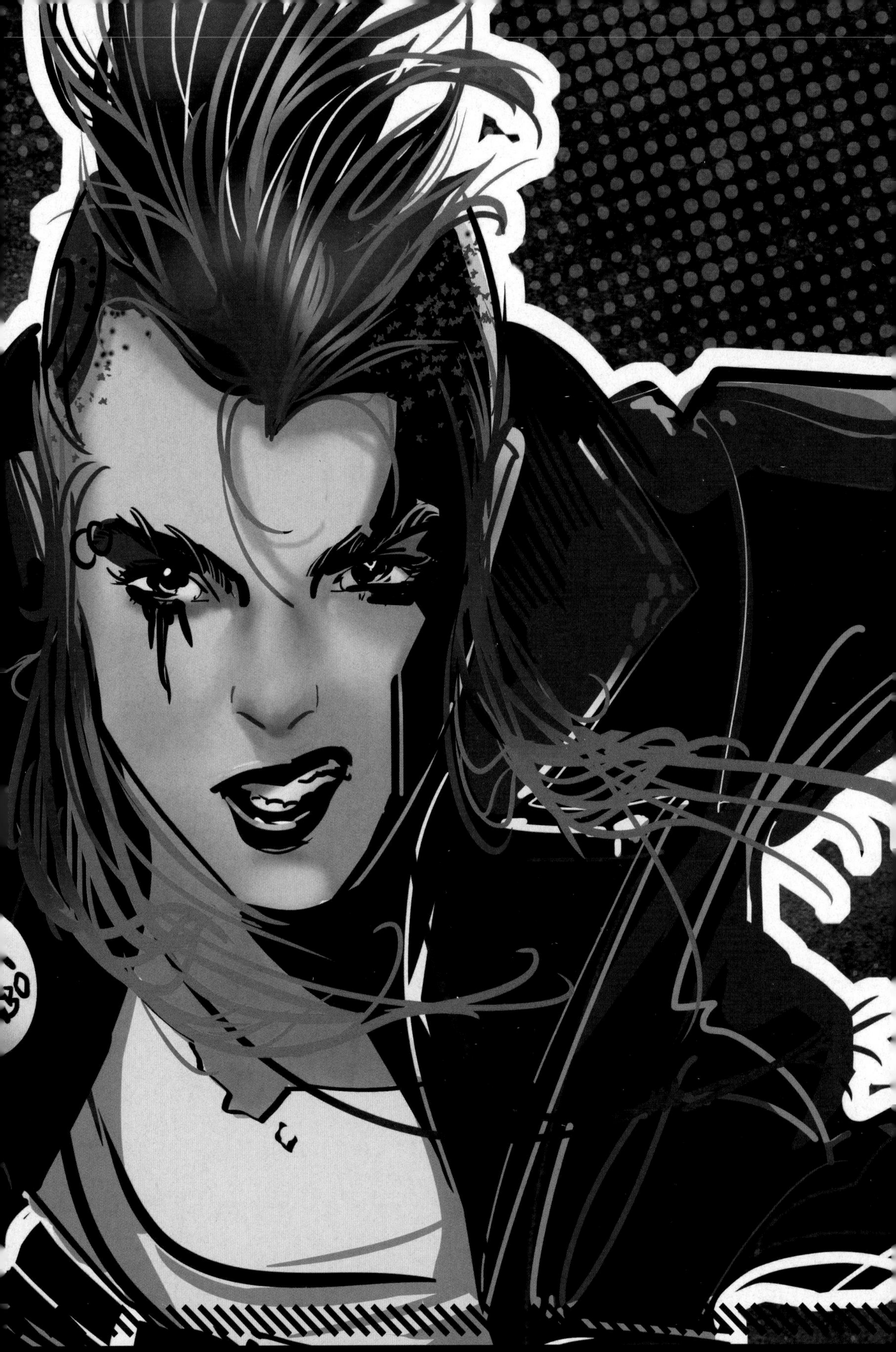
30

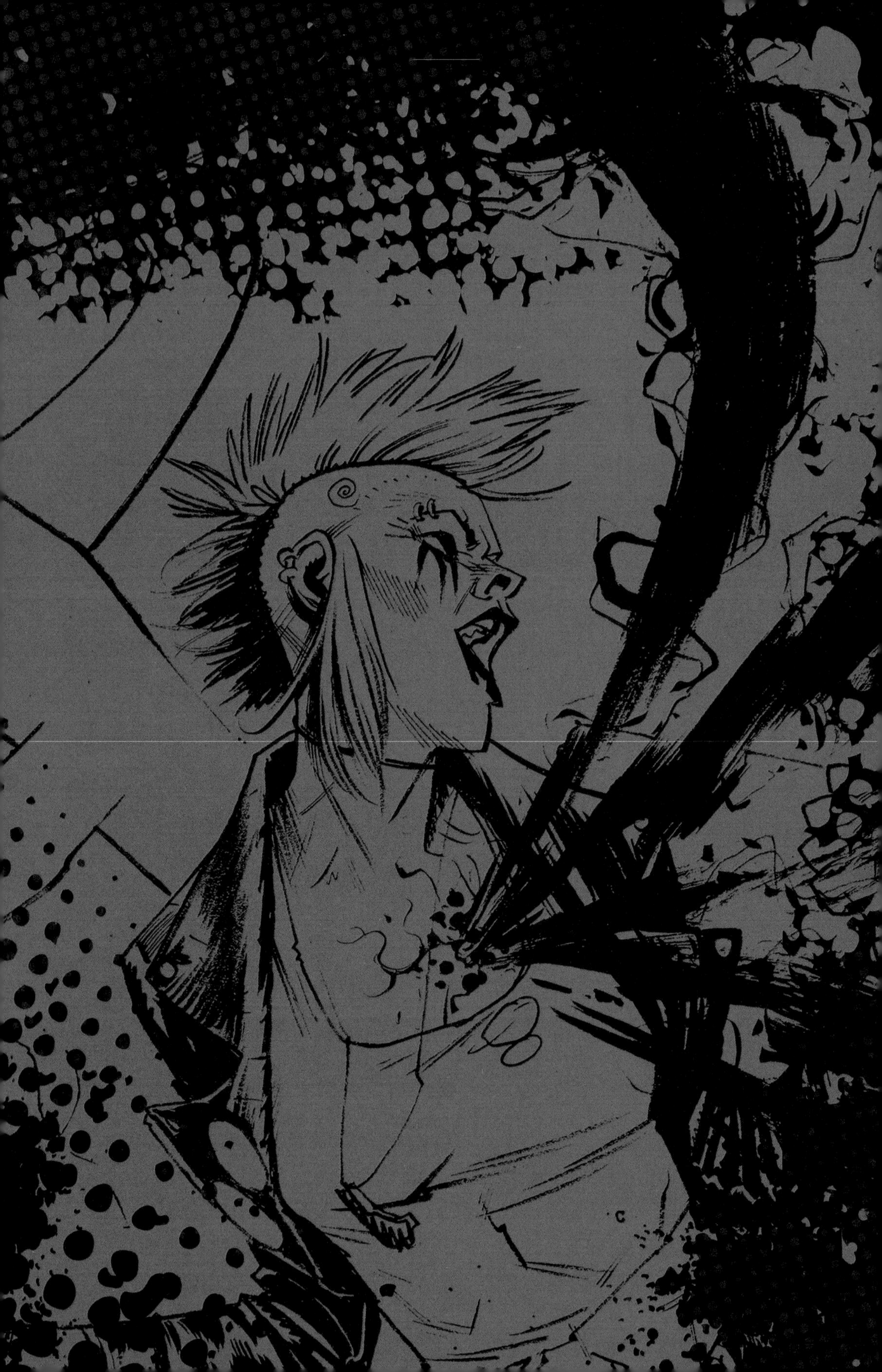

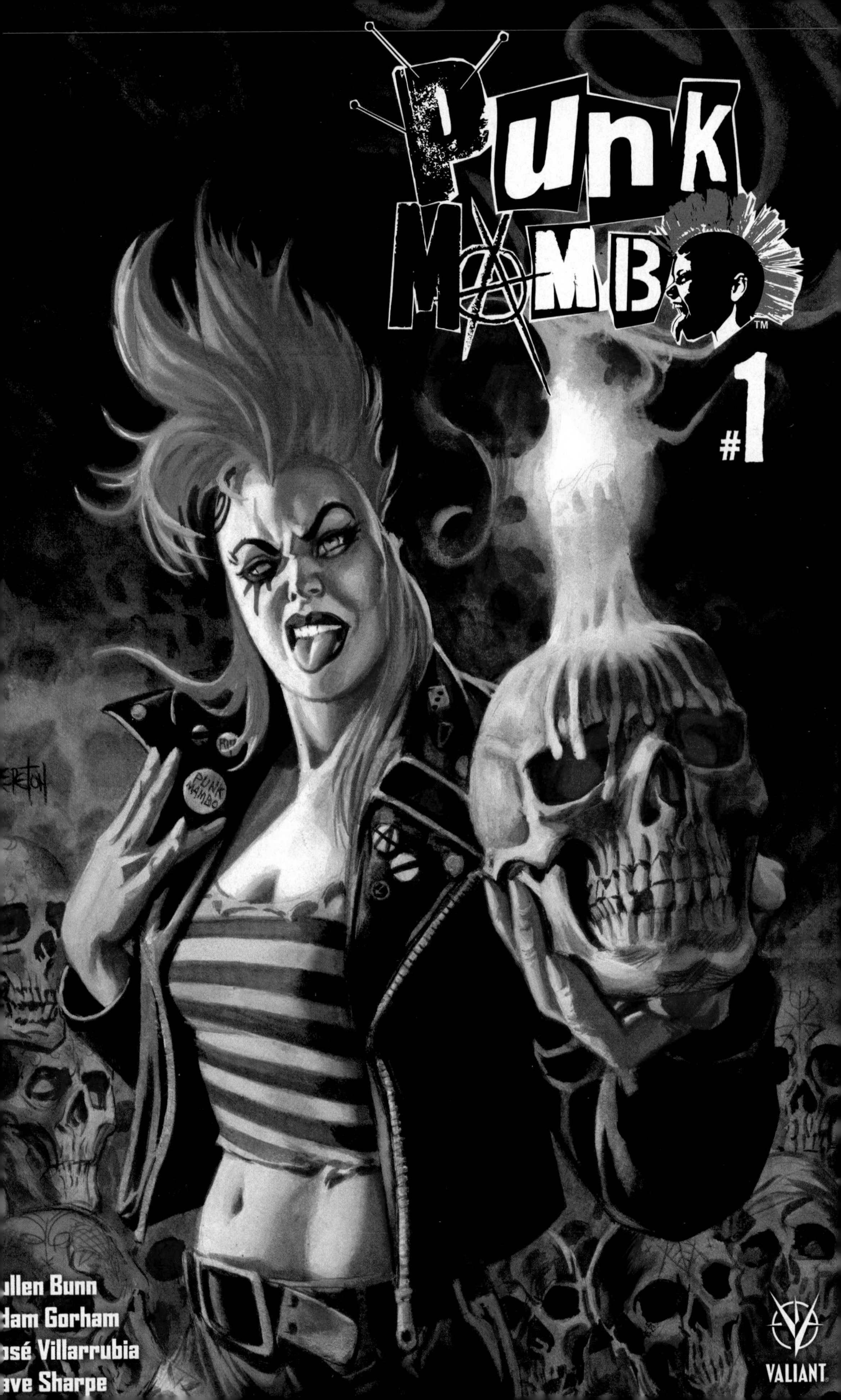
PUNK MAMBO
™
#1
PUNK MAMBO
ullen Bunn
dam Gorham
osé Villarrubia
ave Sharpe
VALIANT

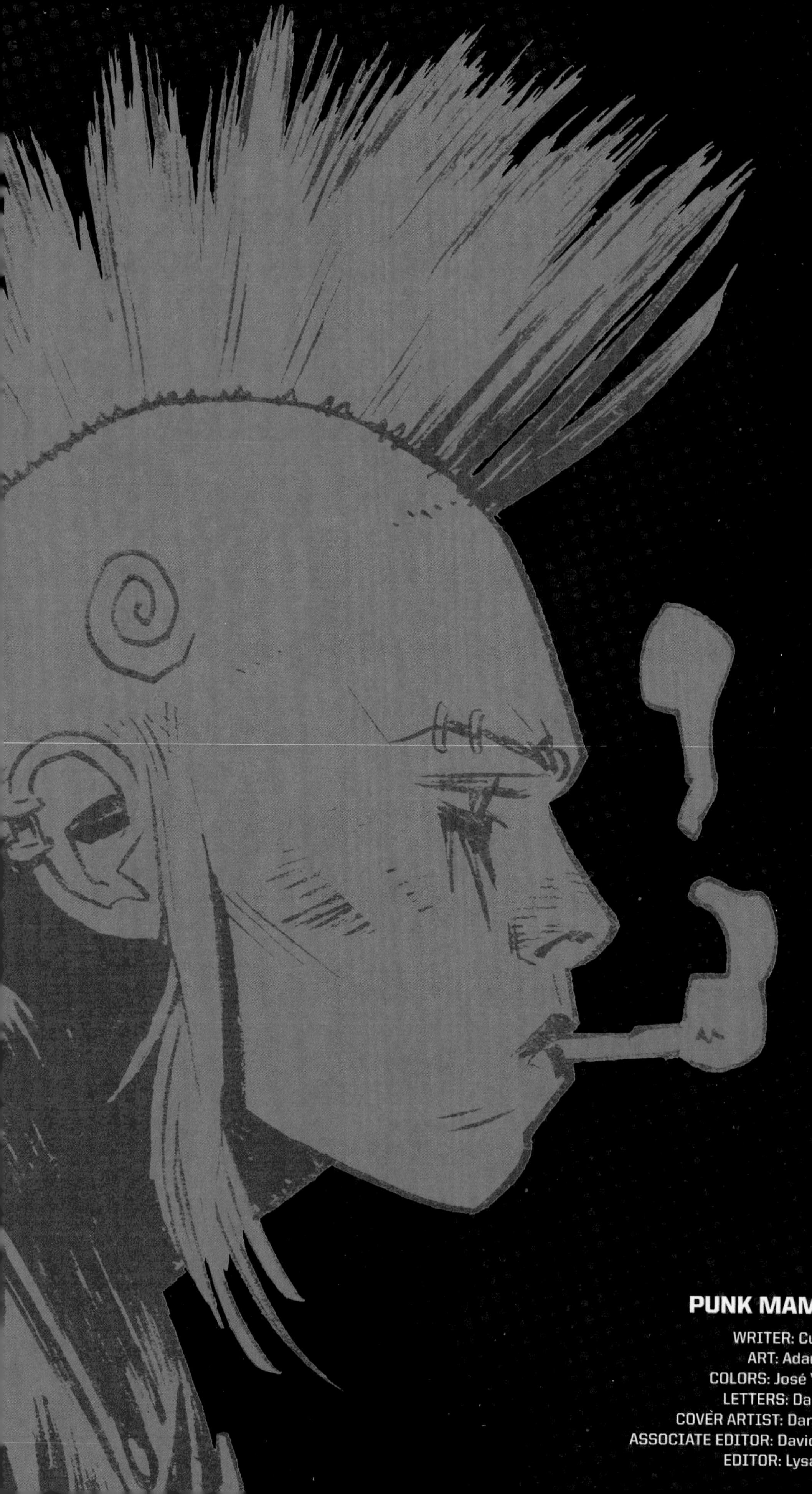

PUNK MAMBO #1

WRITER: Cullen Bunn
ART: Adam Gorham
COLORS: José Villarrubia
LETTERS: Dave Sharpe
COVER ARTIST: Dan Brereton
ASSOCIATE EDITOR: David Menchel
EDITOR: Lysa Hawkins

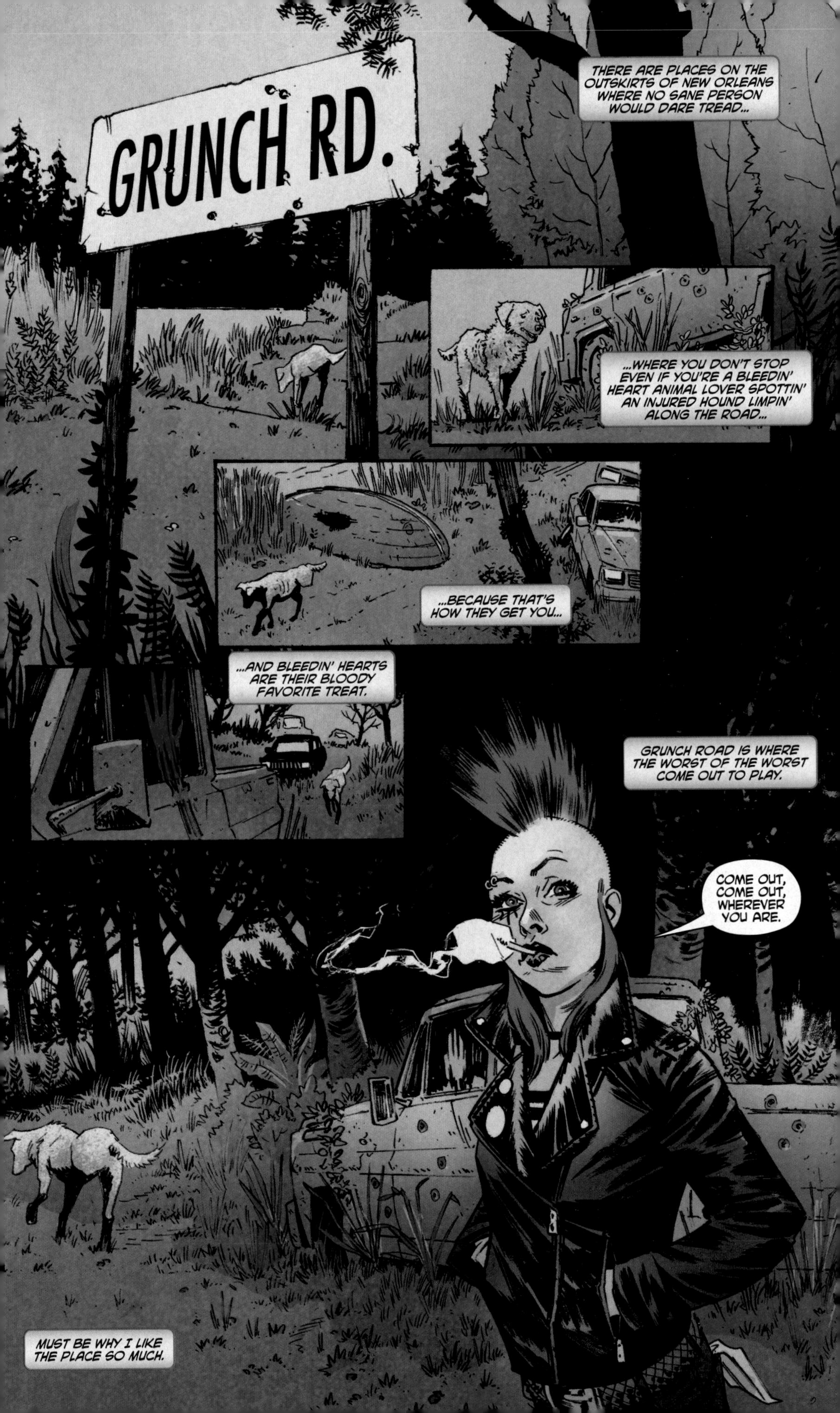
GRUNCH RD.
THERE ARE PLACES ON THE OUTSKIRTS OF NEW ORLEANS WHERE NO SANE PERSON WOULD DARE TREAD...
...WHERE YOU DON'T STOP EVEN IF YOU'RE A BLEEDIN' HEART ANIMAL LOVER SPOTTIN' AN INJURED HOUND LIMPIN' ALONG THE ROAD...
...BECAUSE THAT'S HOW THEY GET YOU...
...AND BLEEDIN' HEARTS ARE THEIR BLOODY FAVORITE TREAT.
GRUNCH ROAD IS WHERE THE WORST OF THE WORST COME OUT TO PLAY.
COME OUT, COME OUT, WHEREVER YOU ARE.
MUST BE WHY I LIKE THE PLACE SO MUCH.

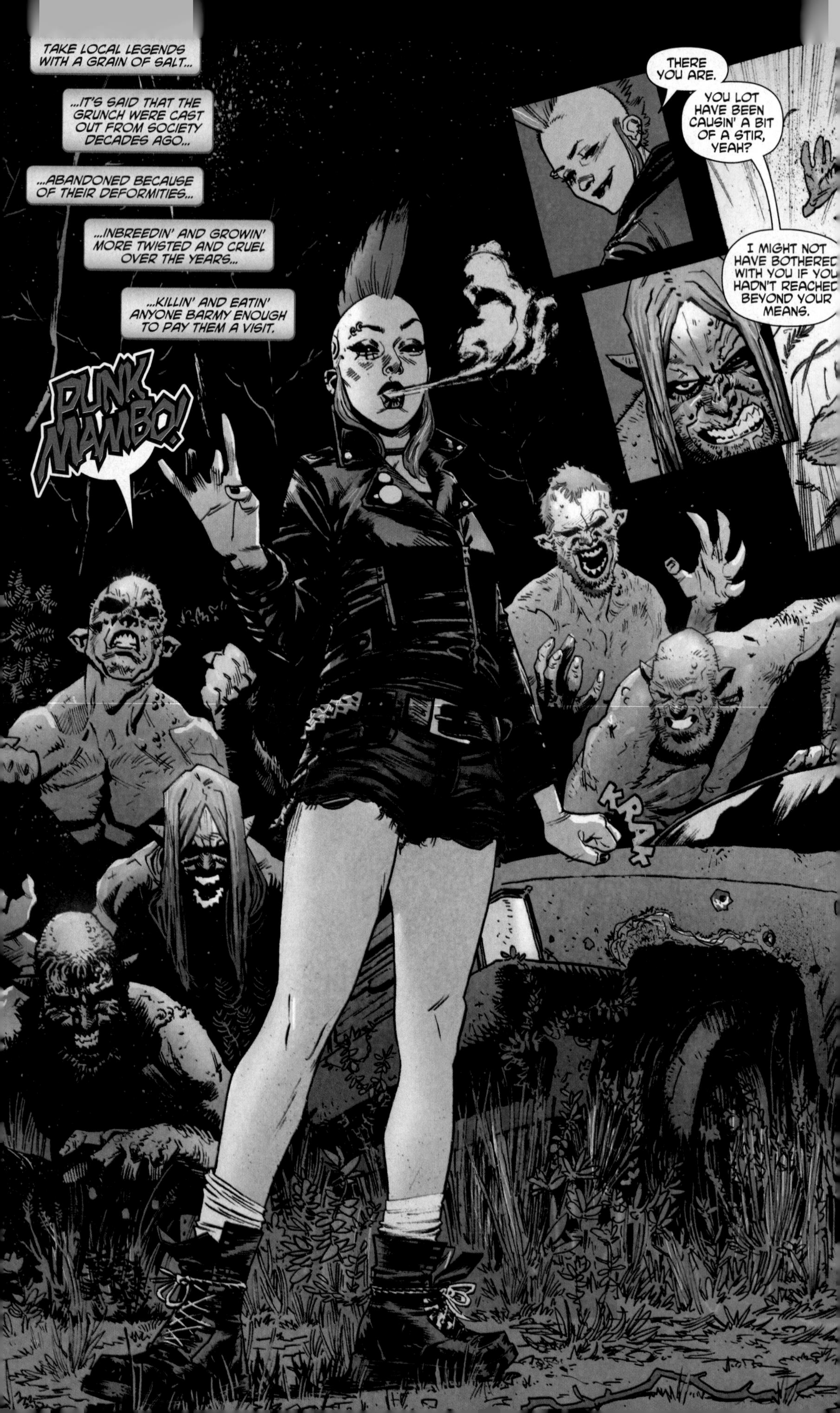
TAKE LOCAL LEGENDS WITH A GRAIN OF SALT...
...IT'S SAID THAT THE GRUNCH WERE CAST OUT FROM SOCIETY DECADES AGO...
...ABANDONED BECAUSE OF THEIR DEFORMITIES...
...INBREEDIN' AND GROWIN' MORE TWISTED AND CRUEL OVER THE YEARS...
...KILLIN' AND EATIN' ANYONE BARMY ENOUGH TO PAY THEM A VISIT.
PUNK MAMBO!
THERE YOU ARE.
YOU LOT HAVE BEEN CAUSIN' A BIT OF A STIR, YEAH?
I MIGHT NOT HAVE BOTHERED WITH YOU IF YOU HADN'T REACHED BEYOND YOUR MEANS.
KRAK

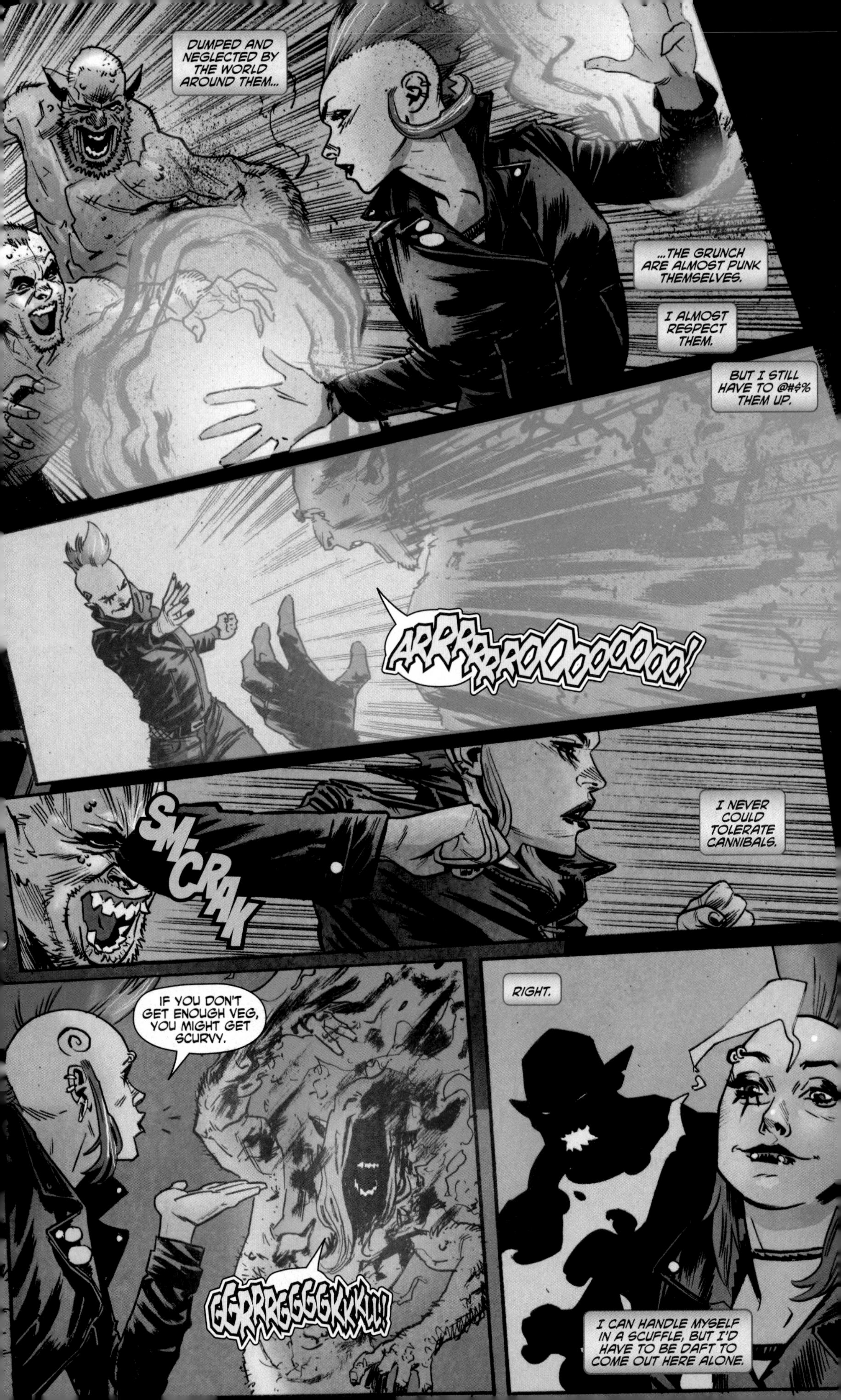
DUMPED AND NEGLECTED BY THE WORLD AROUND THEM...
...THE GRUNCH ARE ALMOST PUNK THEMSELVES.
I ALMOST RESPECT THEM.
BUT I STILL HAVE TO @#$% THEM UP.
ARRRRRROOOOOOOO!
SM-CRAK
I NEVER COULD TOLERATE CANNIBALS.
IF YOU DON'T GET ENOUGH VEG, YOU MIGHT GET SCURVY.
GGRRRGGGGKKKLL!
RIGHT.
I CAN HANDLE MYSELF IN A SCUFFLE, BUT I'D HAVE TO BE DAFT TO COME OUT HERE ALONE.

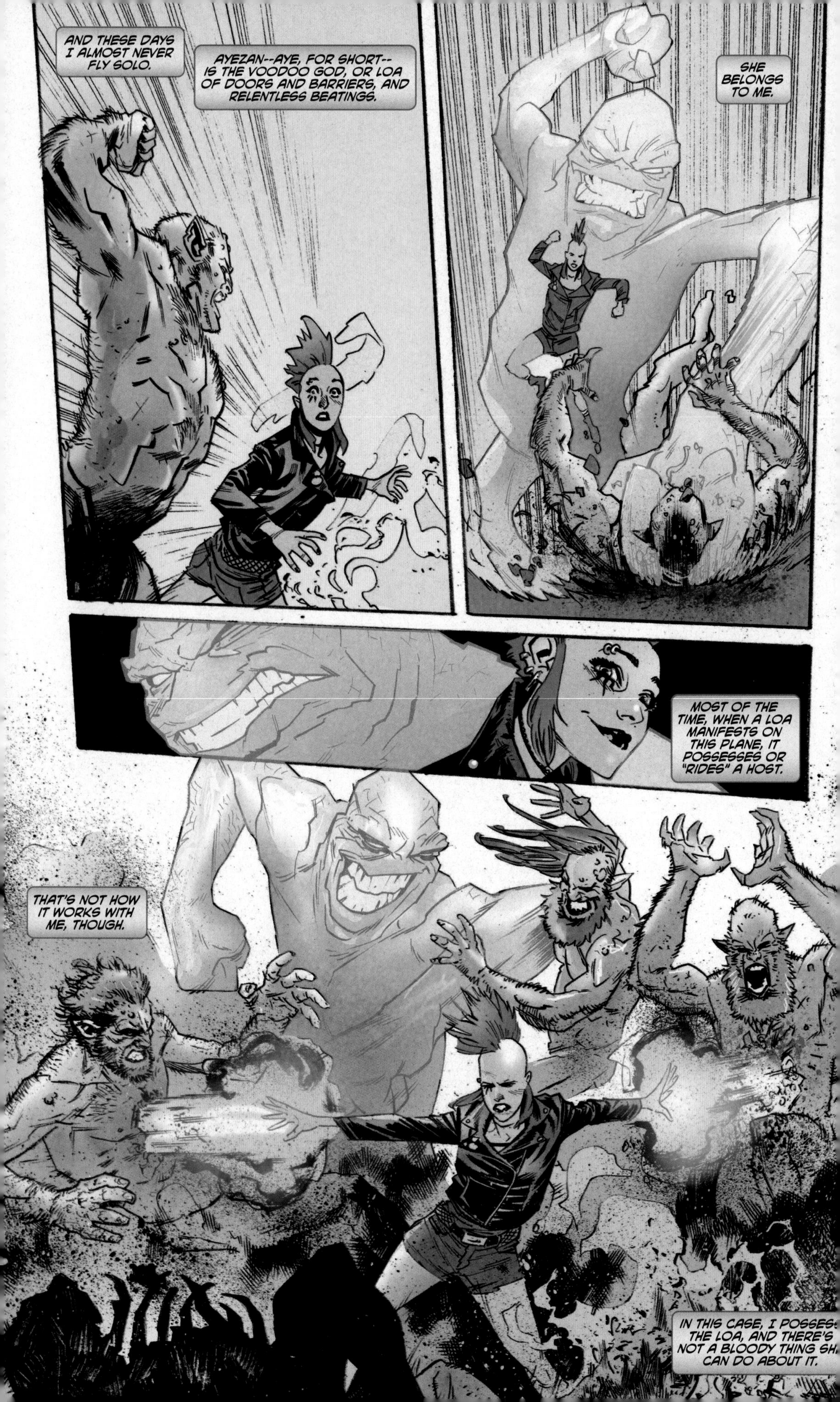
AND THESE DAYS I ALMOST NEVER FLY SOLO.
AYEZAN--AYE, FOR SHORT--IS THE VOODOO GOD, OR LOA OF DOORS AND BARRIERS, AND RELENTLESS BEATINGS.
SHE BELONGS TO ME.
MOST OF THE TIME, WHEN A LOA MANIFESTS ON THIS PLANE, IT POSSESSES OR "RIDES" A HOST.
THAT'S NOT HOW IT WORKS WITH ME, THOUGH.
IN THIS CASE, I POSSESS THE LOA, AND THERE'S NOT A BLOODY THING SHE CAN DO ABOUT IT.

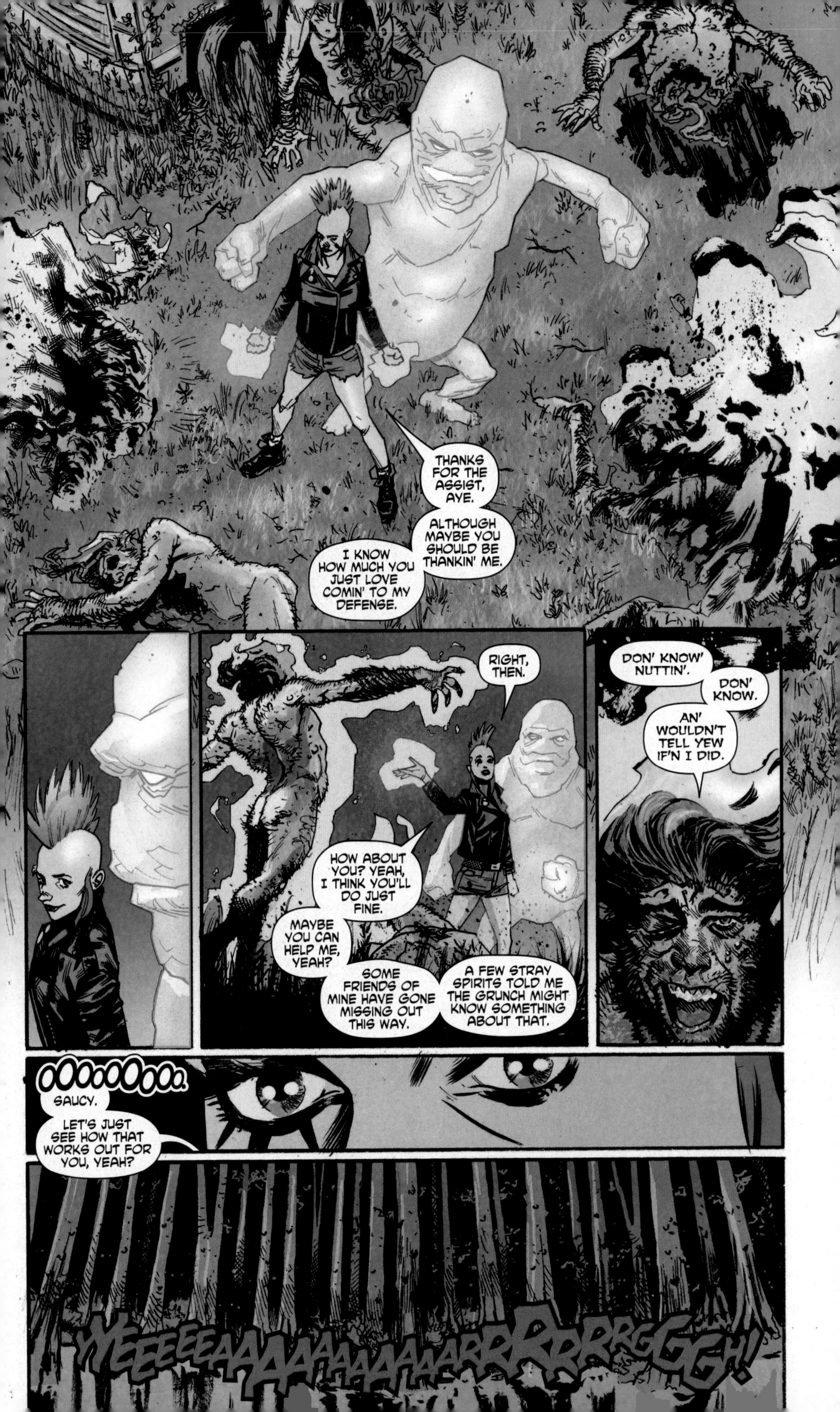
THANKS FOR THE ASSIST, AYE.
ALTHOUGH MAYBE YOU SHOULD BE THANKIN' ME.
I KNOW HOW MUCH YOU JUST LOVE COMIN' TO MY DEFENSE.
RIGHT, THEN.
HOW ABOUT YOU? YEAH, I THINK YOU'LL DO JUST FINE.
MAYBE YOU CAN HELP ME, YEAH?
SOME FRIENDS OF MINE HAVE GONE MISSING OUT THIS WAY.
A FEW STRAY SPIRITS TOLD ME THE GRUNCH MIGHT KNOW SOMETHING ABOUT THAT.
DON' KNOW' NUTTIN'.
DON' KNOW.
AN' WOULDN'T TELL YEW IF'N I DID.
OOOoOOOoo.
SAUCY.
LET'S JUST SEE HOW THAT WORKS OUT FOR YOU, YEAH?
YEEEEEAAAAAAAAAARRRRRRGGGH!

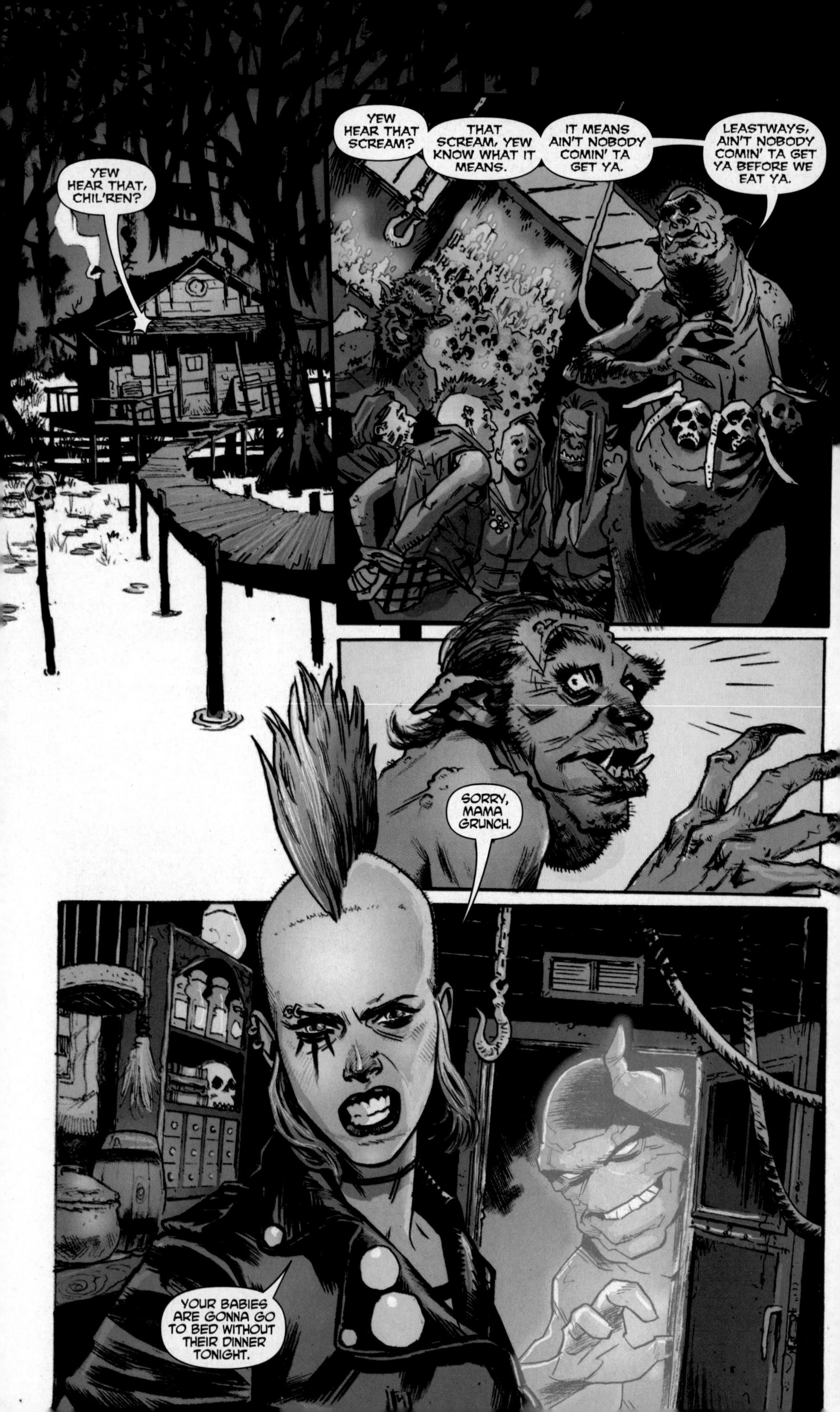
YEW HEAR THAT, CHIL'REN?
YEW HEAR THAT SCREAM?
THAT SCREAM, YEW KNOW WHAT IT MEANS.
IT MEANS AIN'T NOBODY COMIN' TA GET YA.
LEASTWAYS, AIN'T NOBODY COMIN' TA GET YA BEFORE WE EAT YA.
SORRY, MAMA GRUNCH.
YOUR BABIES ARE GONNA GO TO BED WITHOUT THEIR DINNER TONIGHT.

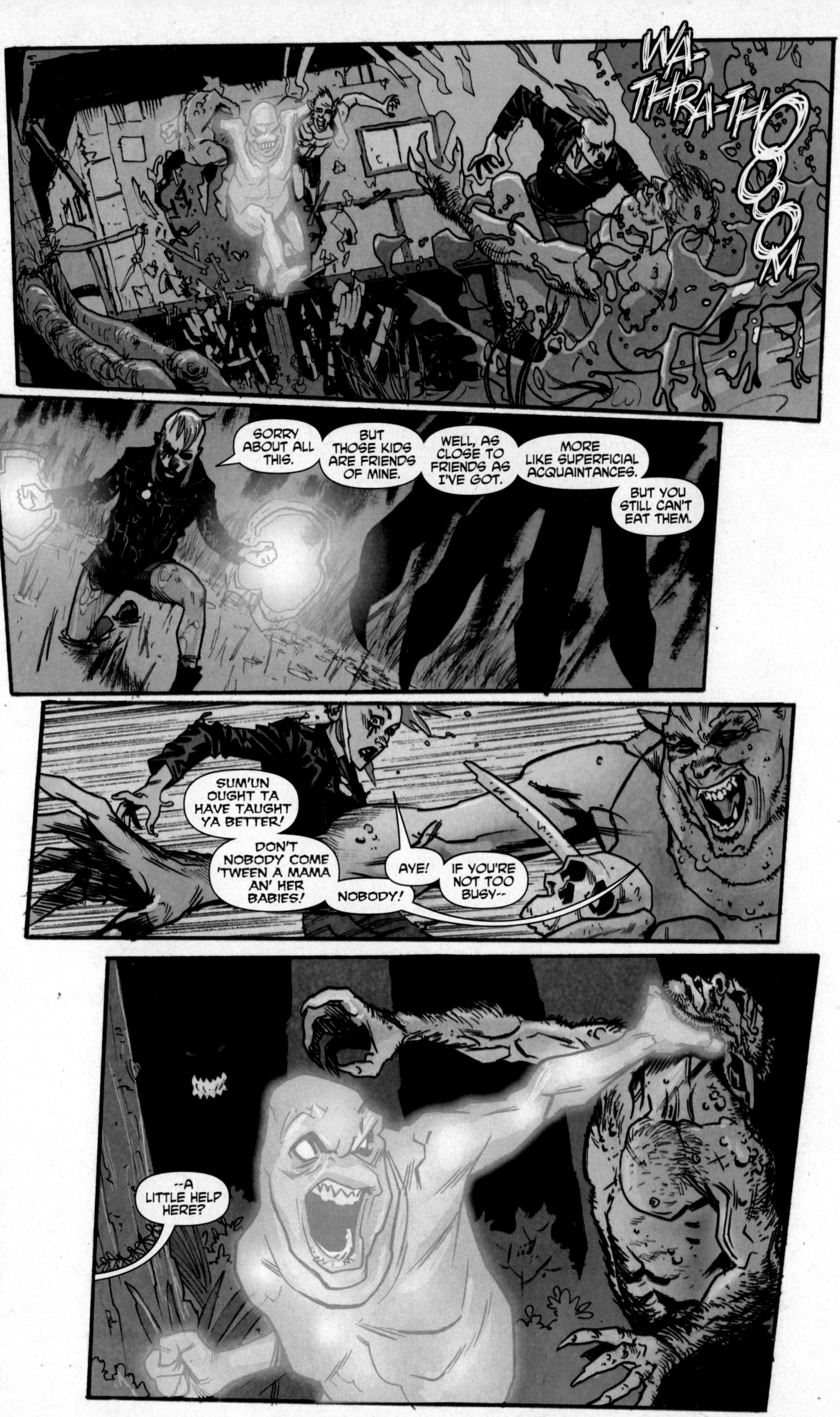
WA-THRA-THOOOOM
SORRY ABOUT ALL THIS.
BUT THOSE KIDS ARE FRIENDS OF MINE.
WELL, AS CLOSE TO FRIENDS AS I'VE GOT.
MORE LIKE SUPERFICIAL ACQUAINTANCES.
BUT YOU STILL CAN'T EAT THEM.
SUM'UN OUGHT TA HAVE TAUGHT YA BETTER!
DON'T NOBODY COME 'TWEEN A MAMA AN' HER BABIES!
NOBODY!
AYE!
IF YOU'RE NOT TOO BUSY--
--A LITTLE HELP HERE?

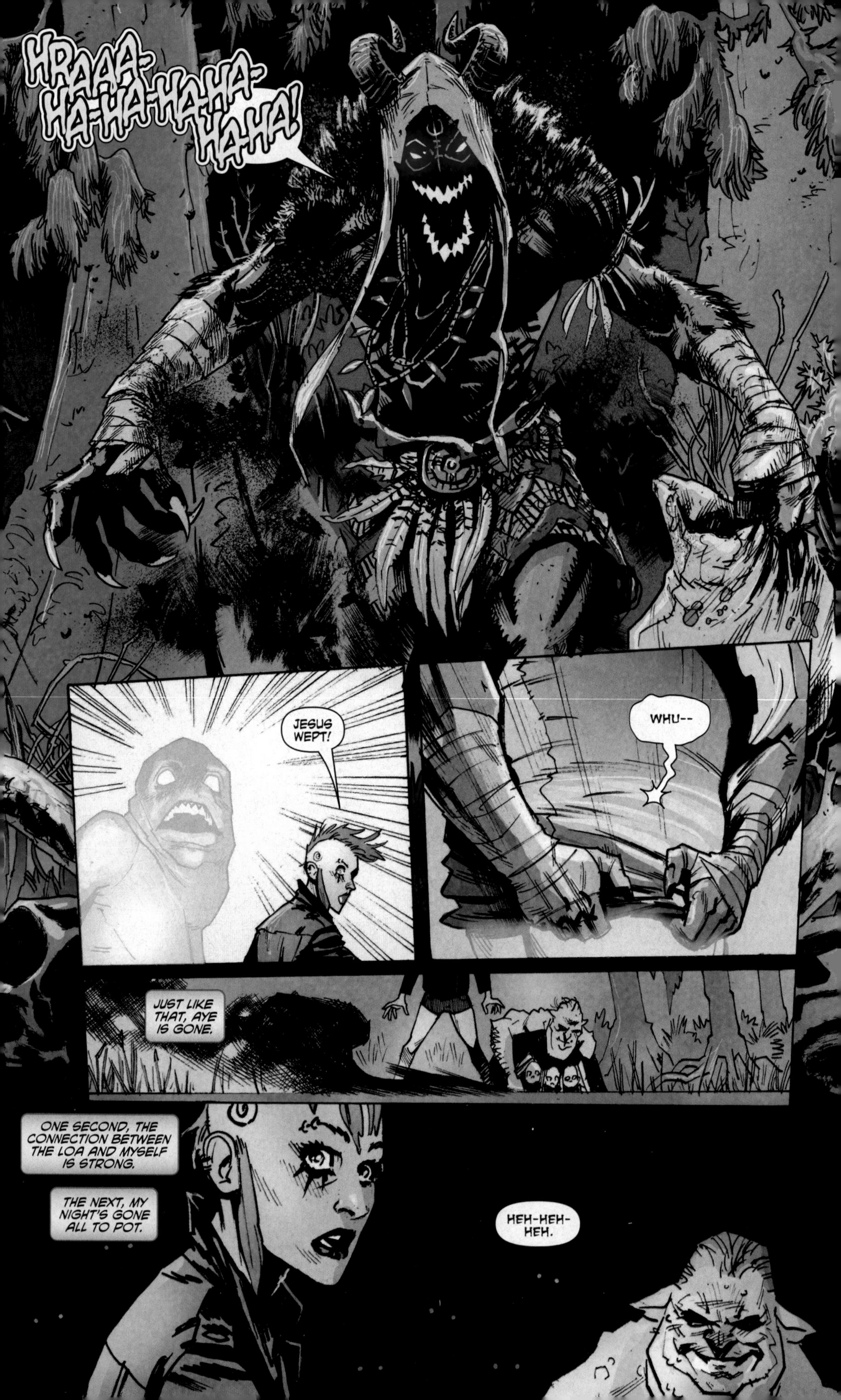
HRAAA-HA-HA-HA-HAHA-HAHA!
JESUS WEPT!
WHU--
JUST LIKE THAT, AYE IS GONE.
ONE SECOND, THE CONNECTION BETWEEN THE LOA AND MYSELF IS STRONG.
THE NEXT, MY NIGHT'S GONE ALL TO POT.
HEH-HEH-HEH.

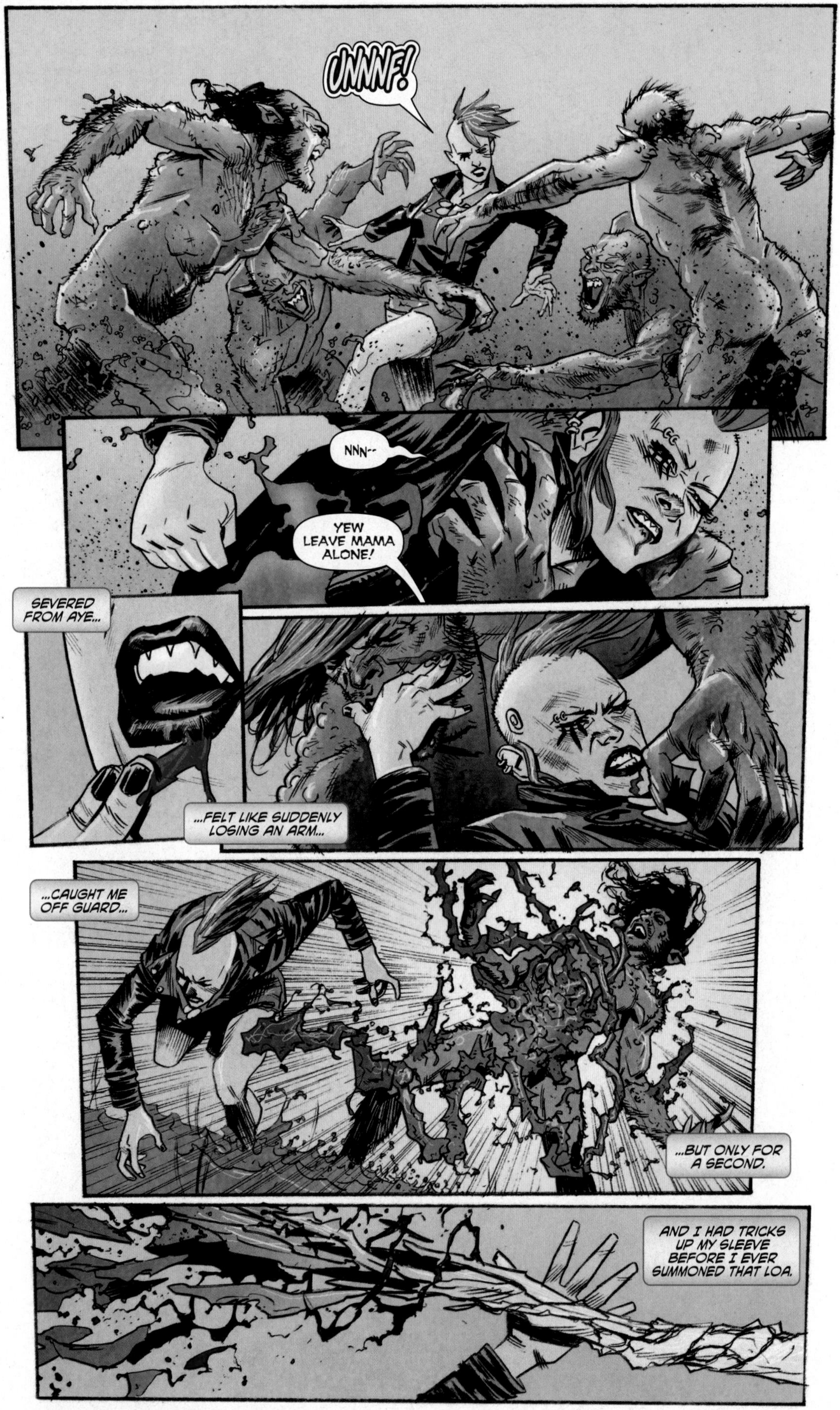
UNNNF!
NNN--
YEW LEAVE MAMA ALONE!
SEVERED FROM AYE...
...FELT LIKE SUDDENLY LOSING AN ARM...
...CAUGHT ME OFF GUARD...
...BUT ONLY FOR A SECOND.
AND I HAD TRICKS UP MY SLEEVE BEFORE I EVER SUMMONED THAT LOA.

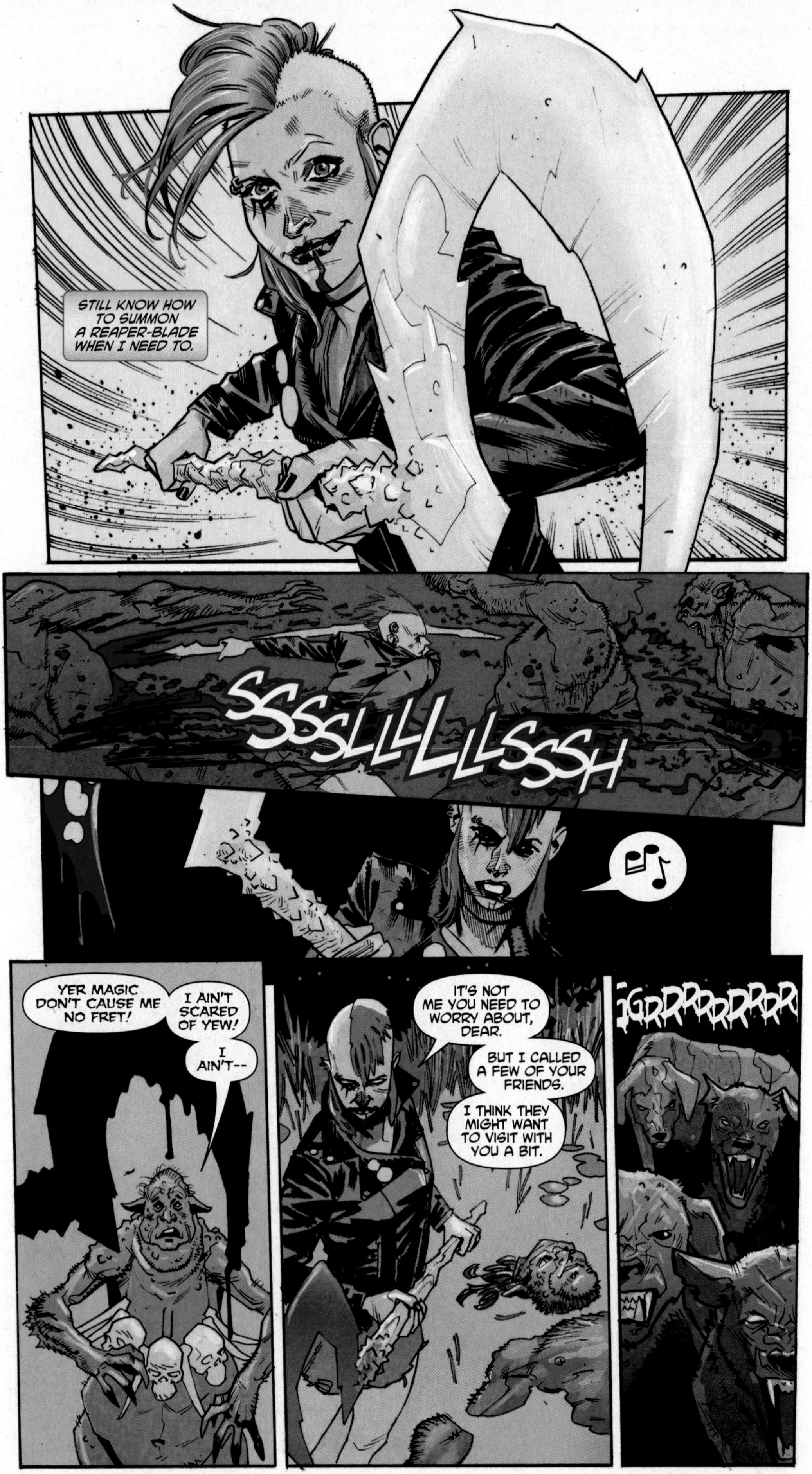
STILL KNOW HOW TO SUMMON A REAPER-BLADE WHEN I NEED TO.
SSSSLLLLLLLSSSH
YER MAGIC DON'T CAUSE ME NO FRET!
I AIN'T SCARED OF YEW!
I AIN'T--
IT'S NOT ME YOU NEED TO WORRY ABOUT, DEAR.
BUT I CALLED A FEW OF YOUR FRIENDS.
I THINK THEY MIGHT WANT TO VISIT WITH YOU A BIT.
GDRRRRRRRR

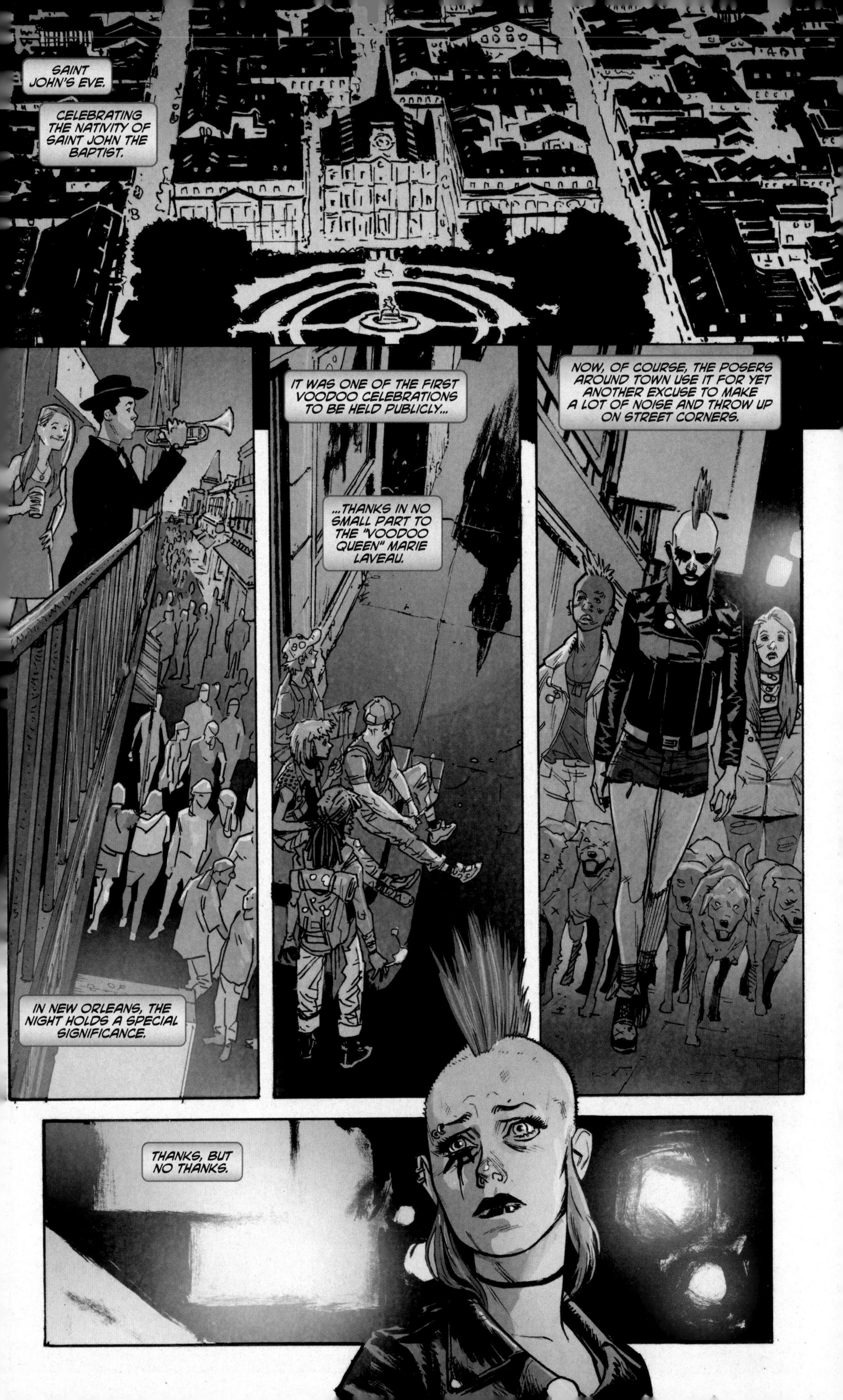
SAINT JOHN'S EVE.
CELEBRATING THE NATIVITY OF SAINT JOHN THE BAPTIST.
IN NEW ORLEANS, THE NIGHT HOLDS A SPECIAL SIGNIFICANCE.
IT WAS ONE OF THE FIRST VOODOO CELEBRATIONS TO BE HELD PUBLICLY...
...THANKS IN NO SMALL PART TO THE "VOODOO QUEEN" MARIE LAVEAU.
NOW, OF COURSE, THE POSERS AROUND TOWN USE IT FOR YET ANOTHER EXCUSE TO MAKE A LOT OF NOISE AND THROW UP ON STREET CORNERS.
THANKS, BUT NO THANKS.

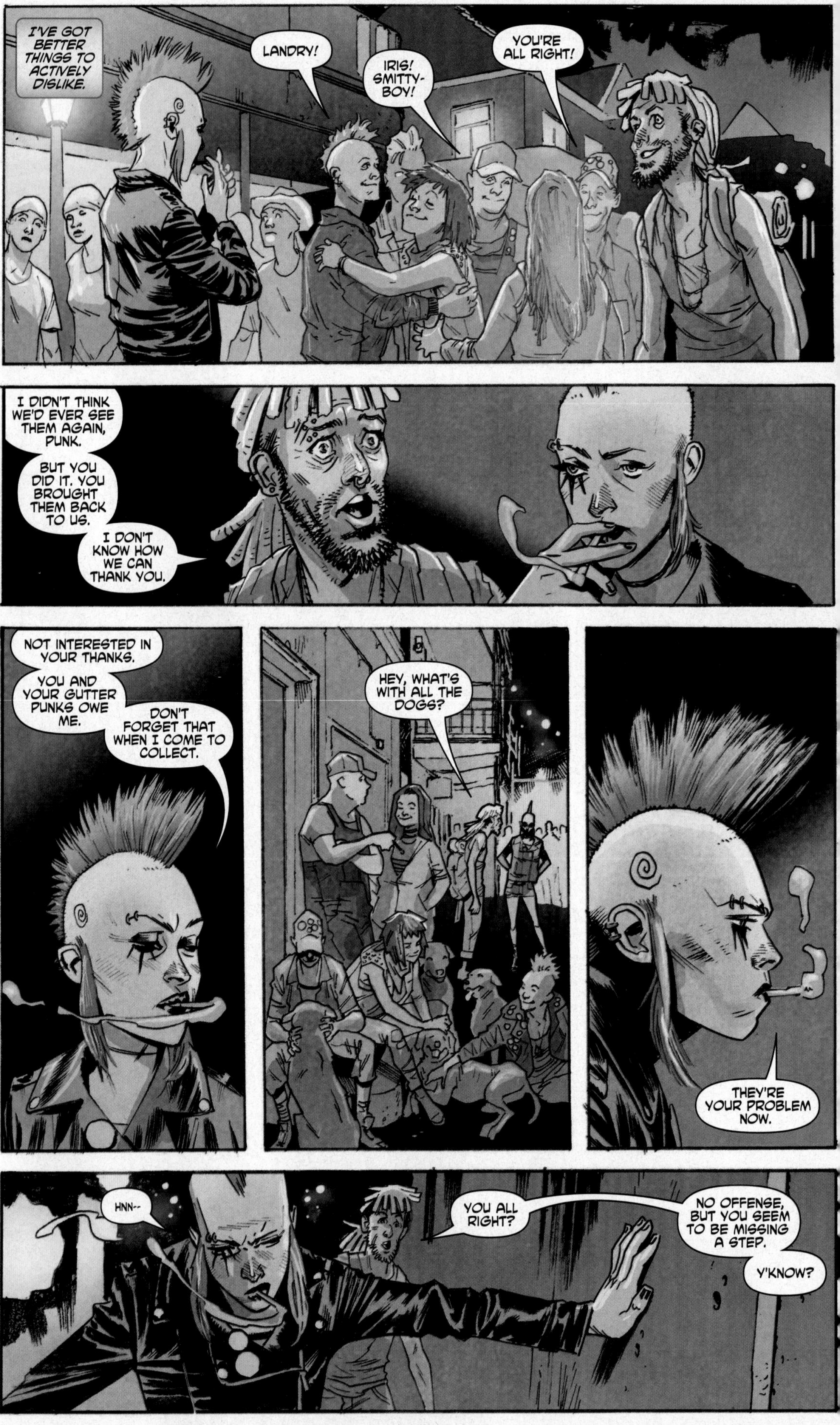
I'VE GOT BETTER THINGS TO ACTIVELY DISLIKE.
LANDRY!
IRIS! SMITTY-BOY!
YOU'RE ALL RIGHT!
I DIDN'T THINK WE'D EVER SEE THEM AGAIN, PUNK.
BUT YOU DID IT. YOU BROUGHT THEM BACK TO US.
I DON'T KNOW HOW WE CAN THANK YOU.
NOT INTERESTED IN YOUR THANKS.
YOU AND YOUR GUTTER PUNKS OWE ME.
DON'T FORGET THAT WHEN I COME TO COLLECT.
HEY, WHAT'S WITH ALL THE DOGS?
THEY'RE YOUR PROBLEM NOW.
HNN--
YOU ALL RIGHT?
NO OFFENSE, BUT YOU SEEM TO BE MISSING A STEP.
Y'KNOW?

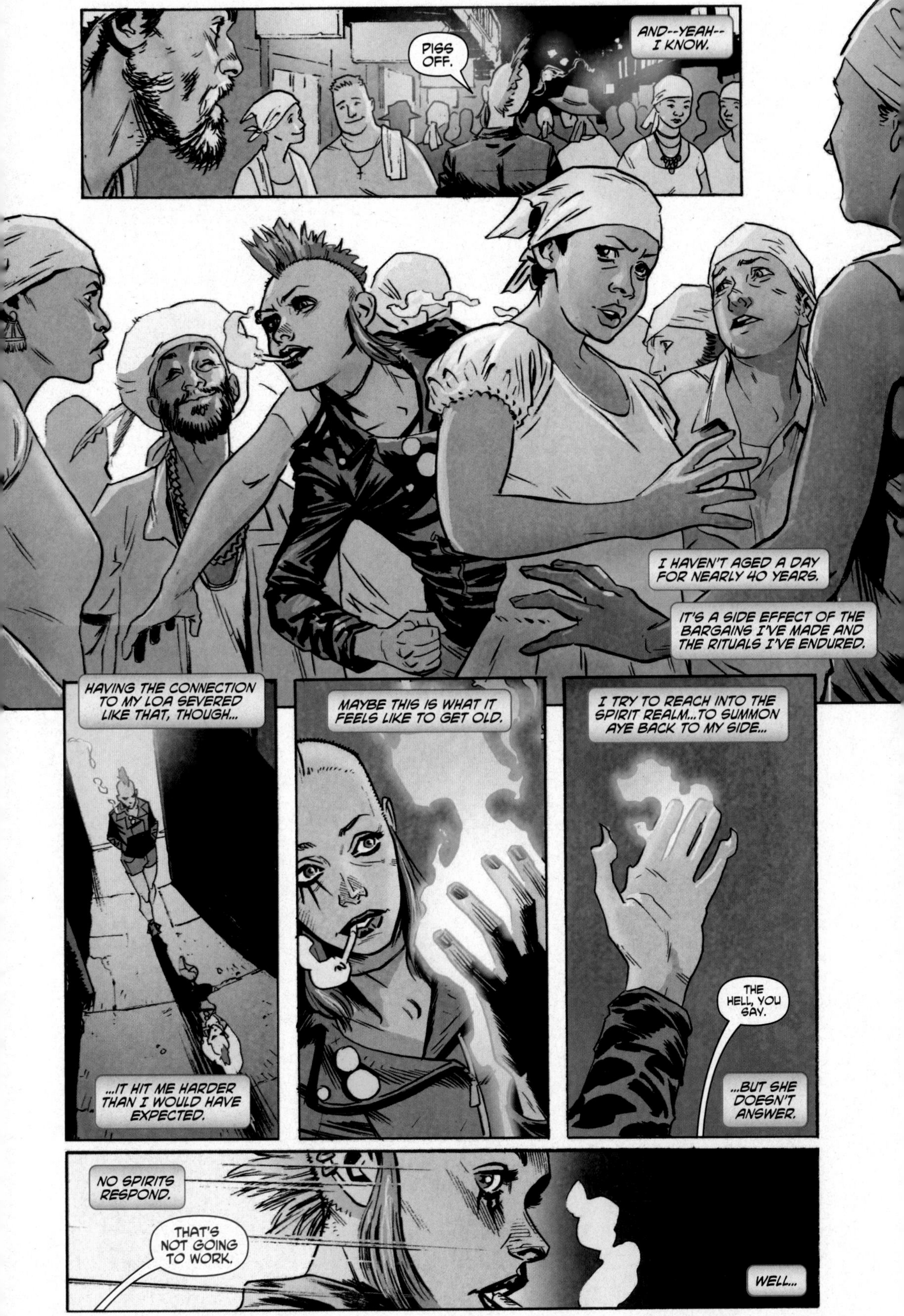
PISS OFF.
AND--YEAH-- I KNOW.
I HAVEN'T AGED A DAY FOR NEARLY 40 YEARS.
IT'S A SIDE EFFECT OF THE BARGAINS I'VE MADE AND THE RITUALS I'VE ENDURED.
HAVING THE CONNECTION TO MY LOA SEVERED LIKE THAT, THOUGH...
...IT HIT ME HARDER THAN I WOULD HAVE EXPECTED.
MAYBE THIS IS WHAT IT FEELS LIKE TO GET OLD.
I TRY TO REACH INTO THE SPIRIT REALM...TO SUMMON AYE BACK TO MY SIDE...
THE HELL, YOU SAY.
...BUT SHE DOESN'T ANSWER.
NO SPIRITS RESPOND.
THAT'S NOT GOING TO WORK.
WELL...

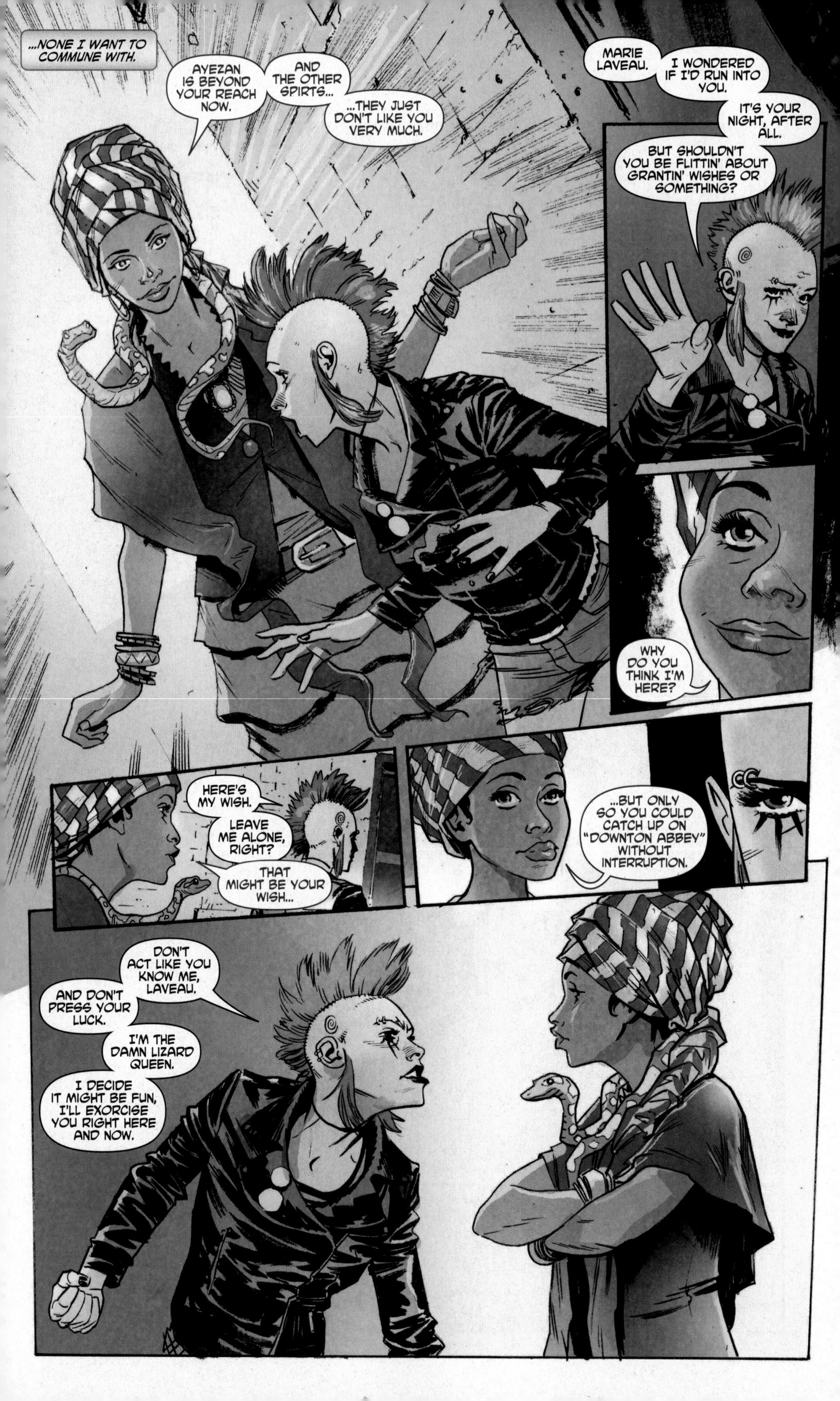
...NONE I WANT TO COMMUNE WITH.
AYEZAN IS BEYOND YOUR REACH NOW.
AND THE OTHER SPIRTS...
...THEY JUST DON'T LIKE YOU VERY MUCH.
MARIE LAVEAU.
I WONDERED IF I'D RUN INTO YOU.
IT'S YOUR NIGHT, AFTER ALL.
BUT SHOULDN'T YOU BE FLITTIN' ABOUT GRANTIN' WISHES OR SOMETHING?
WHY DO YOU THINK I'M HERE?
HERE'S MY WISH.
LEAVE ME ALONE, RIGHT?
THAT MIGHT BE YOUR WISH...
...BUT ONLY SO YOU COULD CATCH UP ON "DOWNTON ABBEY" WITHOUT INTERRUPTION.
DON'T ACT LIKE YOU KNOW ME, LAVEAU.
AND DON'T PRESS YOUR LUCK.
I'M THE DAMN LIZARD QUEEN.
I DECIDE IT MIGHT BE FUN, I'LL EXORCISE YOU RIGHT HERE AND NOW.

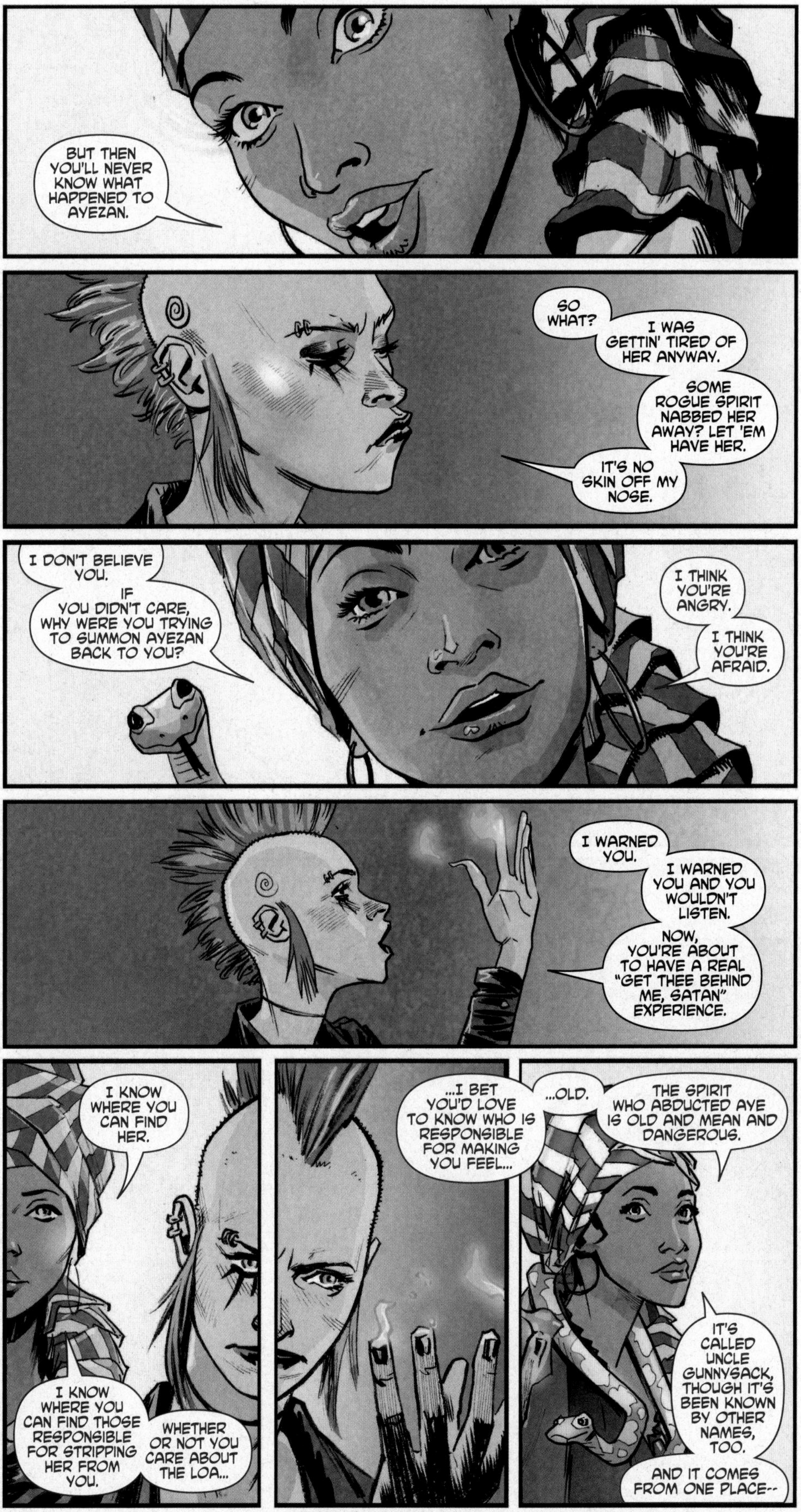
BUT THEN YOU'LL NEVER KNOW WHAT HAPPENED TO AYEZAN.
SO WHAT?
I WAS GETTIN' TIRED OF HER ANYWAY.
SOME ROGUE SPIRIT NABBED HER AWAY? LET 'EM HAVE HER.
IT'S NO SKIN OFF MY NOSE.
I DON'T BELIEVE YOU.
IF YOU DIDN'T CARE, WHY WERE YOU TRYING TO SUMMON AYEZAN BACK TO YOU?
I THINK YOU'RE ANGRY.
I THINK YOU'RE AFRAID.
I WARNED YOU.
I WARNED YOU AND YOU WOULDN'T LISTEN.
NOW, YOU'RE ABOUT TO HAVE A REAL "GET THEE BEHIND ME, SATAN" EXPERIENCE.
I KNOW WHERE YOU CAN FIND HER.
I KNOW WHERE YOU CAN FIND THOSE RESPONSIBLE FOR STRIPPING HER FROM YOU.
WHETHER OR NOT YOU CARE ABOUT THE LOA...
...I BET YOU'D LOVE TO KNOW WHO IS RESPONSIBLE FOR MAKING YOU FEEL...
...OLD.
THE SPIRIT WHO ABDUCTED AYE IS OLD AND MEAN AND DANGEROUS.
IT'S CALLED UNCLE GUNNYSACK, THOUGH IT'S BEEN KNOWN BY OTHER NAMES, TOO.
AND IT COMES FROM ONE PLACE--

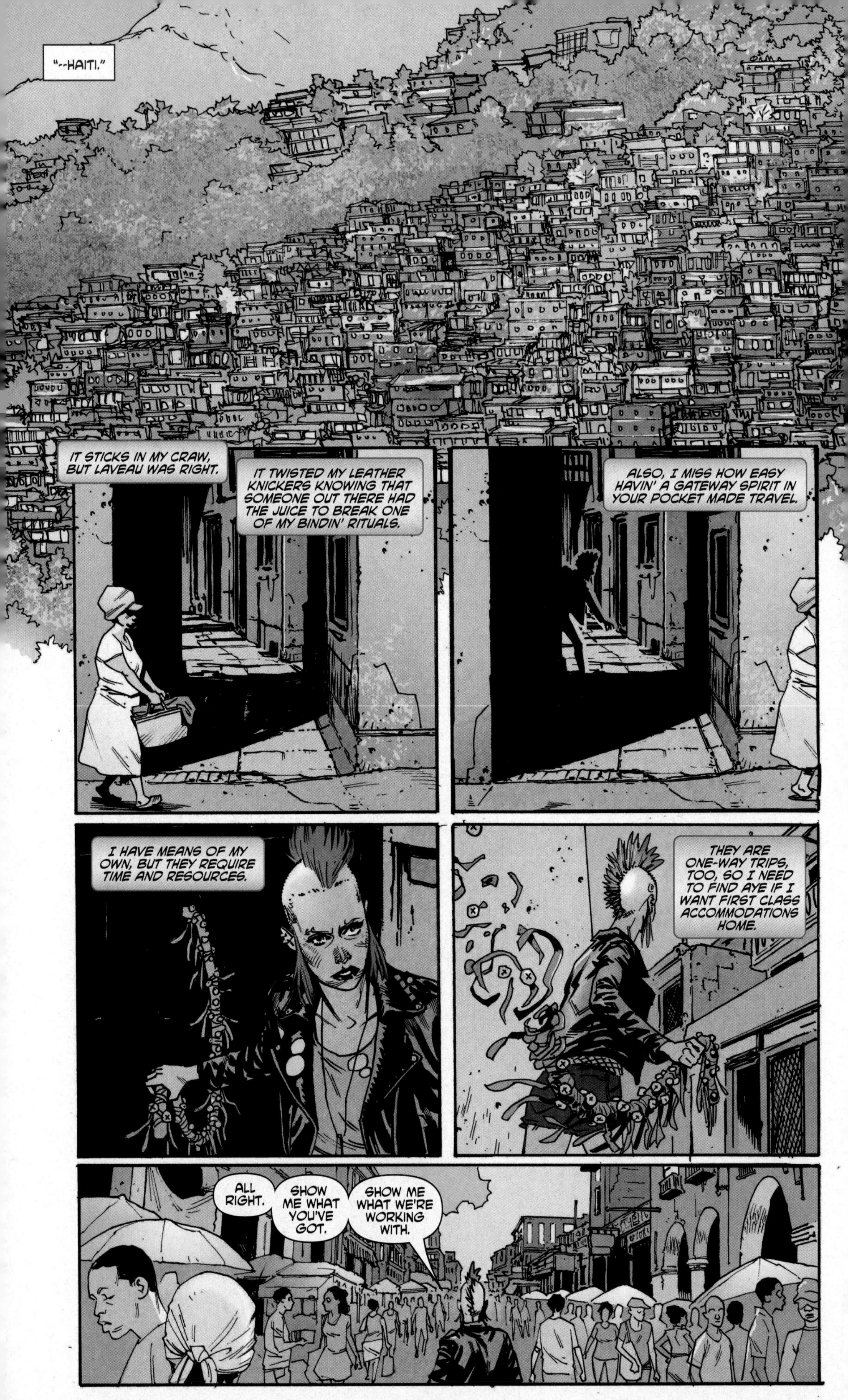
"--HAITI."
IT STICKS IN MY CRAW, BUT LAVEAU WAS RIGHT.
IT TWISTED MY LEATHER KNICKERS KNOWING THAT SOMEONE OUT THERE HAD THE JUICE TO BREAK ONE OF MY BINDIN' RITUALS.
ALSO, I MISS HOW EASY HAVIN' A GATEWAY SPIRIT IN YOUR POCKET MADE TRAVEL.
I HAVE MEANS OF MY OWN, BUT THEY REQUIRE TIME AND RESOURCES.
THEY ARE ONE-WAY TRIPS, TOO, SO I NEED TO FIND AYE IF I WANT FIRST CLASS ACCOMMODATIONS HOME.
ALL RIGHT.
SHOW ME WHAT YOU'VE GOT.
SHOW ME WHAT WE'RE WORKING WITH.

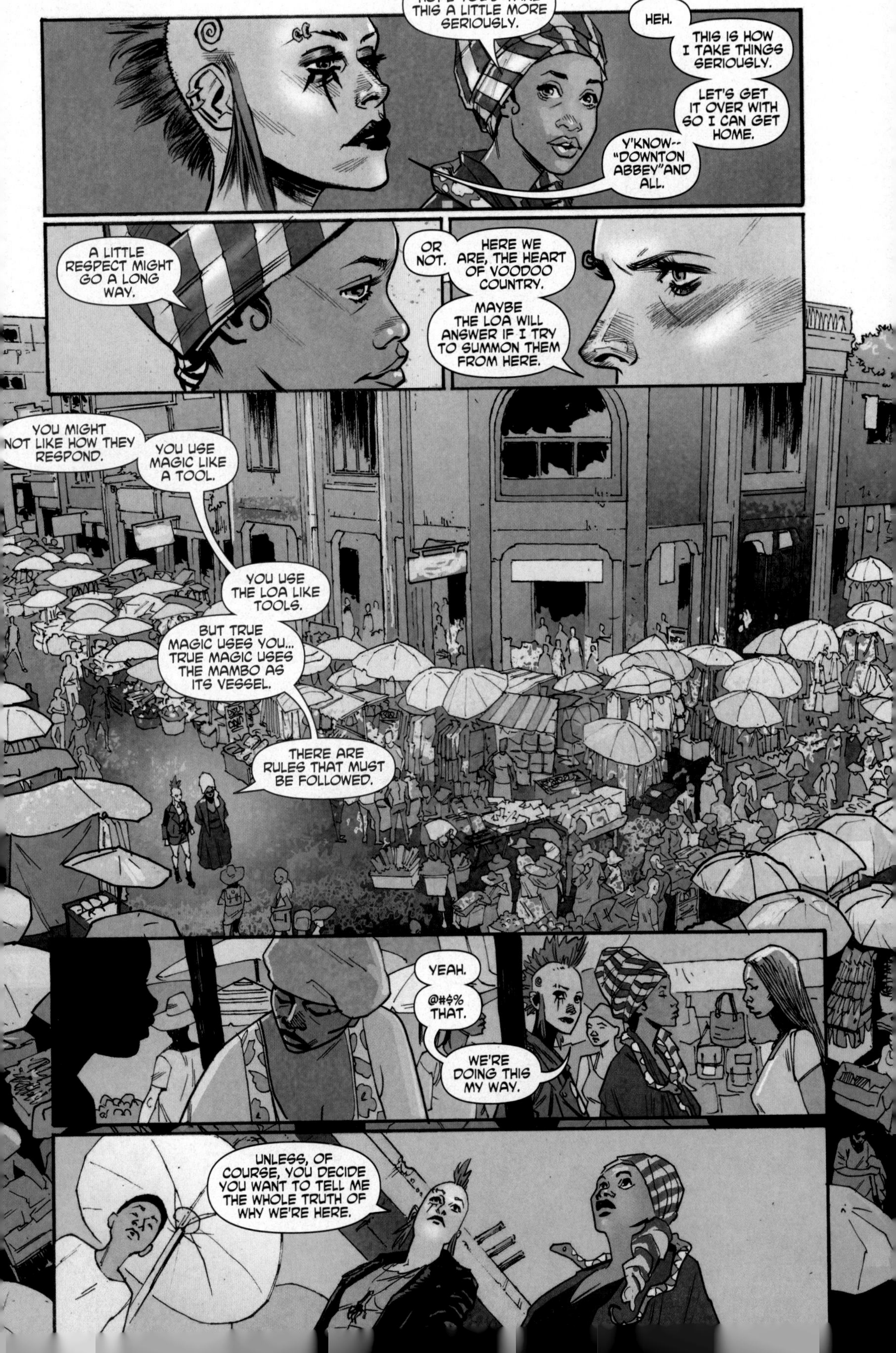

I WOULD HOPE YOU'D TAKE THIS A LITTLE MORE SERIOUSLY.
HEH.
THIS IS HOW I TAKE THINGS SERIOUSLY.
LET'S GET IT OVER WITH SO I CAN GET HOME.
Y'KNOW-- "DOWNTON ABBEY" AND ALL.
A LITTLE RESPECT MIGHT GO A LONG WAY.
OR NOT.
HERE WE ARE, THE HEART OF VOODOO COUNTRY.
MAYBE THE LOA WILL ANSWER IF I TRY TO SUMMON THEM FROM HERE.
YOU MIGHT NOT LIKE HOW THEY RESPOND.
YOU USE MAGIC LIKE A TOOL.
YOU USE THE LOA LIKE TOOLS.
BUT TRUE MAGIC USES YOU... TRUE MAGIC USES THE MAMBO AS ITS VESSEL.
THERE ARE RULES THAT MUST BE FOLLOWED.
YEAH.
@#$% THAT.
WE'RE DOING THIS MY WAY.
UNLESS, OF COURSE, YOU DECIDE YOU WANT TO TELL ME THE WHOLE TRUTH OF WHY WE'RE HERE.

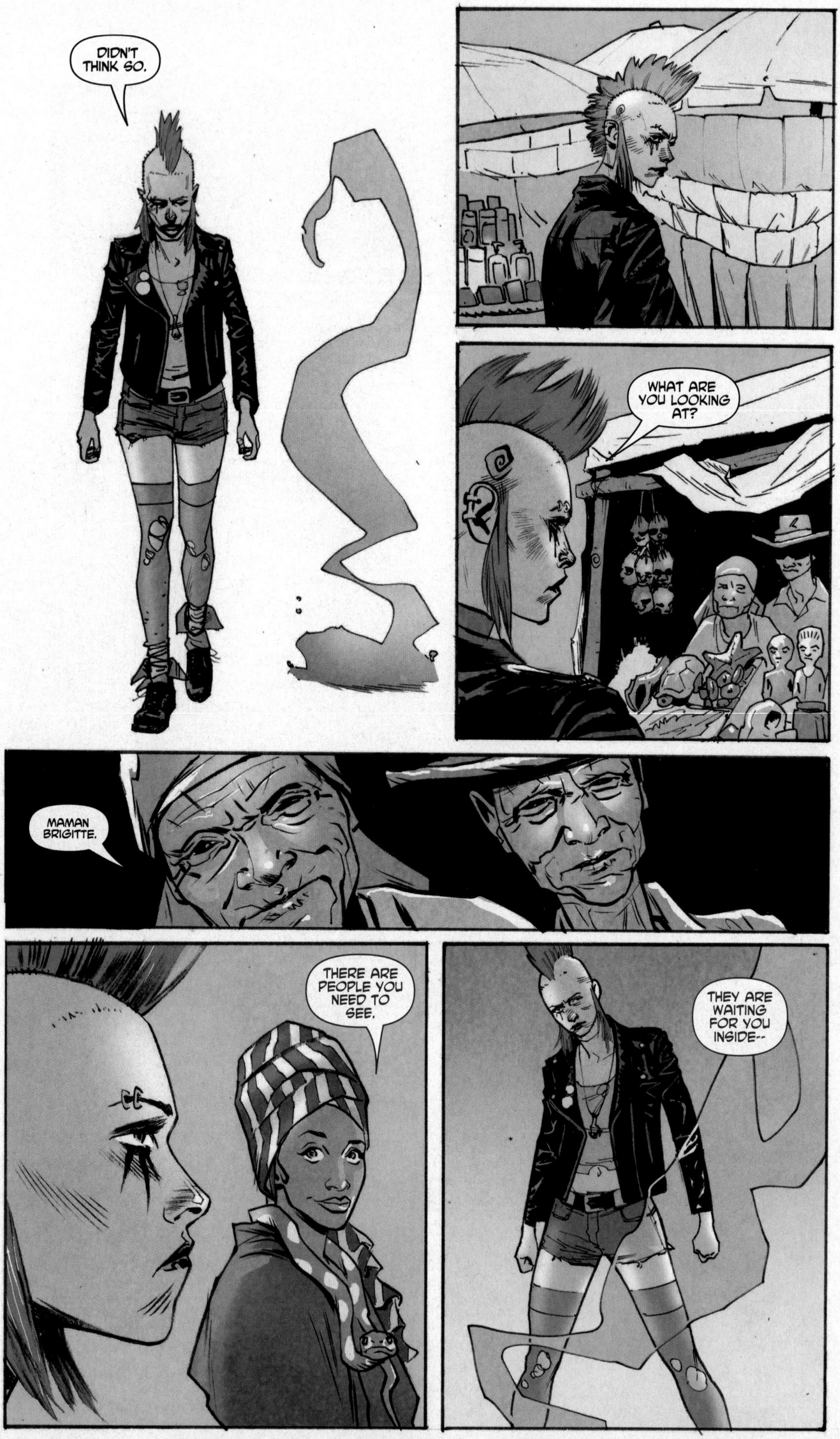
DIDN'T THINK SO.
WHAT ARE YOU LOOKING AT?
MAMAN BRIGITTE.
THERE ARE PEOPLE YOU NEED TO SEE.
THEY ARE WAITING FOR YOU INSIDE--

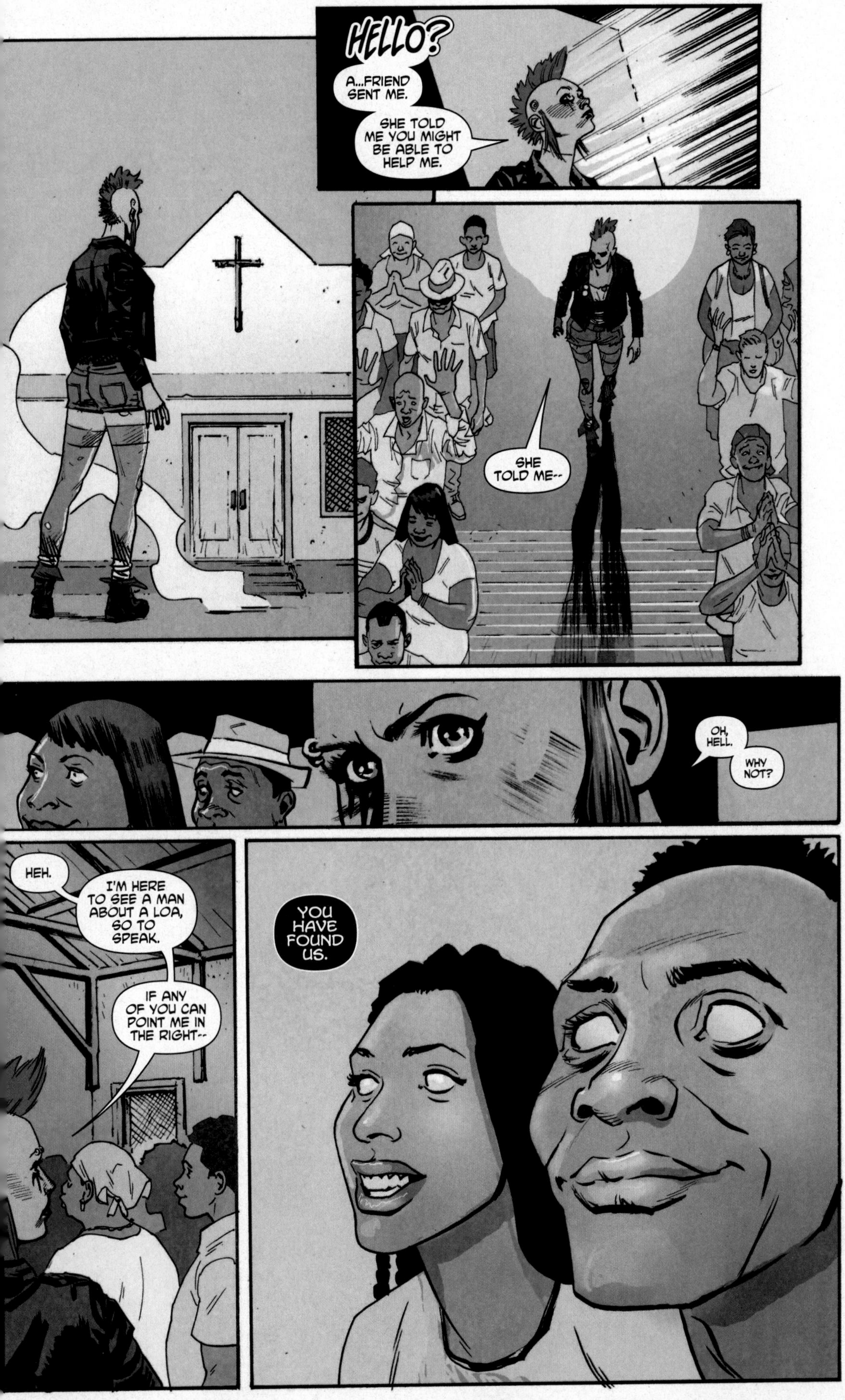
HELLO?
A...FRIEND SENT ME.
SHE TOLD ME YOU MIGHT BE ABLE TO HELP ME.
SHE TOLD ME--
OH, HELL.
WHY NOT?
HEH.
I'M HERE TO SEE A MAN ABOUT A LOA, SO TO SPEAK.
IF ANY OF YOU CAN POINT ME IN THE RIGHT--
YOU HAVE FOUND US.

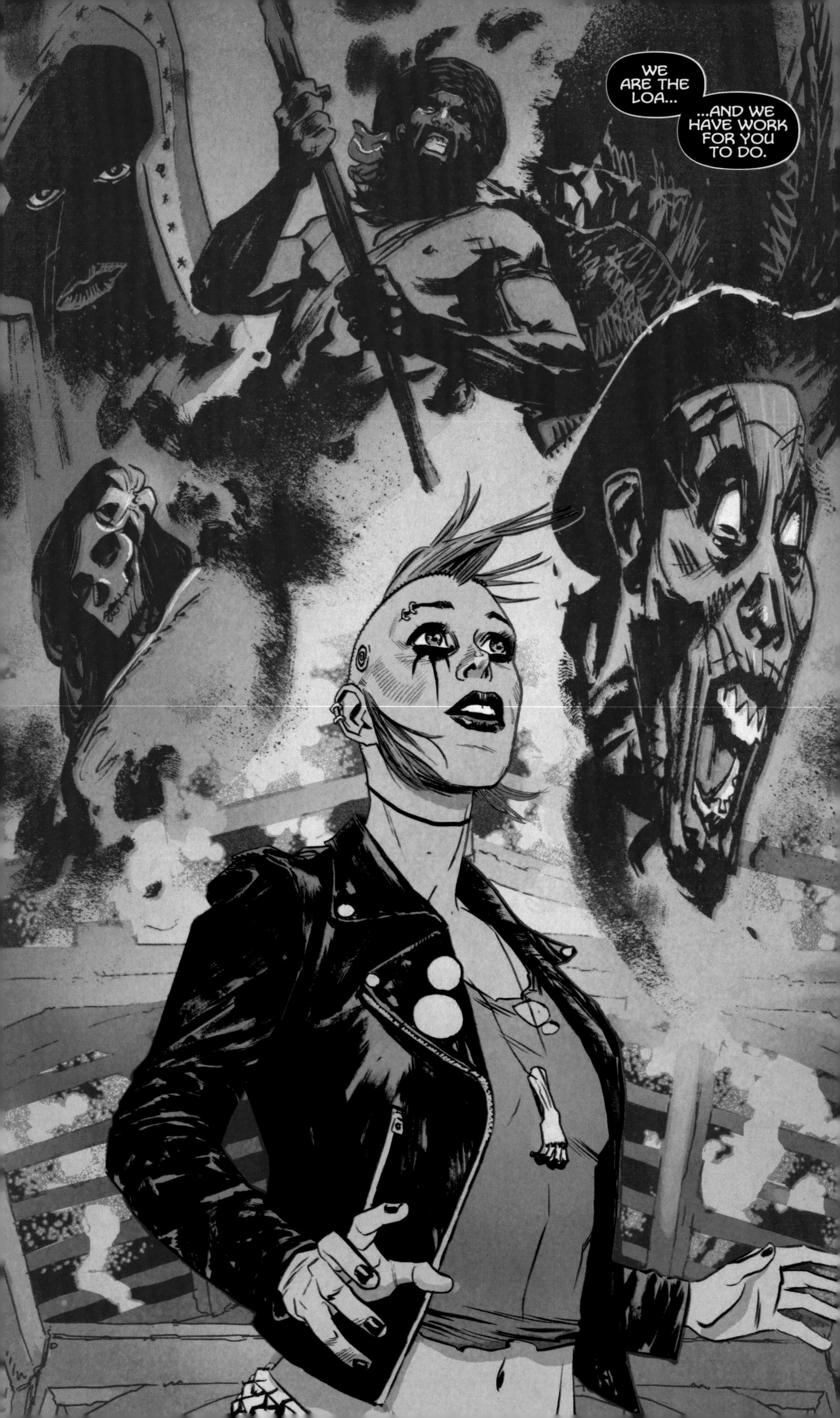
WE ARE THE LOA...
...AND WE HAVE WORK FOR YOU TO DO.

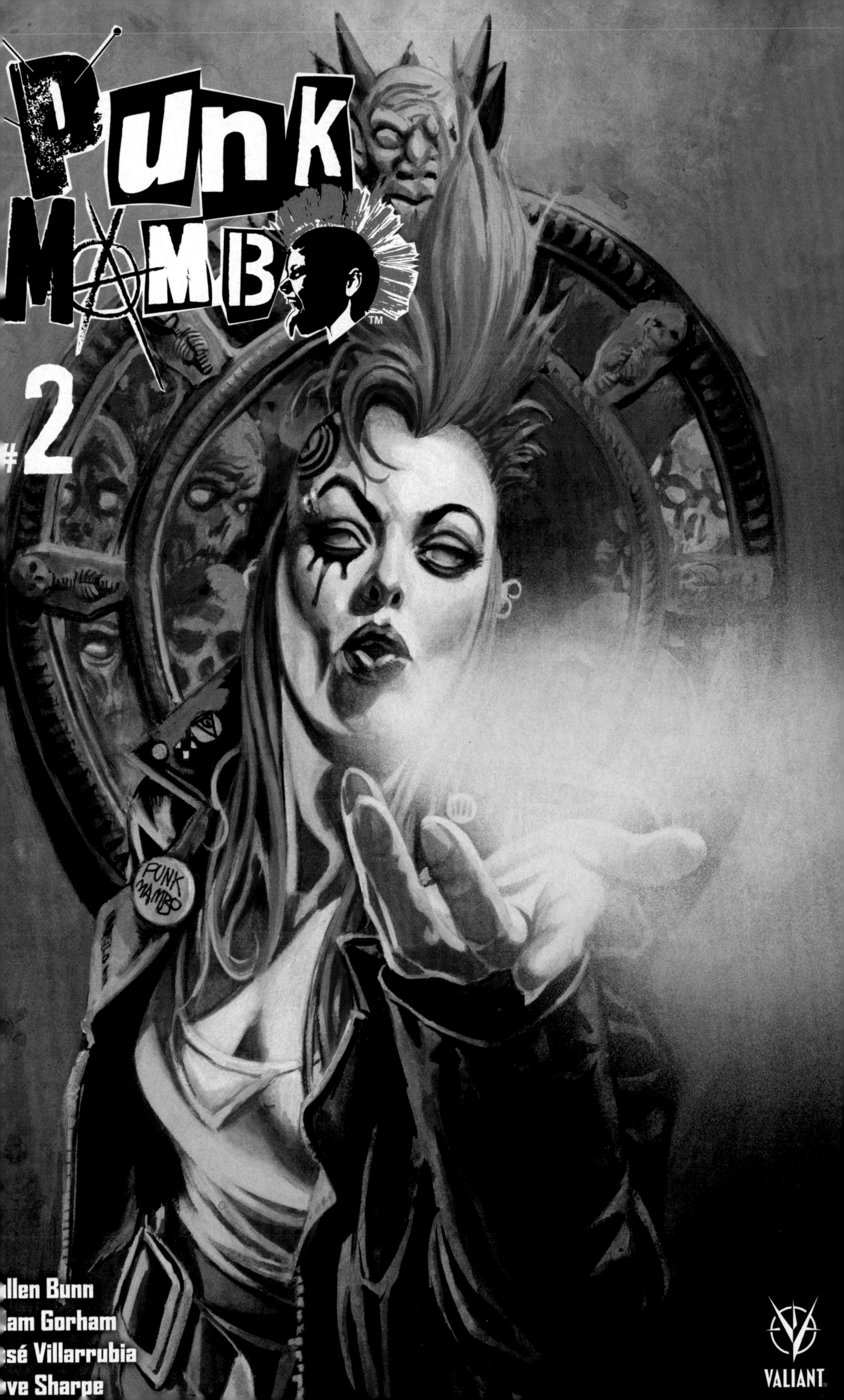
PUNK MAMBO
#2
PUNK MAMBO
llen Bunn
am Gorham
sé Villarrubia
ve Sharpe
VALIANT

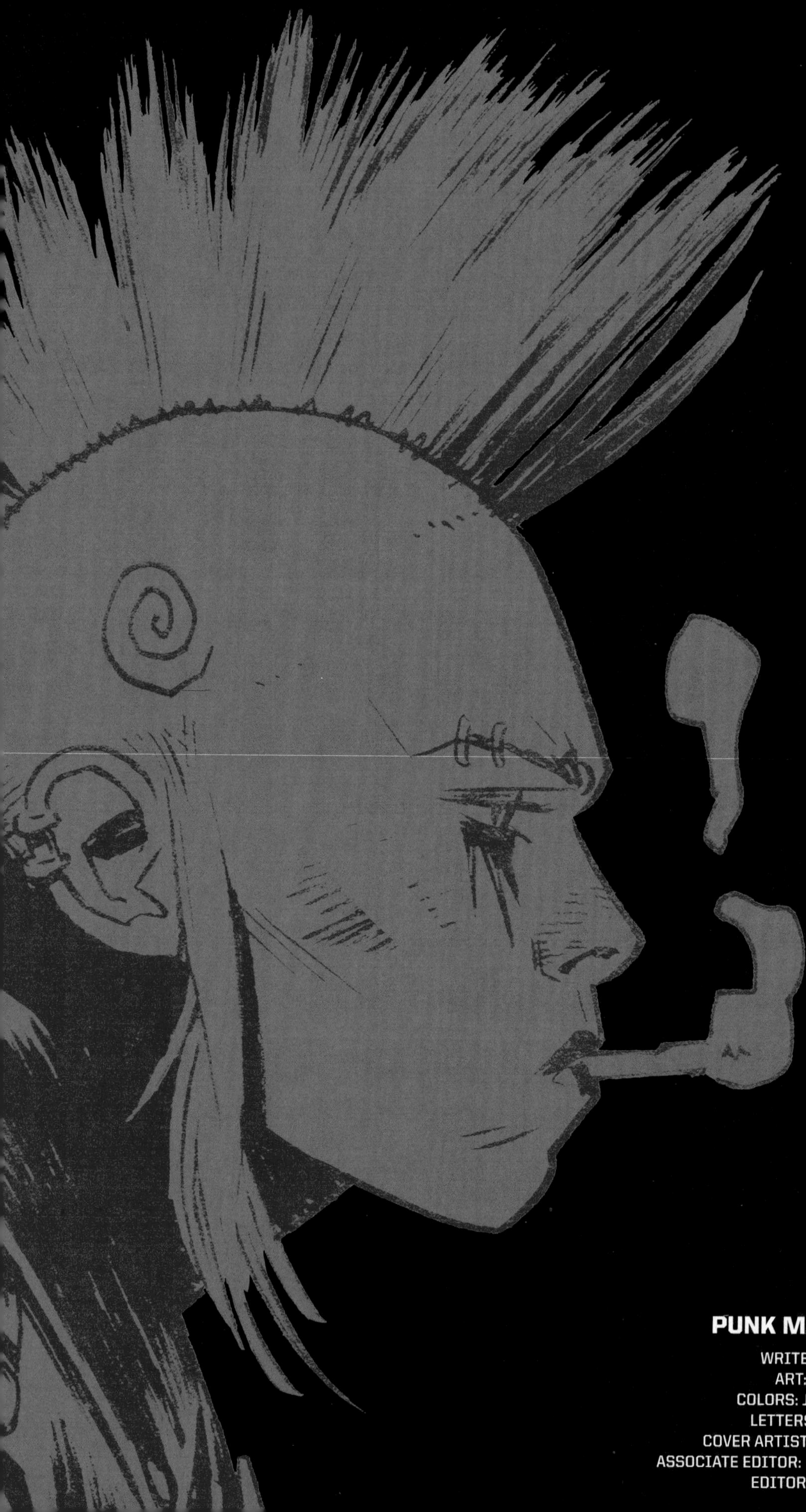

PUNK MAMBO #2

WRITER: Cullen Bunn
ART: Adam Gorham
COLORS: José Villarrubia
LETTERS: Dave Sharpe
COVER ARTIST: Dan Brereton
ASSOCIATE EDITOR: David Menchel
EDITOR: Lysa Hawkins

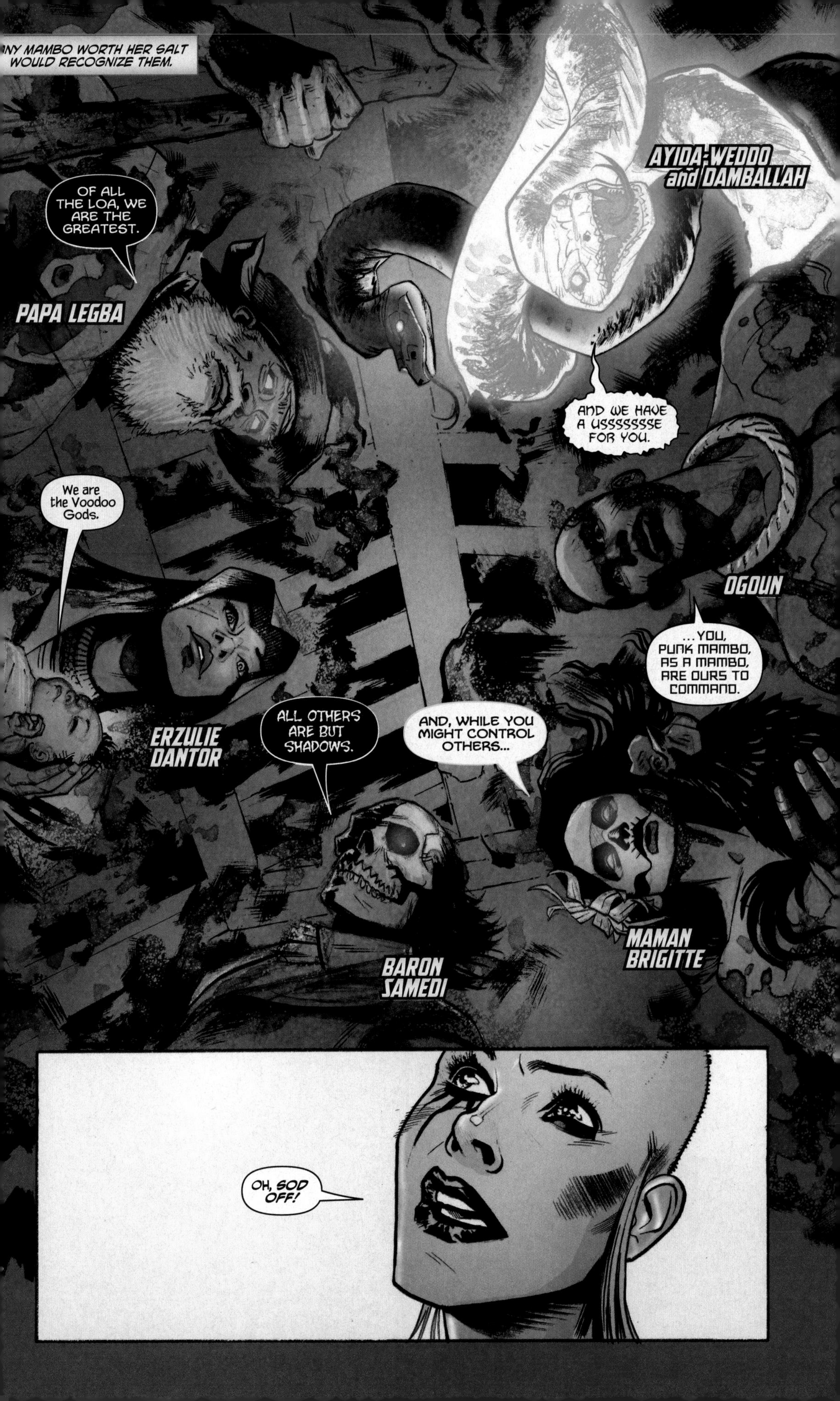

ANY MAMBO WORTH HER SALT WOULD RECOGNIZE THEM.
AYIDA-WEDDO and DAMBALLAH
OF ALL THE LOA, WE ARE THE GREATEST.
PAPA LEGBA
AND WE HAVE A USSSSSSSE FOR YOU.
We are the Voodoo Gods.
OGOUN
...YOU, PUNK MAMBO, AS A MAMBO, ARE OURS TO COMMAND.
ERZULIE DANTOR
ALL OTHERS ARE BUT SHADOWS.
AND, WHILE YOU MIGHT CONTROL OTHERS...
MAMAN BRIGITTE
BARON SAMEDI
OH, SOD OFF!

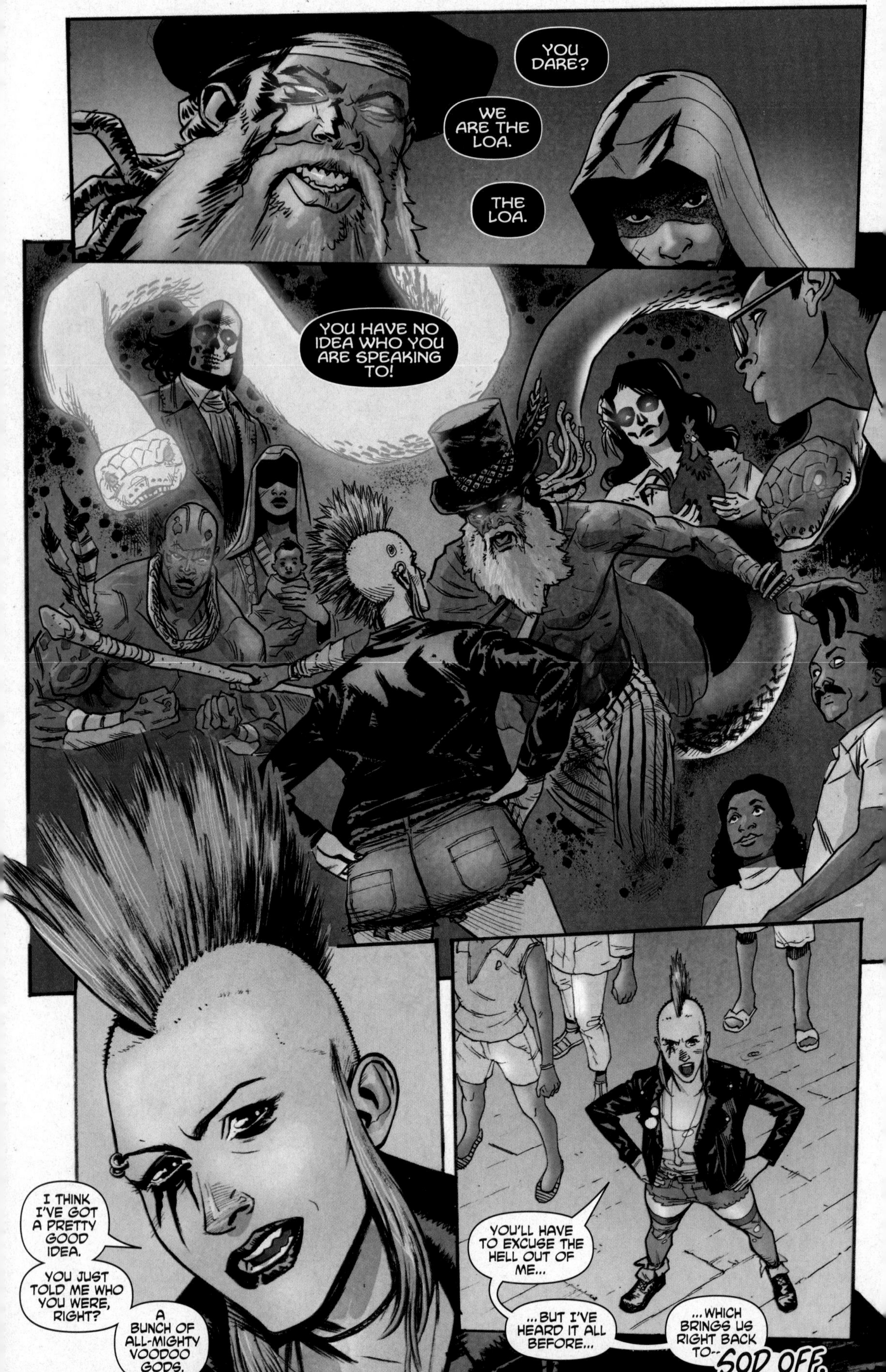
YOU DARE?
WE ARE THE LOA.
THE LOA.
YOU HAVE NO IDEA WHO YOU ARE SPEAKING TO!
I THINK I'VE GOT A PRETTY GOOD IDEA.
YOU JUST TOLD ME WHO YOU WERE, RIGHT?
A BUNCH OF ALL-MIGHTY VOODOO GODS.
YOU'LL HAVE TO EXCUSE THE HELL OUT OF ME...
...BUT I'VE HEARD IT ALL BEFORE...
...WHICH BRINGS US RIGHT BACK TO--
SOD OFF.

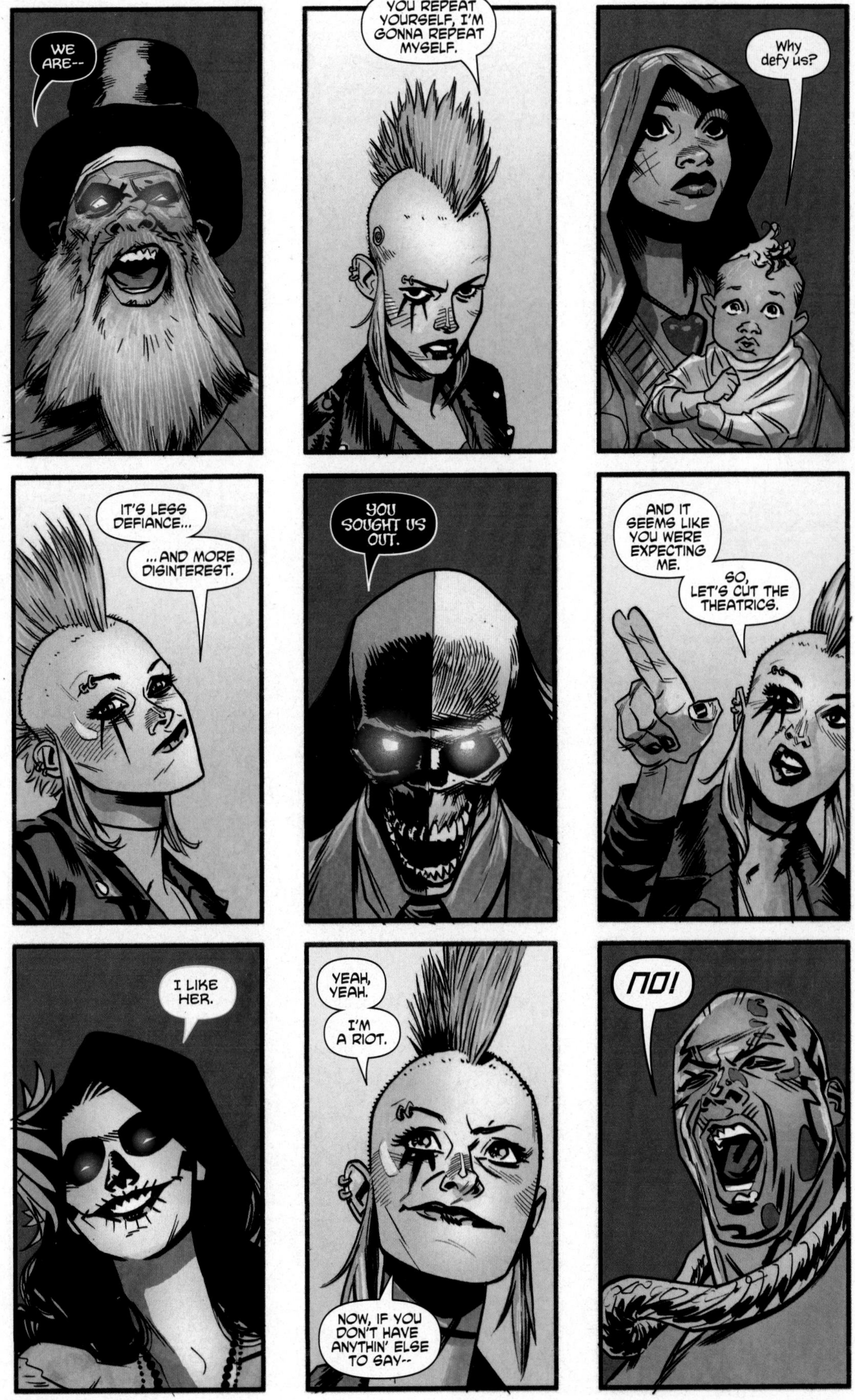
WE ARE--
YOU REPEAT YOURSELF, I'M GONNA REPEAT MYSELF.
Why defy us?
IT'S LESS DEFIANCE...
...AND MORE DISINTEREST.
YOU SOUGHT US OUT.
AND IT SEEMS LIKE YOU WERE EXPECTING ME.
SO, LET'S CUT THE THEATRICS.
I LIKE HER.
YEAH, YEAH.
I'M A RIOT.
NOW, IF YOU DON'T HAVE ANYTHIN' ELSE TO SAY--
NO!

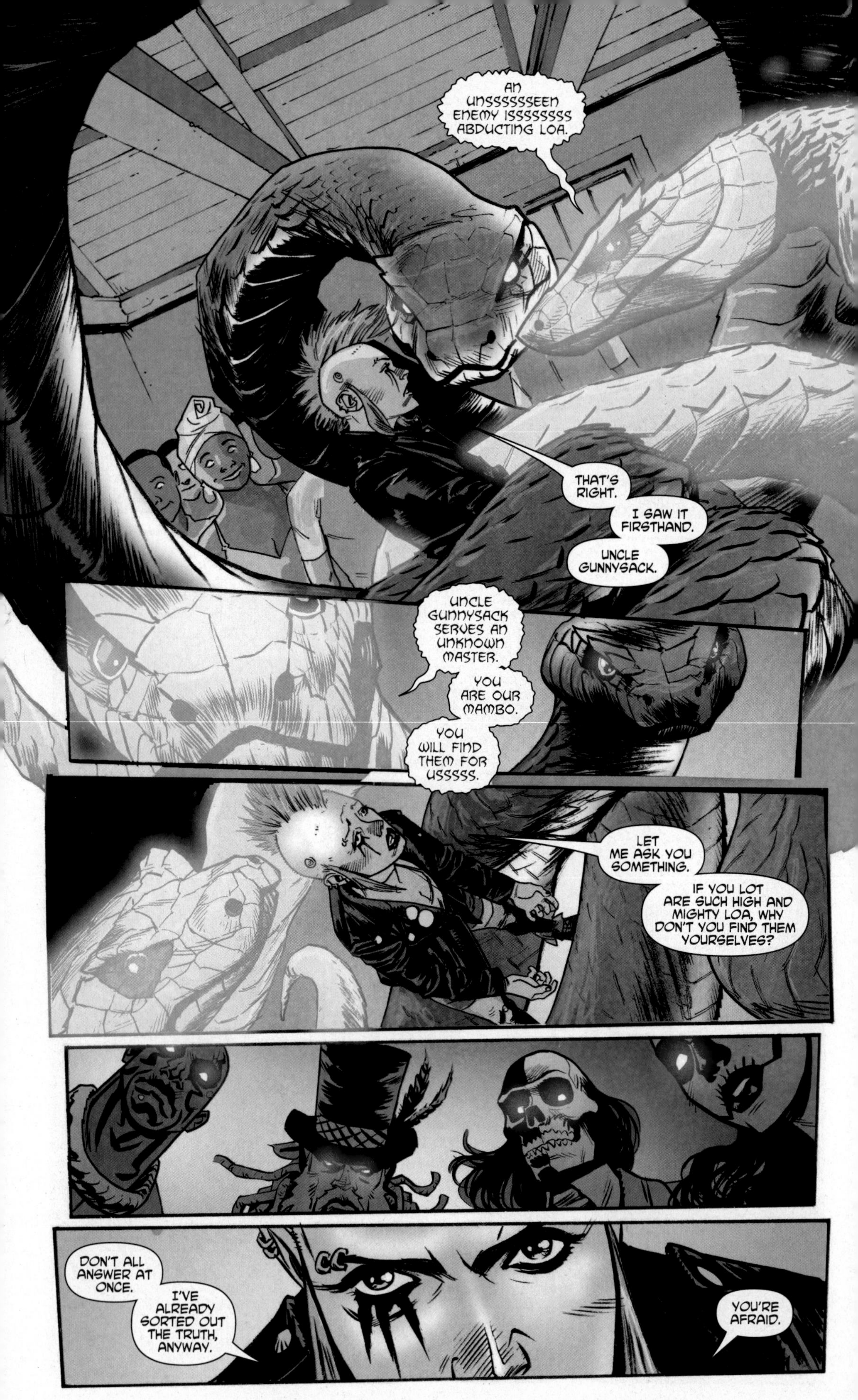
AN UNSSSSSSEEN ENEMY ISSSSSSSS ABDUCTING LOA.
THAT'S RIGHT.
I SAW IT FIRSTHAND.
UNCLE GUNNYSACK.
UNCLE GUNNYSACK SERVES AN UNKNOWN MASTER.
YOU ARE OUR MAMBO.
YOU WILL FIND THEM FOR USSSSS.
LET ME ASK YOU SOMETHING.
IF YOU LOT ARE SUCH HIGH AND MIGHTY LOA, WHY DON'T YOU FIND THEM YOURSELVES?
DON'T ALL ANSWER AT ONCE.
I'VE ALREADY SORTED OUT THE TRUTH, ANYWAY.
YOU'RE AFRAID.

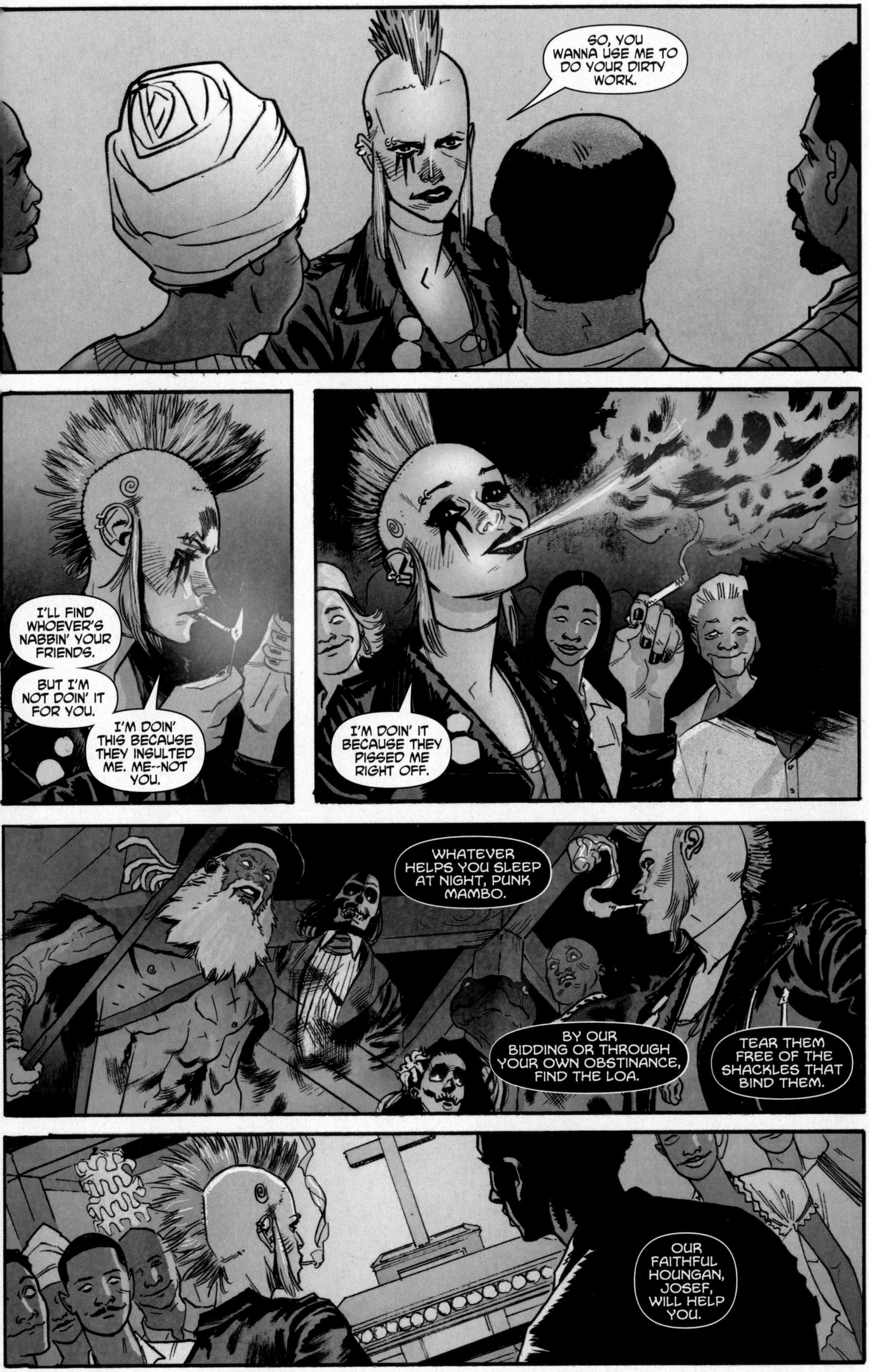

SO, YOU WANNA USE ME TO DO YOUR DIRTY WORK.
I'LL FIND WHOEVER'S NABBIN' YOUR FRIENDS.
BUT I'M NOT DOIN' IT FOR YOU.
I'M DOIN' THIS BECAUSE THEY INSULTED ME. ME--NOT YOU.
I'M DOIN' IT BECAUSE THEY PISSED ME RIGHT OFF.
WHATEVER HELPS YOU SLEEP AT NIGHT, PUNK MAMBO.
BY OUR BIDDING OR THROUGH YOUR OWN OBSTINANCE, FIND THE LOA.
TEAR THEM FREE OF THE SHACKLES THAT BIND THEM.
OUR FAITHFUL HOUNGAN, JOSEF, WILL HELP YOU.

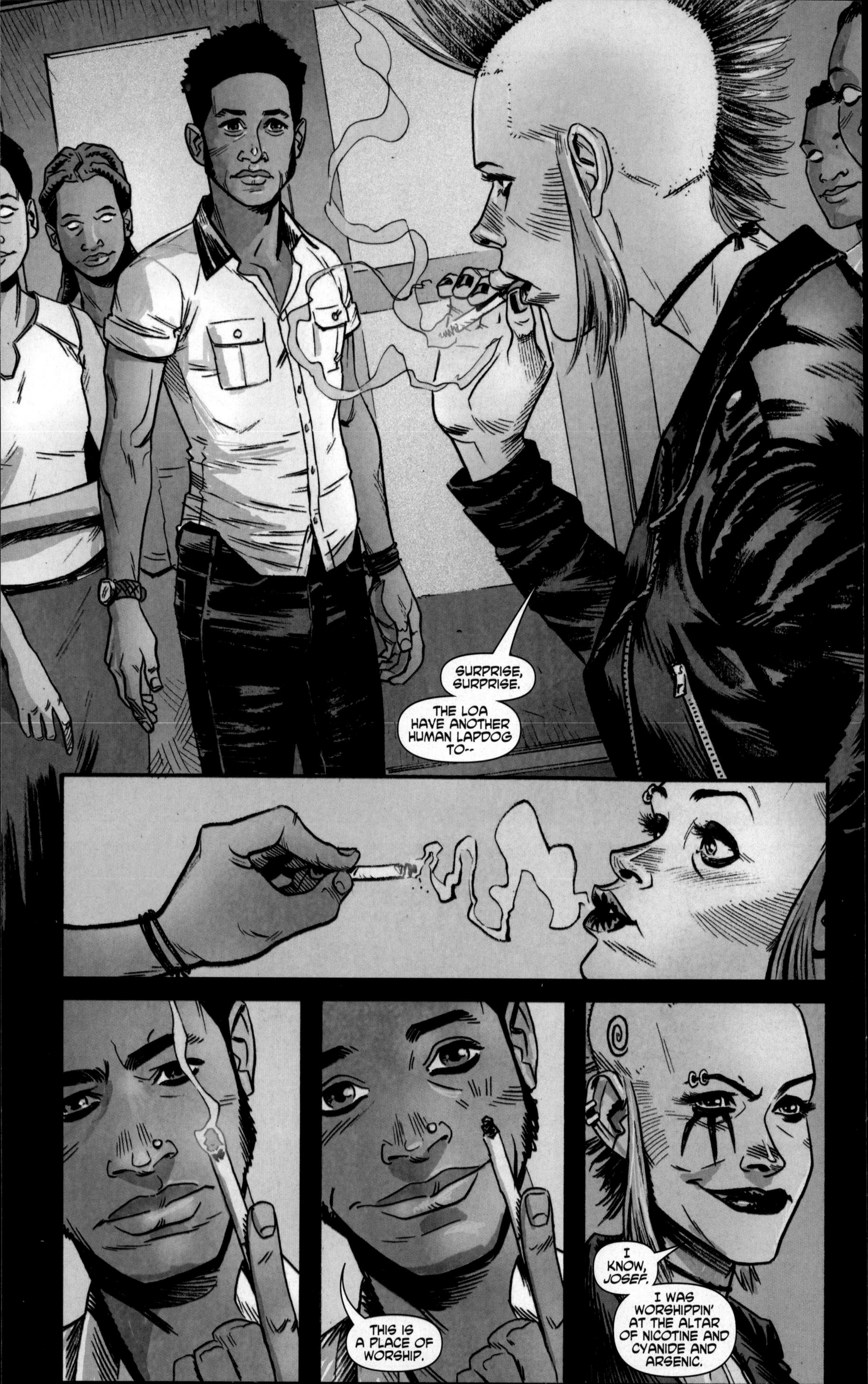
SURPRISE, SURPRISE.
THE LOA HAVE ANOTHER HUMAN LAPDOG TO--
THIS IS A PLACE OF WORSHIP.
I KNOW, JOSEF.
I WAS WORSHIPPIN' AT THE ALTAR OF NICOTINE AND CYANIDE AND ARSENIC.

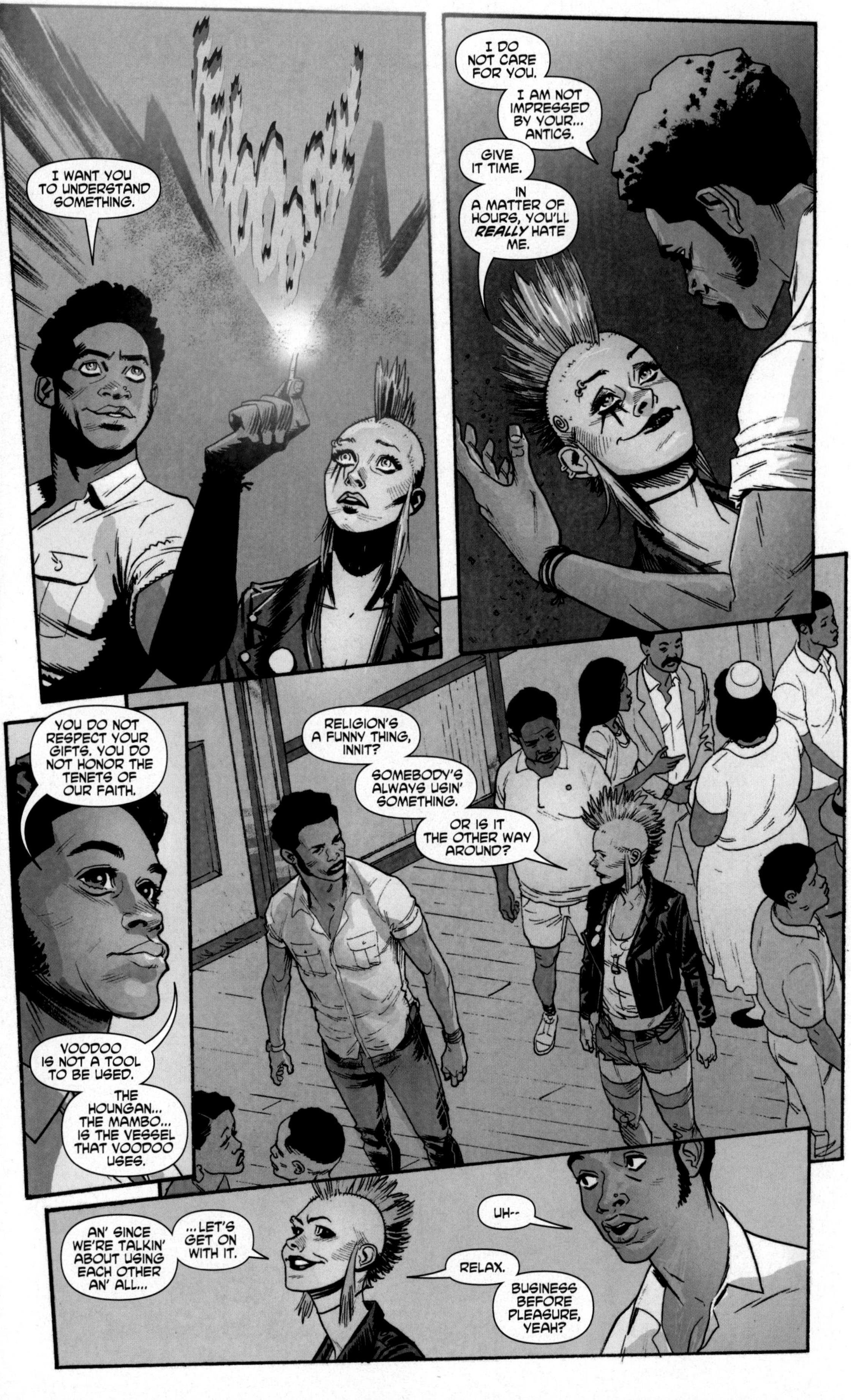
I WANT YOU TO UNDERSTAND SOMETHING.
I DO NOT CARE FOR YOU.
I AM NOT IMPRESSED BY YOUR... ANTICS.
GIVE IT TIME.
IN A MATTER OF HOURS, YOU'LL *REALLY* HATE ME.
YOU DO NOT RESPECT YOUR GIFTS. YOU DO NOT HONOR THE TENETS OF OUR FAITH.
VOODOO IS NOT A TOOL TO BE USED.
THE HOUNGAN... THE MAMBO... IS THE VESSEL THAT VOODOO USES.
RELIGION'S A FUNNY THING, INNIT?
SOMEBODY'S ALWAYS USIN' SOMETHING.
OR IS IT THE OTHER WAY AROUND?
AN' SINCE WE'RE TALKIN' ABOUT USING EACH OTHER AN' ALL...
...LET'S GET ON WITH IT.
UH--
RELAX.
BUSINESS BEFORE PLEASURE, YEAH?

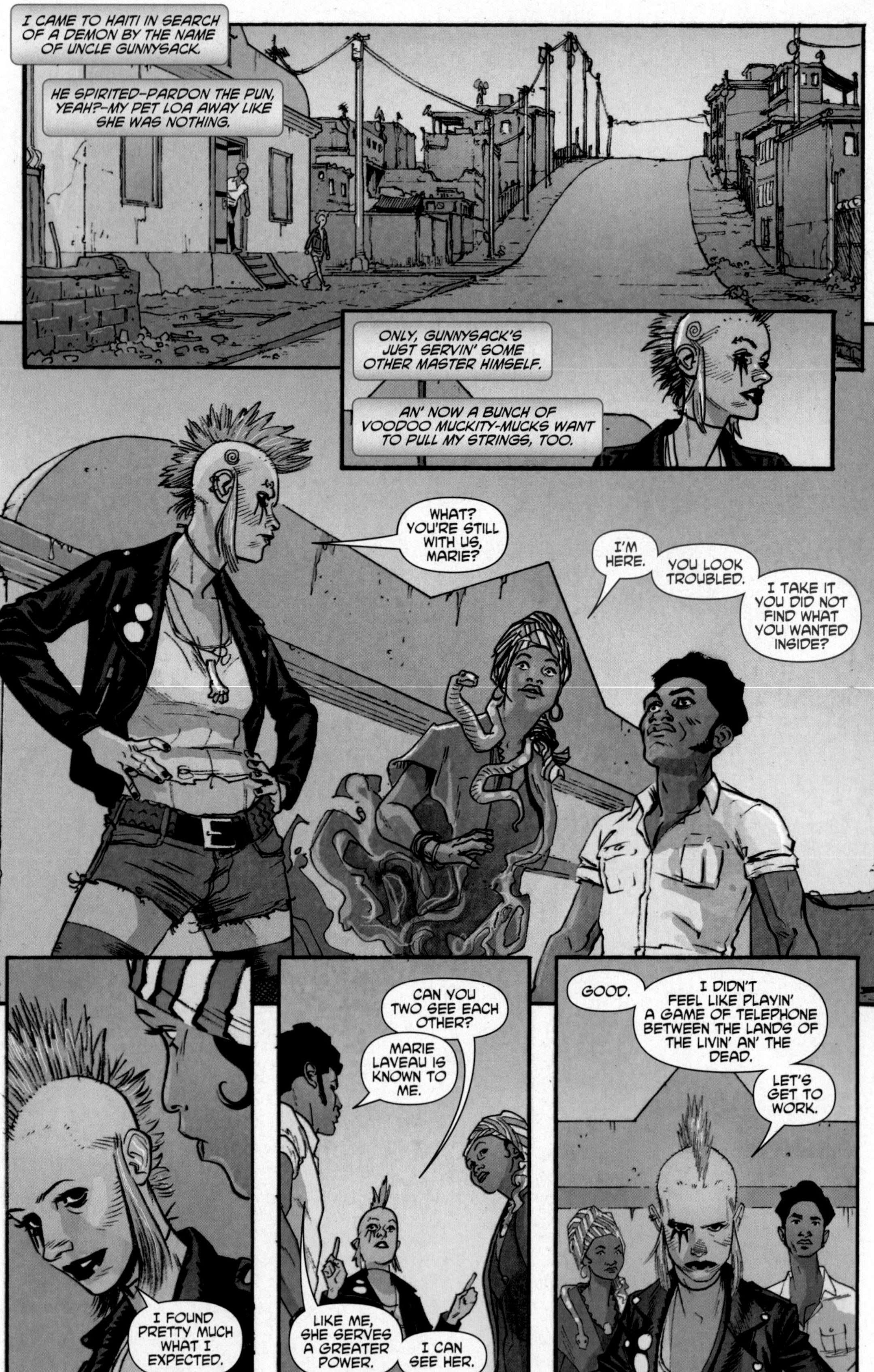

I CAME TO HAITI IN SEARCH OF A DEMON BY THE NAME OF UNCLE GUNNYSACK.
HE SPIRITED–PARDON THE PUN, YEAH?–MY PET LOA AWAY LIKE SHE WAS NOTHING.
ONLY, GUNNYSACK'S JUST SERVIN' SOME OTHER MASTER HIMSELF.
AN' NOW A BUNCH OF VOODOO MUCKITY-MUCKS WANT TO PULL MY STRINGS, TOO.
WHAT? YOU'RE STILL WITH US, MARIE?
I'M HERE.
YOU LOOK TROUBLED.
I TAKE IT YOU DID NOT FIND WHAT YOU WANTED INSIDE?
I FOUND PRETTY MUCH WHAT I EXPECTED.
CAN YOU TWO SEE EACH OTHER?
MARIE LAVEAU IS KNOWN TO ME.
LIKE ME, SHE SERVES A GREATER POWER.
I CAN SEE HER.
GOOD.
I DIDN'T FEEL LIKE PLAYIN' A GAME OF TELEPHONE BETWEEN THE LANDS OF THE LIVIN' AN' THE DEAD.
LET'S GET TO WORK.

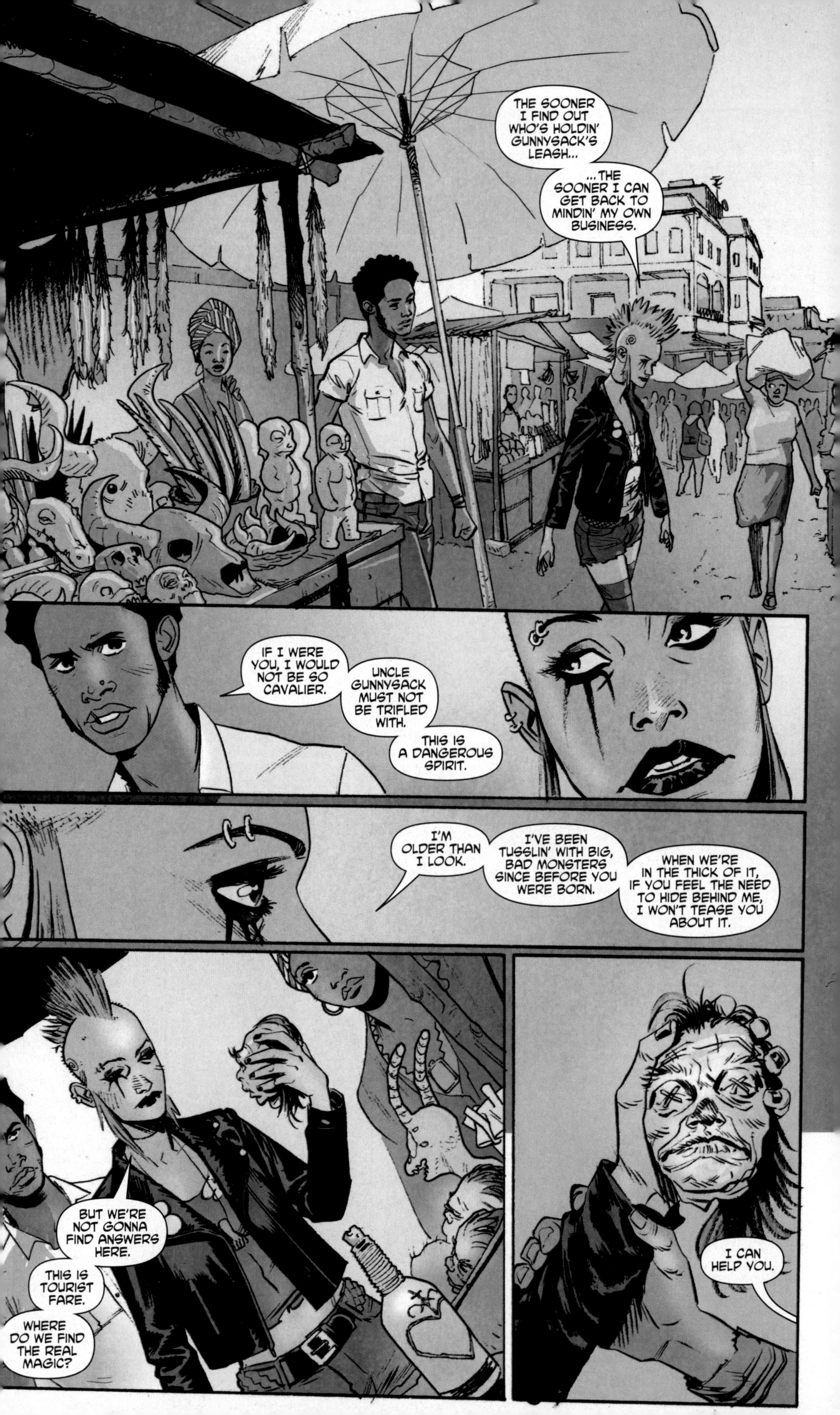
THE SOONER I FIND OUT WHO'S HOLDIN' GUNNYSACK'S LEASH...
...THE SOONER I CAN GET BACK TO MINDIN' MY OWN BUSINESS.
IF I WERE YOU, I WOULD NOT BE SO CAVALIER.
UNCLE GUNNYSACK MUST NOT BE TRIFLED WITH.
THIS IS A DANGEROUS SPIRIT.
I'M OLDER THAN I LOOK.
I'VE BEEN TUSSLIN' WITH BIG, BAD MONSTERS SINCE BEFORE YOU WERE BORN.
WHEN WE'RE IN THE THICK OF IT, IF YOU FEEL THE NEED TO HIDE BEHIND ME, I WON'T TEASE YOU ABOUT IT.
BUT WE'RE NOT GONNA FIND ANSWERS HERE.
THIS IS TOURIST FARE.
WHERE DO WE FIND THE REAL MAGIC?
I CAN HELP YOU.

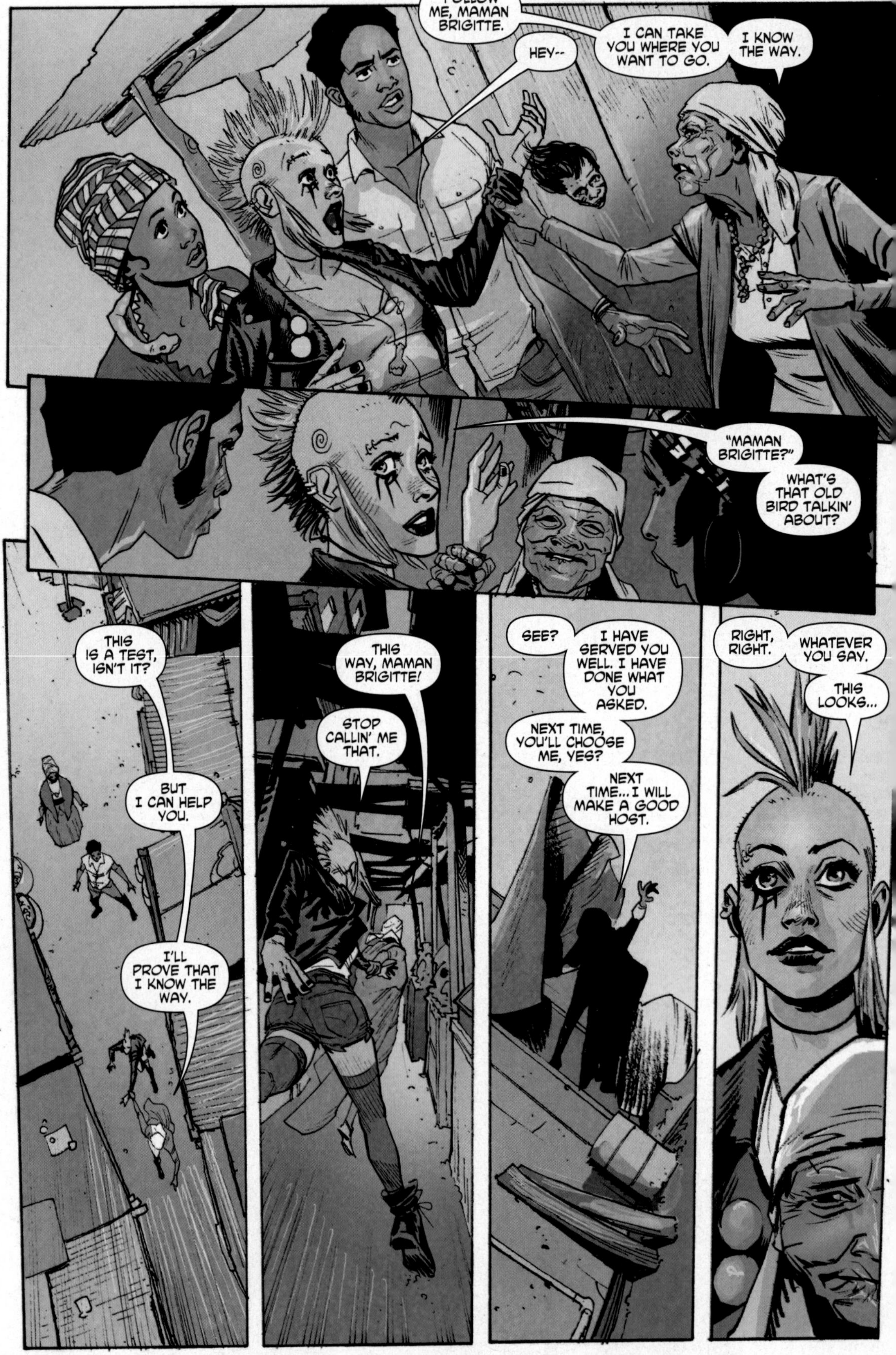
FOLLOW ME, MAMAN BRIGITTE.
HEY--
I CAN TAKE YOU WHERE YOU WANT TO GO.
I KNOW THE WAY.
"MAMAN BRIGITTE?"
WHAT'S THAT OLD BIRD TALKIN' ABOUT?
THIS IS A TEST, ISN'T IT?
BUT I CAN HELP YOU.
I'LL PROVE THAT I KNOW THE WAY.
THIS WAY, MAMAN BRIGITTE!
STOP CALLIN' ME THAT.
SEE?
I HAVE SERVED YOU WELL. I HAVE DONE WHAT YOU ASKED.
NEXT TIME, YOU'LL CHOOSE ME, YES?
NEXT TIME... I WILL MAKE A GOOD HOST.
RIGHT, RIGHT.
WHATEVER YOU SAY.
THIS LOOKS...

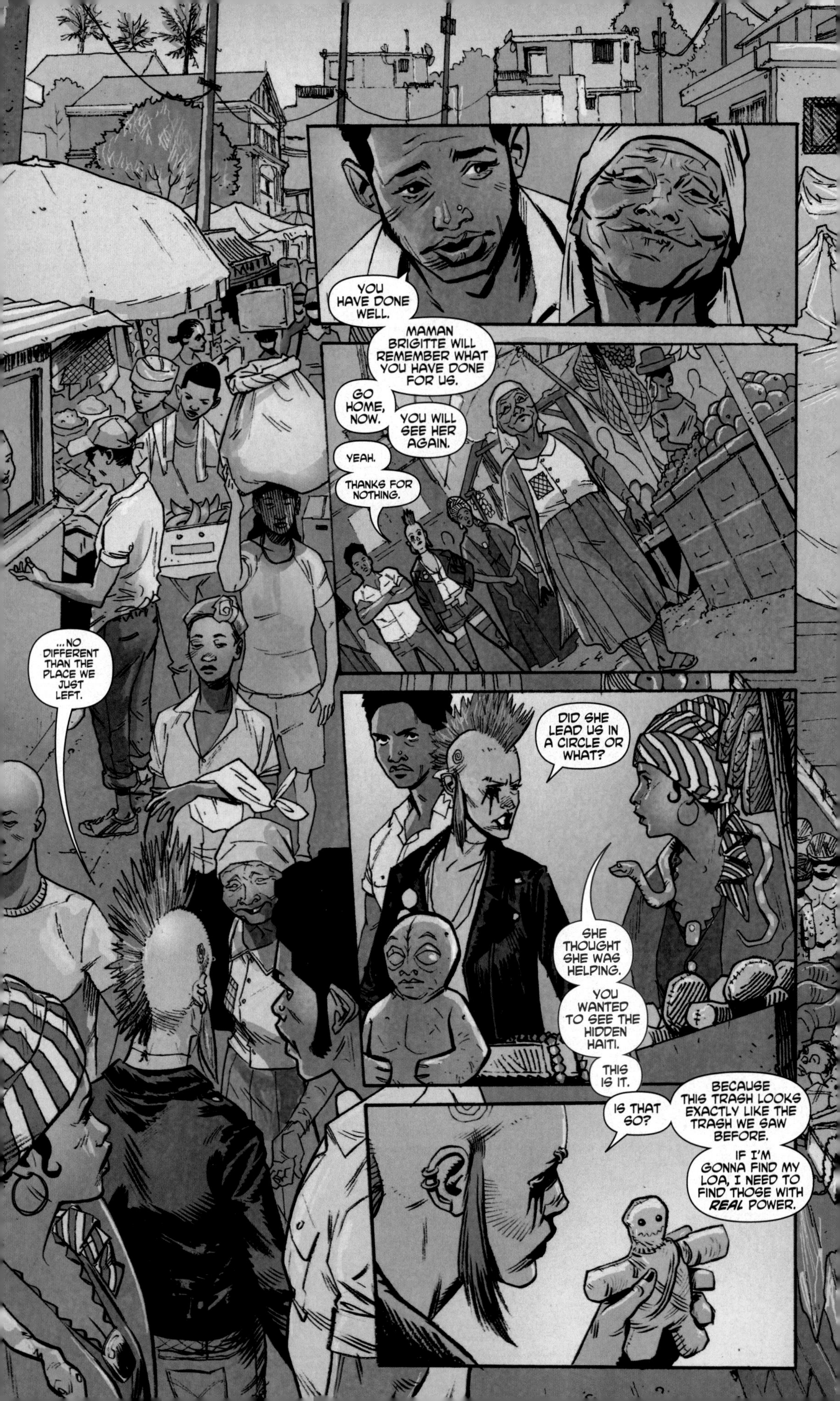
YOU HAVE DONE WELL.
MAMAN BRIGITTE WILL REMEMBER WHAT YOU HAVE DONE FOR US.
GO HOME, NOW.
YOU WILL SEE HER AGAIN.
YEAH.
THANKS FOR NOTHING.
...NO DIFFERENT THAN THE PLACE WE JUST LEFT.
DID SHE LEAD US IN A CIRCLE OR WHAT?
SHE THOUGHT SHE WAS HELPING.
YOU WANTED TO SEE THE HIDDEN HAITI.
THIS IS IT.
IS THAT SO?
BECAUSE THIS TRASH LOOKS EXACTLY LIKE THE TRASH WE SAW BEFORE.
IF I'M GONNA FIND MY LOA, I NEED TO FIND THOSE WITH *REAL* POWER.

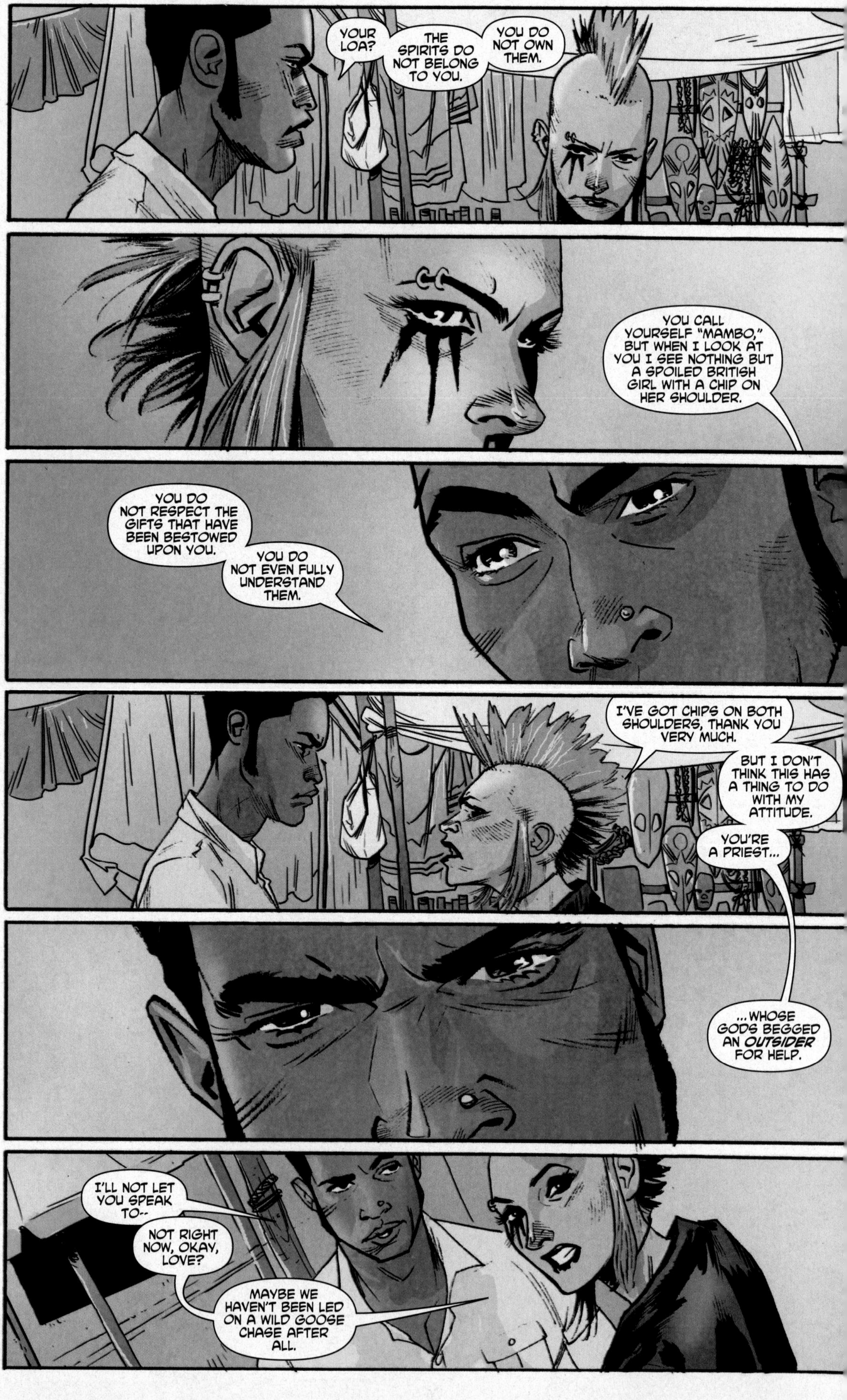

YOUR LOA?
THE SPIRITS DO NOT BELONG TO YOU.
YOU DO NOT OWN THEM.
YOU CALL YOURSELF "MAMBO," BUT WHEN I LOOK AT YOU I SEE NOTHING BUT A SPOILED BRITISH GIRL WITH A CHIP ON HER SHOULDER.
YOU DO NOT RESPECT THE GIFTS THAT HAVE BEEN BESTOWED UPON YOU.
YOU DO NOT EVEN FULLY UNDERSTAND THEM.
I'VE GOT CHIPS ON BOTH SHOULDERS, THANK YOU VERY MUCH.
BUT I DON'T THINK THIS HAS A THING TO DO WITH MY ATTITUDE.
YOU'RE A PRIEST...
...WHOSE GODS BEGGED AN *OUTSIDER* FOR HELP.
I'LL NOT LET YOU SPEAK TO--
NOT RIGHT NOW, OKAY, LOVE?
MAYBE WE HAVEN'T BEEN LED ON A WILD GOOSE CHASE AFTER ALL.

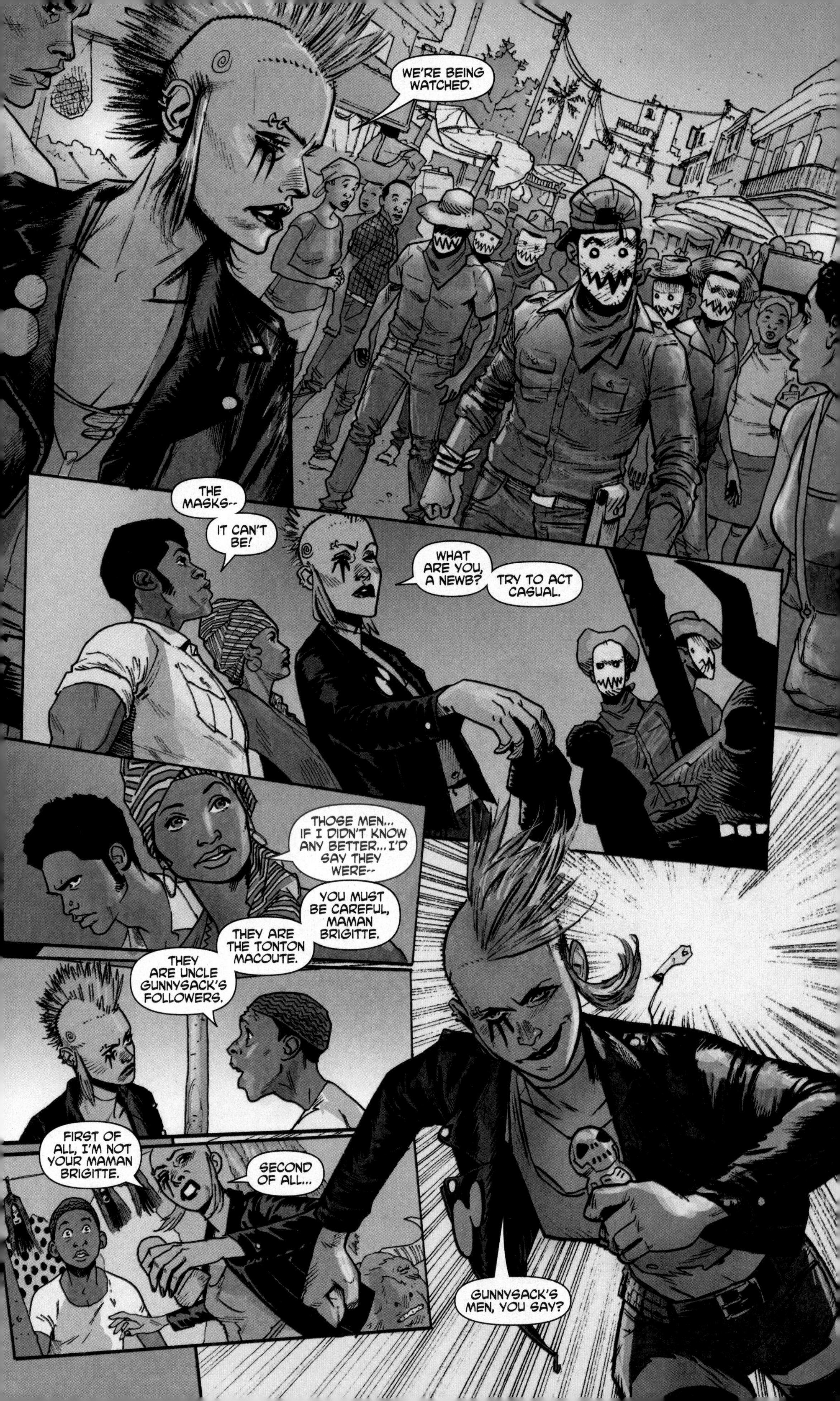
WE'RE BEING WATCHED.
THE MASKS--
IT CAN'T BE!
WHAT ARE YOU, A NEWB?
TRY TO ACT CASUAL.
THOSE MEN... IF I DIDN'T KNOW ANY BETTER... I'D SAY THEY WERE--
YOU MUST BE CAREFUL, MAMAN BRIGITTE.
THEY ARE THE TONTON MACOUTE.
THEY ARE UNCLE GUNNYSACK'S FOLLOWERS.
FIRST OF ALL, I'M NOT YOUR MAMAN BRIGITTE.
SECOND OF ALL...
GUNNYSACK'S MEN, YOU SAY?

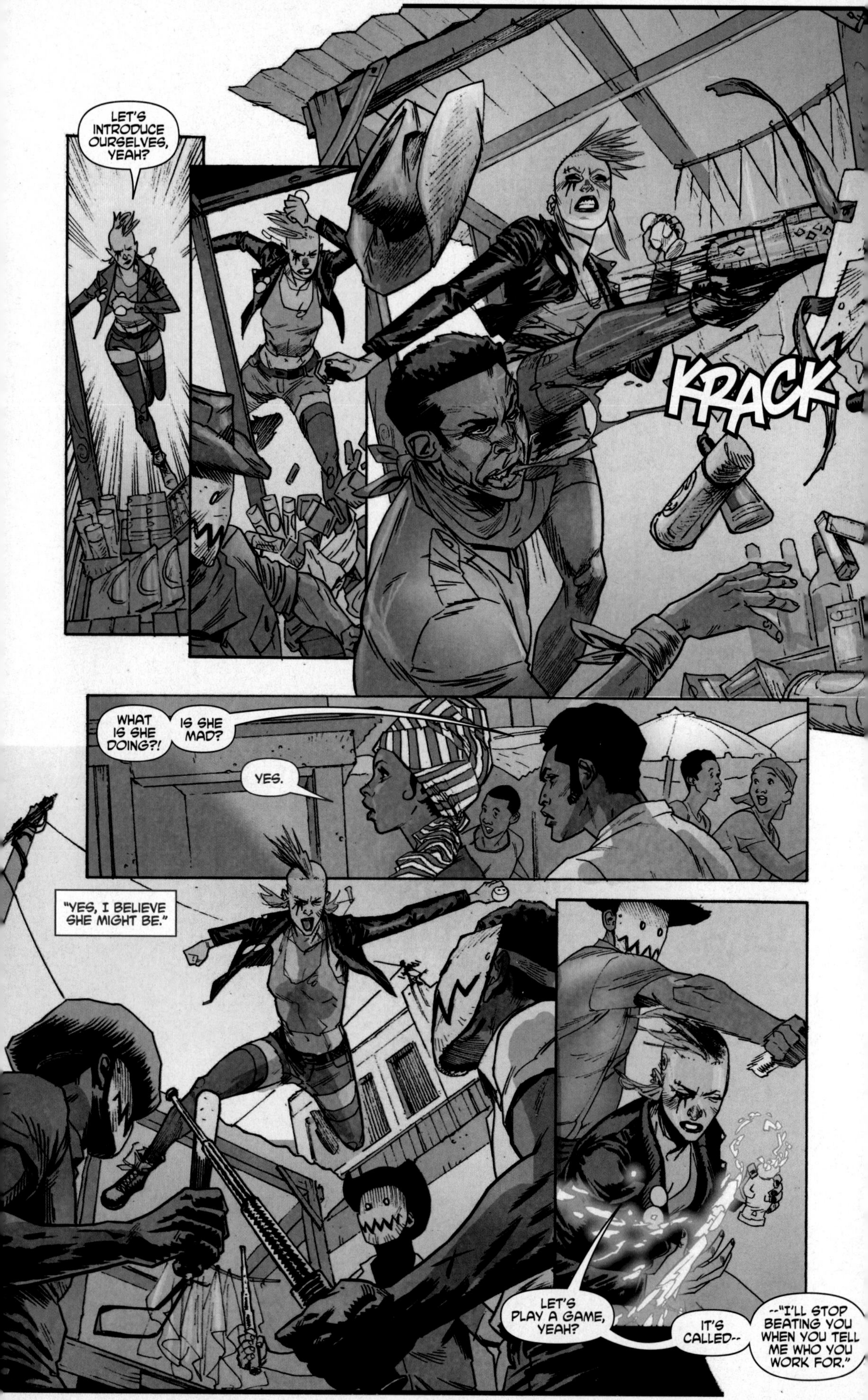
LET'S INTRODUCE OURSELVES, YEAH?
KRACK
WHAT IS SHE DOING?!
IS SHE MAD?
YES.
"YES, I BELIEVE SHE MIGHT BE."
LET'S PLAY A GAME, YEAH?
IT'S CALLED--
--"I'LL STOP BEATING YOU WHEN YOU TELL ME WHO YOU WORK FOR."

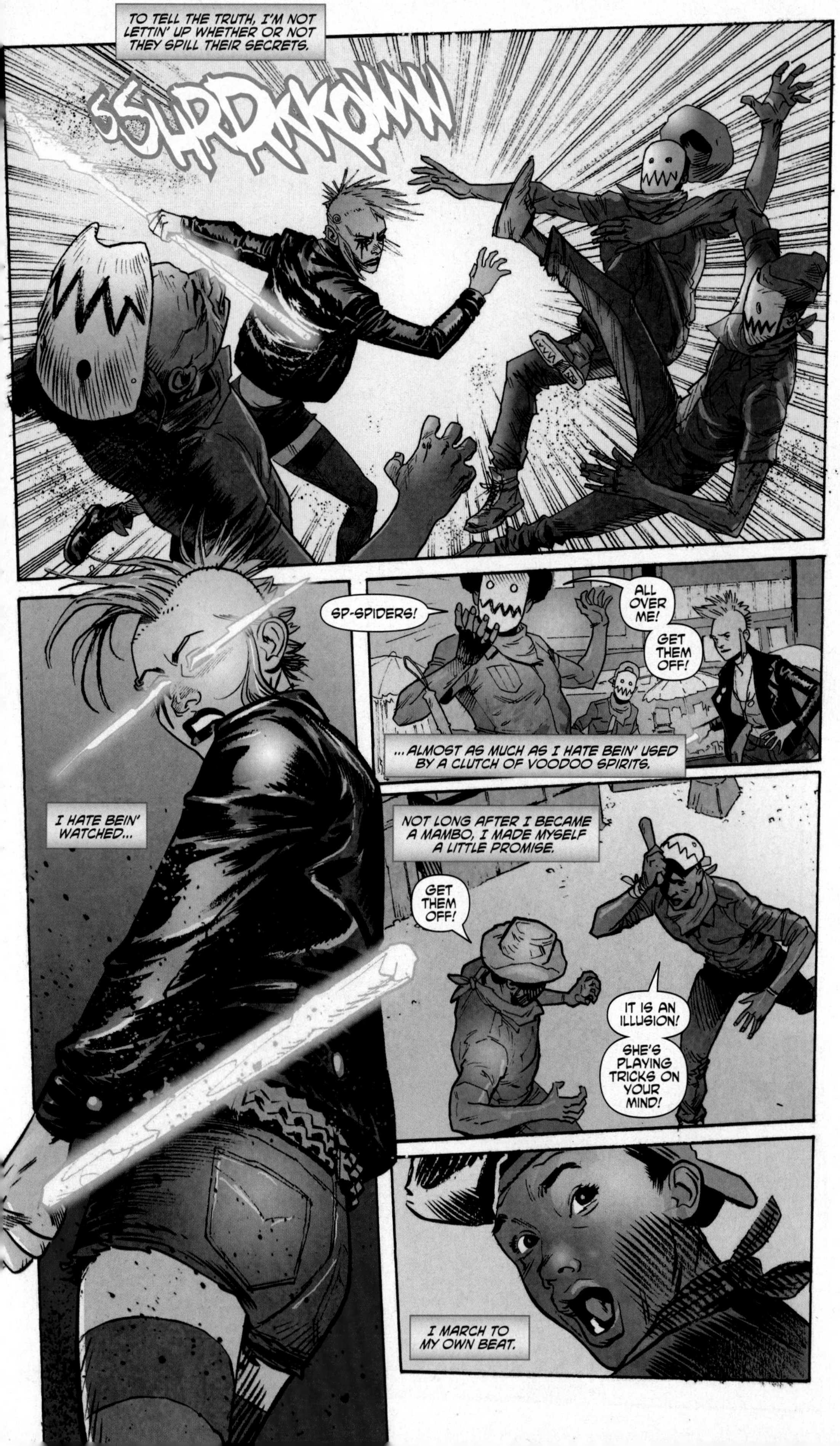
TO TELL THE TRUTH, I'M NOT LETTIN' UP WHETHER OR NOT THEY SPILL THEIR SECRETS.
SSHRDKKOWW
I HATE BEIN' WATCHED...
SP-SPIDERS!
ALL OVER ME!
GET THEM OFF!
...ALMOST AS MUCH AS I HATE BEIN' USED BY A CLUTCH OF VOODOO SPIRITS.
NOT LONG AFTER I BECAME A MAMBO, I MADE MYSELF A LITTLE PROMISE.
GET THEM OFF!
IT IS AN ILLUSION!
SHE'S PLAYING TRICKS ON YOUR MIND!
I MARCH TO MY OWN BEAT.

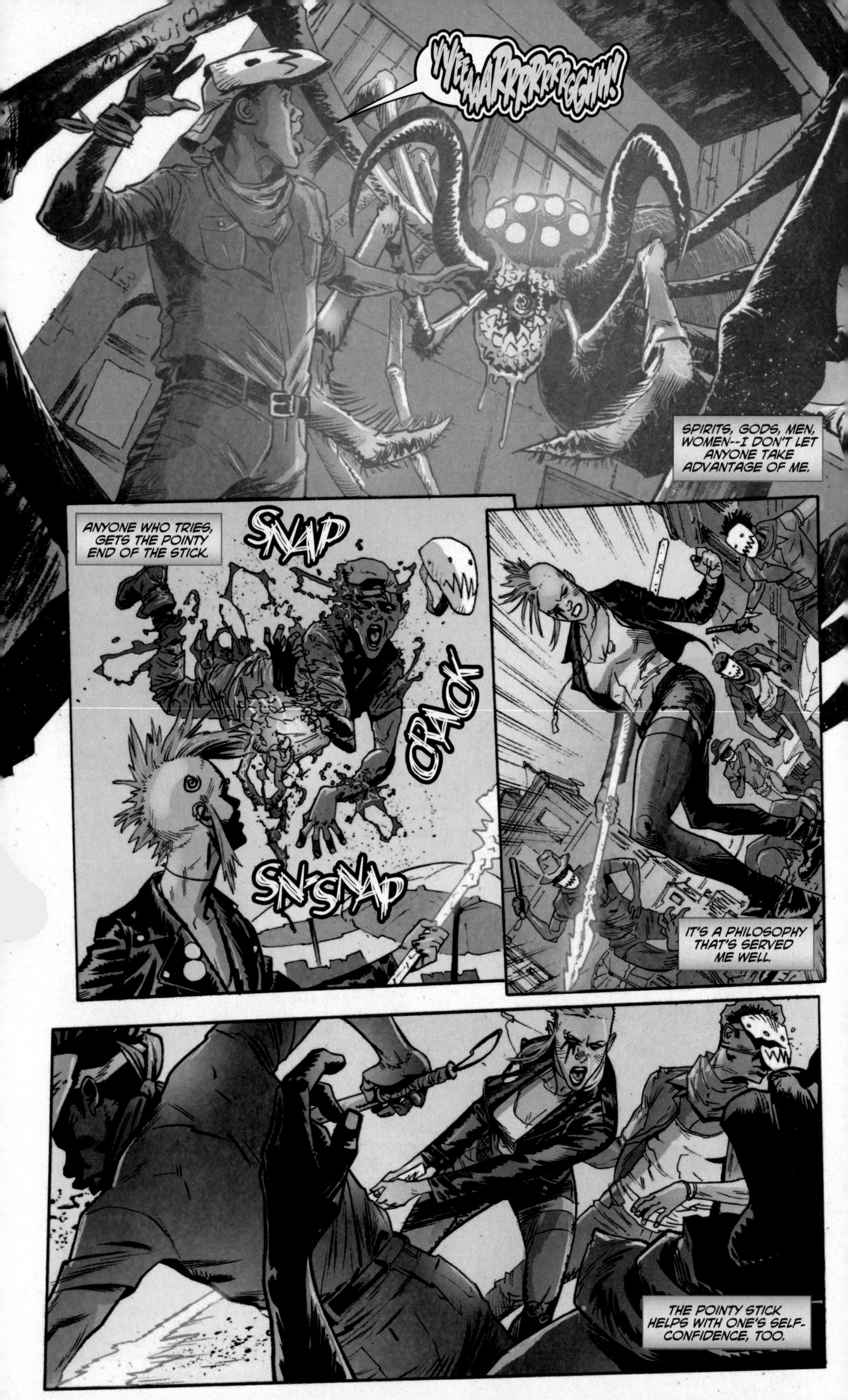
YYEEAAARRRRRRRRGGHHH!
SPIRITS, GODS, MEN, WOMEN--I DON'T LET ANYONE TAKE ADVANTAGE OF ME.
ANYONE WHO TRIES, GETS THE POINTY END OF THE STICK.
SNAP
CRACK
SN-SNAP
IT'S A PHILOSOPHY THAT'S SERVED ME WELL.
THE POINTY STICK HELPS WITH ONE'S SELF-CONFIDENCE, TOO.

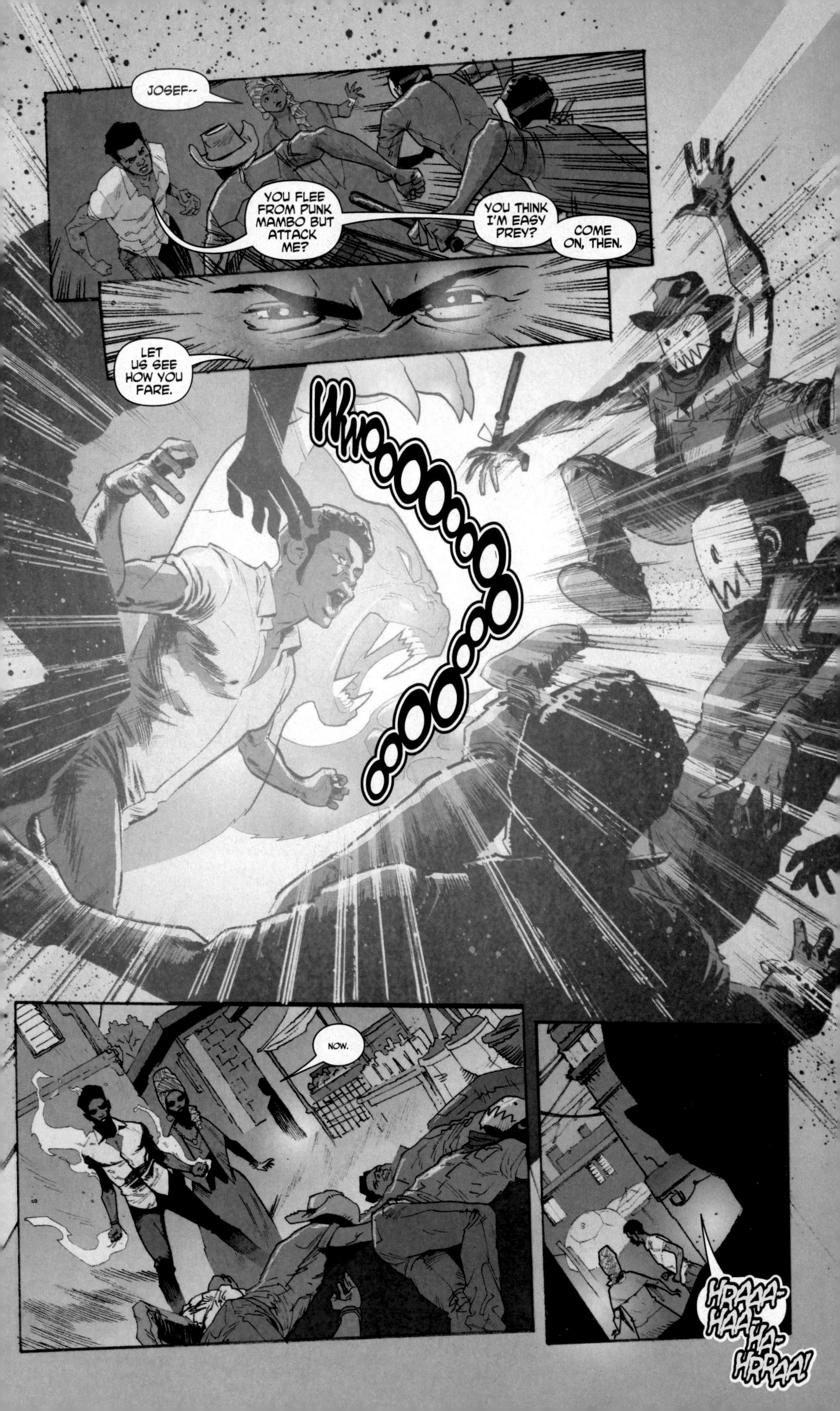

JOSEF--
YOU FLEE FROM PUNK MAMBO BUT ATTACK ME?
YOU THINK I'M EASY PREY?
COME ON, THEN.
LET US SEE HOW YOU FARE.
WHOOOOOOOOOOO
NOW.
HRAAA-HAA-HA-HRRAA!

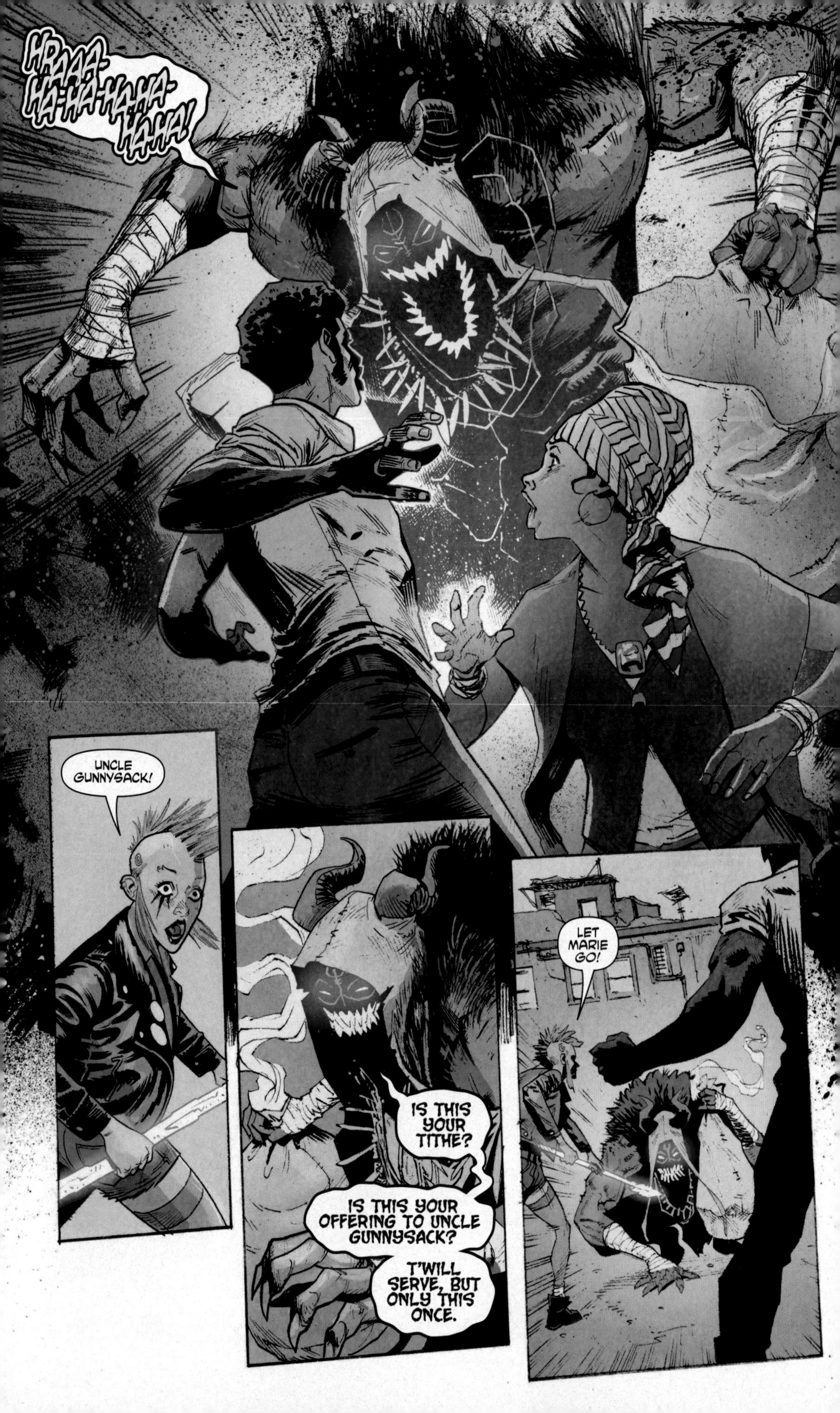
HRAAA-HA-HA-HA-HA-HA-HA-HA!
UNCLE GUNNYSACK!
IS THIS YOUR TITHE?
IS THIS YOUR OFFERING TO UNCLE GUNNYSACK?
T'WILL SERVE, BUT ONLY THIS ONCE.
LET MARIE GO!

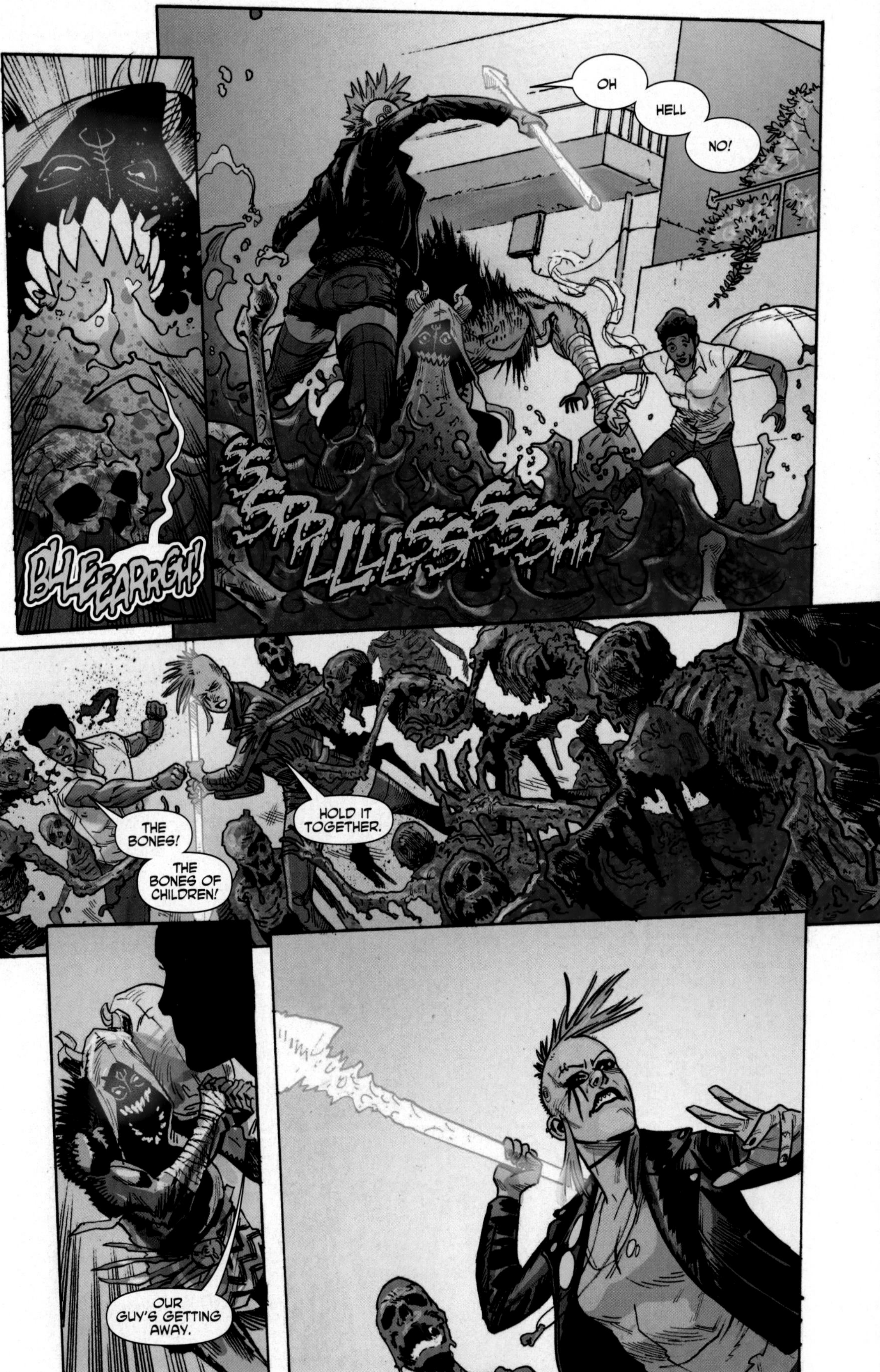
BLLEEARRGH!
OH
HELL
NO!
SSPPLLLSSSSHH
THE BONES!
THE BONES OF CHILDREN!
HOLD IT TOGETHER.
OUR GUY'S GETTING AWAY.

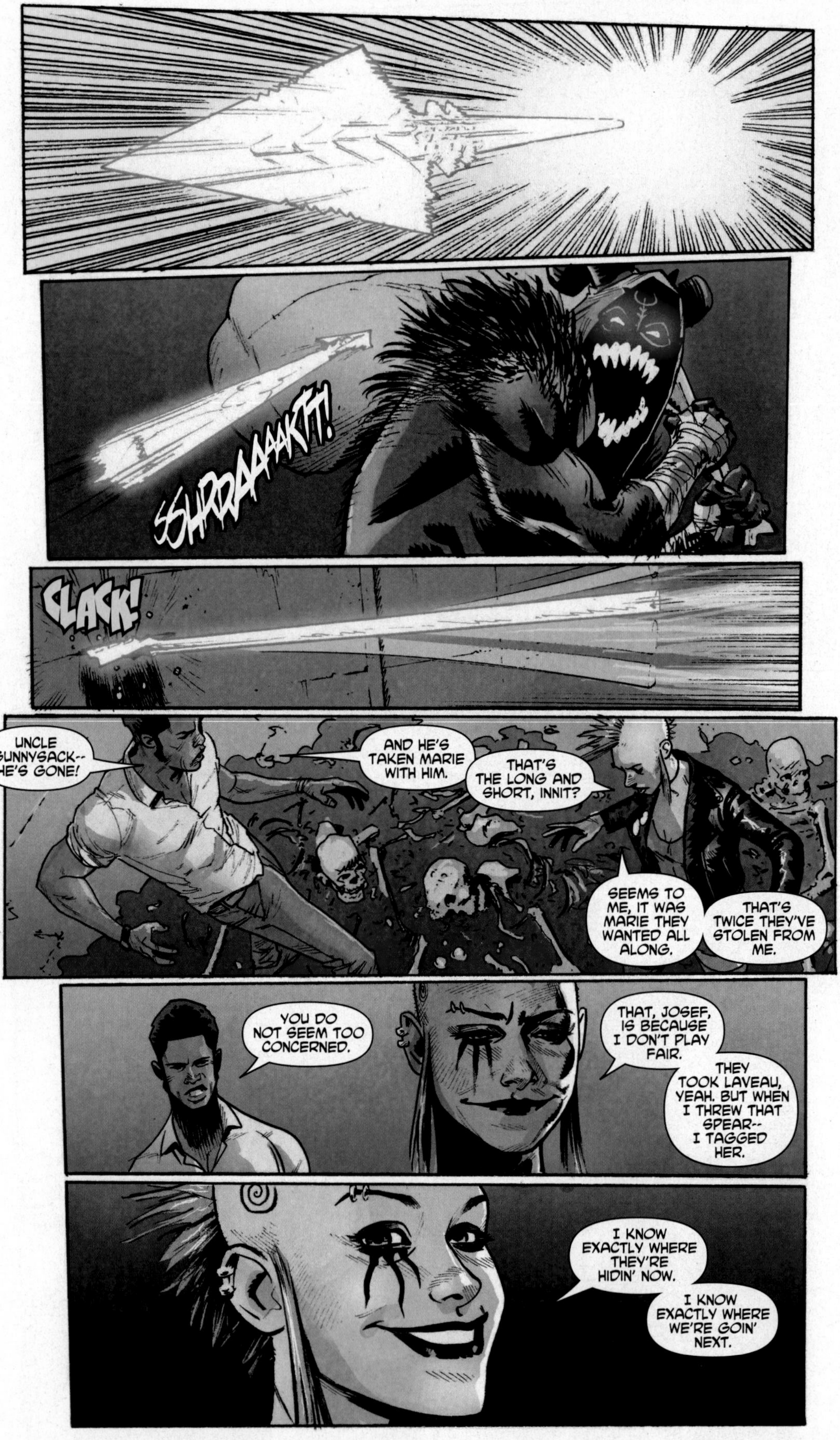
SSHRDAAAAKTT!
CLACK!
UNCLE GUNNYSACK-- HE'S GONE!
AND HE'S TAKEN MARIE WITH HIM.
THAT'S THE LONG AND SHORT, INNIT?
SEEMS TO ME, IT WAS MARIE THEY WANTED ALL ALONG.
THAT'S TWICE THEY'VE STOLEN FROM ME.
YOU DO NOT SEEM TOO CONCERNED.
THAT, JOSEF, IS BECAUSE I DON'T PLAY FAIR.
THEY TOOK LAVEAU, YEAH. BUT WHEN I THREW THAT SPEAR-- I TAGGED HER.
I KNOW EXACTLY WHERE THEY'RE HIDIN' NOW.
I KNOW EXACTLY WHERE WE'RE GOIN' NEXT.

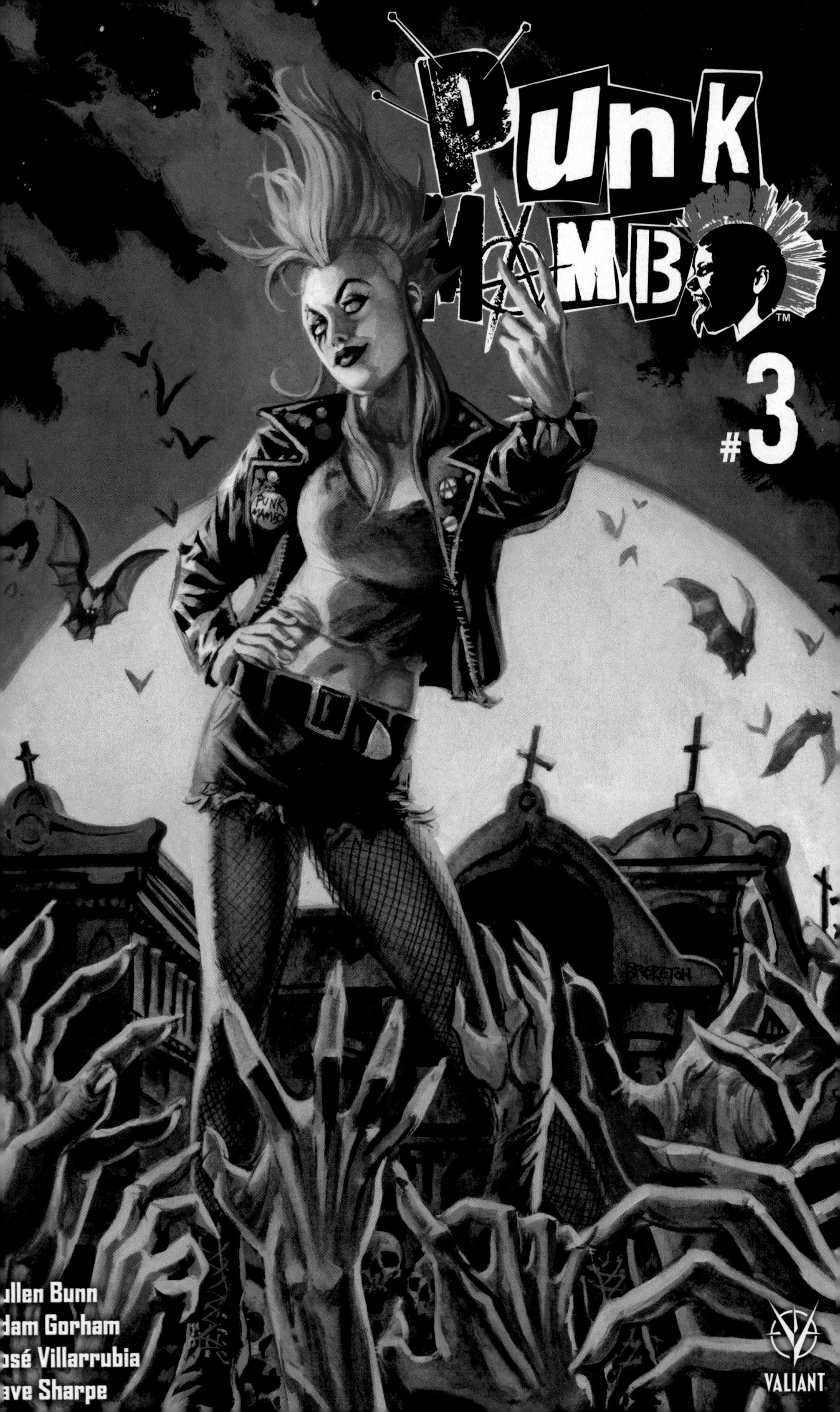
PUNK MAMBO
#3
ullen Bunn
dam Gorham
osé Villarrubia
ave Sharpe
VALIANT

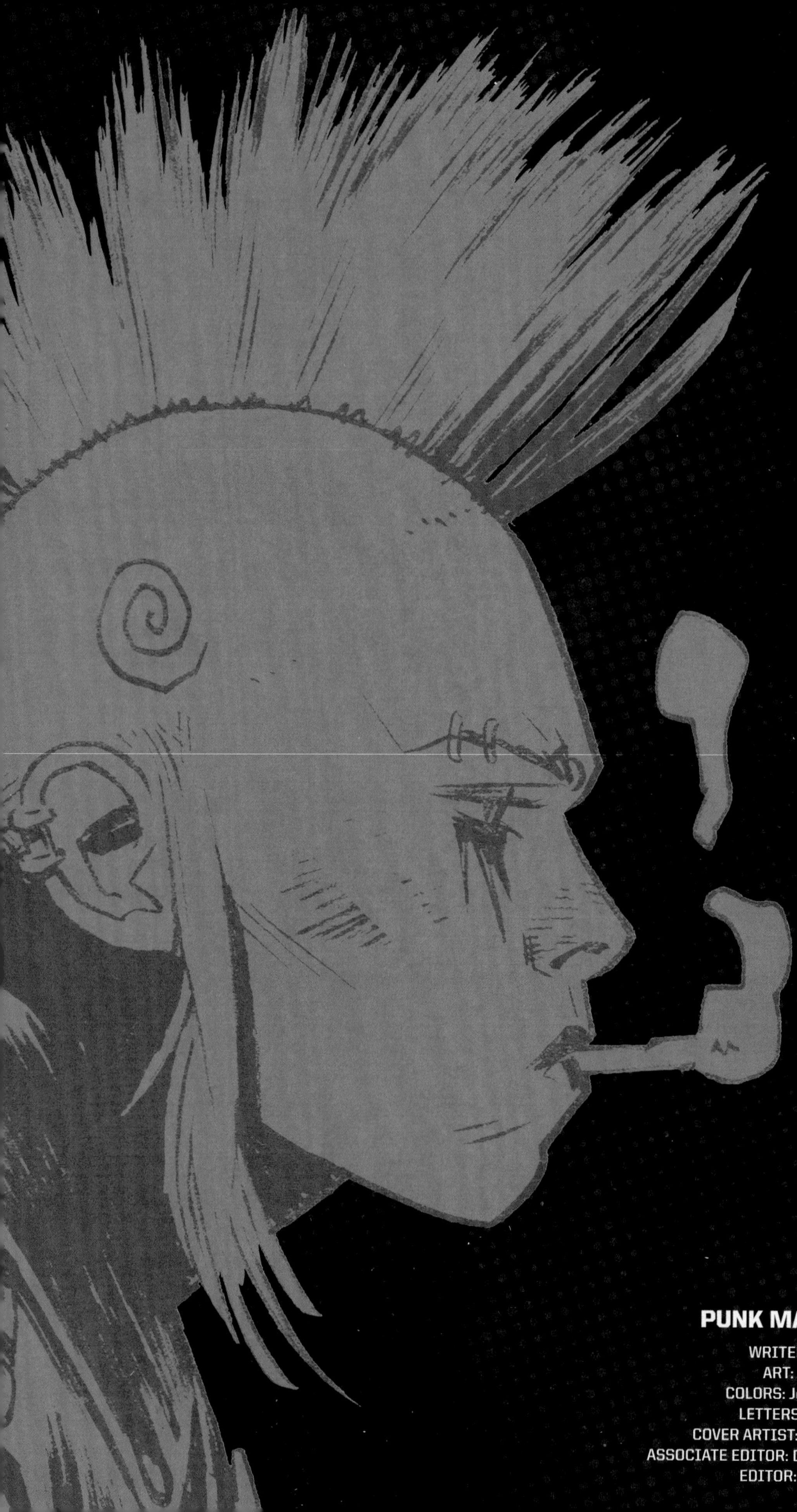

PUNK MAMBO #3

WRITER: Cullen Bunn
ART: Adam Gorham
COLORS: José Villarrubia
LETTERS: Dave Sharpe
COVER ARTIST: Dan Brereton
ASSOCIATE EDITOR: David Menchel
EDITOR: Lysa Hawkins

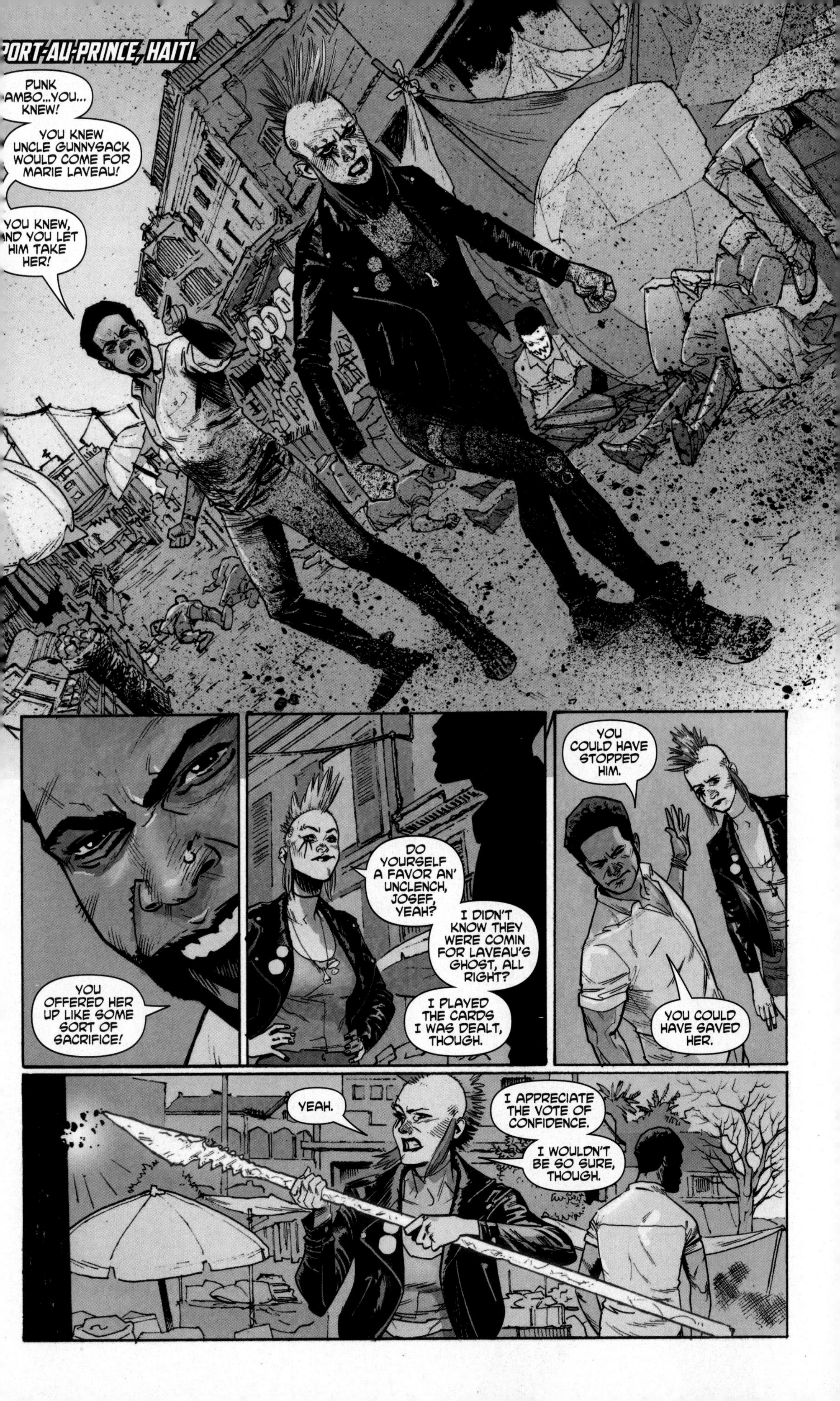
PORT-AU-PRINCE, HAITI.
PUNK MAMBO...YOU... KNEW!
YOU KNEW UNCLE GUNNYSACK WOULD COME FOR MARIE LAVEAU!
YOU KNEW, AND YOU LET HIM TAKE HER!
YOU OFFERED HER UP LIKE SOME SORT OF SACRIFICE!
DO YOURSELF A FAVOR AN' UNCLENCH, JOSEF, YEAH?
I DIDN'T KNOW THEY WERE COMIN FOR LAVEAU'S GHOST, ALL RIGHT?
I PLAYED THE CARDS I WAS DEALT, THOUGH.
YOU COULD HAVE STOPPED HIM.
YOU COULD HAVE SAVED HER.
YEAH.
I APPRECIATE THE VOTE OF CONFIDENCE.
I WOULDN'T BE SO SURE, THOUGH.

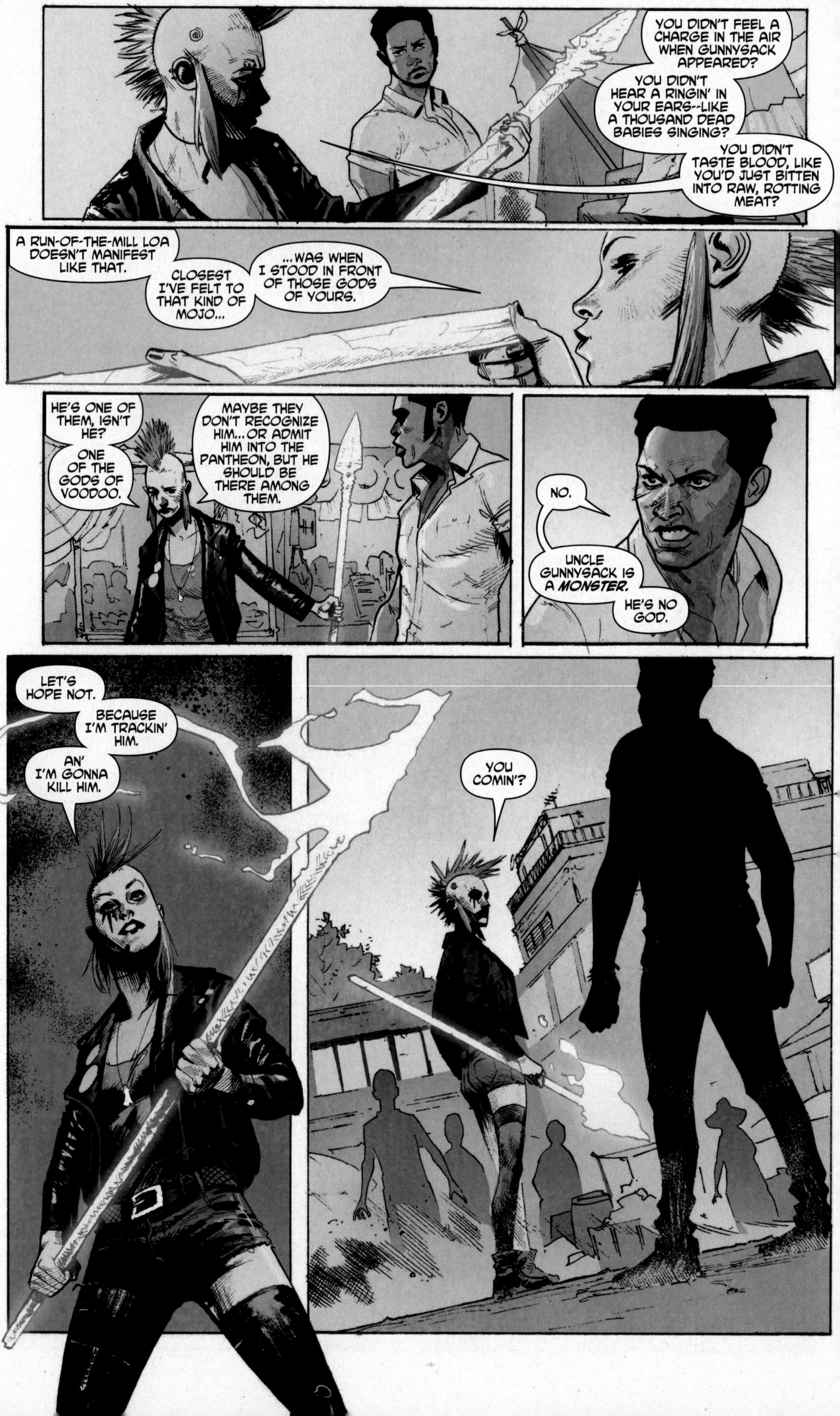
YOU DIDN'T FEEL A CHARGE IN THE AIR WHEN GUNNYSACK APPEARED?
YOU DIDN'T HEAR A RINGIN' IN YOUR EARS--LIKE A THOUSAND DEAD BABIES SINGING?
YOU DIDN'T TASTE BLOOD, LIKE YOU'D JUST BITTEN INTO RAW, ROTTING MEAT?
A RUN-OF-THE-MILL LOA DOESN'T MANIFEST LIKE THAT.
CLOSEST I'VE FELT TO THAT KIND OF MOJO...
...WAS WHEN I STOOD IN FRONT OF THOSE GODS OF YOURS.
HE'S ONE OF THEM, ISN'T HE?
ONE OF THE GODS OF VOODOO.
MAYBE THEY DON'T RECOGNIZE HIM...OR ADMIT HIM INTO THE PANTHEON, BUT HE SHOULD BE THERE AMONG THEM.
NO.
UNCLE GUNNYSACK IS A ***MONSTER.***
HE'S NO GOD.
LET'S HOPE NOT.
BECAUSE I'M TRACKIN' HIM.
AN' I'M GONNA KILL HIM.
YOU COMIN'?

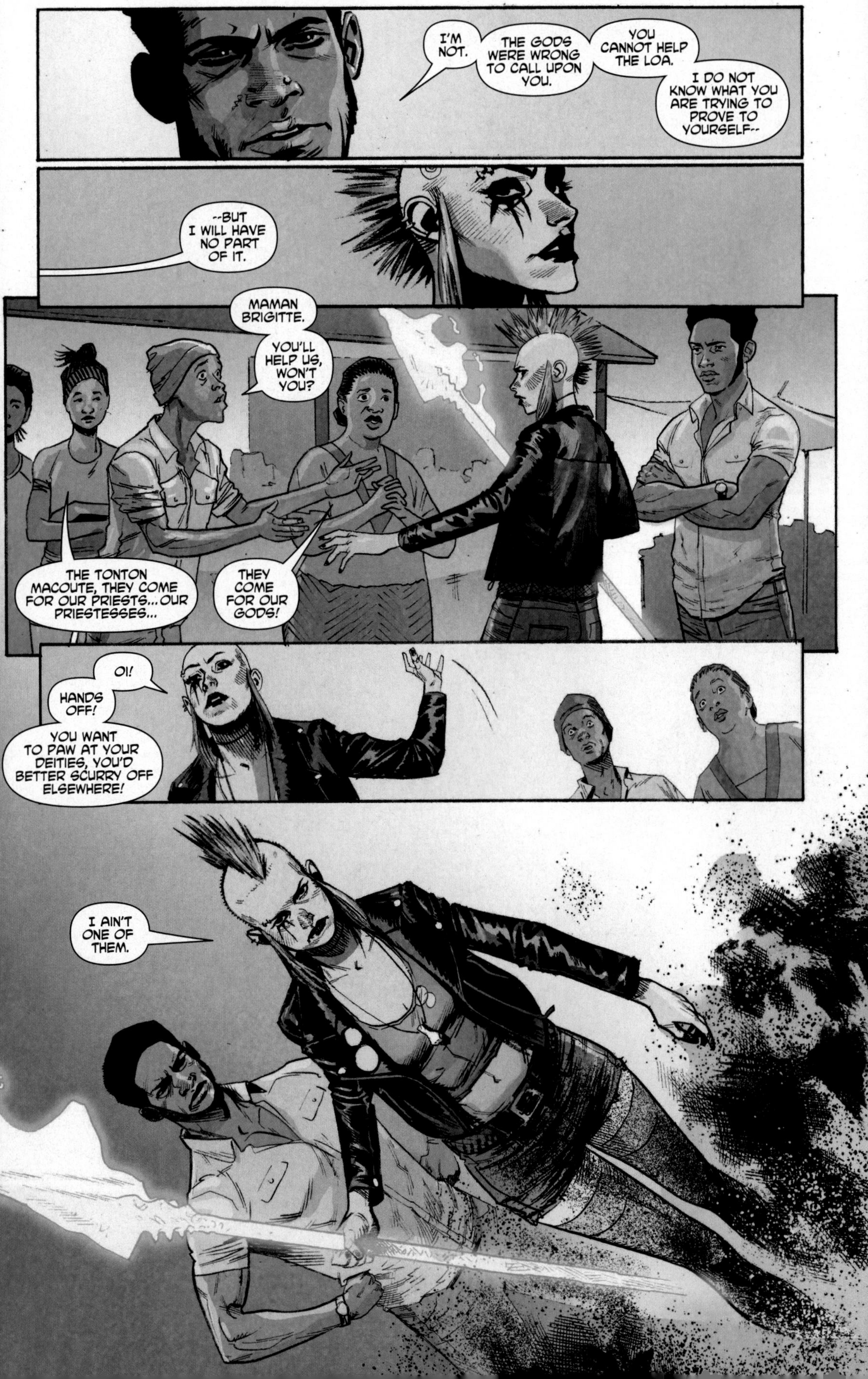
I'M NOT.
THE GODS WERE WRONG TO CALL UPON YOU.
YOU CANNOT HELP THE LOA.
I DO NOT KNOW WHAT YOU ARE TRYING TO PROVE TO YOURSELF--
--BUT I WILL HAVE NO PART OF IT.
MAMAN BRIGITTE.
YOU'LL HELP US, WON'T YOU?
THE TONTON MACOUTE, THEY COME FOR OUR PRIESTS...OUR PRIESTESSES...
THEY COME FOR OUR GODS!
OI!
HANDS OFF!
YOU WANT TO PAW AT YOUR DEITIES, YOU'D BETTER SCURRY OFF ELSEWHERE!
I AIN'T ONE OF THEM.

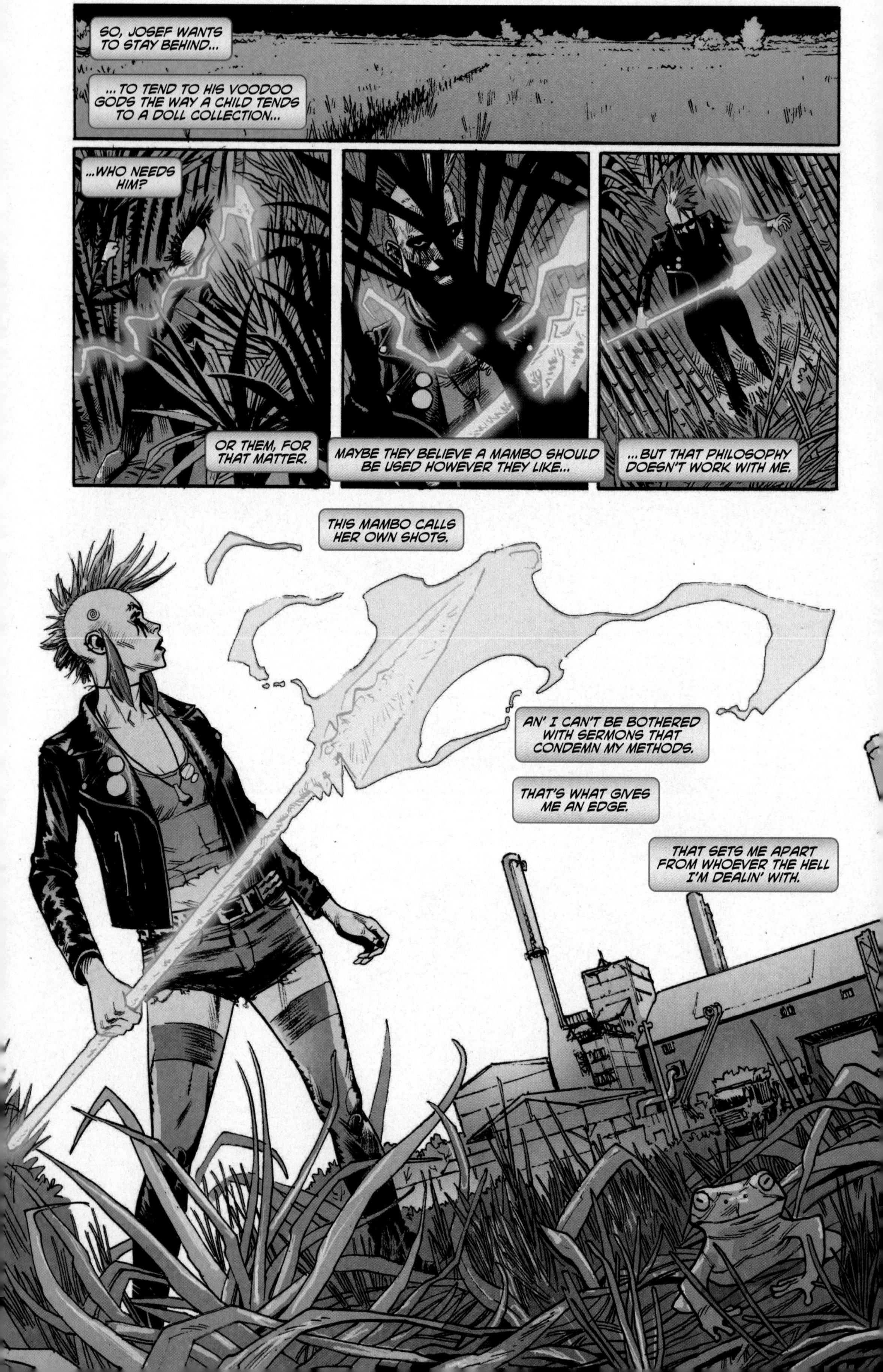
SO, JOSEF WANTS TO STAY BEHIND...
...TO TEND TO HIS VOODOO GODS THE WAY A CHILD TENDS TO A DOLL COLLECTION...
...WHO NEEDS HIM?
OR THEM, FOR THAT MATTER.
MAYBE THEY BELIEVE A MAMBO SHOULD BE USED HOWEVER THEY LIKE...
...BUT THAT PHILOSOPHY DOESN'T WORK WITH ME.
THIS MAMBO CALLS HER OWN SHOTS.
AN' I CAN'T BE BOTHERED WITH SERMONS THAT CONDEMN MY METHODS.
THAT'S WHAT GIVES ME AN EDGE.
THAT SETS ME APART FROM WHOEVER THE HELL I'M DEALIN' WITH.

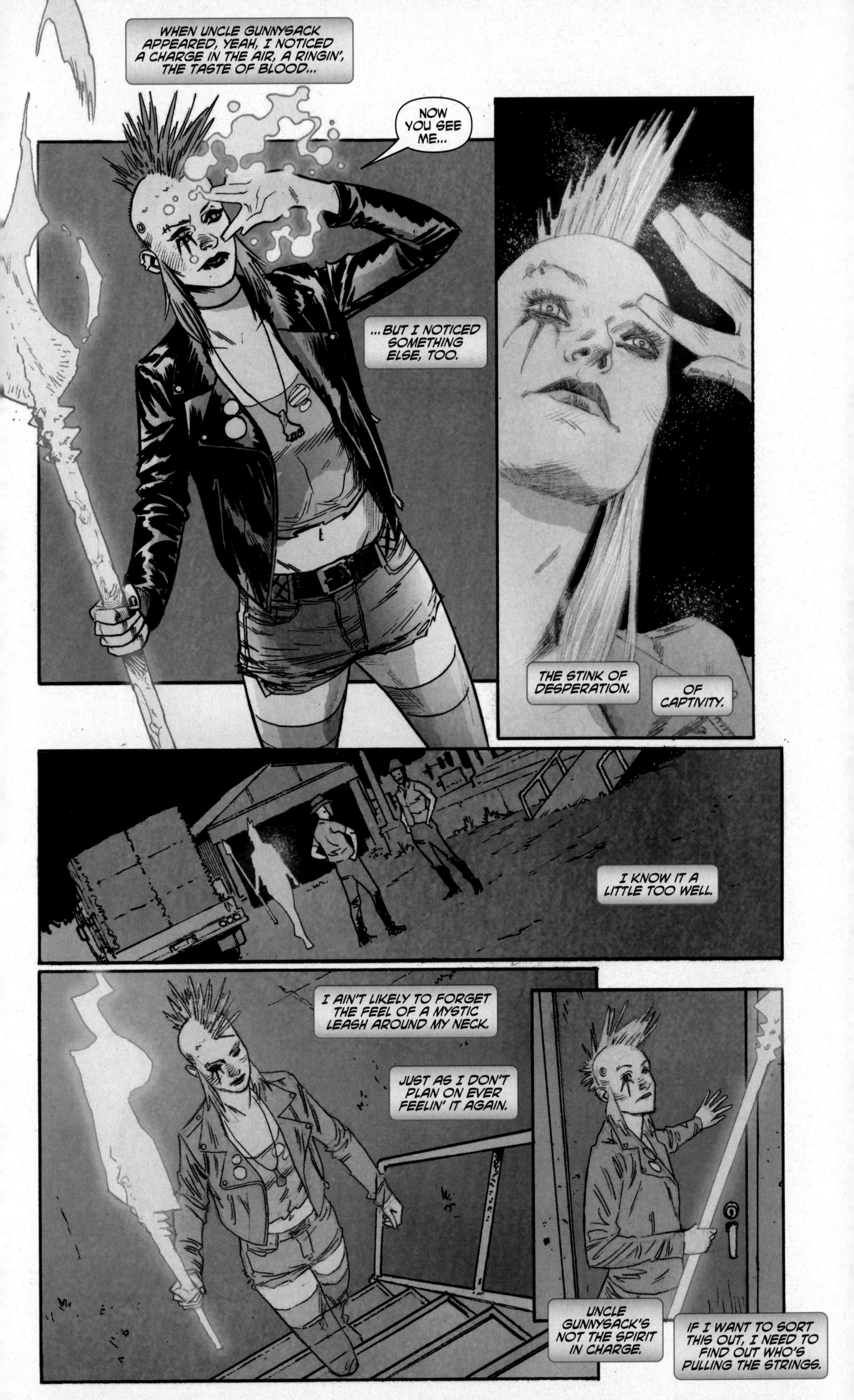
WHEN UNCLE GUNNYSACK APPEARED, YEAH, I NOTICED A CHARGE IN THE AIR, A RINGIN', THE TASTE OF BLOOD...
NOW YOU SEE ME...
...BUT I NOTICED SOMETHING ELSE, TOO.
THE STINK OF DESPERATION.
OF CAPTIVITY.
I KNOW IT A LITTLE TOO WELL.
I AIN'T LIKELY TO FORGET THE FEEL OF A MYSTIC LEASH AROUND MY NECK.
JUST AS I DON'T PLAN ON EVER FEELIN' IT AGAIN.
UNCLE GUNNYSACK'S NOT THE SPIRIT IN CHARGE.
IF I WANT TO SORT THIS OUT, I NEED TO FIND OUT WHO'S PULLING THE STRINGS.

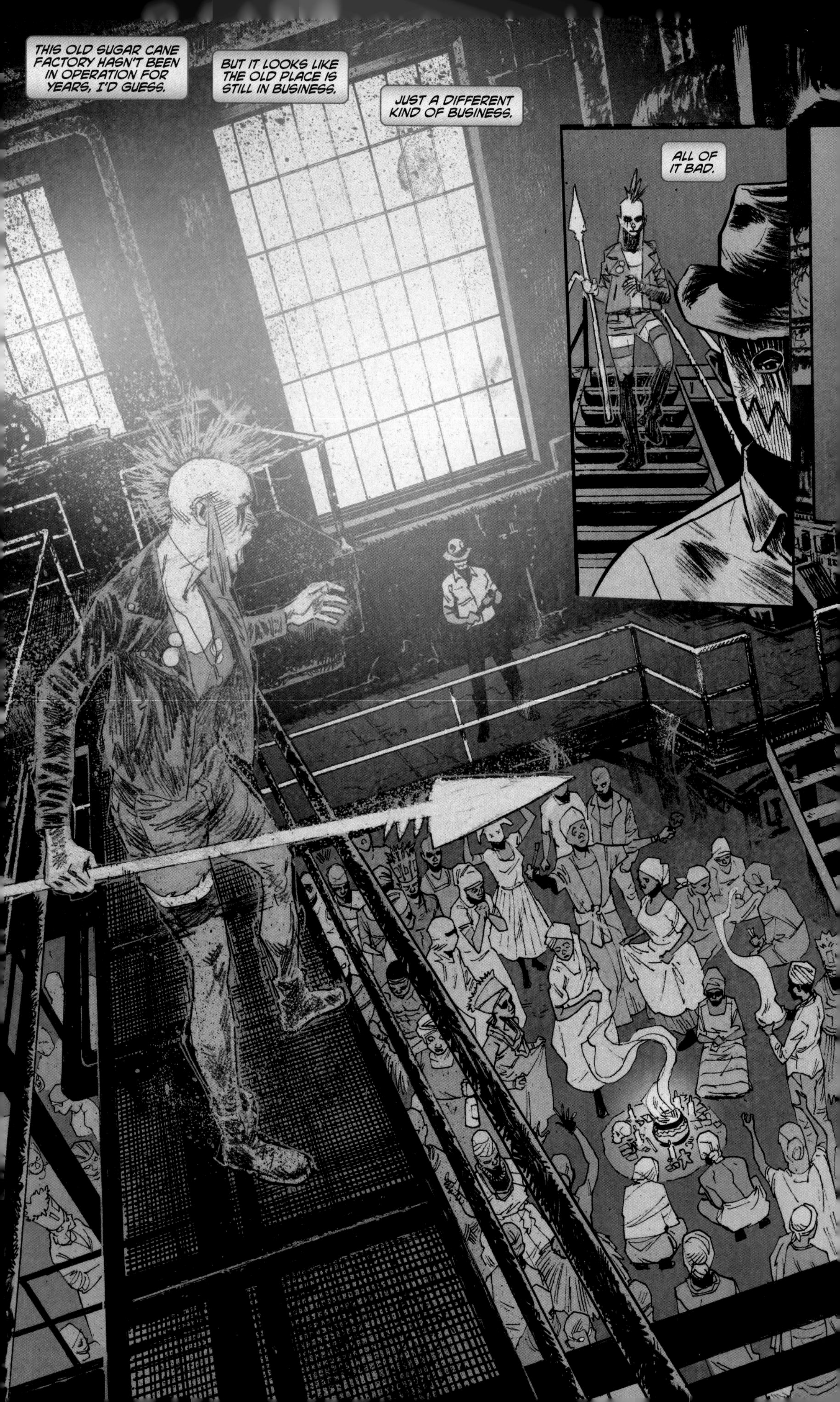
THIS OLD SUGAR CANE FACTORY HASN'T BEEN IN OPERATION FOR YEARS, I'D GUESS.
BUT IT LOOKS LIKE THE OLD PLACE IS STILL IN BUSINESS.
JUST A DIFFERENT KIND OF BUSINESS.
ALL OF IT BAD.

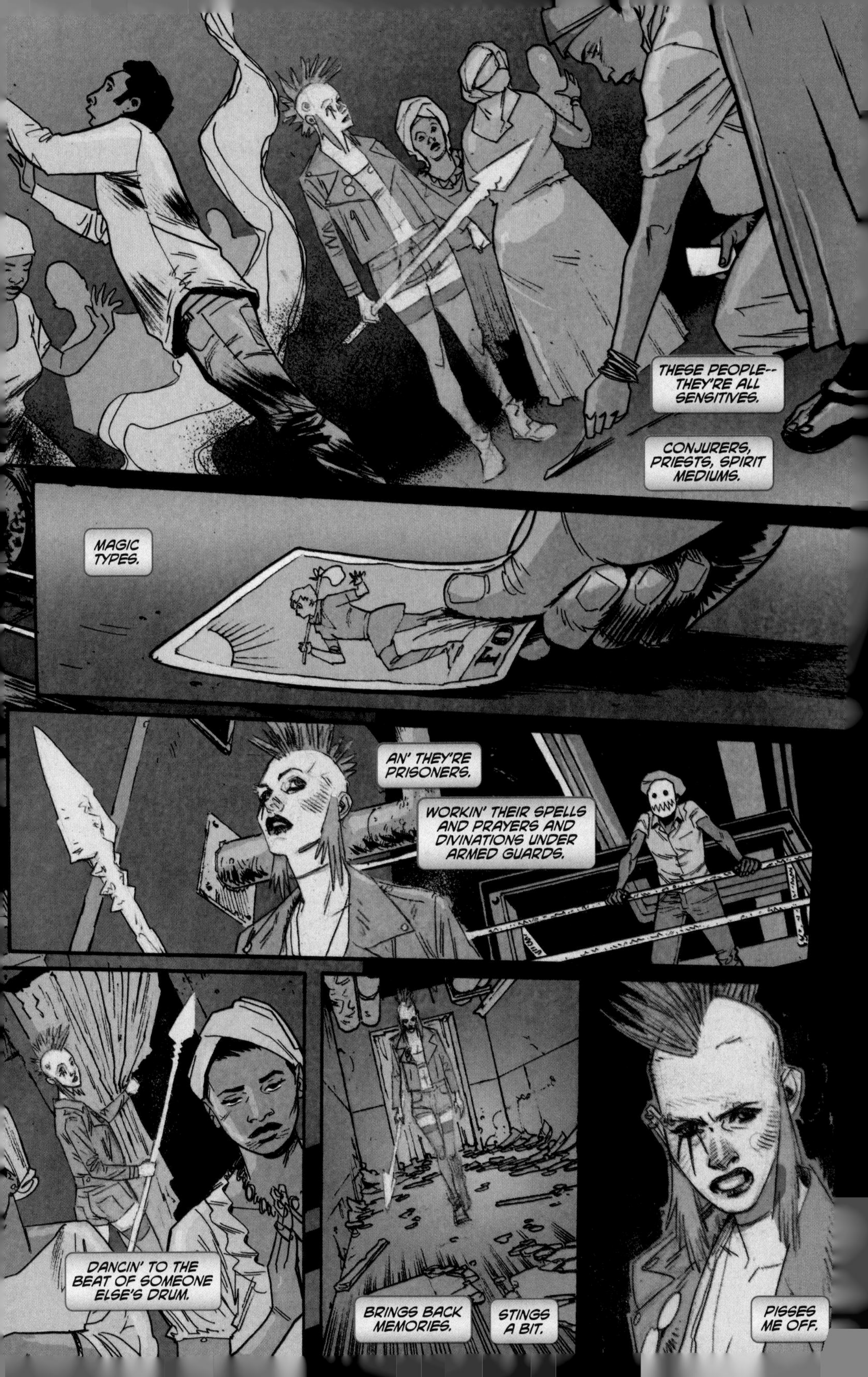

THESE PEOPLE-- THEY'RE ALL SENSITIVES.
CONJURERS, PRIESTS, SPIRIT MEDIUMS.
MAGIC TYPES.
AN' THEY'RE PRISONERS.
WORKIN' THEIR SPELLS AND PRAYERS AND DIVINATIONS UNDER ARMED GUARDS.
DANCIN' TO THE BEAT OF SOMEONE ELSE'S DRUM.
BRINGS BACK MEMORIES.
STINGS A BIT.
PISSES ME OFF.

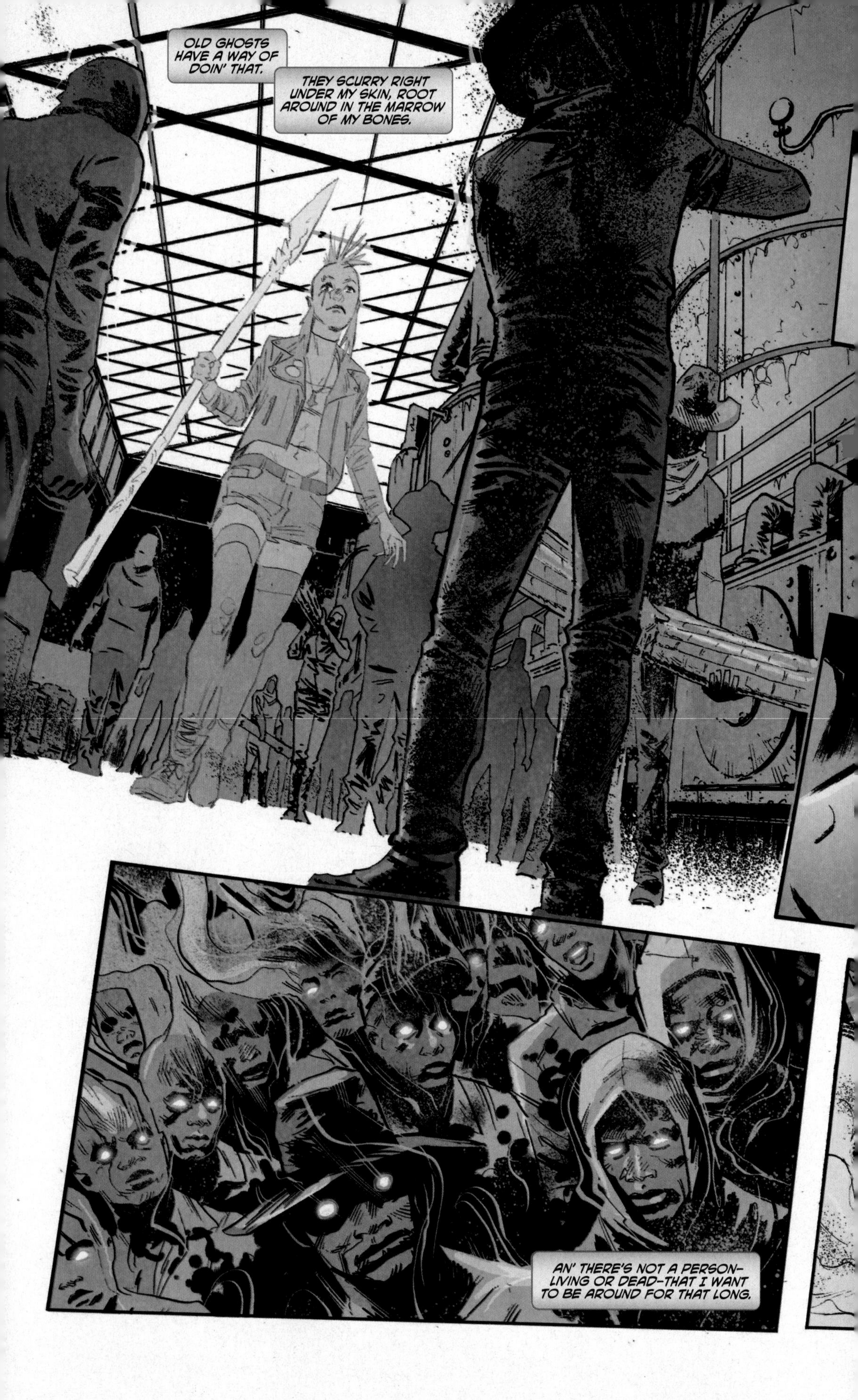
OLD GHOSTS HAVE A WAY OF DOIN' THAT.
THEY SCURRY RIGHT UNDER MY SKIN, ROOT AROUND IN THE MARROW OF MY BONES.
AN' THERE'S NOT A PERSON--LIVING OR DEAD--THAT I WANT TO BE AROUND FOR THAT LONG.

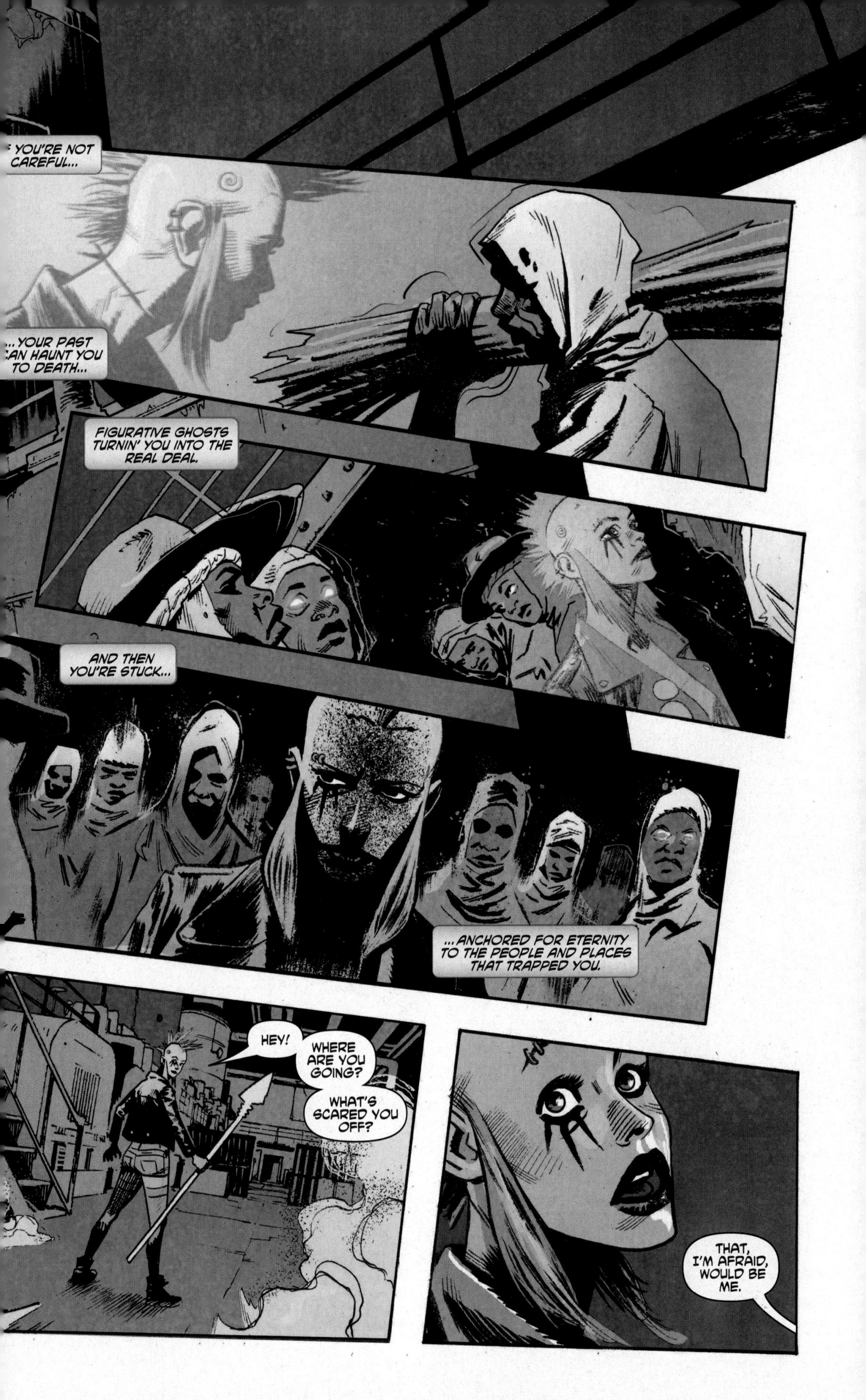

F YOU'RE NOT CAREFUL...
...YOUR PAST CAN HAUNT YOU TO DEATH...
FIGURATIVE GHOSTS TURNIN' YOU INTO THE REAL DEAL.
AND THEN YOU'RE STUCK...
...ANCHORED FOR ETERNITY TO THE PEOPLE AND PLACES THAT TRAPPED YOU.
HEY!
WHERE ARE YOU GOING?
WHAT'S SCARED YOU OFF?
THAT, I'M AFRAID, WOULD BE ME.

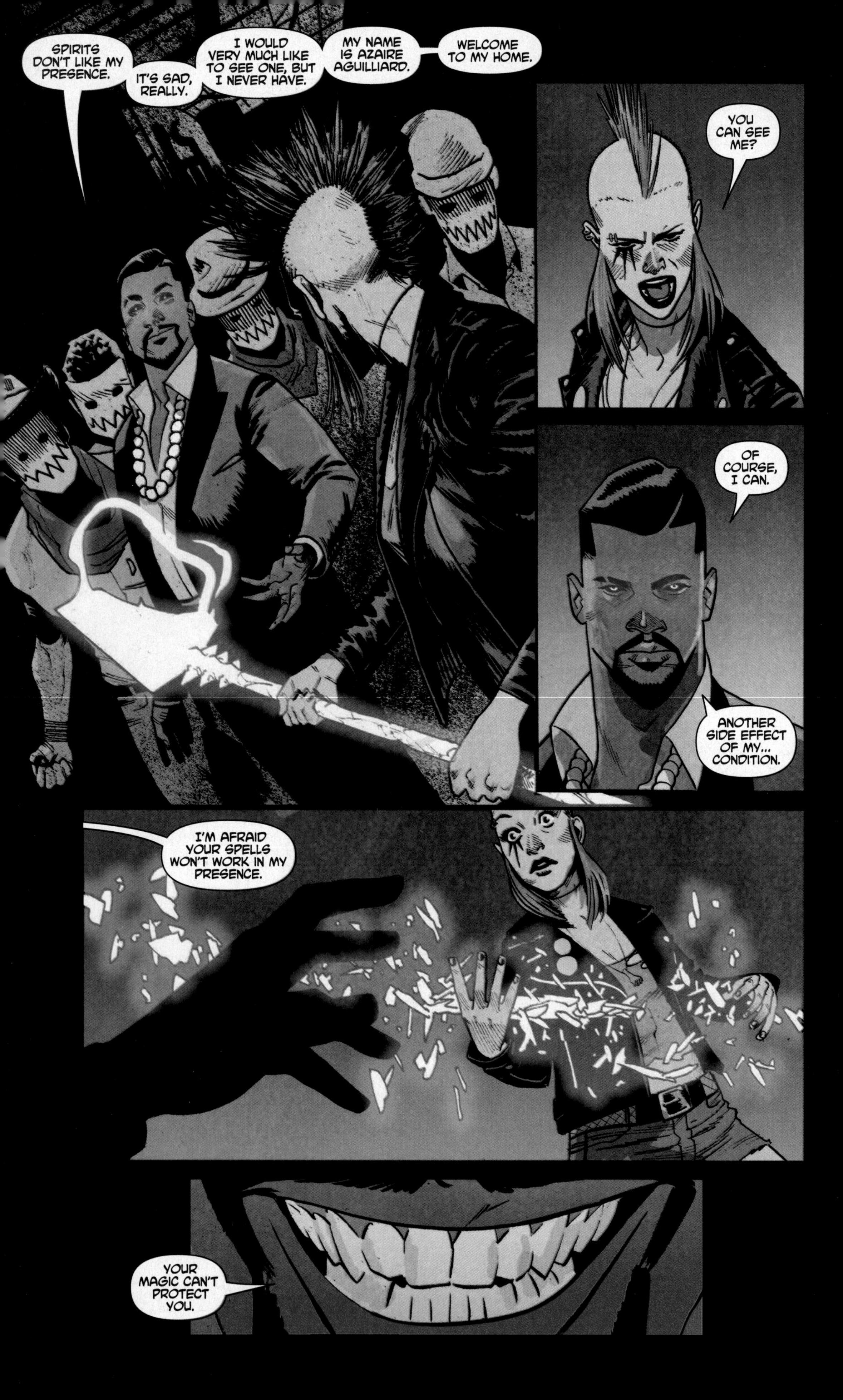
SPIRITS DON'T LIKE MY PRESENCE.
IT'S SAD, REALLY.
I WOULD VERY MUCH LIKE TO SEE ONE, BUT I NEVER HAVE.
MY NAME IS AZAIRE AGUILLIARD.
WELCOME TO MY HOME.
YOU CAN SEE ME?
OF COURSE, I CAN.
ANOTHER SIDE EFFECT OF MY... CONDITION.
I'M AFRAID YOUR SPELLS WON'T WORK IN MY PRESENCE.
YOUR MAGIC CAN'T PROTECT YOU.

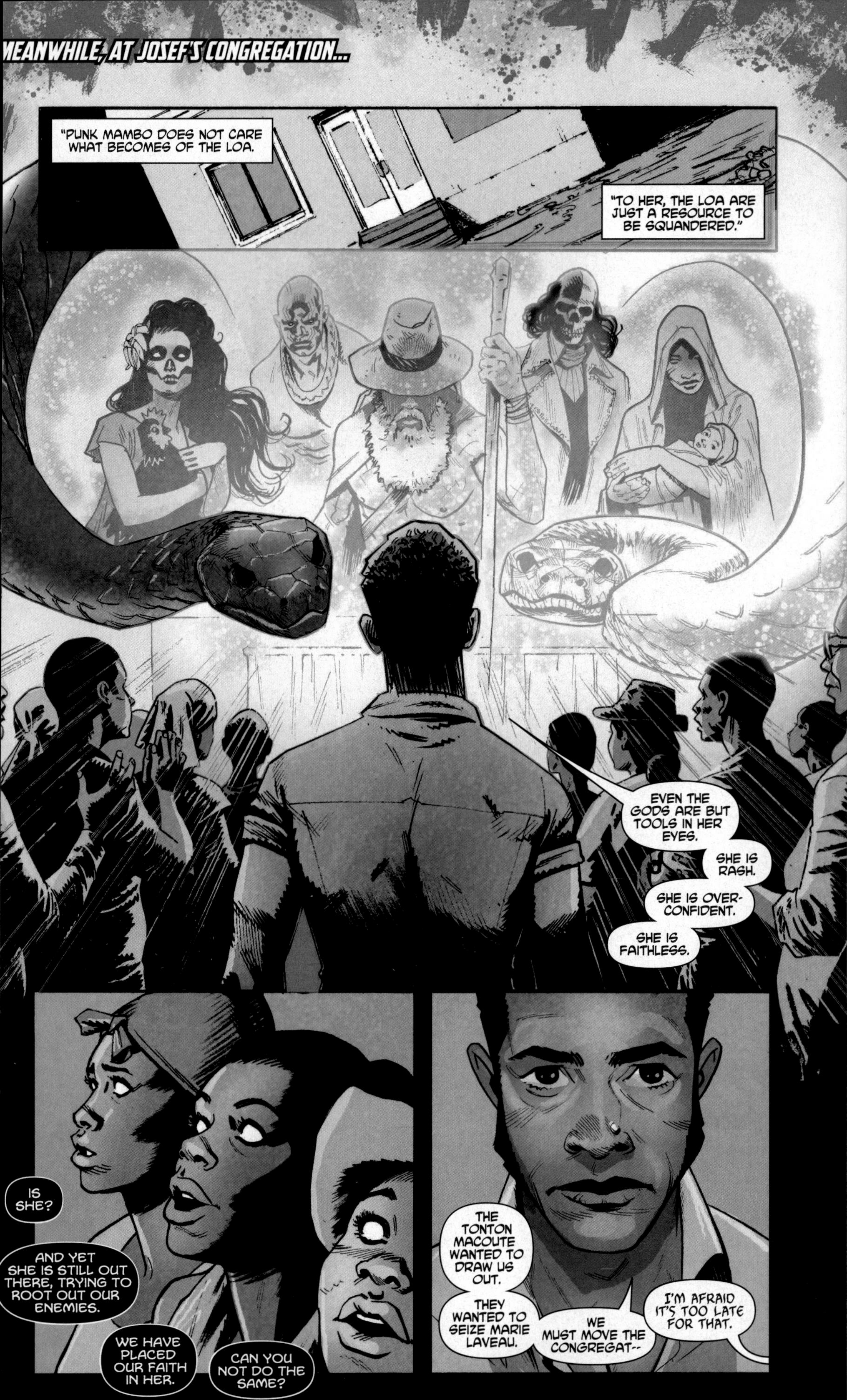
MEANWHILE, AT JOSEF'S CONGREGATION...
"PUNK MAMBO DOES NOT CARE WHAT BECOMES OF THE LOA.
"TO HER, THE LOA ARE JUST A RESOURCE TO BE SQUANDERED."
EVEN THE GODS ARE BUT TOOLS IN HER EYES.
SHE IS RASH.
SHE IS OVER-CONFIDENT.
SHE IS FAITHLESS.
IS SHE?
AND YET SHE IS STILL OUT THERE, TRYING TO ROOT OUT OUR ENEMIES.
WE HAVE PLACED OUR FAITH IN HER.
CAN YOU NOT DO THE SAME?
THE TONTON MACOUTE WANTED TO DRAW US OUT.
THEY WANTED TO SEIZE MARIE LAVEAU.
WE MUST MOVE THE CONGREGAT--
I'M AFRAID IT'S TOO LATE FOR THAT.

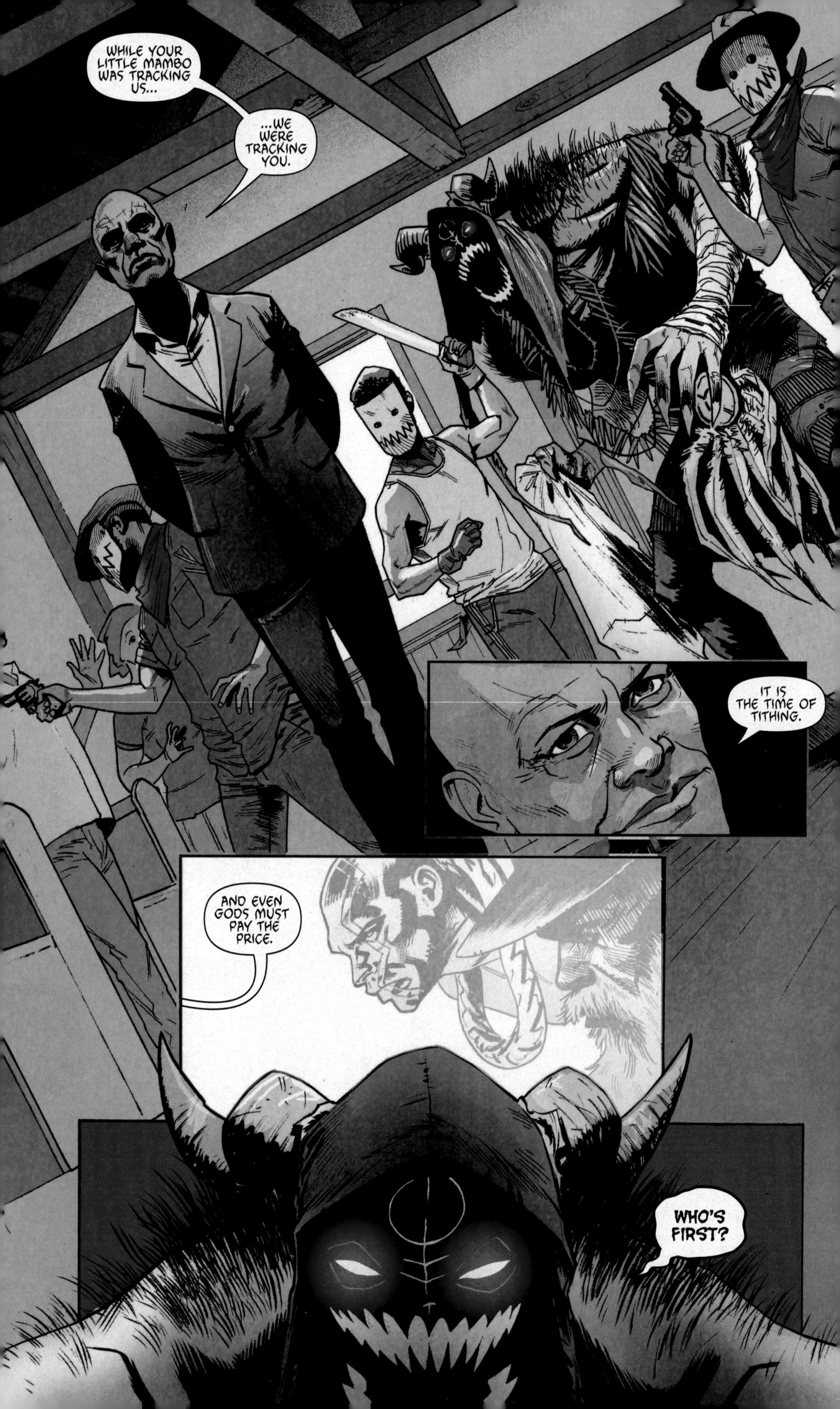
WHILE YOUR LITTLE MAMBO WAS TRACKING US...
...WE WERE TRACKING YOU.
IT IS THE TIME OF TITHING.
AND EVEN GODS MUST PAY THE PRICE.
WHO'S FIRST?

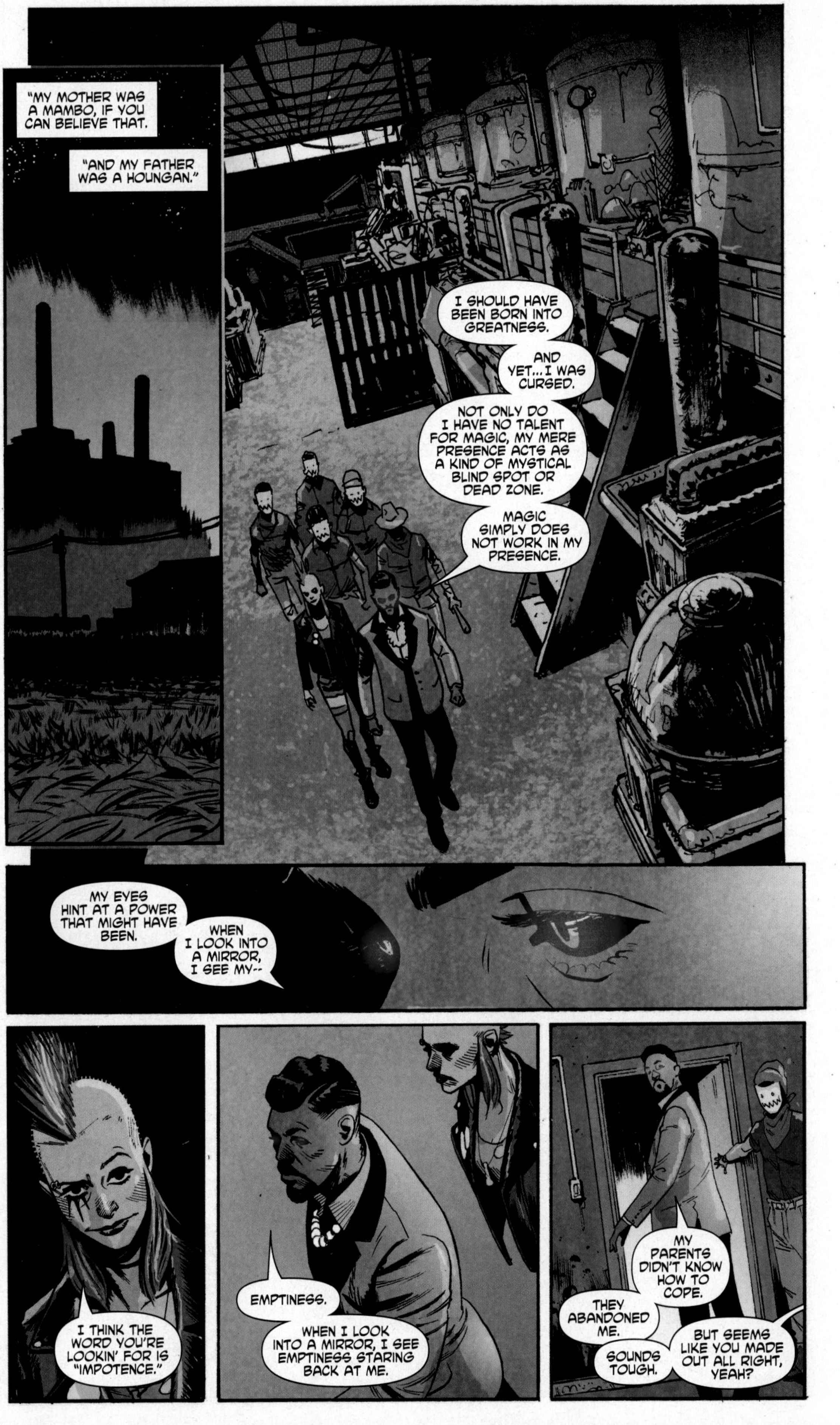

"MY MOTHER WAS A MAMBO, IF YOU CAN BELIEVE THAT.
"AND MY FATHER WAS A HOUNGAN."
I SHOULD HAVE BEEN BORN INTO GREATNESS.
AND YET... I WAS CURSED.
NOT ONLY DO I HAVE NO TALENT FOR MAGIC, MY MERE PRESENCE ACTS AS A KIND OF MYSTICAL BLIND SPOT OR DEAD ZONE.
MAGIC SIMPLY DOES NOT WORK IN MY PRESENCE.
MY EYES HINT AT A POWER THAT MIGHT HAVE BEEN.
WHEN I LOOK INTO A MIRROR, I SEE MY--
I THINK THE WORD YOU'RE LOOKIN' FOR IS "IMPOTENCE."
EMPTINESS.
WHEN I LOOK INTO A MIRROR, I SEE EMPTINESS STARING BACK AT ME.
MY PARENTS DIDN'T KNOW HOW TO COPE.
THEY ABANDONED ME.
SOUNDS TOUGH.
BUT SEEMS LIKE YOU MADE OUT ALL RIGHT, YEAH?

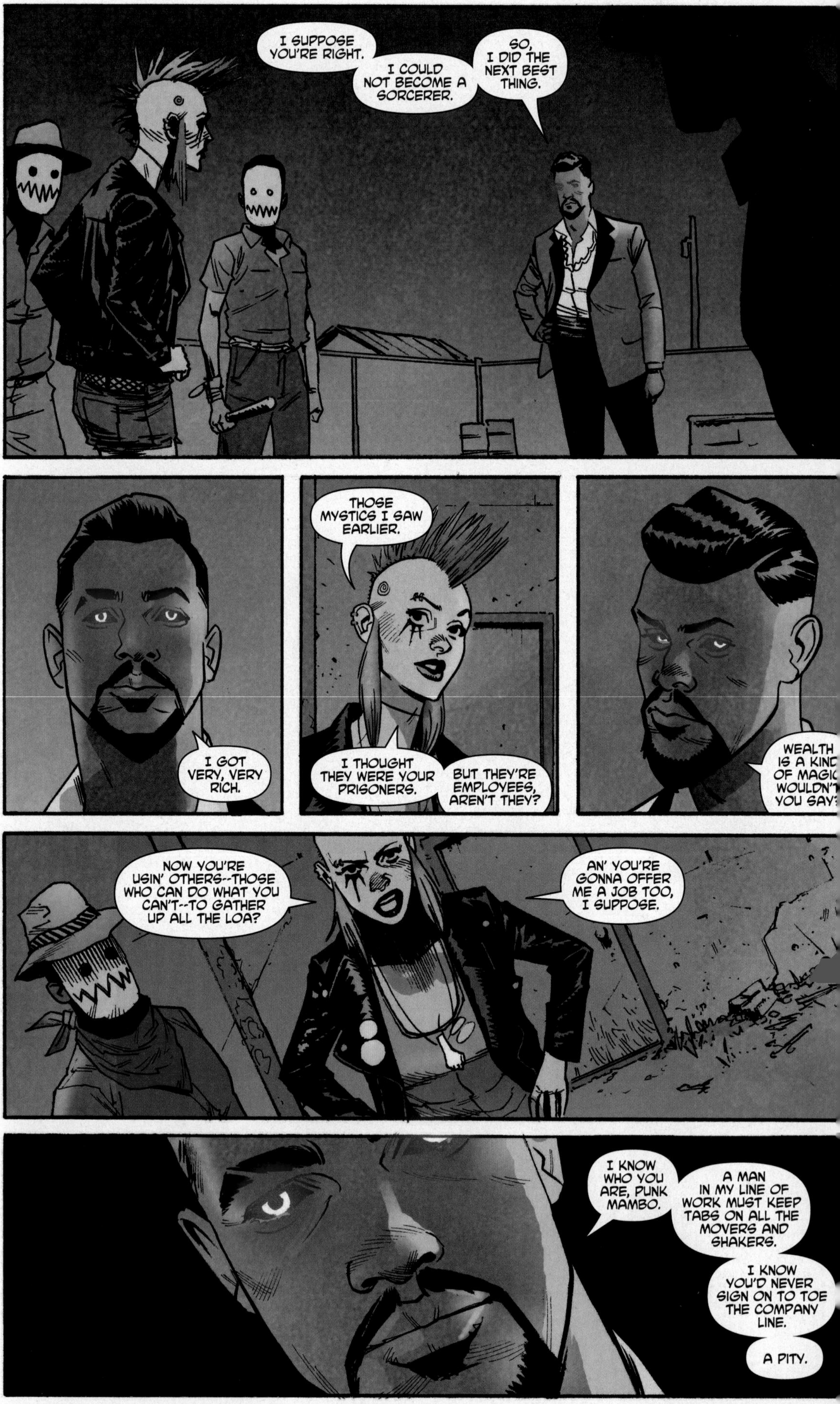
I SUPPOSE YOU'RE RIGHT.
I COULD NOT BECOME A SORCERER.
SO, I DID THE NEXT BEST THING.
I GOT VERY, VERY RICH.
THOSE MYSTICS I SAW EARLIER.
I THOUGHT THEY WERE YOUR PRISONERS.
BUT THEY'RE EMPLOYEES, AREN'T THEY?
WEALTH IS A KIND OF MAGIC, WOULDN'T YOU SAY?
NOW YOU'RE USIN' OTHERS--THOSE WHO CAN DO WHAT YOU CAN'T--TO GATHER UP ALL THE LOA?
AN' YOU'RE GONNA OFFER ME A JOB TOO, I SUPPOSE.
I KNOW WHO YOU ARE, PUNK MAMBO.
A MAN IN MY LINE OF WORK MUST KEEP TABS ON ALL THE MOVERS AND SHAKERS.
I KNOW YOU'D NEVER SIGN ON TO TOE THE COMPANY LINE.
A PITY.

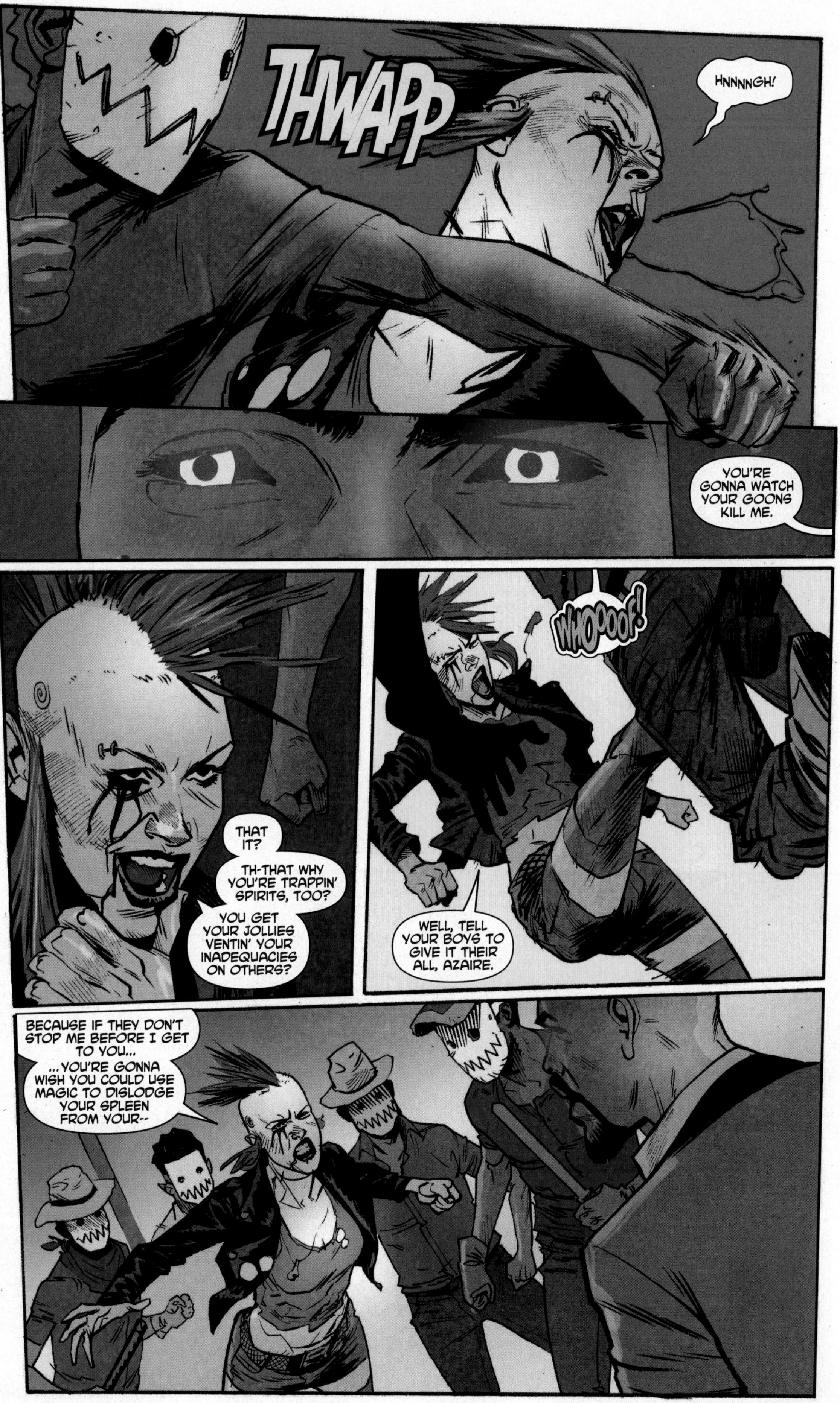
THWAPP
HNNNNGH!
YOU'RE GONNA WATCH YOUR GOONS KILL ME.
THAT IT?
TH-THAT WHY YOU'RE TRAPPIN' SPIRITS, TOO?
YOU GET YOUR JOLLIES VENTIN' YOUR INADEQUACIES ON OTHERS?
WHOOOOF!
WELL, TELL YOUR BOYS TO GIVE IT THEIR ALL, AZAIRE.
BECAUSE IF THEY DON'T STOP ME BEFORE I GET TO YOU...
...YOU'RE GONNA WISH YOU COULD USE MAGIC TO DISLODGE YOUR SPLEEN FROM YOUR--

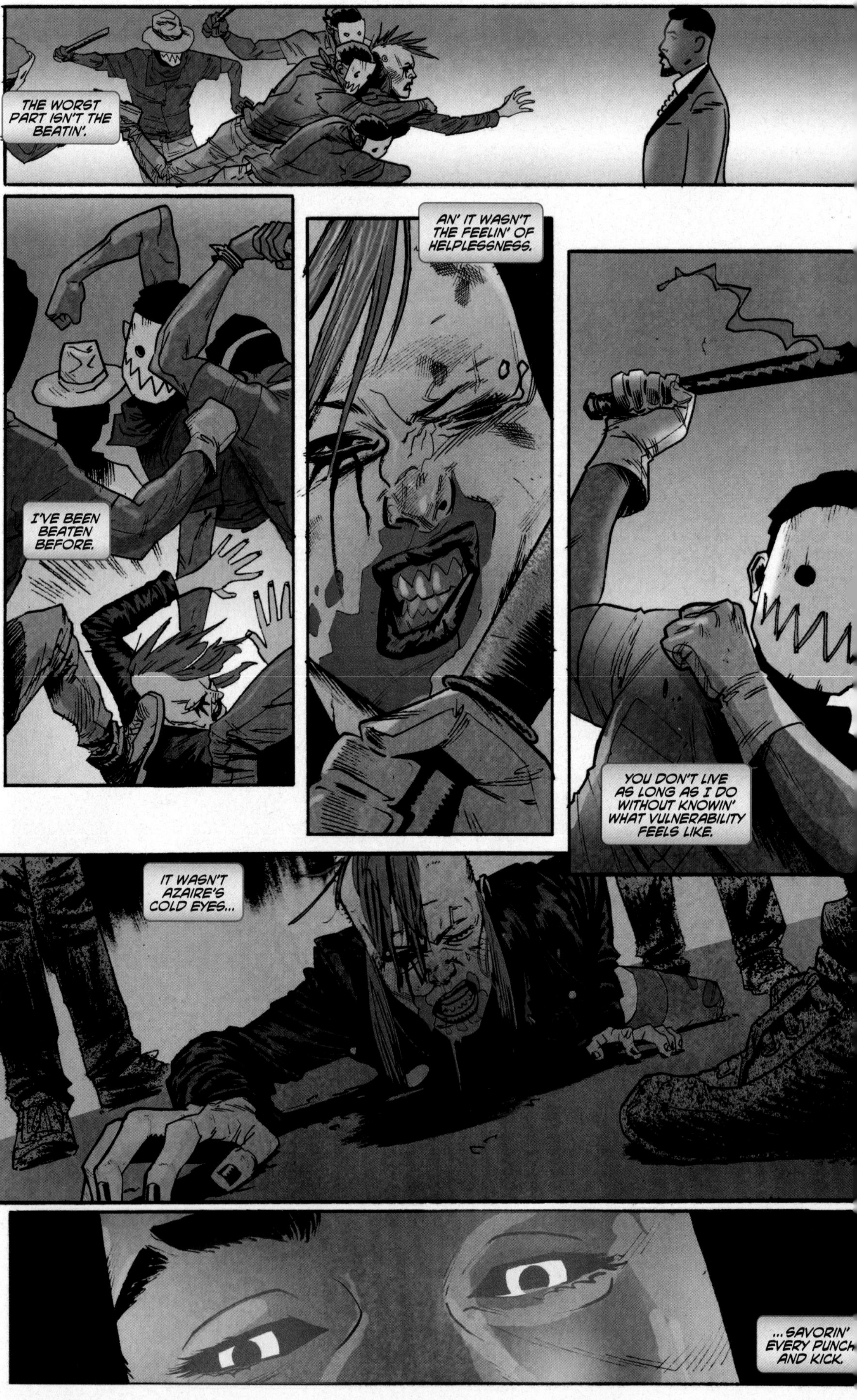
THE WORST PART ISN'T THE BEATIN'.
I'VE BEEN BEATEN BEFORE.
AN' IT WASN'T THE FEELIN' OF HELPLESSNESS.
YOU DON'T LIVE AS LONG AS I DO WITHOUT KNOWIN' WHAT VULNERABILITY FEELS LIKE.
IT WASN'T AZAIRE'S COLD EYES...
...SAVORIN' EVERY PUNCH AND KICK.

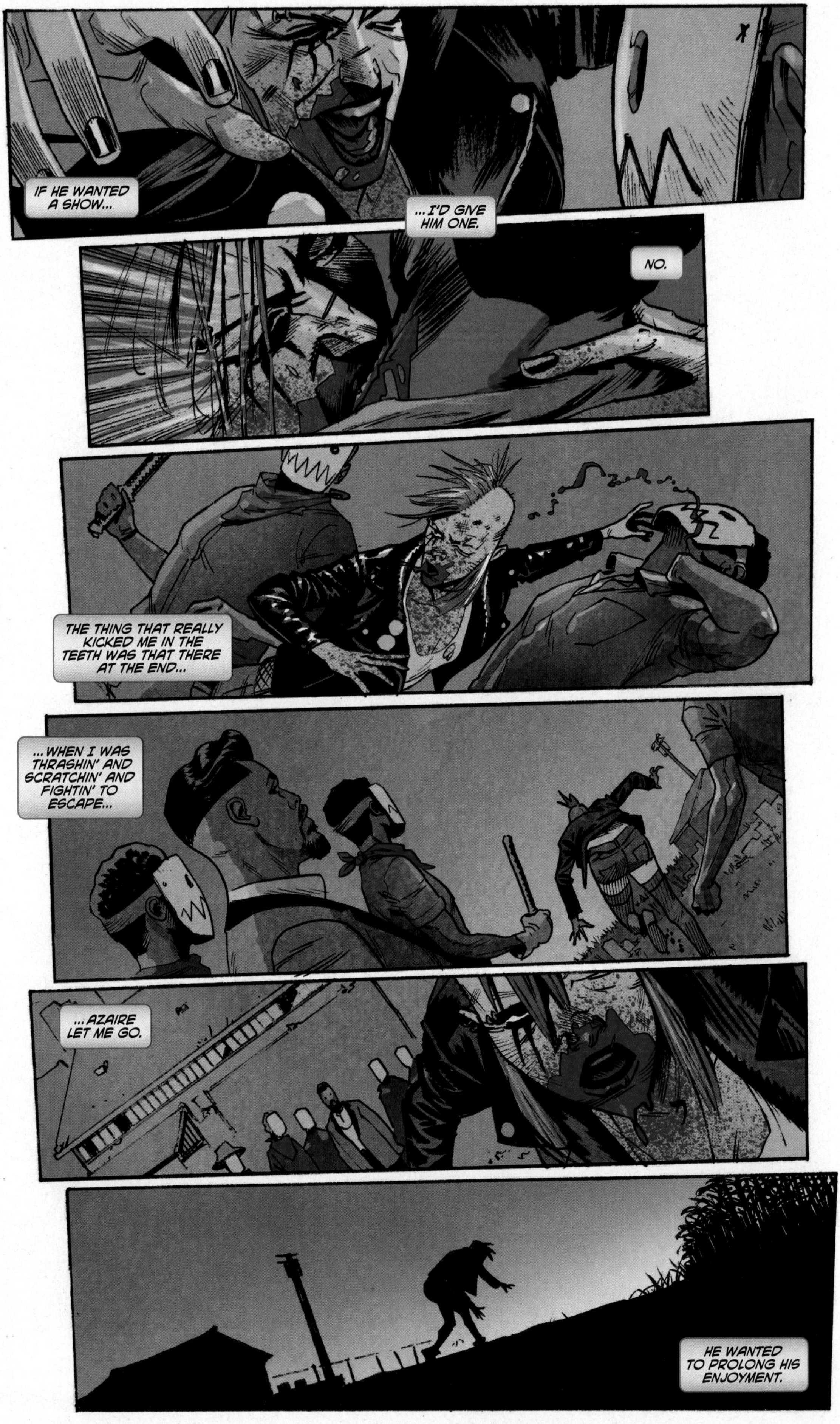
IF HE WANTED A SHOW...
...I'D GIVE HIM ONE.
NO.
THE THING THAT REALLY KICKED ME IN THE TEETH WAS THAT THERE AT THE END...
...WHEN I WAS THRASHIN' AND SCRATCHIN' AND FIGHTIN' TO ESCAPE...
...AZAIRE LET ME GO.
HE WANTED TO PROLONG HIS ENJOYMENT.

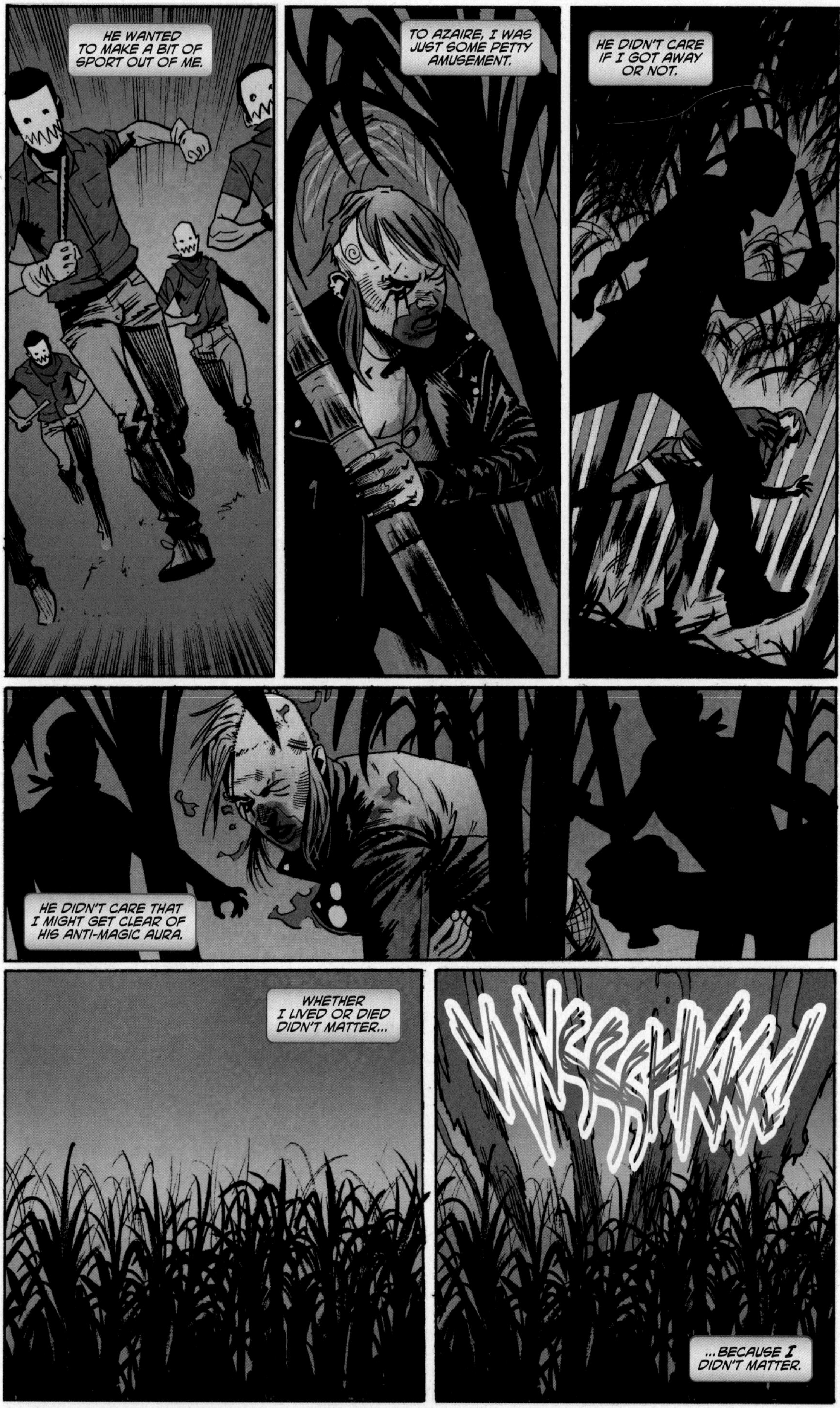
HE WANTED TO MAKE A BIT OF SPORT OUT OF ME.
TO AZAIRE, I WAS JUST SOME PETTY AMUSEMENT.
HE DIDN'T CARE IF I GOT AWAY OR NOT.
HE DIDN'T CARE THAT I MIGHT GET CLEAR OF HIS ANTI-MAGIC AURA.
WHETHER I LIVED OR DIED DIDN'T MATTER...
...BECAUSE I DIDN'T MATTER.

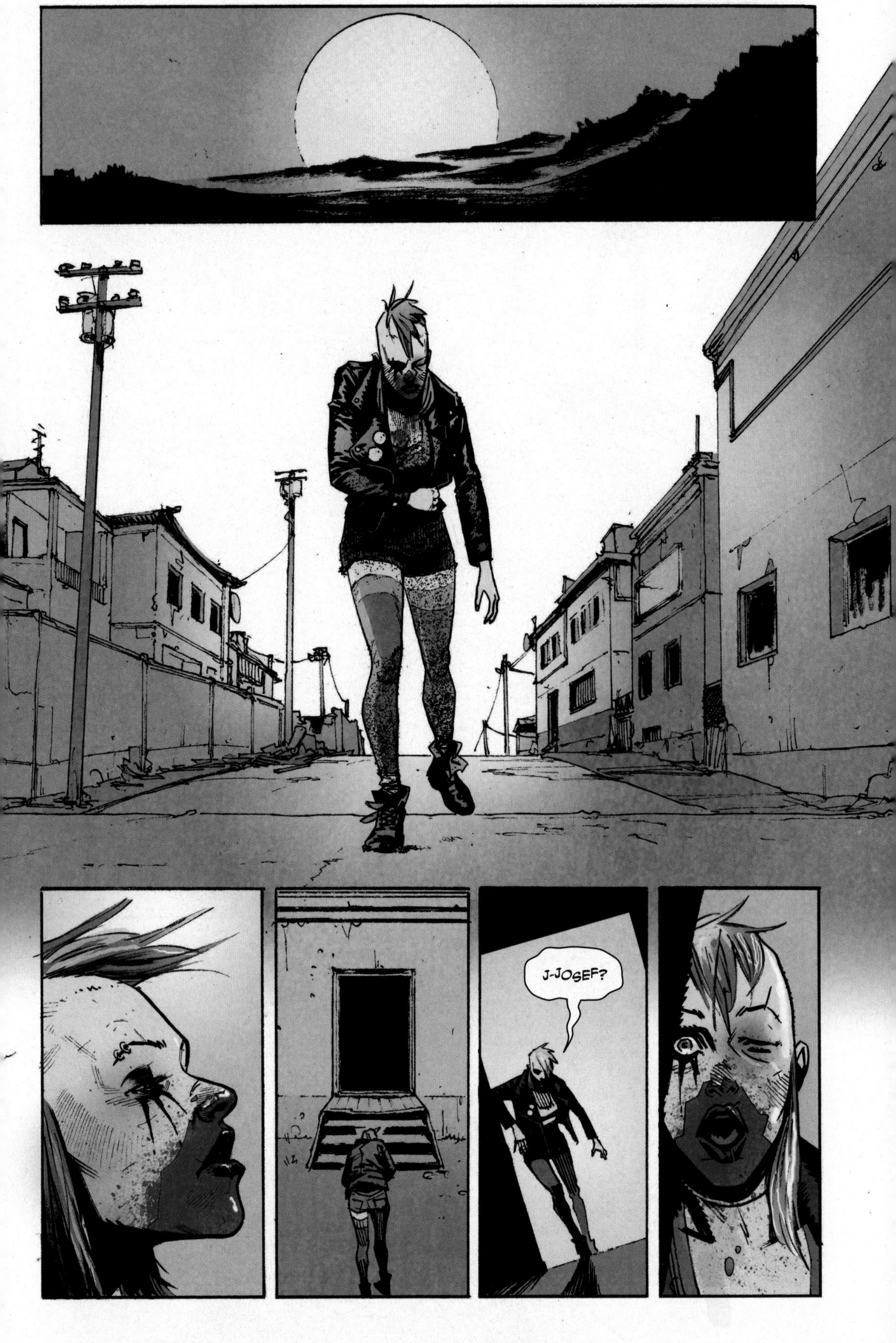
J-JOSEF?

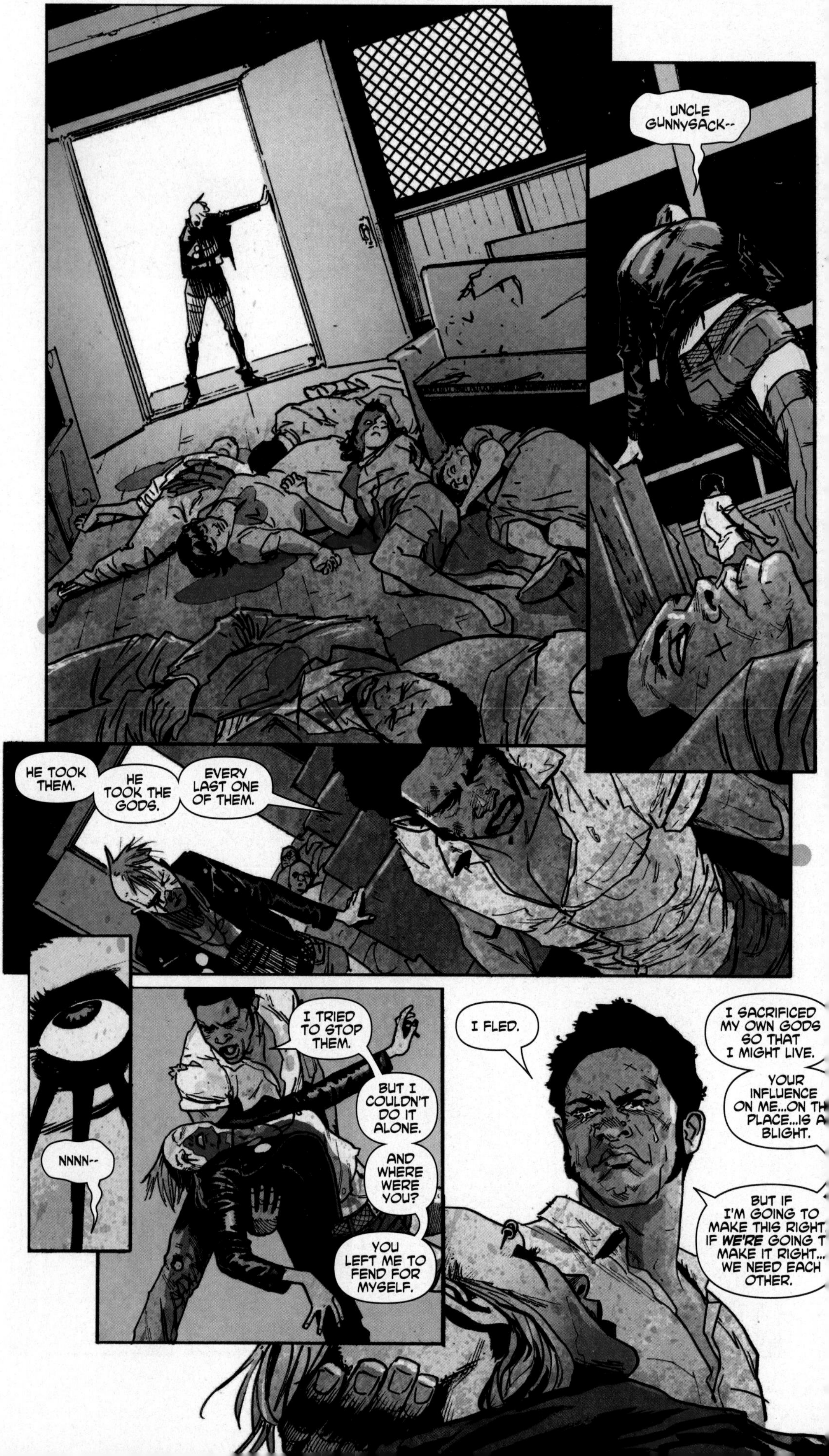
UNCLE GUNNYSACK--
HE TOOK THEM.
HE TOOK THE GODS.
EVERY LAST ONE OF THEM.
NNNN--
I TRIED TO STOP THEM.
BUT I COULDN'T DO IT ALONE.
AND WHERE WERE YOU?
YOU LEFT ME TO FEND FOR MYSELF.
I FLED.
I SACRIFICED MY OWN GODS SO THAT I MIGHT LIVE.
YOUR INFLUENCE ON ME...ON TH PLACE...IS A BLIGHT.
BUT IF I'M GOING TO MAKE THIS RIGHT IF *WE'RE* GOING T MAKE IT RIGHT... WE NEED EACH OTHER.

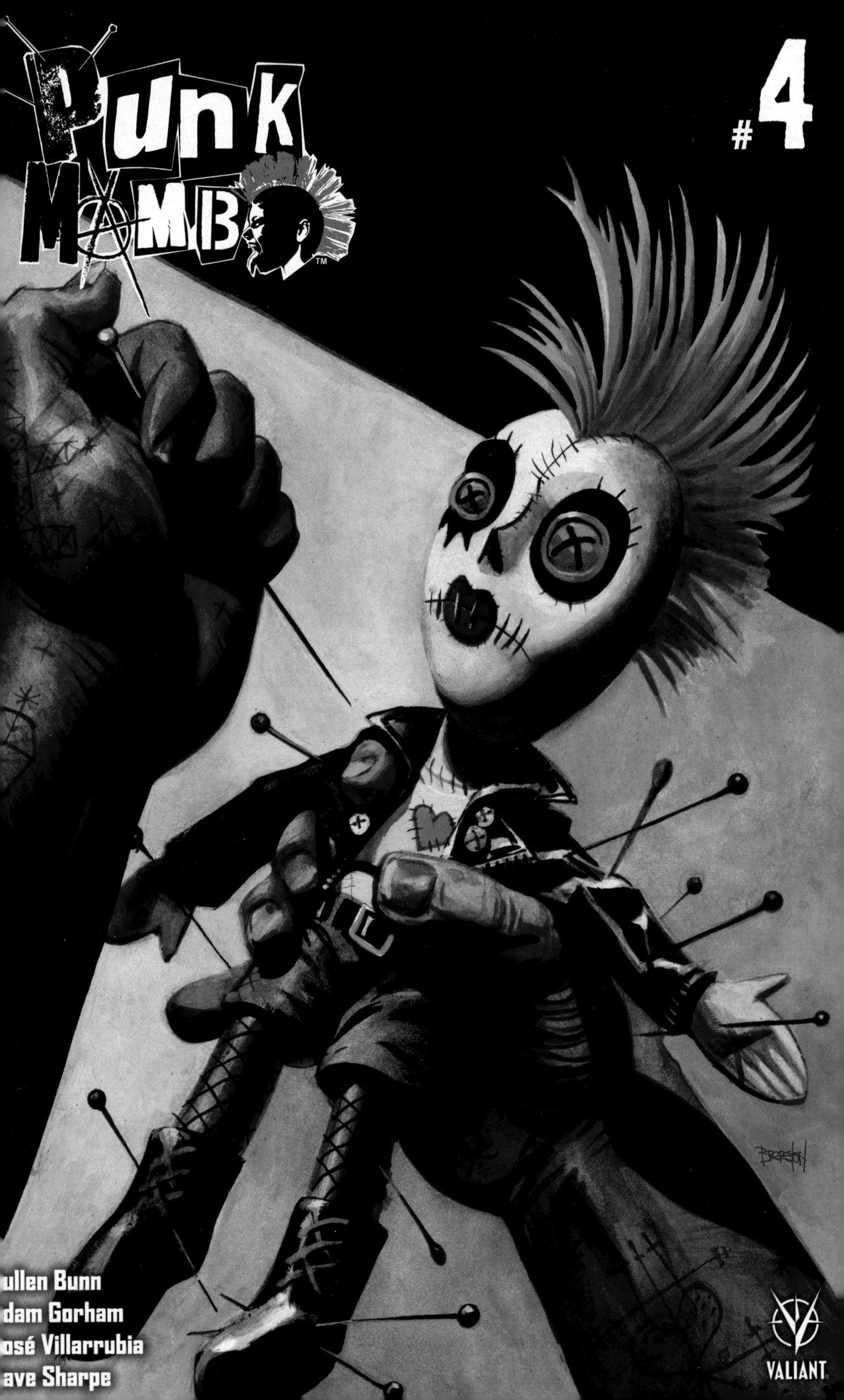

PUNK MAMBO™
#4
ullen Bunn
dam Gorham
osé Villarrubia
ave Sharpe
VALIANT

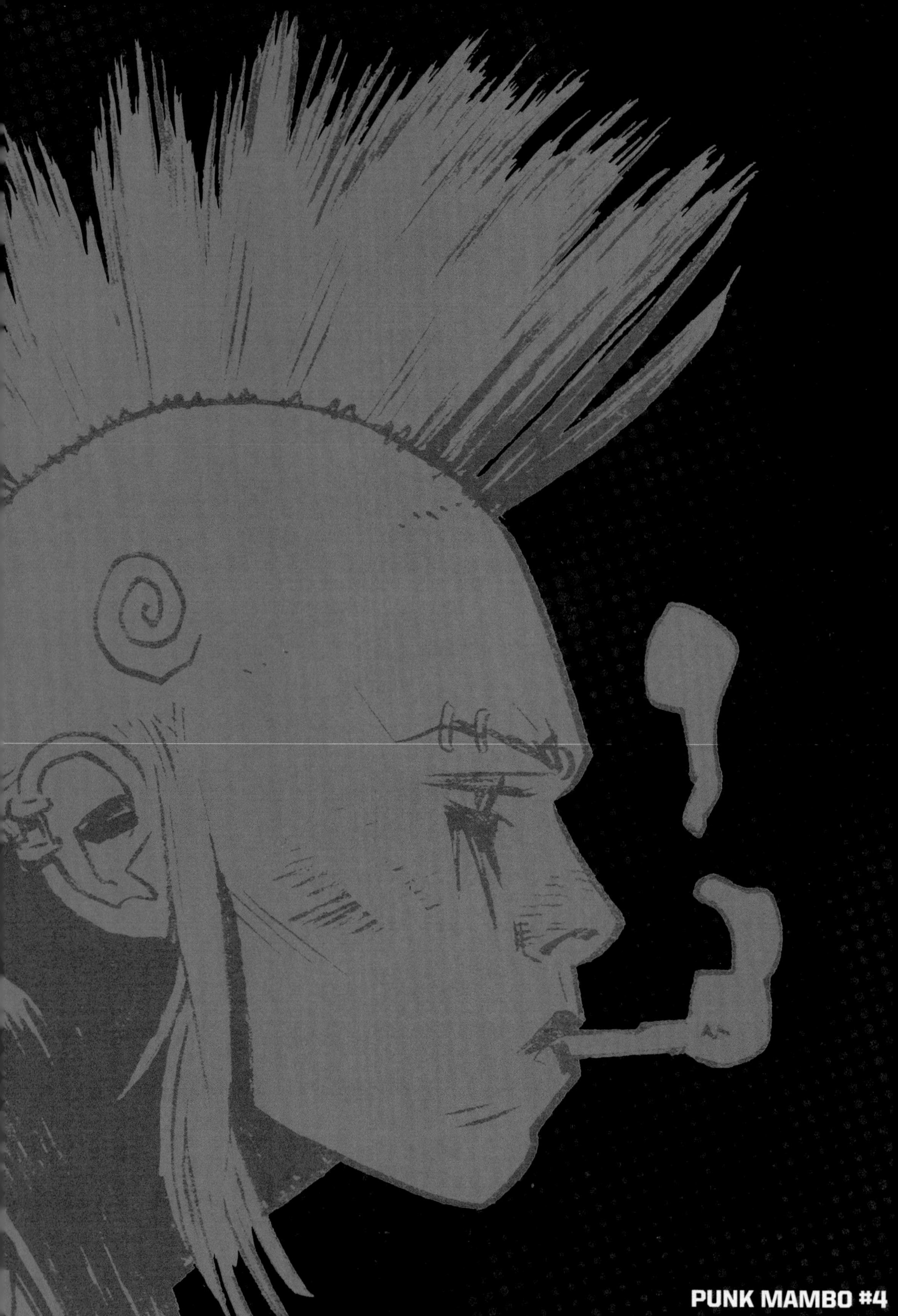

PUNK MAMBO #4

WRITER: Cullen Bunn
ART: Adam Gorham
COLORS: José Villarrubia
LETTERS: Dave Sharpe
COVER ARTIST: Dan Brereton
ASSOCIATE EDITOR: David Menchel
EDITOR: Lysa Hawkins

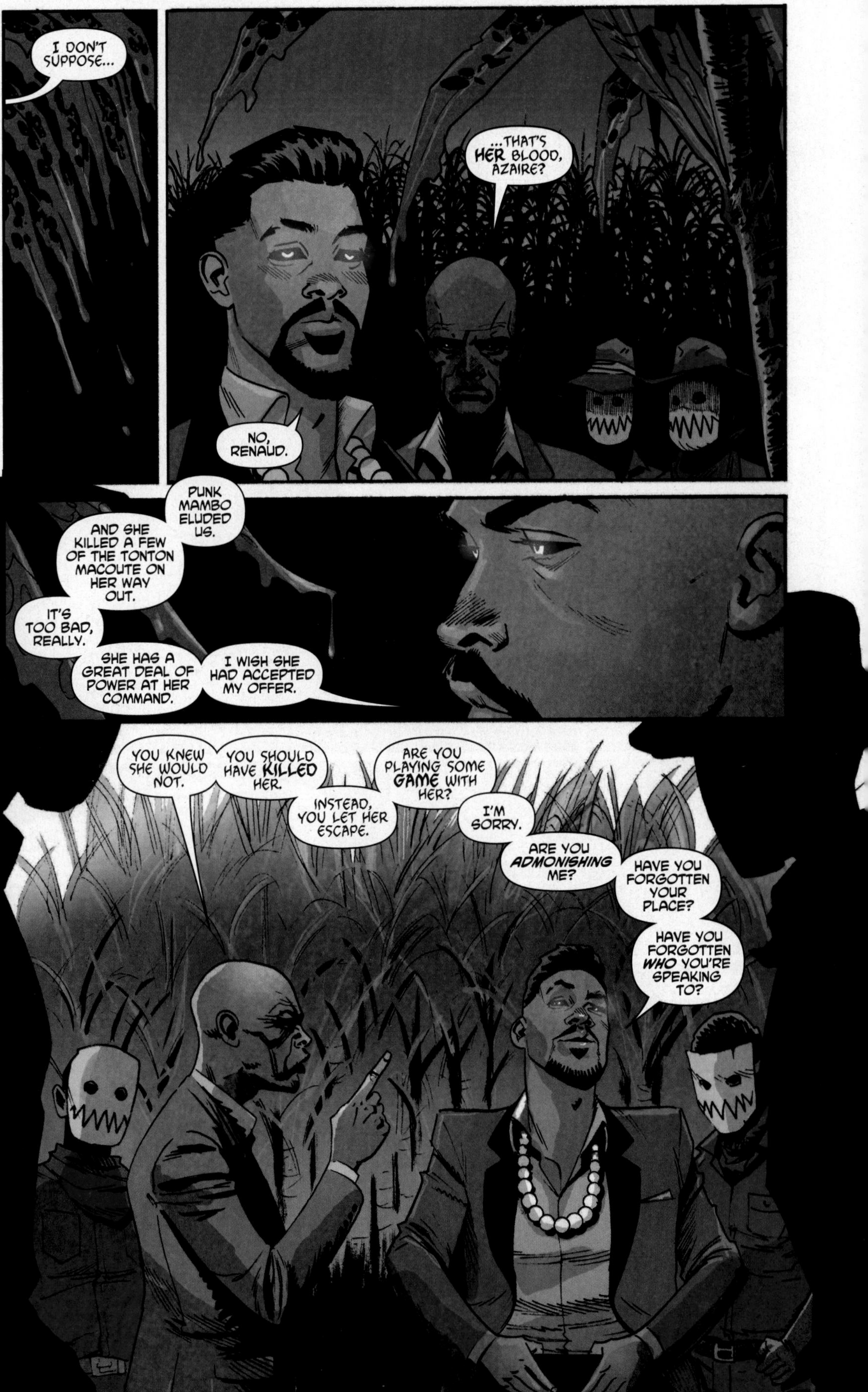
I DON'T SUPPOSE...
...THAT'S HER BLOOD, AZAIRE?
NO, RENAUD.
PUNK MAMBO ELUDED US.
AND SHE KILLED A FEW OF THE TONTON MACOUTE ON HER WAY OUT.
IT'S TOO BAD, REALLY.
SHE HAS A GREAT DEAL OF POWER AT HER COMMAND.
I WISH SHE HAD ACCEPTED MY OFFER.
YOU KNEW SHE WOULD NOT.
YOU SHOULD HAVE KILLED HER.
INSTEAD, YOU LET HER ESCAPE.
ARE YOU PLAYING SOME GAME WITH HER?
I'M SORRY.
ARE YOU ADMONISHING ME?
HAVE YOU FORGOTTEN YOUR PLACE?
HAVE YOU FORGOTTEN WHO YOU'RE SPEAKING TO?

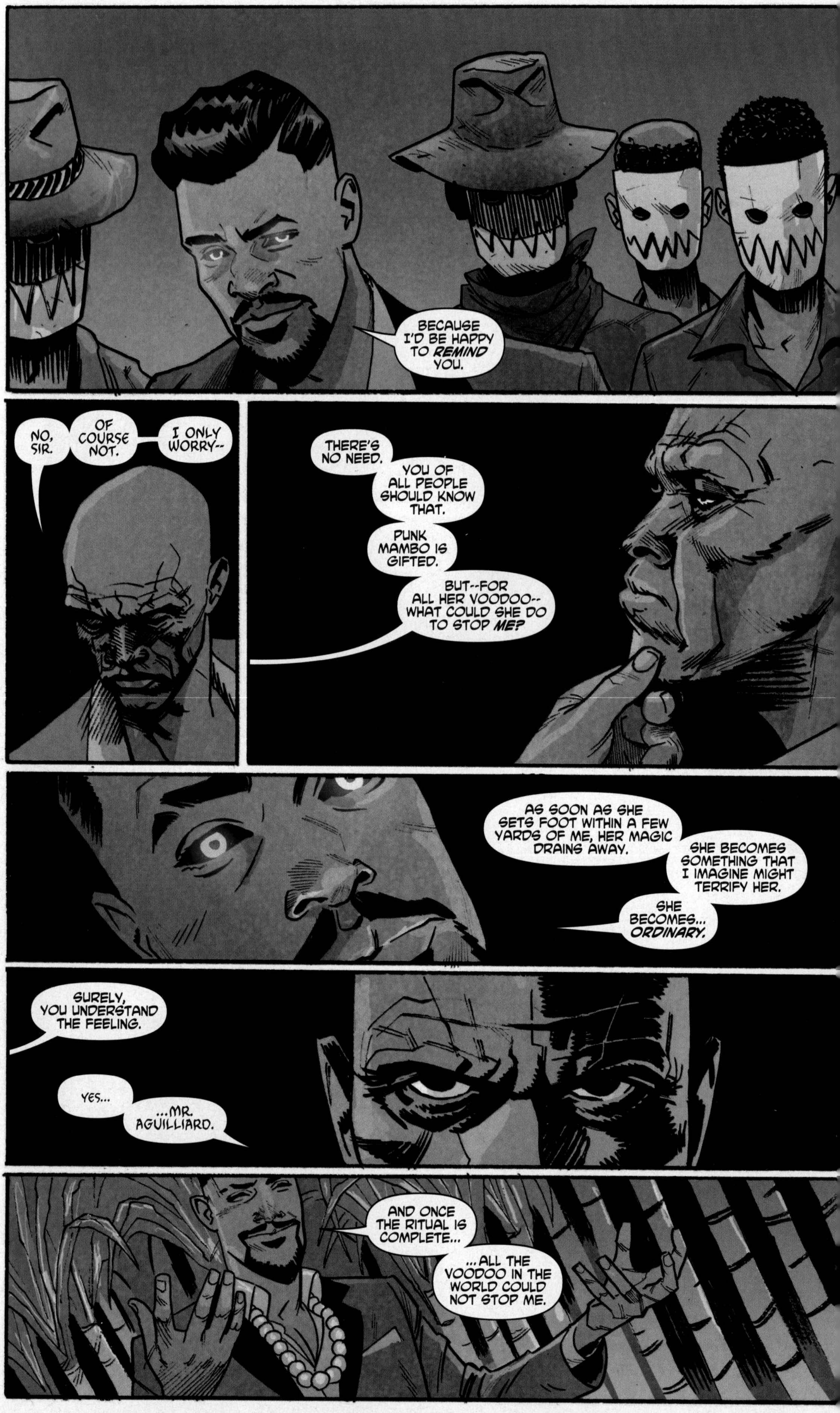
BECAUSE I'D BE HAPPY TO *REMIND* YOU.
NO, SIR.
OF COURSE NOT.
I ONLY WORRY--
THERE'S NO NEED.
YOU OF ALL PEOPLE SHOULD KNOW THAT.
PUNK MAMBO IS GIFTED.
BUT--FOR ALL HER VOODOO--WHAT COULD SHE DO TO STOP *ME?*
AS SOON AS SHE SETS FOOT WITHIN A FEW YARDS OF ME, HER MAGIC DRAINS AWAY.
SHE BECOMES SOMETHING THAT I IMAGINE MIGHT TERRIFY HER.
SHE BECOMES... *ORDINARY.*
SURELY, YOU UNDERSTAND THE FEELING.
YES...
...MR. AGUILLIARD.
AND ONCE THE RITUAL IS COMPLETE...
...ALL THE VOODOO IN THE WORLD COULD NOT STOP ME.

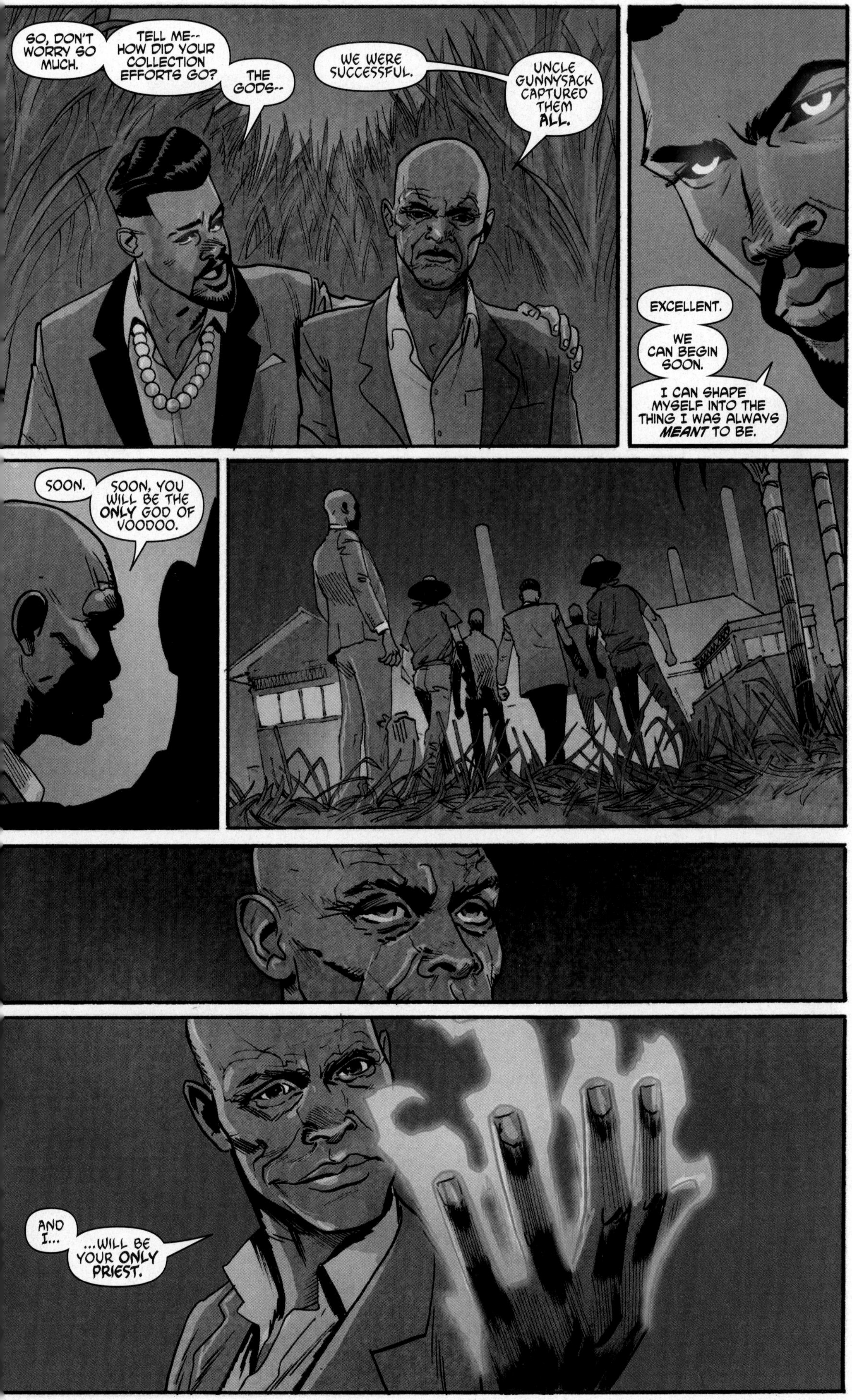

SO, DON'T WORRY SO MUCH.
TELL ME-- HOW DID YOUR COLLECTION EFFORTS GO?
THE GODS--
WE WERE SUCCESSFUL.
UNCLE GUNNYSACK CAPTURED THEM **ALL.**
EXCELLENT.
WE CAN BEGIN SOON.
I CAN SHAPE MYSELF INTO THE THING I WAS ALWAYS ***MEANT*** TO BE.
SOON.
SOON, YOU WILL BE THE **ONLY** GOD OF VOODOO.
AND I...
...WILL BE YOUR **ONLY** **PRIEST.**

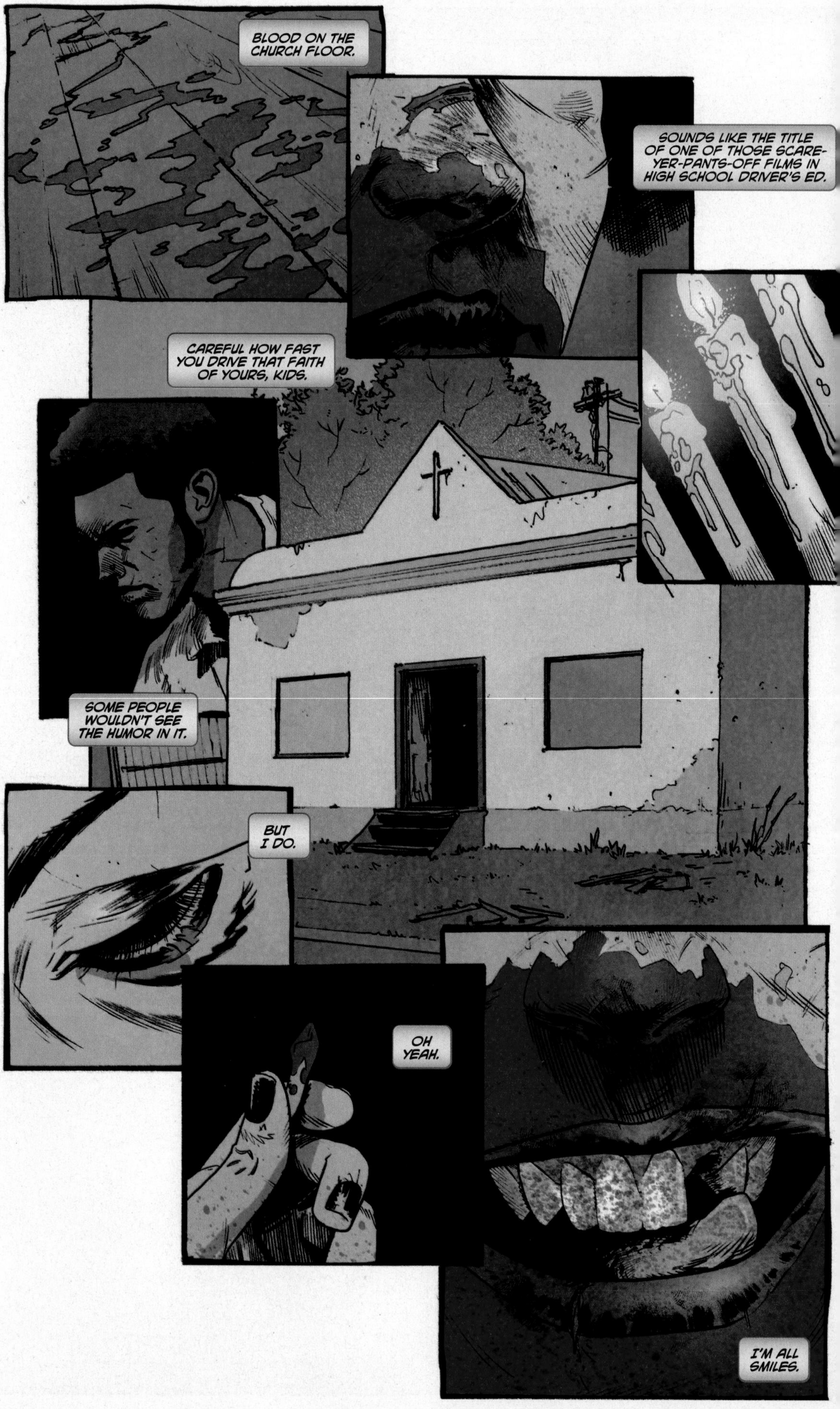
BLOOD ON THE CHURCH FLOOR.
SOUNDS LIKE THE TITLE OF ONE OF THOSE SCARE-YER-PANTS-OFF FILMS IN HIGH SCHOOL DRIVER'S ED.
CAREFUL HOW FAST YOU DRIVE THAT FAITH OF YOURS, KIDS.
SOME PEOPLE WOULDN'T SEE THE HUMOR IN IT.
BUT I DO.
OH YEAH.
I'M ALL SMILES.

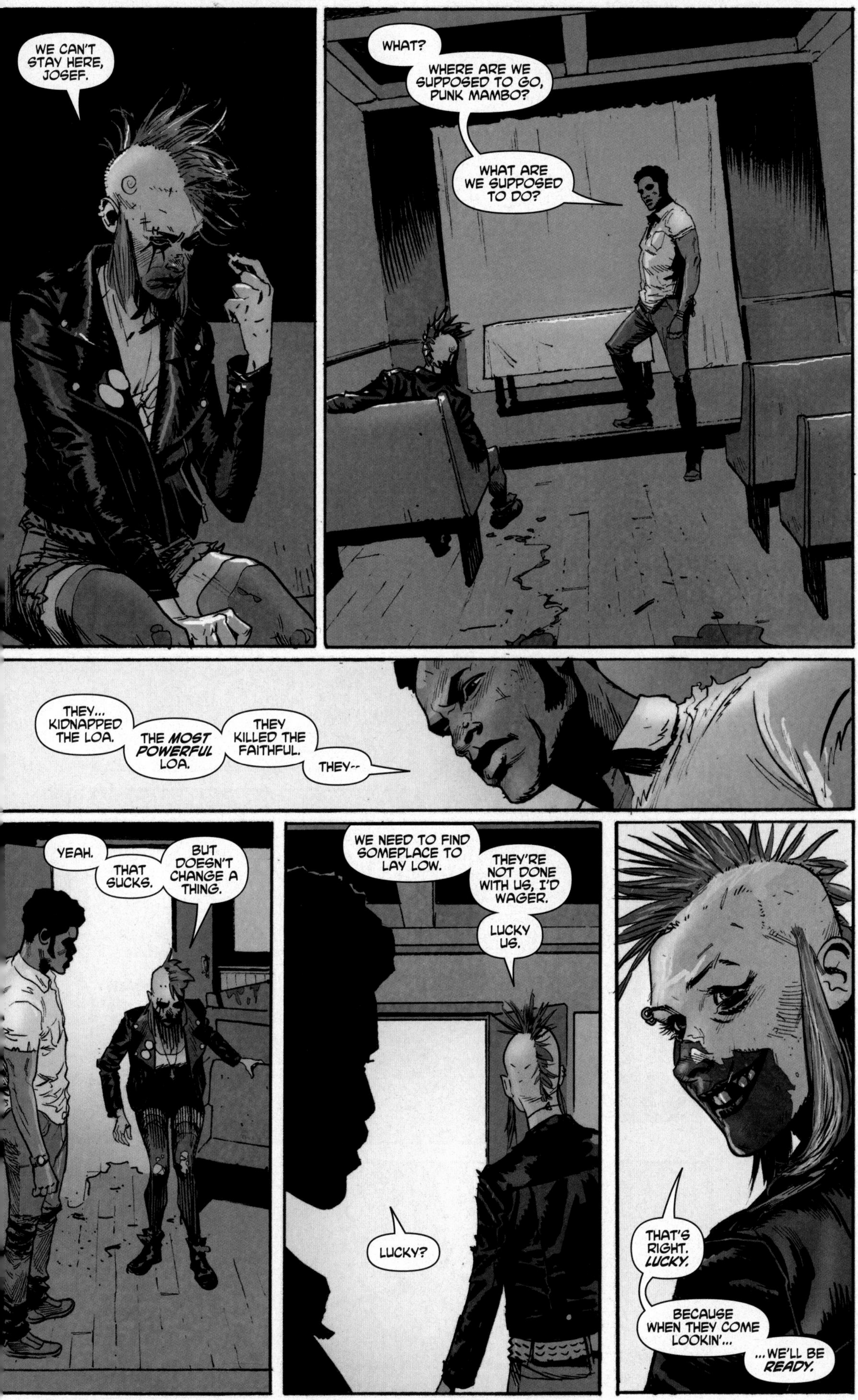

WE CAN'T STAY HERE, JOSEF.
WHAT?
WHERE ARE WE SUPPOSED TO GO, PUNK MAMBO?
WHAT ARE WE SUPPOSED TO DO?
THEY... KIDNAPPED THE LOA.
THE *MOST POWERFUL* LOA.
THEY KILLED THE FAITHFUL.
THEY--
YEAH.
THAT SUCKS.
BUT DOESN'T CHANGE A THING.
WE NEED TO FIND SOMEPLACE TO LAY LOW.
THEY'RE NOT DONE WITH US, I'D WAGER.
LUCKY US.
LUCKY?
THAT'S RIGHT. *LUCKY.*
BECAUSE WHEN THEY COME LOOKIN'...
...WE'LL BE *READY.*

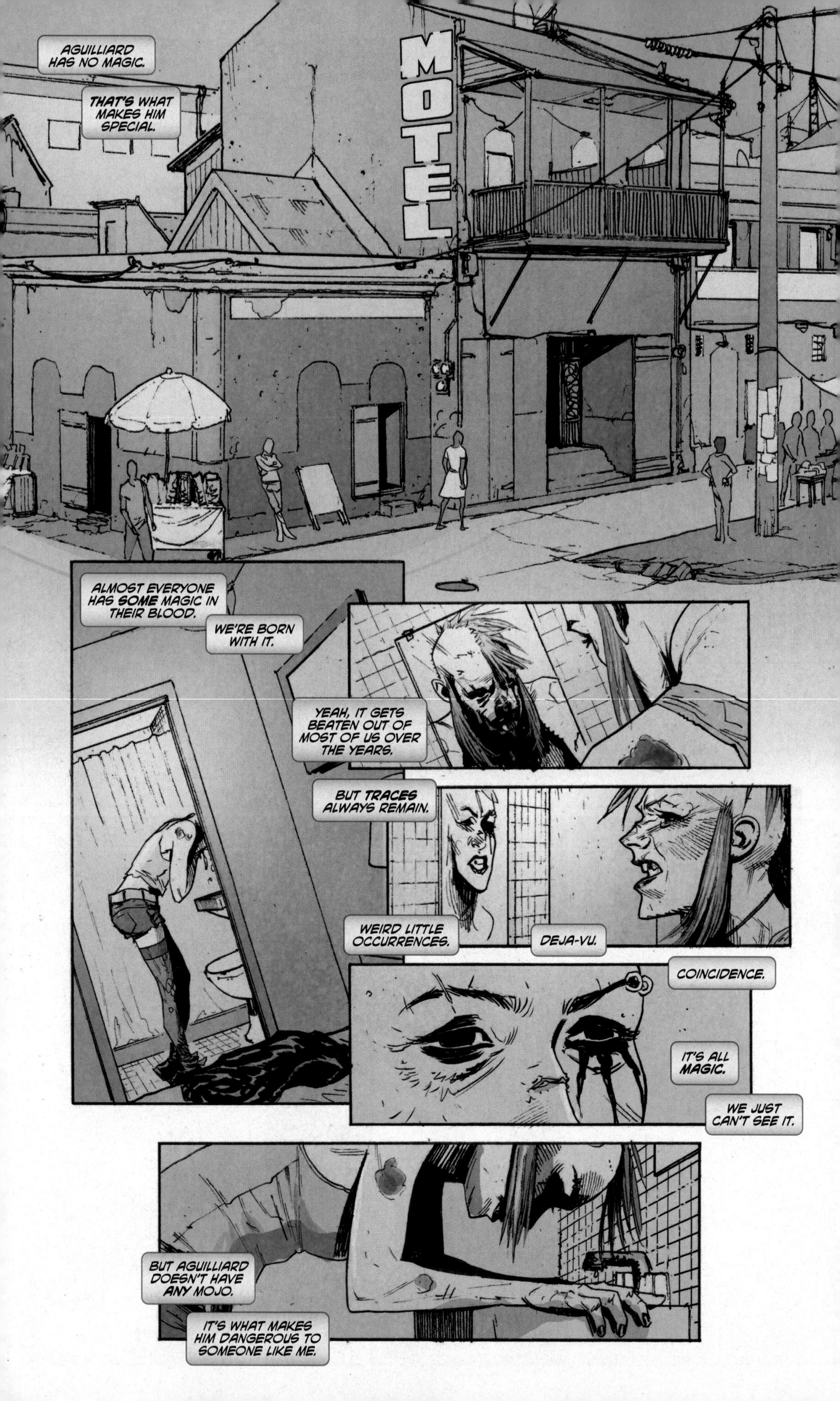
AGUILLIARD HAS NO MAGIC.
THAT'S WHAT MAKES HIM SPECIAL.
MOTEL
ALMOST EVERYONE HAS SOME MAGIC IN THEIR BLOOD.
WE'RE BORN WITH IT.
YEAH, IT GETS BEATEN OUT OF MOST OF US OVER THE YEARS.
BUT TRACES ALWAYS REMAIN.
WEIRD LITTLE OCCURRENCES.
DEJA-VU.
COINCIDENCE.
IT'S ALL MAGIC.
WE JUST CAN'T SEE IT.
BUT AGUILLIARD DOESN'T HAVE ANY MOJO.
IT'S WHAT MAKES HIM DANGEROUS TO SOMEONE LIKE ME.

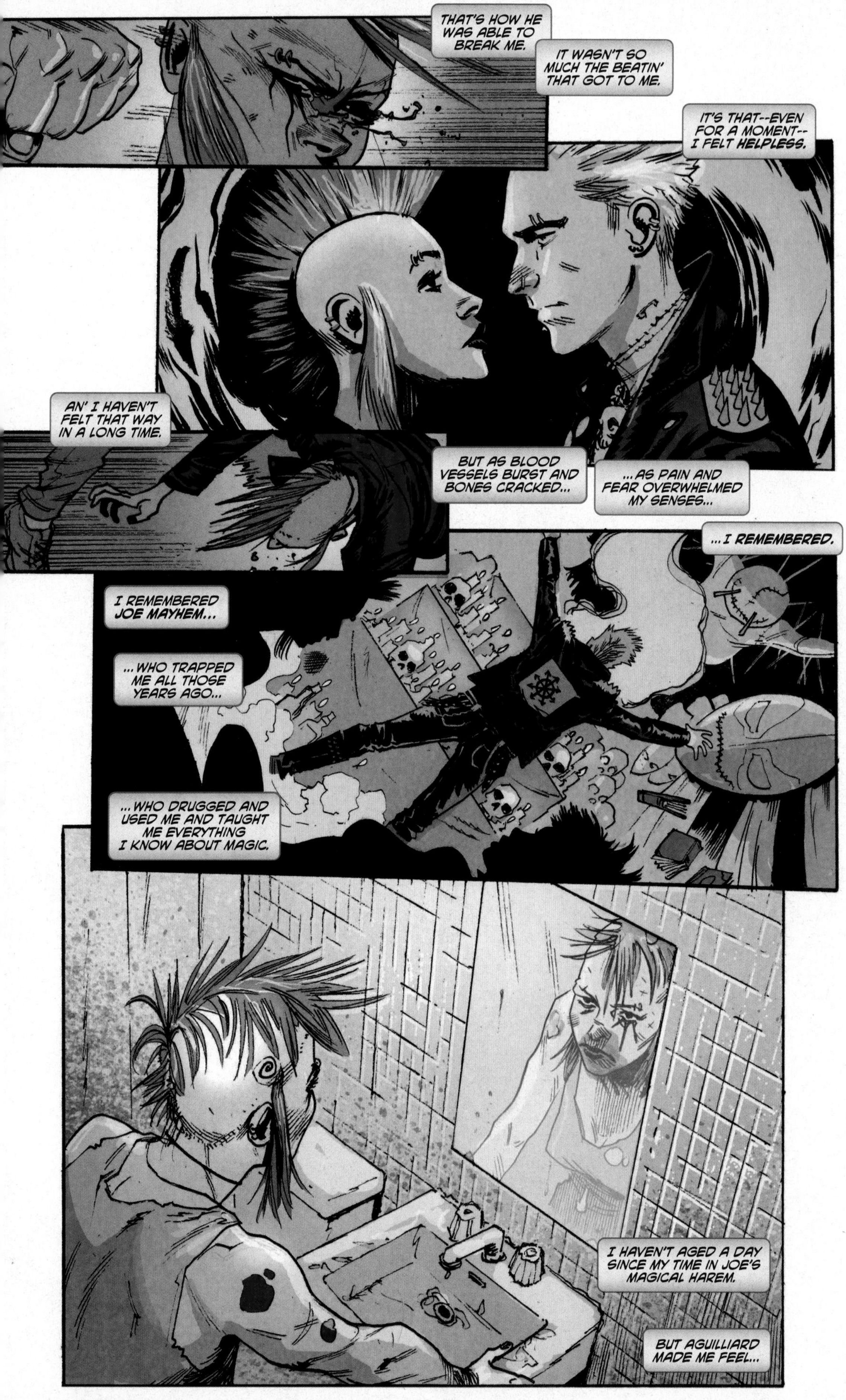
THAT'S HOW HE WAS ABLE TO BREAK ME.
IT WASN'T SO MUCH THE BEATIN' THAT GOT TO ME.
IT'S THAT--EVEN FOR A MOMENT-- I FELT HELPLESS.
AN' I HAVEN'T FELT THAT WAY IN A LONG TIME.
BUT AS BLOOD VESSELS BURST AND BONES CRACKED...
...AS PAIN AND FEAR OVERWHELMED MY SENSES...
...I REMEMBERED.
I REMEMBERED JOE MAYHEM...
...WHO TRAPPED ME ALL THOSE YEARS AGO...
...WHO DRUGGED AND USED ME AND TAUGHT ME EVERYTHING I KNOW ABOUT MAGIC.
I HAVEN'T AGED A DAY SINCE MY TIME IN JOE'S MAGICAL HAREM.
BUT AGUILLIARD MADE ME FEEL...

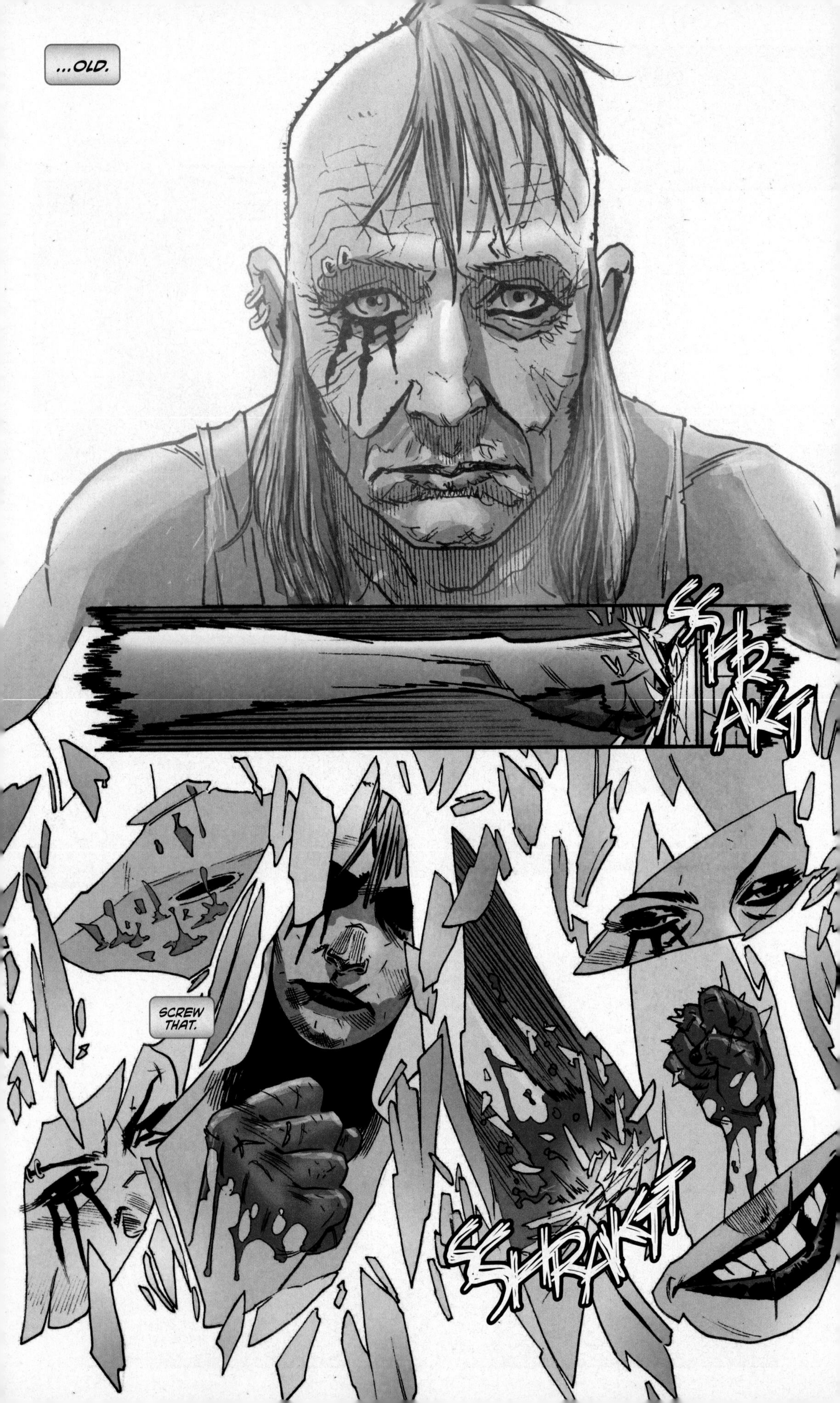
...OLD.
SHRAKT
SCREW THAT.
SHRAKT

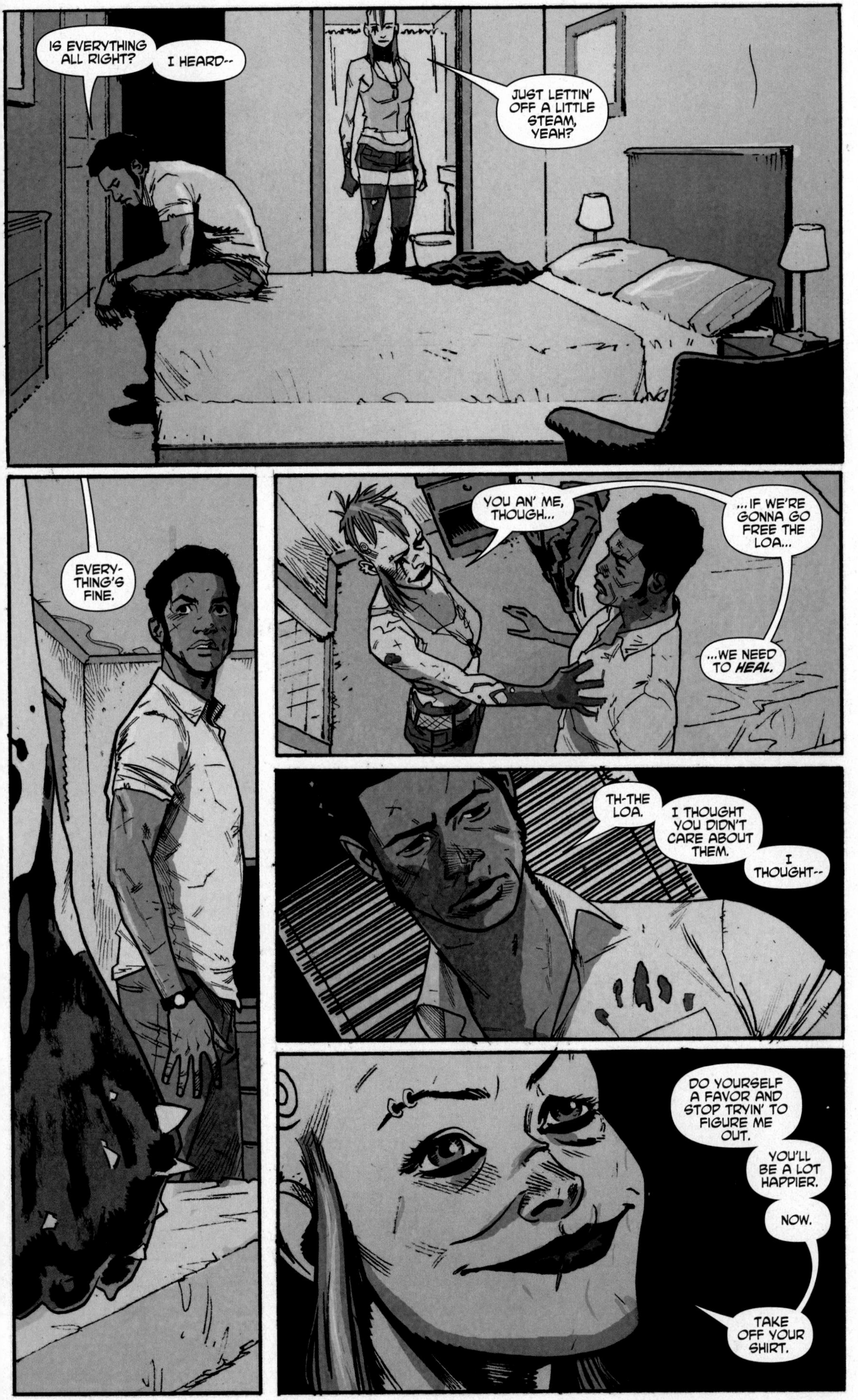
IS EVERYTHING ALL RIGHT?
I HEARD--
JUST LETTIN' OFF A LITTLE STEAM, YEAH?
EVERY-THING'S FINE.
YOU AN' ME, THOUGH...
...IF WE'RE GONNA GO FREE THE LOA...
...WE NEED TO HEAL.
TH-THE LOA.
I THOUGHT YOU DIDN'T CARE ABOUT THEM.
I THOUGHT--
DO YOURSELF A FAVOR AND STOP TRYIN' TO FIGURE ME OUT.
YOU'LL BE A LOT HAPPIER.
NOW.
TAKE OFF YOUR SHIRT.

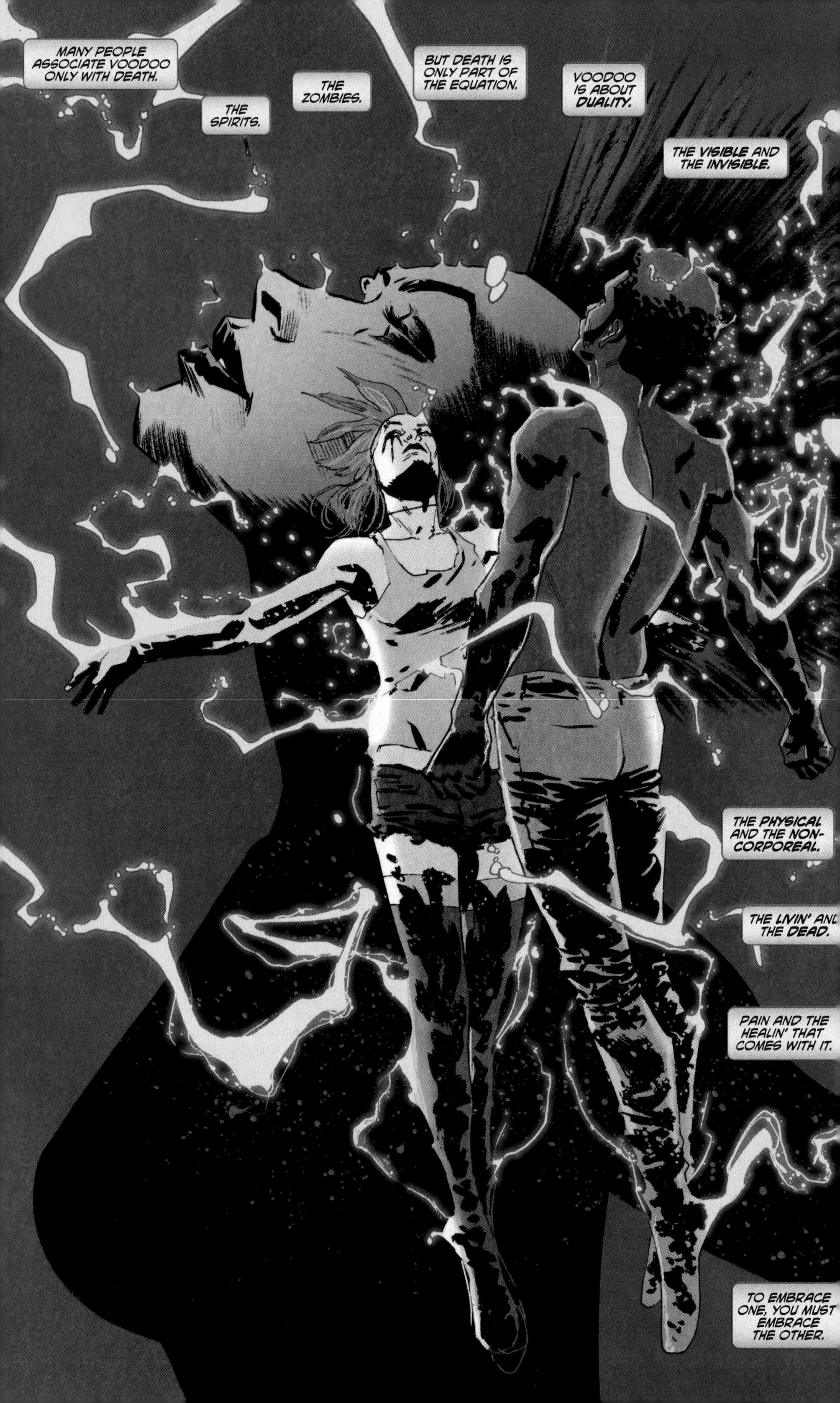
MANY PEOPLE ASSOCIATE VOODOO ONLY WITH DEATH.
THE SPIRITS.
THE ZOMBIES.
BUT DEATH IS ONLY PART OF THE EQUATION.
VOODOO IS ABOUT DUALITY.
THE VISIBLE AND THE INVISIBLE.
THE PHYSICAL AND THE NON-CORPOREAL.
THE LIVIN' AND THE DEAD.
PAIN AND THE HEALIN' THAT COMES WITH IT.
TO EMBRACE ONE, YOU MUST EMBRACE THE OTHER.

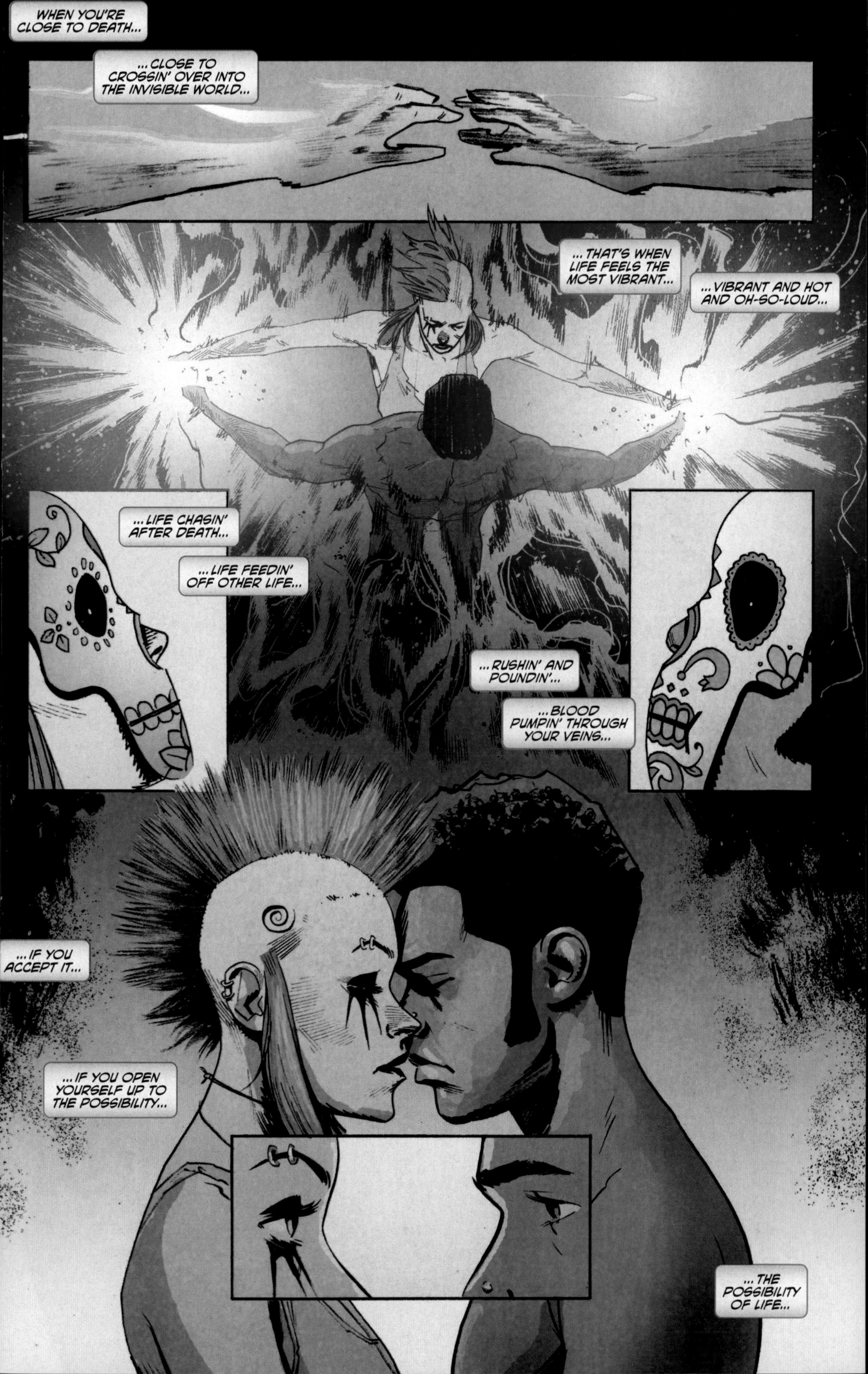
WHEN YOU'RE CLOSE TO DEATH...
...CLOSE TO CROSSIN' OVER INTO THE INVISIBLE WORLD...
...THAT'S WHEN LIFE FEELS THE MOST VIBRANT...
...VIBRANT AND HOT AND OH-SO-LOUD...
...LIFE CHASIN' AFTER DEATH...
...LIFE FEEDIN' OFF OTHER LIFE...
...RUSHIN' AND POUNDIN'...
...BLOOD PUMPIN' THROUGH YOUR VEINS...
...IF YOU ACCEPT IT...
...IF YOU OPEN YOURSELF UP TO THE POSSIBILITY...
...THE POSSIBILITY OF LIFE...

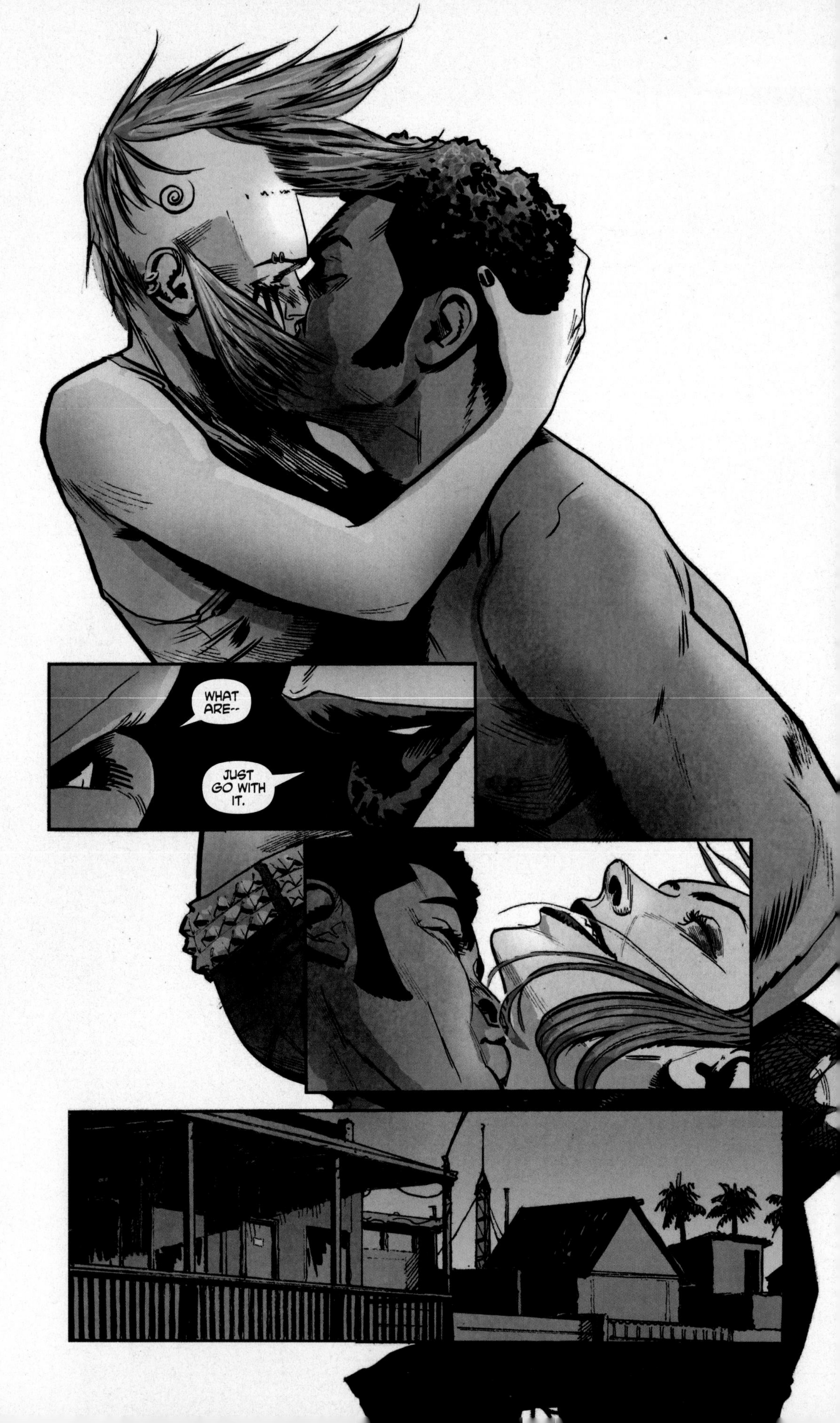
WHAT ARE--
JUST GO WITH IT.

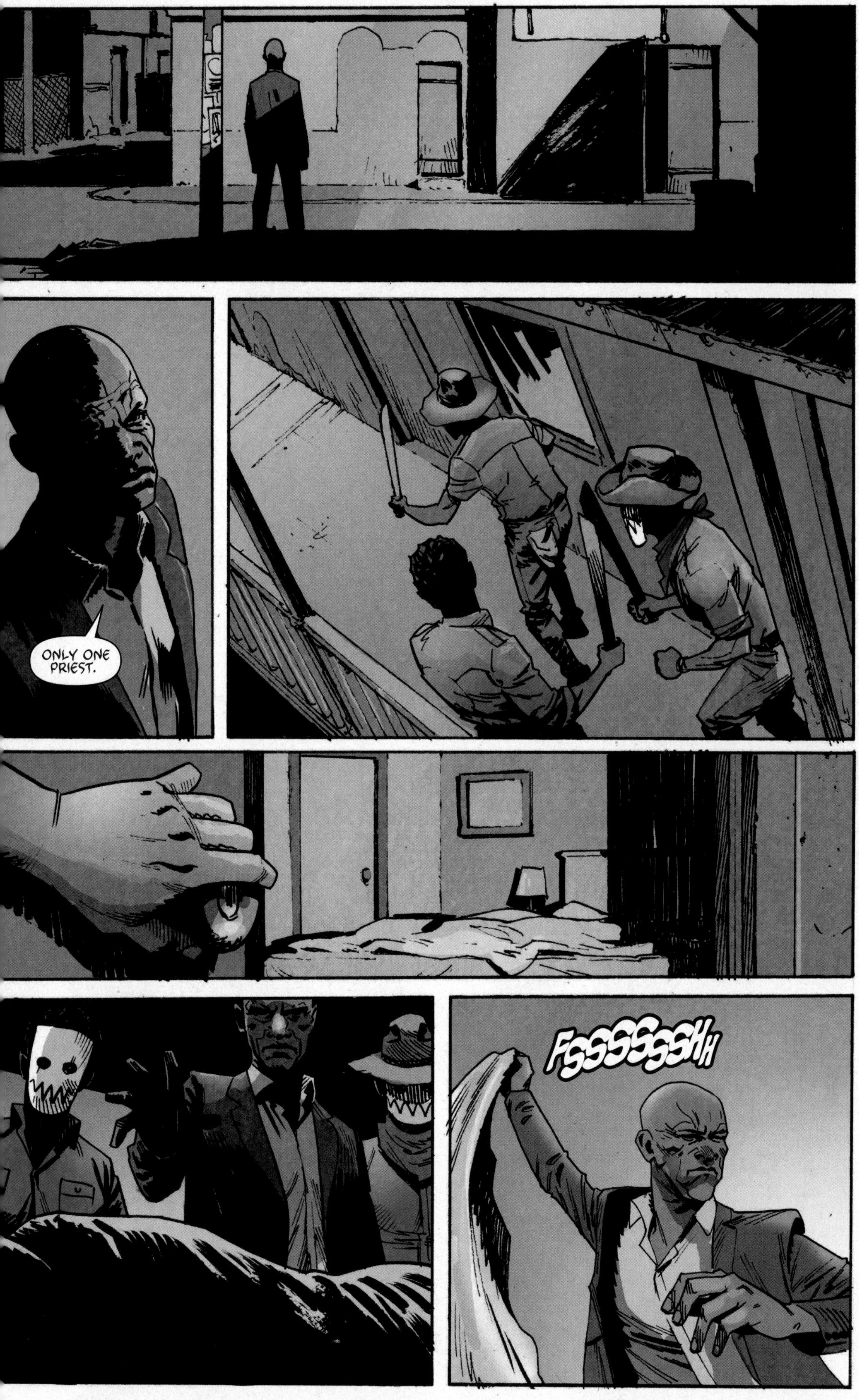
ONLY ONE PRIEST.
FSSSSSSHH

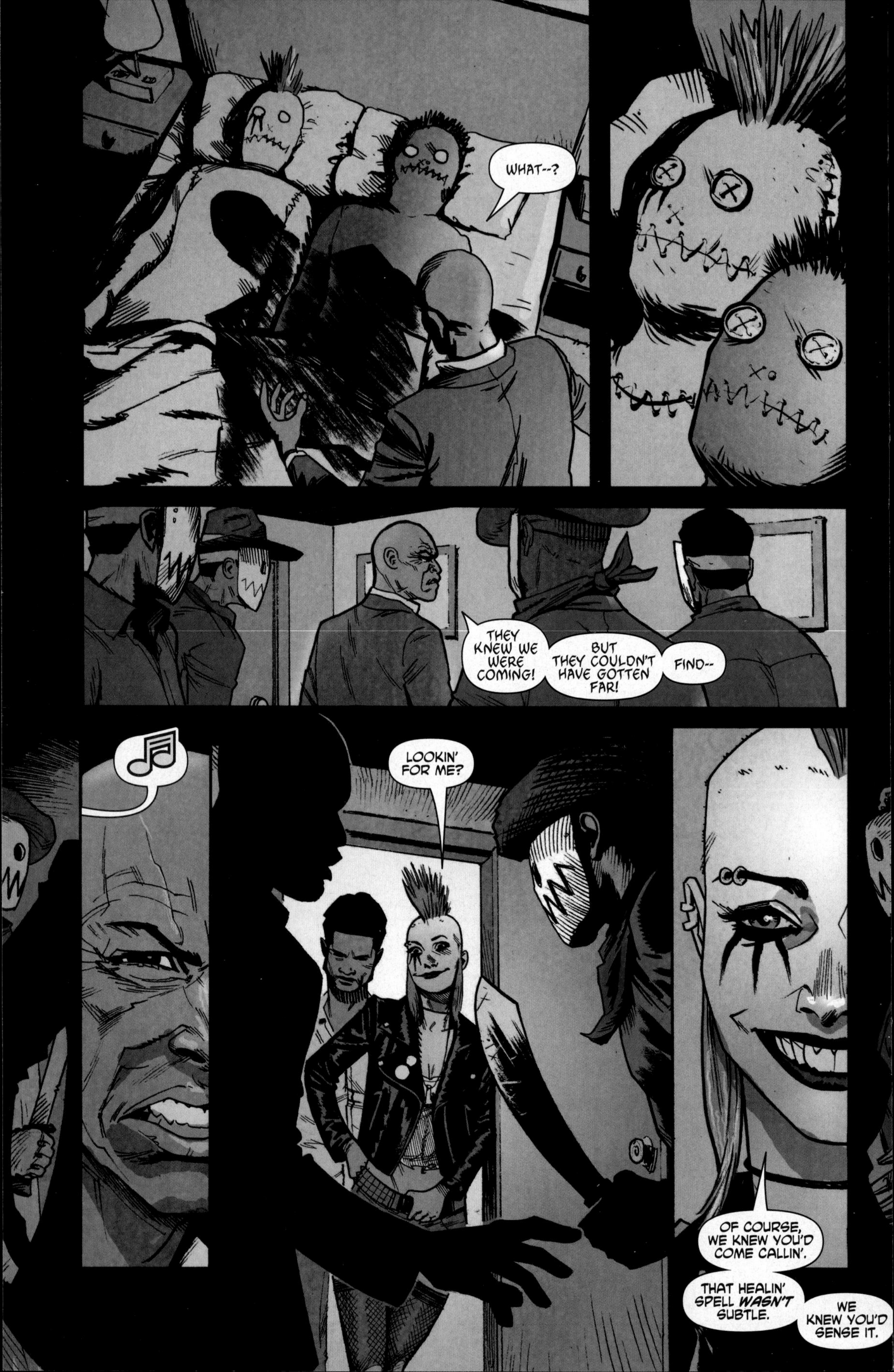

WHAT--?
THEY KNEW WE WERE COMING!
BUT THEY COULDN'T HAVE GOTTEN FAR!
FIND--
LOOKIN' FOR ME?
OF COURSE, WE KNEW YOU'D COME CALLIN'.
THAT HEALIN' SPELL *WASN'T* SUBTLE.
WE KNEW YOU'D SENSE IT.

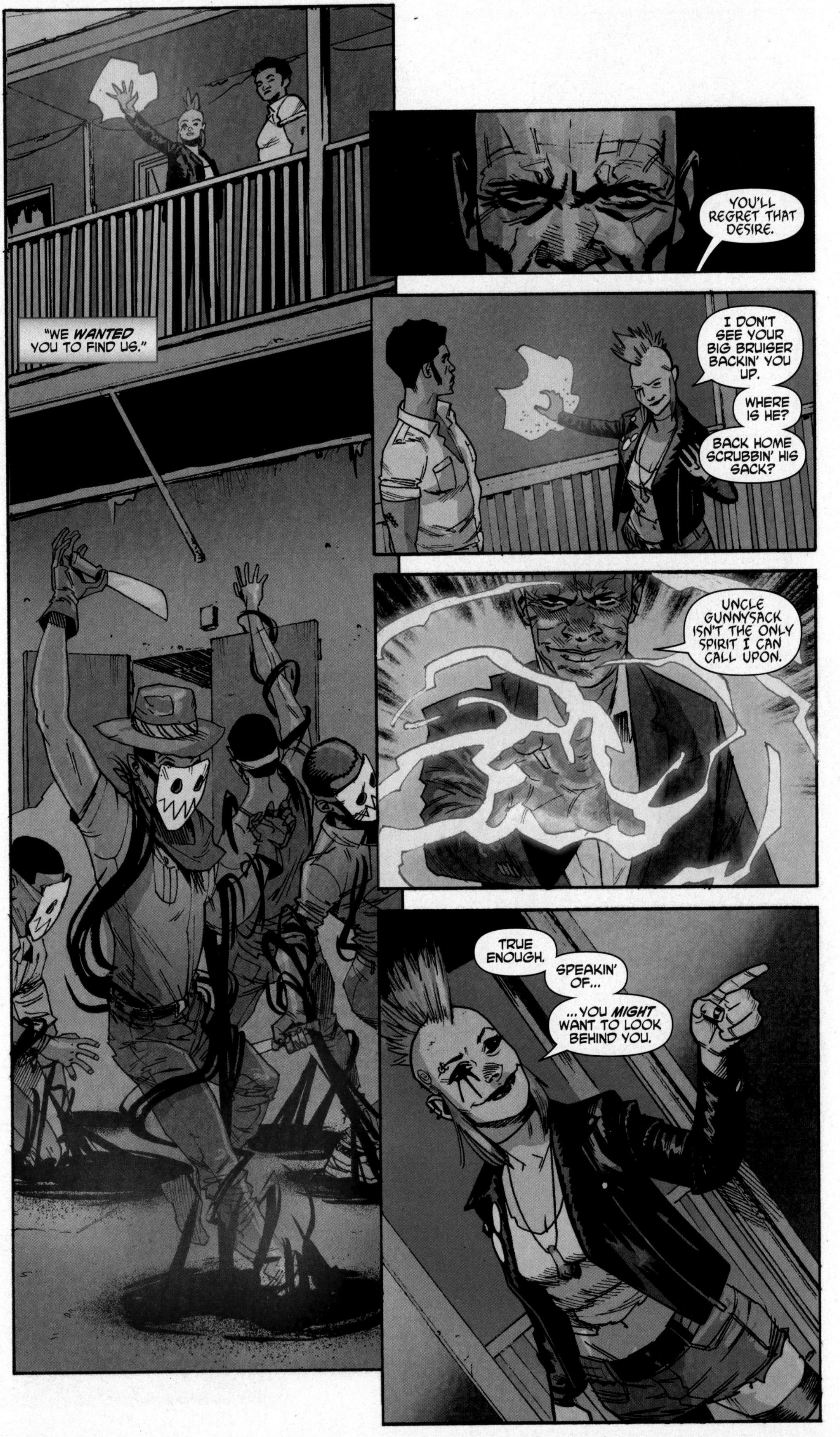
"WE WANTED YOU TO FIND US."
YOU'LL REGRET THAT DESIRE.
I DON'T SEE YOUR BIG BRUISER BACKIN' YOU UP.
WHERE IS HE?
BACK HOME SCRUBBIN' HIS SACK?
UNCLE GUNNYSACK ISN'T THE ONLY SPIRIT I CAN CALL UPON.
TRUE ENOUGH.
SPEAKIN' OF...
...YOU MIGHT WANT TO LOOK BEHIND YOU.

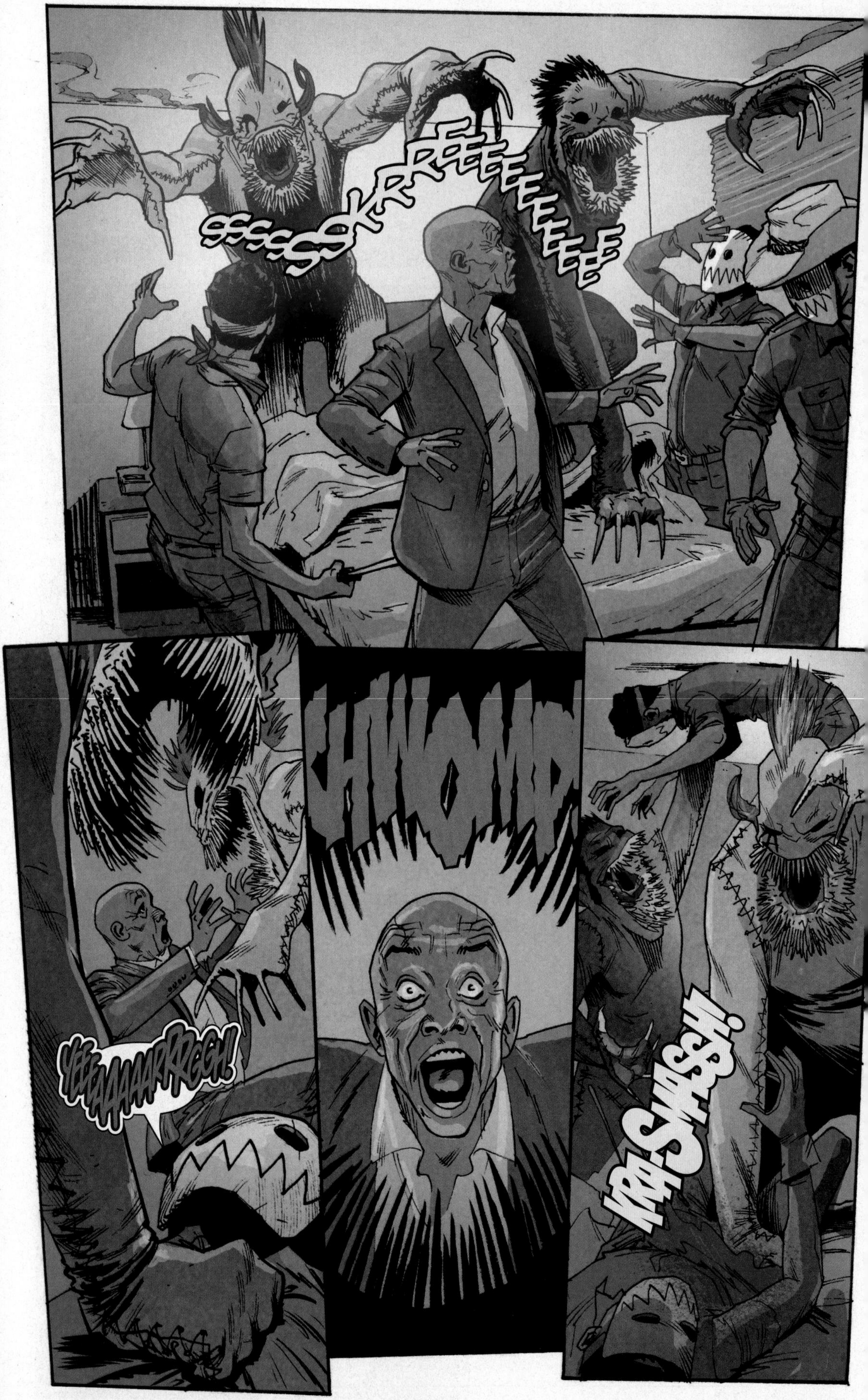
SSSSSSKRREEEEEEEEEEE
YEEEAAAARRRGGH!
CHOMP
KRA-SMASSH!

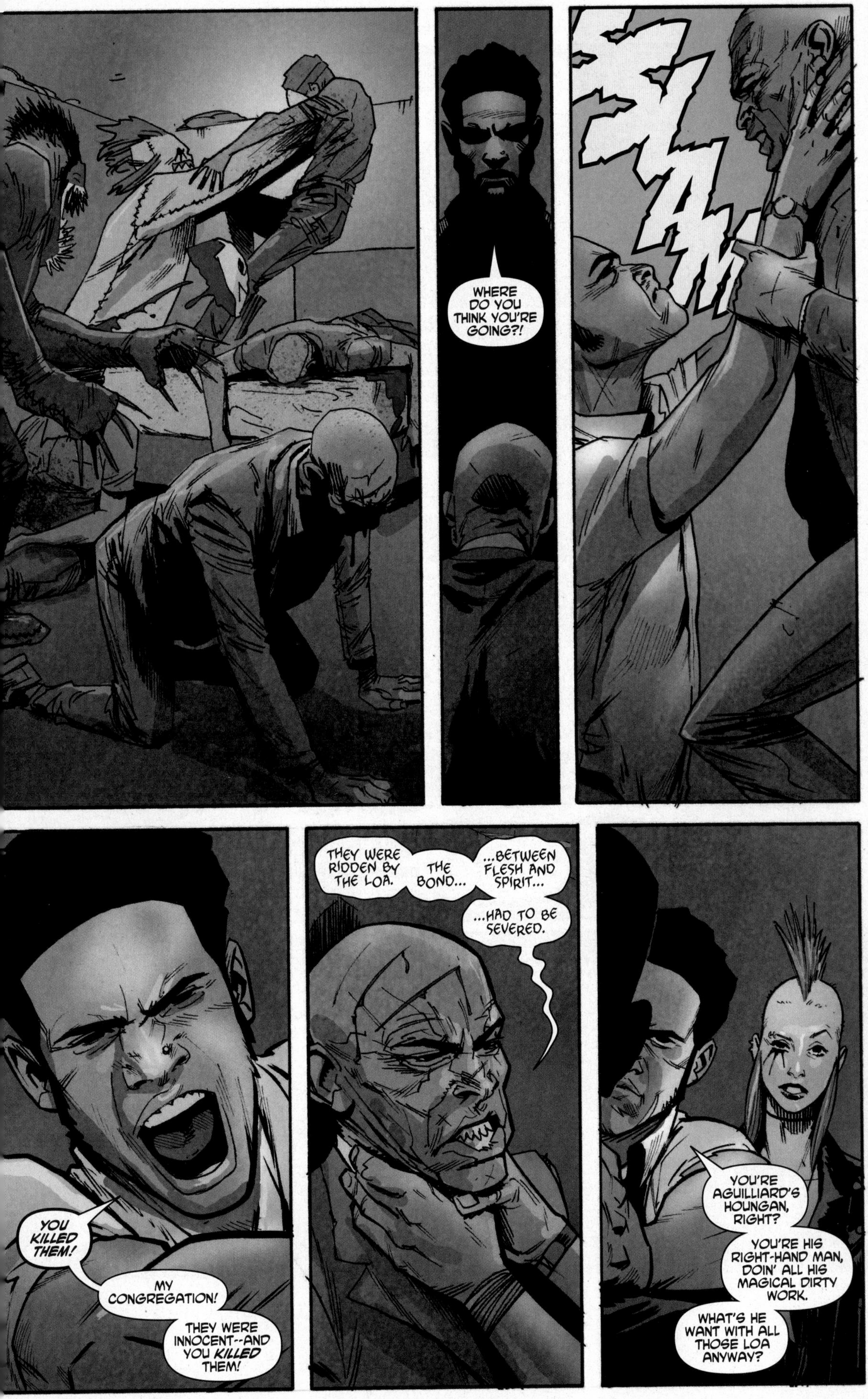
WHERE DO YOU THINK YOU'RE GOING?!
YOU KILLED THEM!
MY CONGREGATION!
THEY WERE INNOCENT--AND YOU KILLED THEM!
THEY WERE RIDDEN BY THE LOA.
THE BOND...
...BETWEEN FLESH AND SPIRIT...
...HAD TO BE SEVERED.
YOU'RE AGUILLIARD'S HOUNGAN, RIGHT?
YOU'RE HIS RIGHT-HAND MAN, DOIN' ALL HIS MAGICAL DIRTY WORK.
WHAT'S HE WANT WITH ALL THOSE LOA ANYWAY?

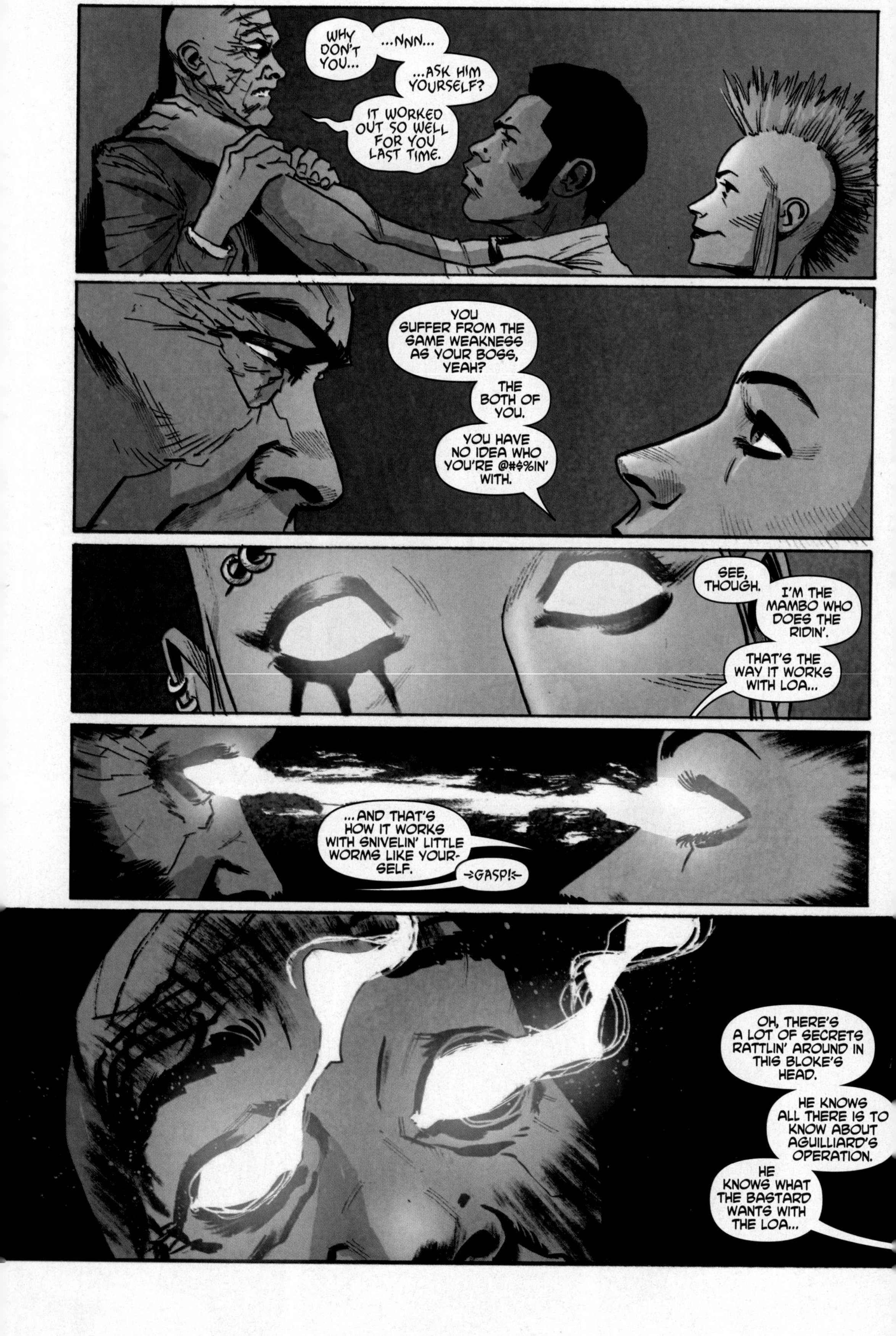
WHY DON'T YOU...
...NNN...
...ASK HIM YOURSELF?
IT WORKED OUT SO WELL FOR YOU LAST TIME.
YOU SUFFER FROM THE SAME WEAKNESS AS YOUR BOSS, YEAH?
THE BOTH OF YOU.
YOU HAVE NO IDEA WHO YOU'RE @#$%IN' WITH.
SEE, THOUGH.
I'M THE MAMBO WHO DOES THE RIDIN'.
THAT'S THE WAY IT WORKS WITH LOA...
...AND THAT'S HOW IT WORKS WITH SNIVELIN' LITTLE WORMS LIKE YOURSELF.
GASP!
OH, THERE'S A LOT OF SECRETS RATTLIN' AROUND IN THIS BLOKE'S HEAD.
HE KNOWS ALL THERE IS TO KNOW ABOUT AGUILLIARD'S OPERATION.
HE KNOWS WHAT THE BASTARD WANTS WITH THE LOA...

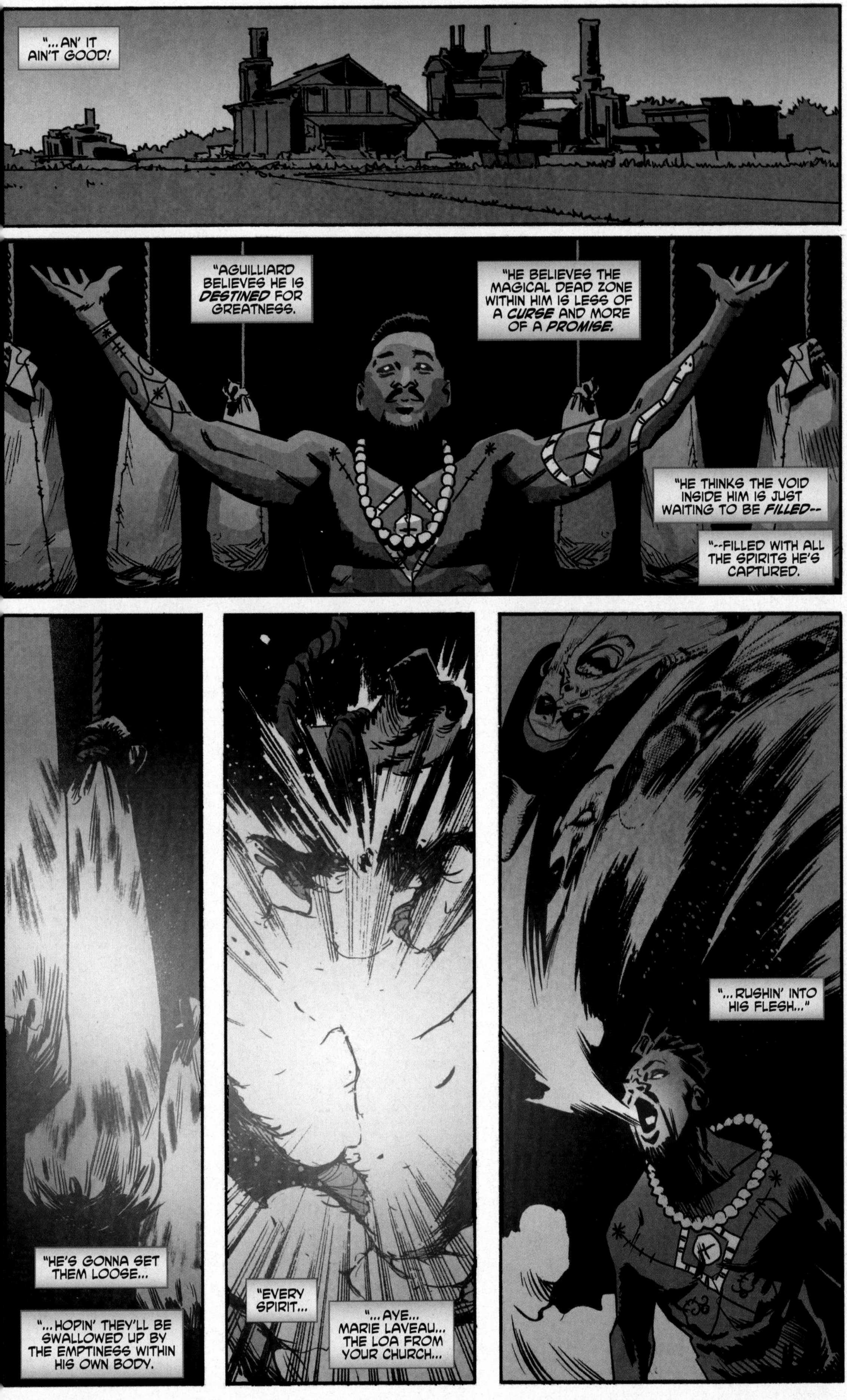
"...AN' IT AIN'T GOOD!
"AGUILLIARD BELIEVES HE IS *DESTINED* FOR GREATNESS.
"HE BELIEVES THE MAGICAL DEAD ZONE WITHIN HIM IS LESS OF A *CURSE* AND MORE OF A *PROMISE*.
"HE THINKS THE VOID INSIDE HIM IS JUST WAITING TO BE *FILLED*--
"--FILLED WITH ALL THE SPIRITS HE'S CAPTURED.
"HE'S GONNA SET THEM LOOSE...
"...HOPIN' THEY'LL BE SWALLOWED UP BY THE EMPTINESS WITHIN HIS OWN BODY.
"EVERY SPIRIT...
"...AYE... MARIE LAVEAU... THE LOA FROM YOUR CHURCH...
"...RUSHIN' INTO HIS FLESH..."

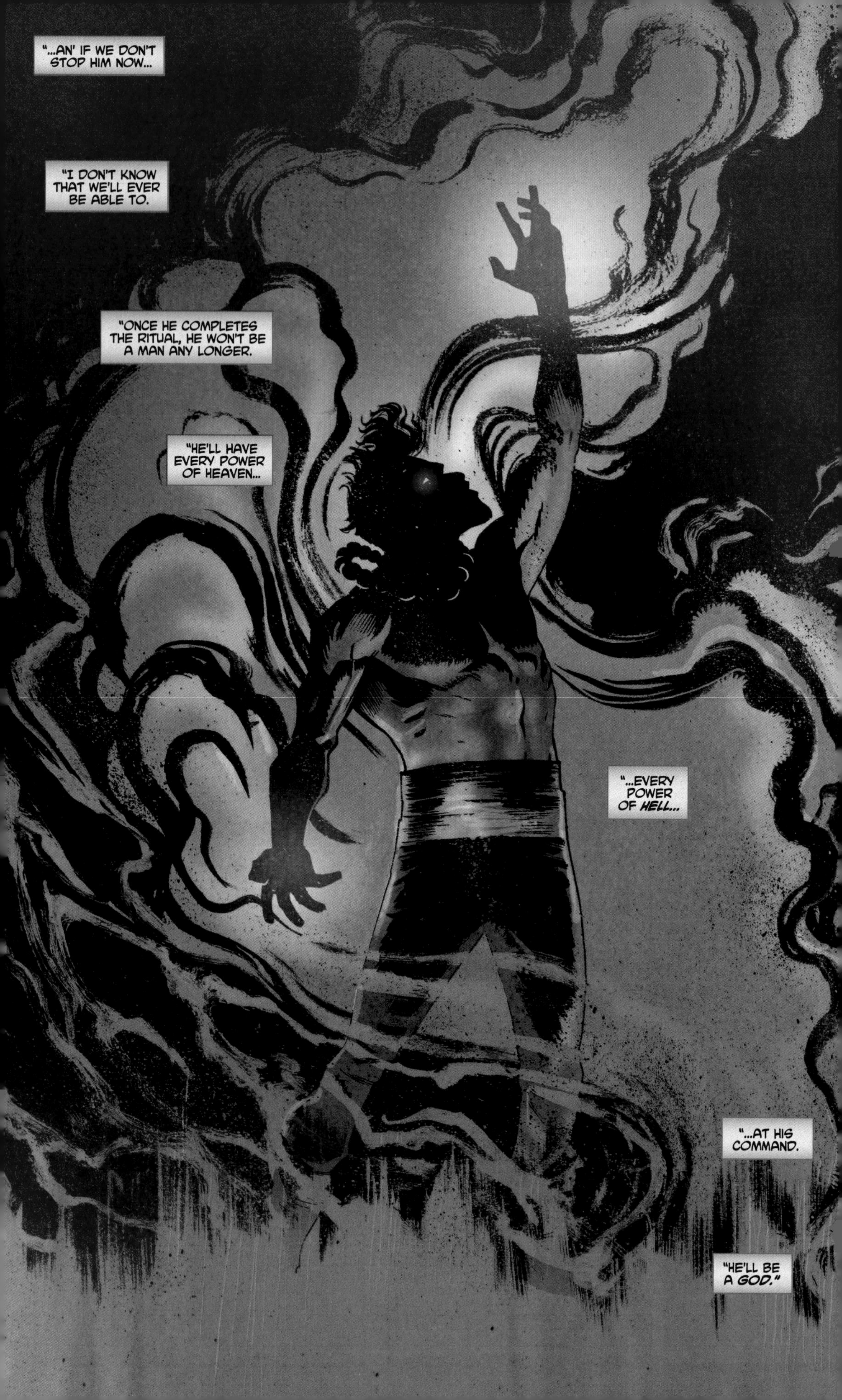
"...AN' IF WE DON'T STOP HIM NOW...
"I DON'T KNOW THAT WE'LL EVER BE ABLE TO.
"ONCE HE COMPLETES THE RITUAL, HE WON'T BE A MAN ANY LONGER.
"HE'LL HAVE EVERY POWER OF HEAVEN...
"...EVERY POWER OF *HELL*...
"...AT HIS COMMAND.
"HE'LL BE A *GOD*."

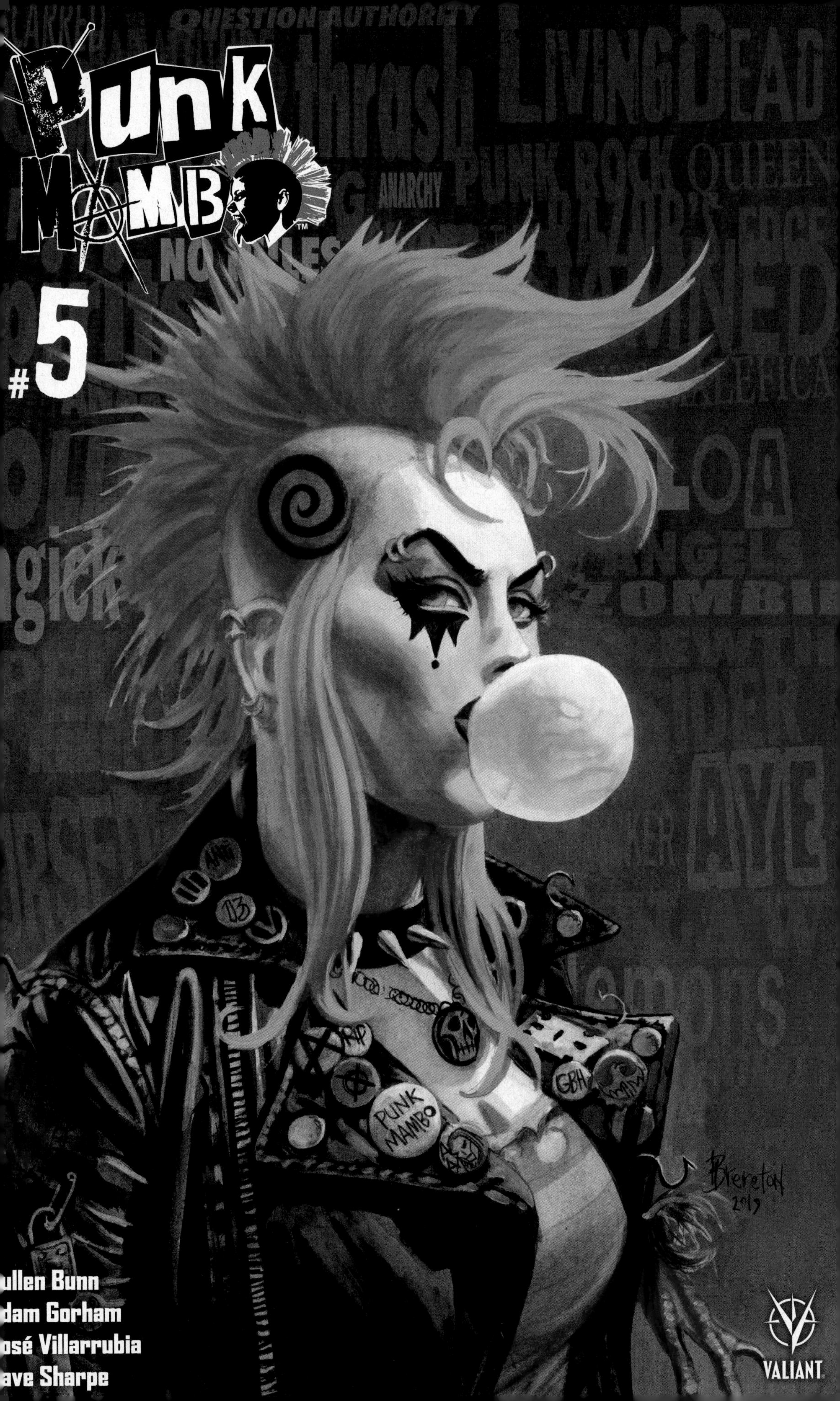
PUNK MAMBO
#5
ullen Bunn
dam Gorham
osé Villarrubia
ave Sharpe
VALIANT

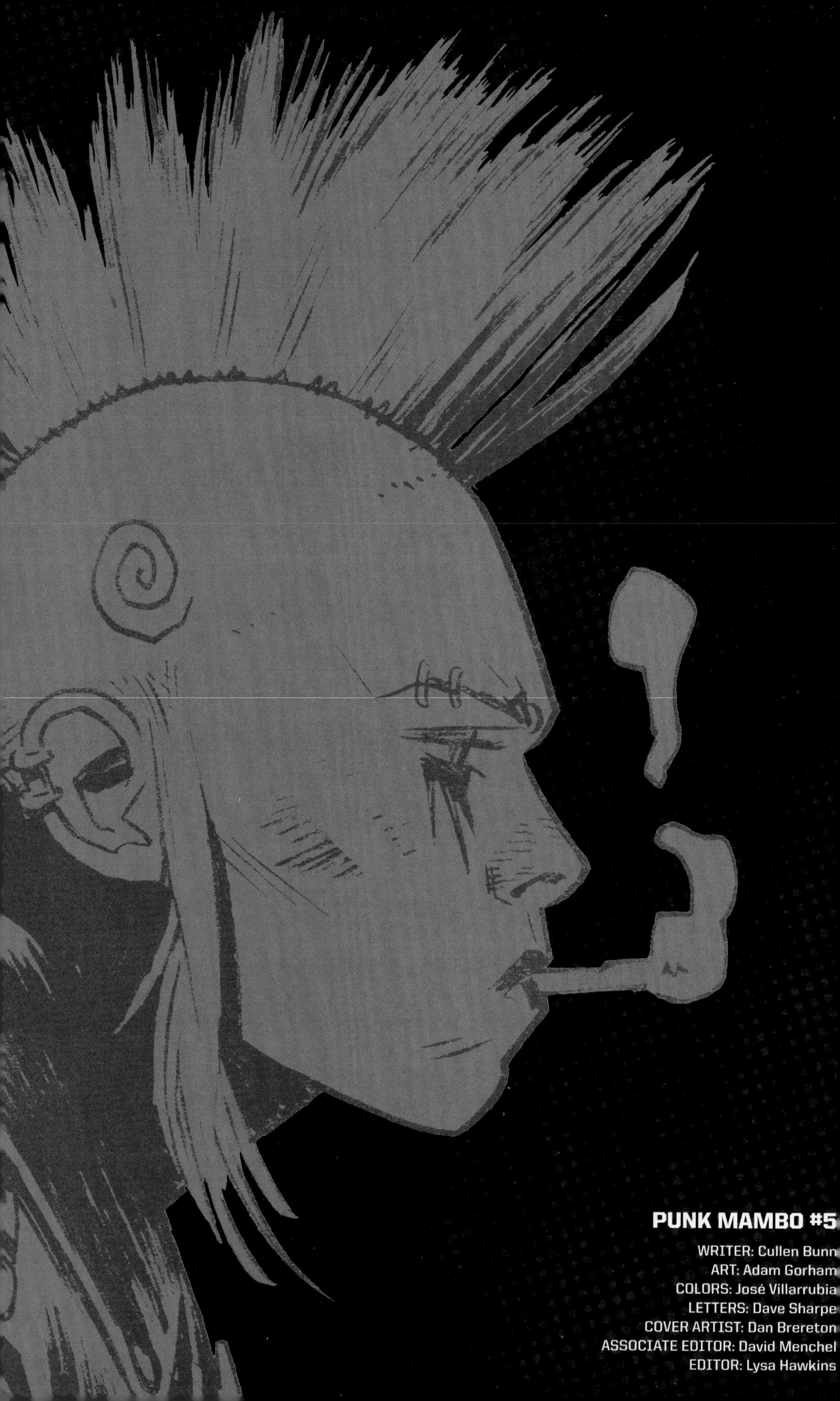

PUNK MAMBO #5

WRITER: Cullen Bunn
ART: Adam Gorham
COLORS: José Villarrubia
LETTERS: Dave Sharpe
COVER ARTIST: Dan Brereton
ASSOCIATE EDITOR: David Menchel
EDITOR: Lysa Hawkins

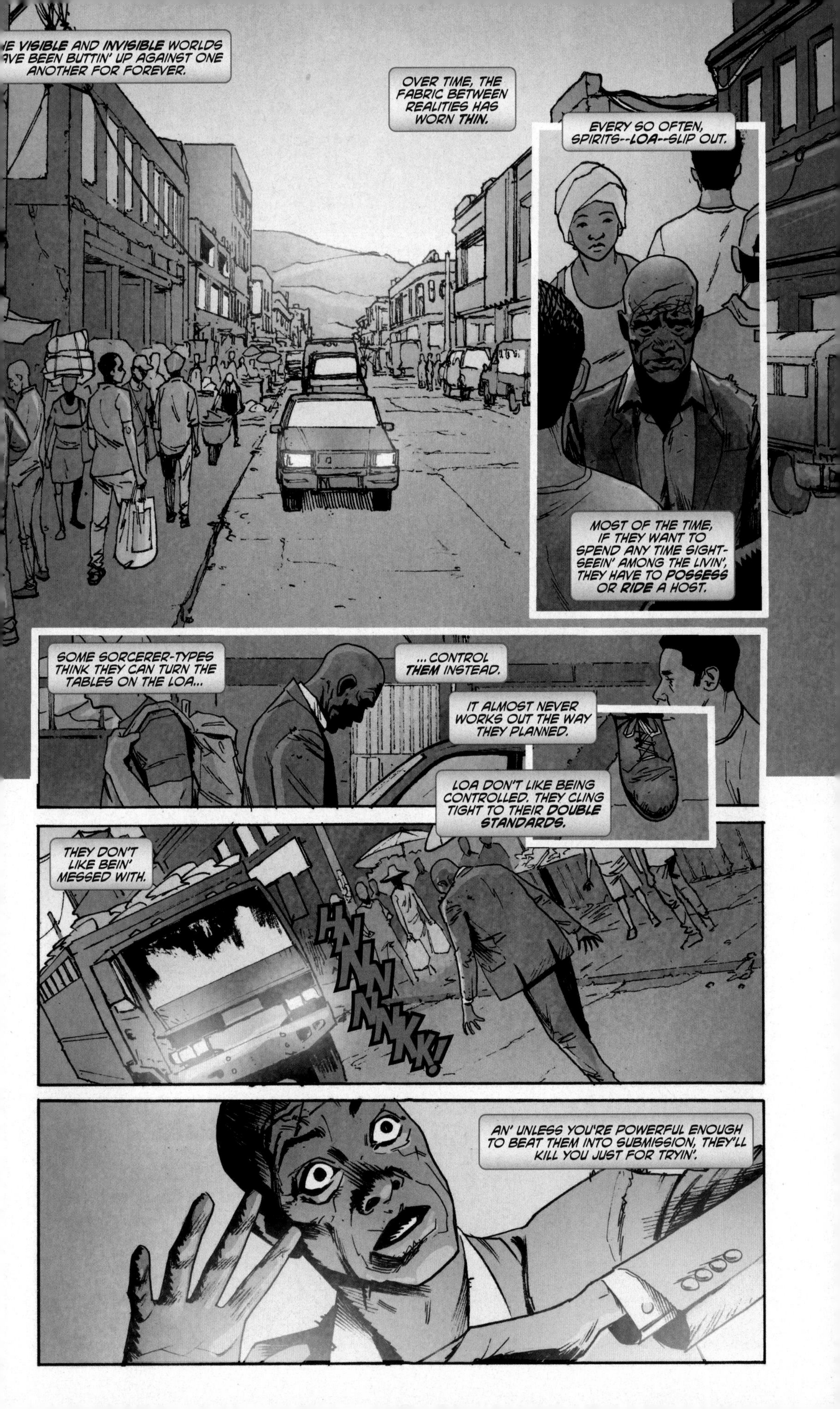

E VISIBLE AND INVISIBLE WORLDS AVE BEEN BUTTIN' UP AGAINST ONE ANOTHER FOR FOREVER.
OVER TIME, THE FABRIC BETWEEN REALITIES HAS WORN THIN.
EVERY SO OFTEN, SPIRITS--LOA--SLIP OUT.
MOST OF THE TIME, IF THEY WANT TO SPEND ANY TIME SIGHT-SEEIN' AMONG THE LIVIN', THEY HAVE TO POSSESS OR RIDE A HOST.
SOME SORCERER-TYPES THINK THEY CAN TURN THE TABLES ON THE LOA...
...CONTROL THEM INSTEAD.
IT ALMOST NEVER WORKS OUT THE WAY THEY PLANNED.
LOA DON'T LIKE BEING CONTROLLED. THEY CLING TIGHT TO THEIR DOUBLE STANDARDS.
THEY DON'T LIKE BEIN' MESSED WITH.
HNNNNNKK!
AN' UNLESS YOU'RE POWERFUL ENOUGH TO BEAT THEM INTO SUBMISSION, THEY'LL KILL YOU JUST FOR TRYIN'.

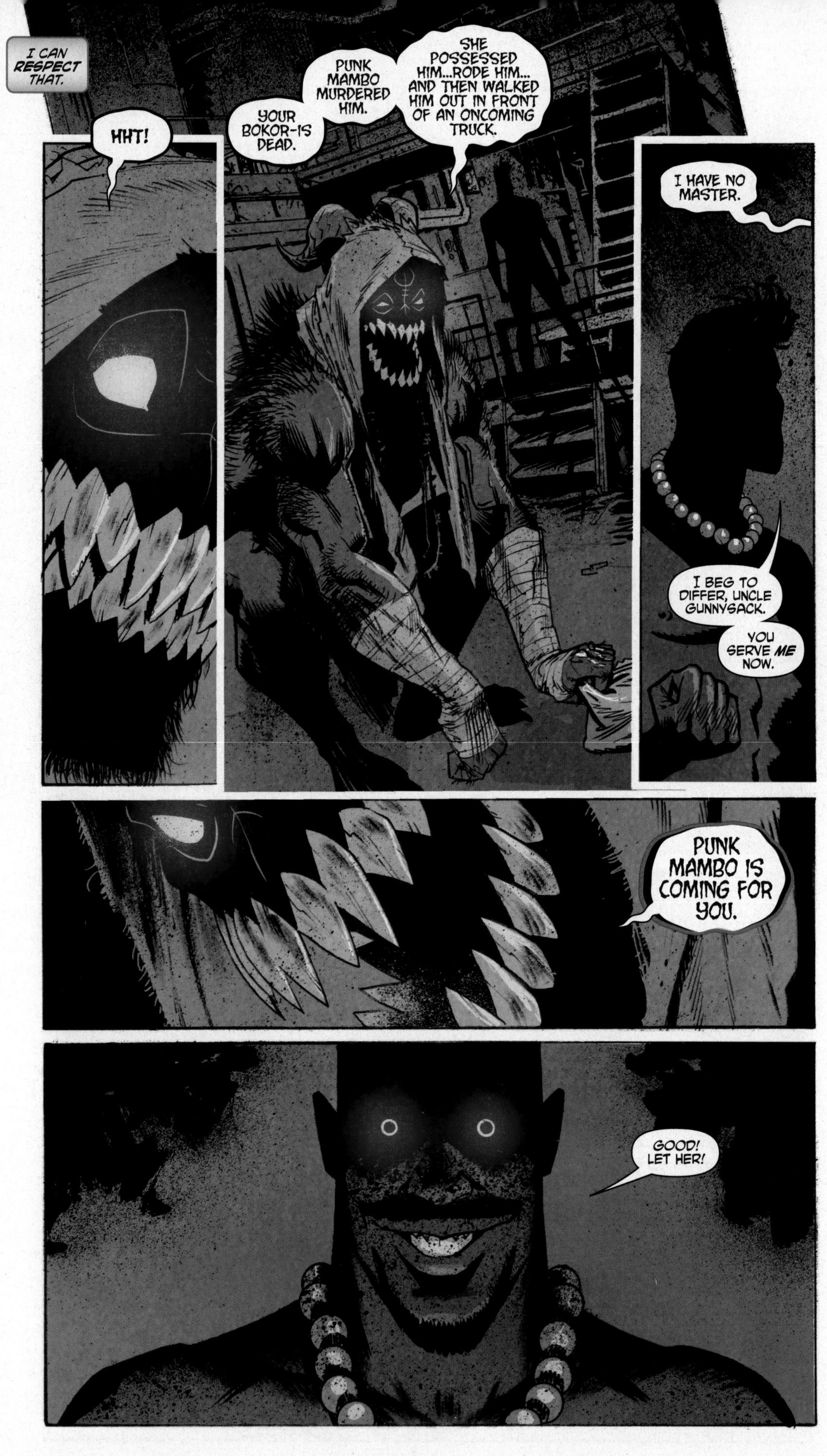

I CAN RESPECT THAT.
HHT!
YOUR BOKOR-IS DEAD.
PUNK MAMBO MURDERED HIM.
SHE POSSESSED HIM...RODE HIM... AND THEN WALKED HIM OUT IN FRONT OF AN ONCOMING TRUCK.
I HAVE NO MASTER.
I BEG TO DIFFER, UNCLE GUNNYSACK.
YOU SERVE ME NOW.
PUNK MAMBO IS COMING FOR YOU.
GOOD! LET HER!

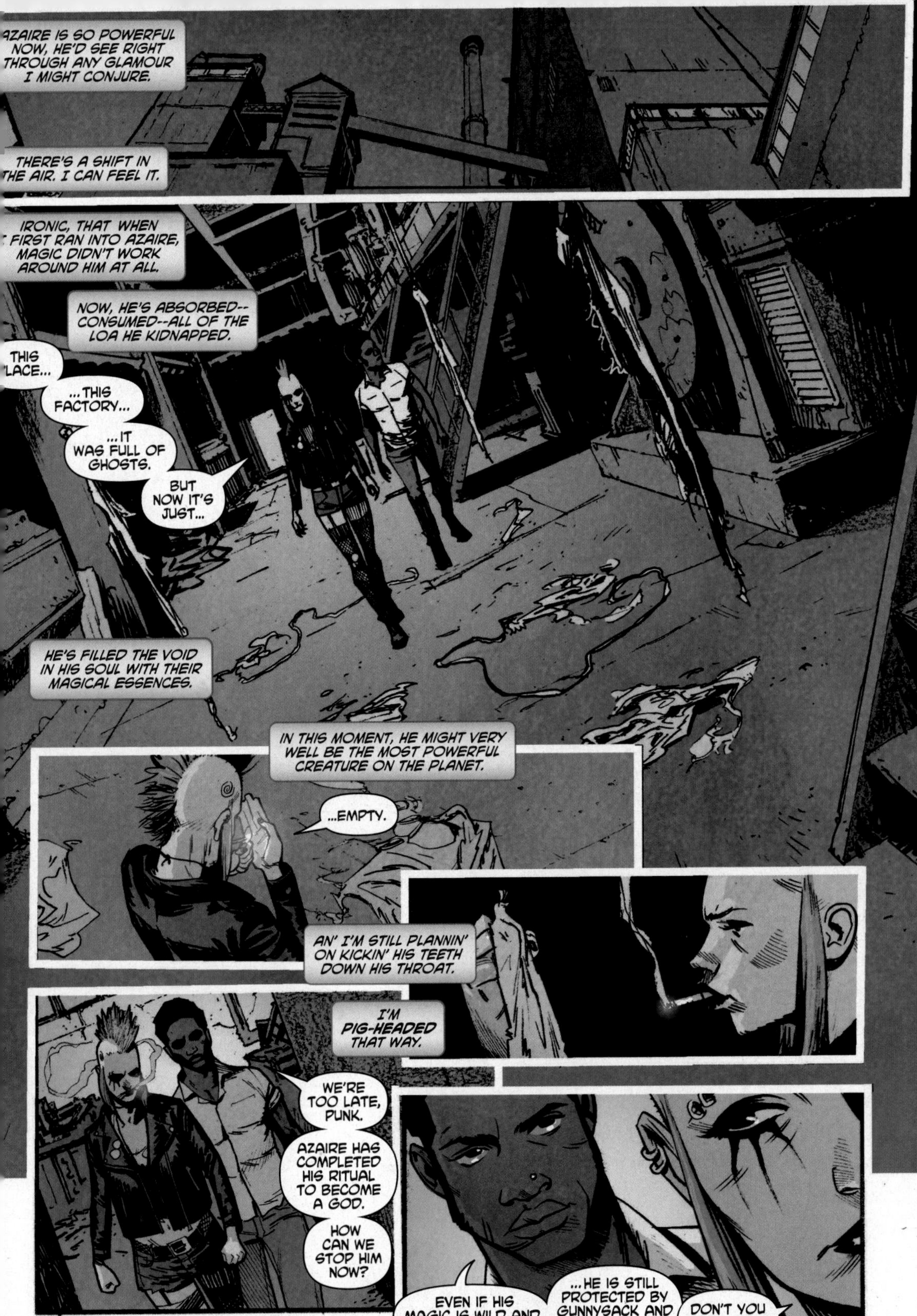
AZAIRE IS SO POWERFUL NOW, HE'D SEE RIGHT THROUGH ANY GLAMOUR I MIGHT CONJURE.
THERE'S A SHIFT IN THE AIR. I CAN FEEL IT.
IRONIC, THAT WHEN I FIRST RAN INTO AZAIRE, MAGIC DIDN'T WORK AROUND HIM AT ALL.
NOW, HE'S ABSORBED--CONSUMED--ALL OF THE LOA HE KIDNAPPED.
THIS PLACE...
...THIS FACTORY...
...IT WAS FULL OF GHOSTS.
BUT NOW IT'S JUST...
HE'S FILLED THE VOID IN HIS SOUL WITH THEIR MAGICAL ESSENCES.
IN THIS MOMENT, HE MIGHT VERY WELL BE THE MOST POWERFUL CREATURE ON THE PLANET.
...EMPTY.
AN' I'M STILL PLANNIN' ON KICKIN' HIS TEETH DOWN HIS THROAT.
I'M PIG-HEADED THAT WAY.
WE'RE TOO LATE, PUNK.
AZAIRE HAS COMPLETED HIS RITUAL TO BECOME A GOD.
HOW CAN WE STOP HIM NOW?
EVEN IF HIS MAGIC IS WILD AND UNCONTROLLED...
...HE IS STILL PROTECTED BY GUNNYSACK AND THE TONTON MACOUTE.
DON'T YOU SMELL THAT, JOSEF?

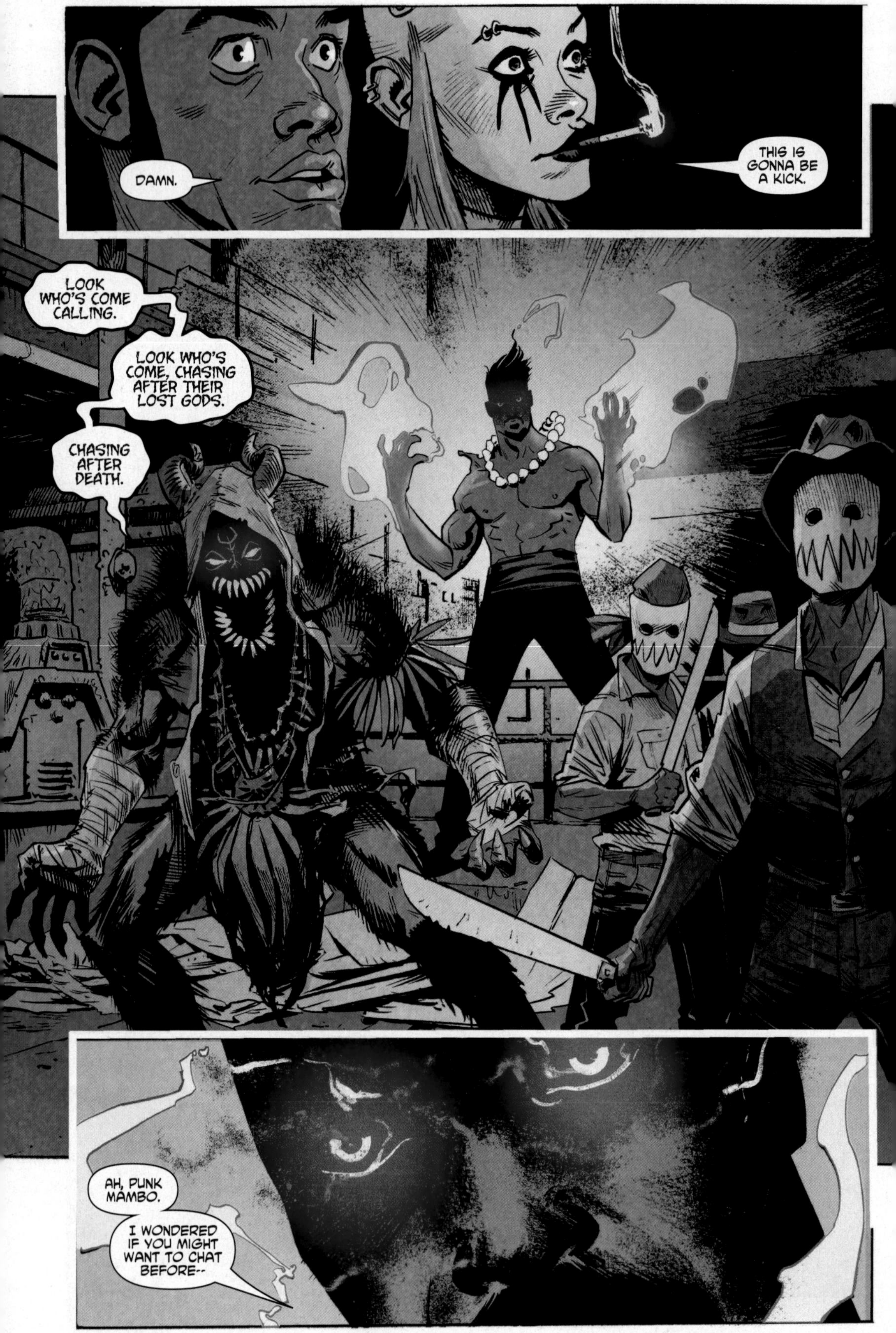
DAMN.
THIS IS GONNA BE A KICK.
LOOK WHO'S COME CALLING.
LOOK WHO'S COME, CHASING AFTER THEIR LOST GODS.
CHASING AFTER DEATH.
AH, PUNK MAMBO.
I WONDERED IF YOU MIGHT WANT TO CHAT BEFORE--

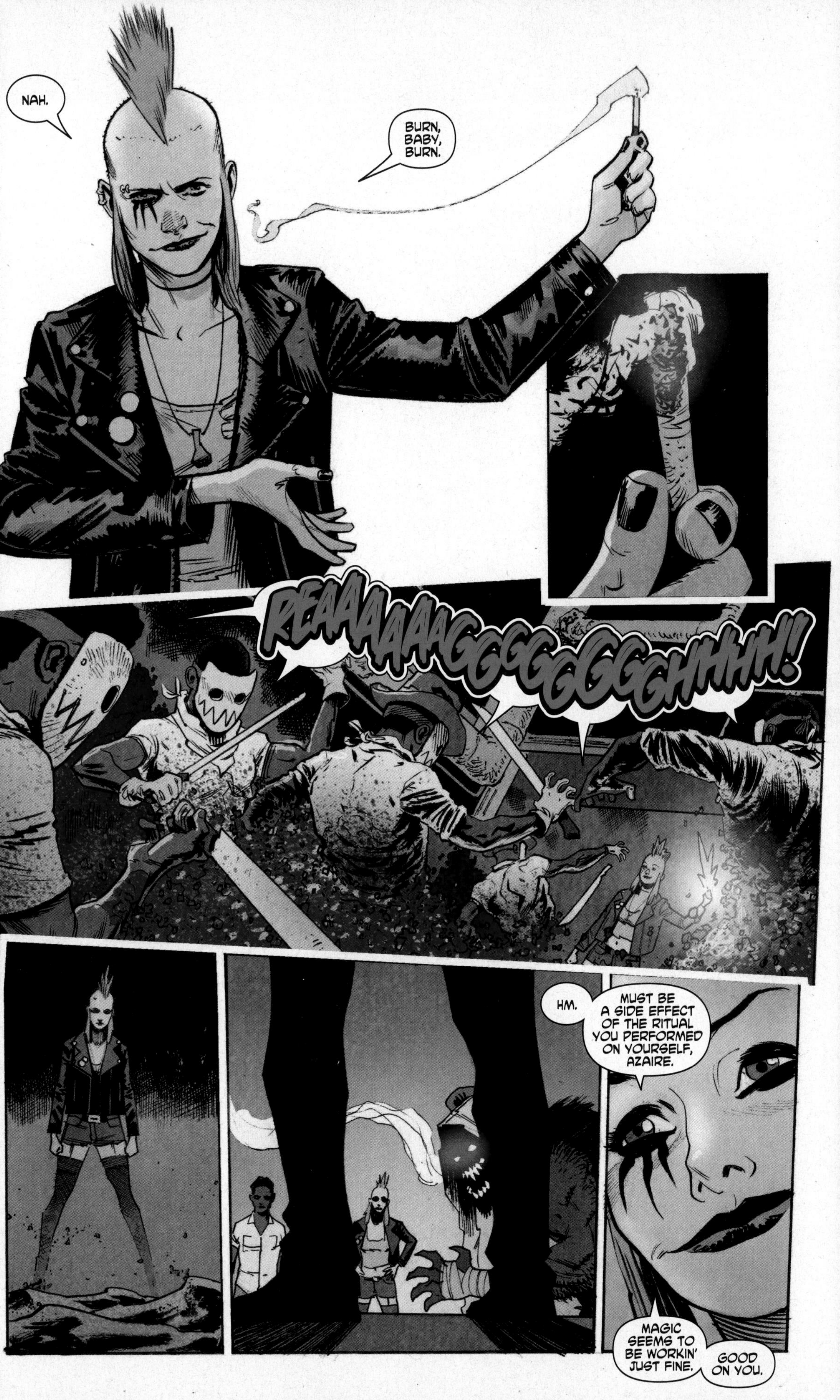
NAH.
BURN, BABY, BURN.
REAAAAAAAAGGGGGGGGHHHHH!!
HM.
MUST BE A SIDE EFFECT OF THE RITUAL YOU PERFORMED ON YOURSELF, AZAIRE.
MAGIC SEEMS TO BE WORKIN' JUST FINE.
GOOD ON YOU.

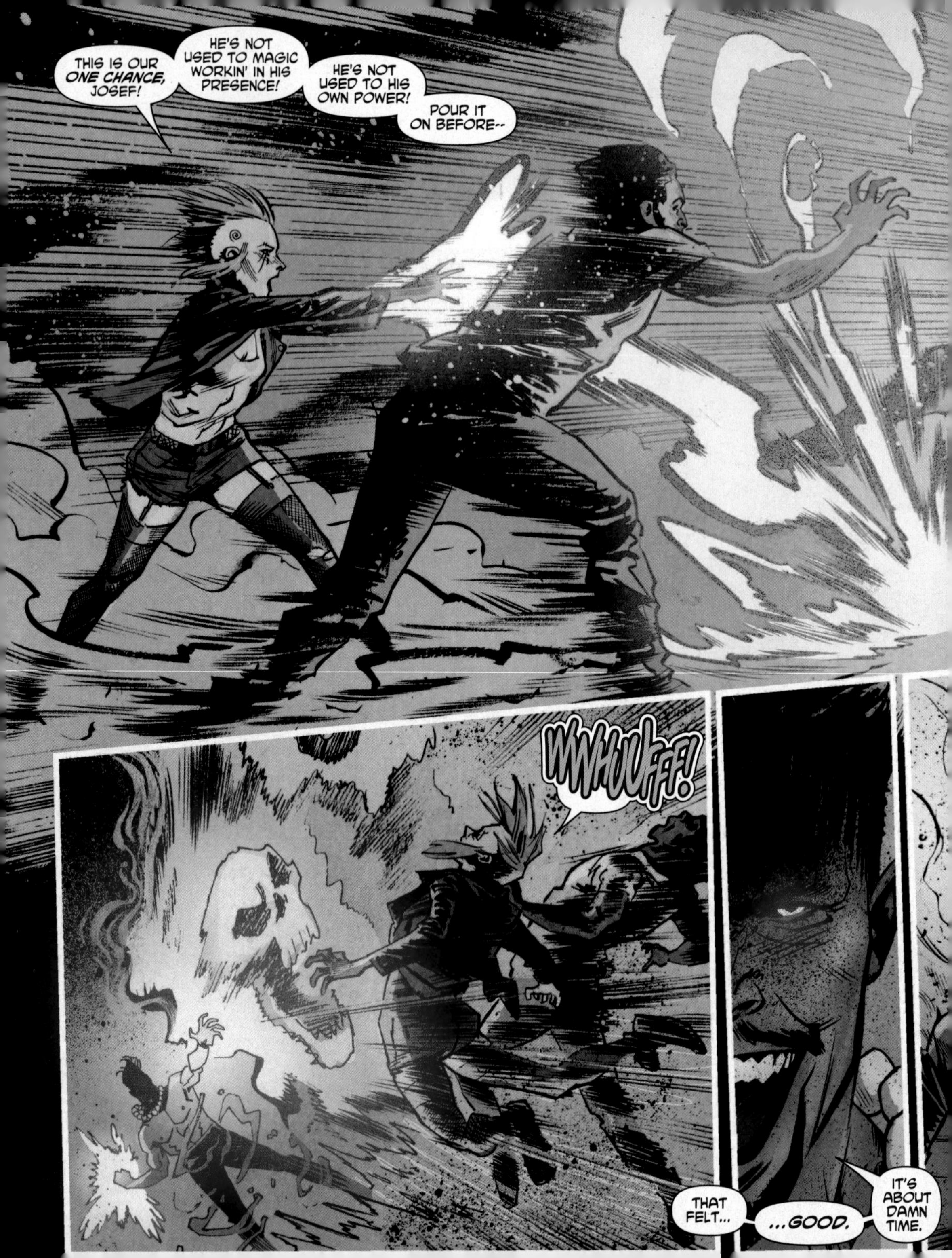
THIS IS OUR ONE CHANCE, JOSEF!
HE'S NOT USED TO MAGIC WORKIN' IN HIS PRESENCE!
HE'S NOT USED TO HIS OWN POWER!
POUR IT ON BEFORE--
WWHUUFFF!
THAT FELT...
...GOOD.
IT'S ABOUT DAMN TIME.

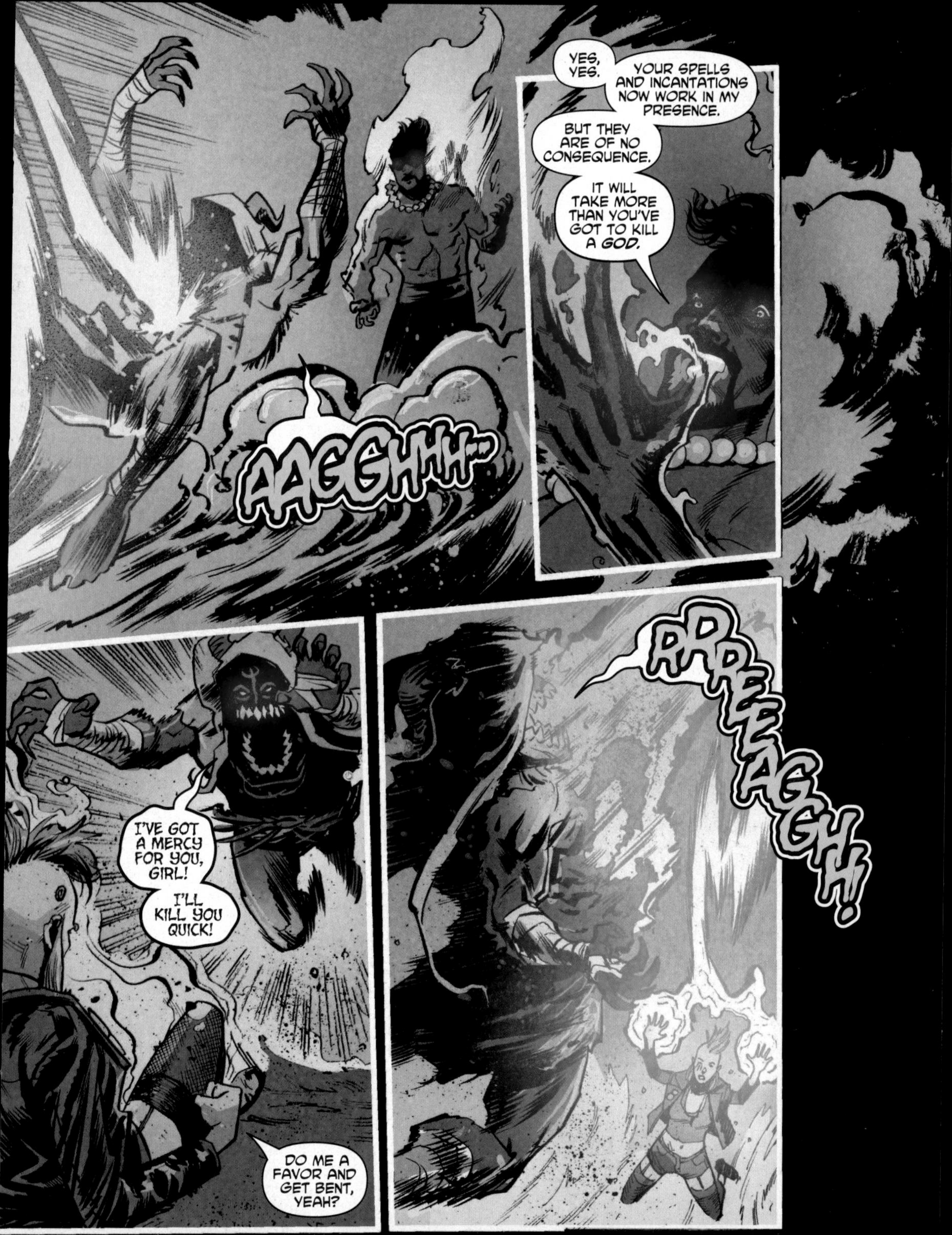
YES, YES.
YOUR SPELLS AND INCANTATIONS NOW WORK IN MY PRESENCE.
BUT THEY ARE OF NO CONSEQUENCE.
IT WILL TAKE MORE THAN YOU'VE GOT TO KILL A GOD.
AAGGHHH--
I'VE GOT A MERCY FOR YOU, GIRL!
I'LL KILL YOU QUICK!
DO ME A FAVOR AND GET BENT, YEAH?
RRREEAGGHH!

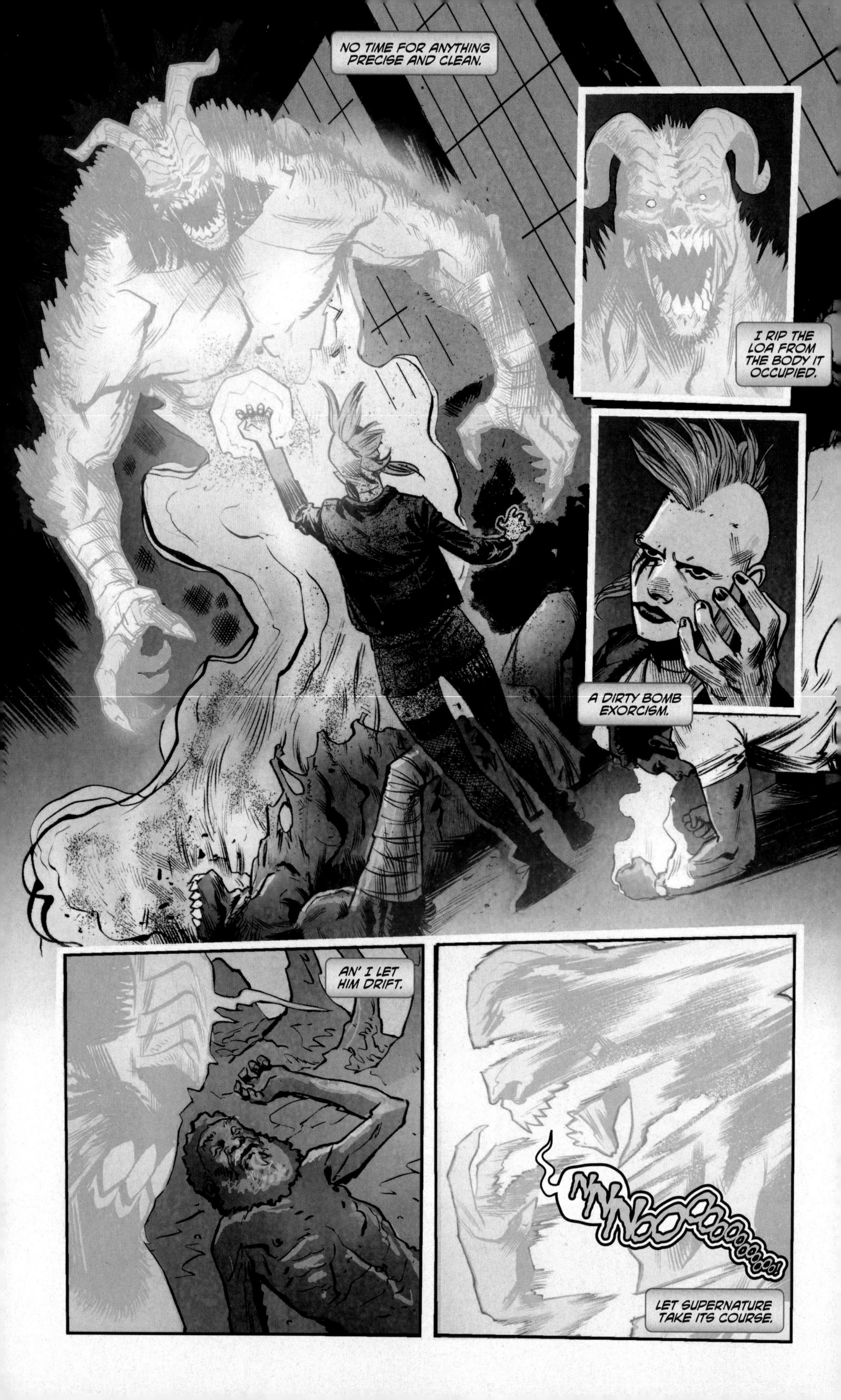
NO TIME FOR ANYTHING PRECISE AND CLEAN.
I RIP THE LOA FROM THE BODY IT OCCUPIED.
A DIRTY BOMB EXORCISM.
AN' I LET HIM DRIFT.
NNNNOOOooooooooo!
LET SUPERNATURE TAKE ITS COURSE.

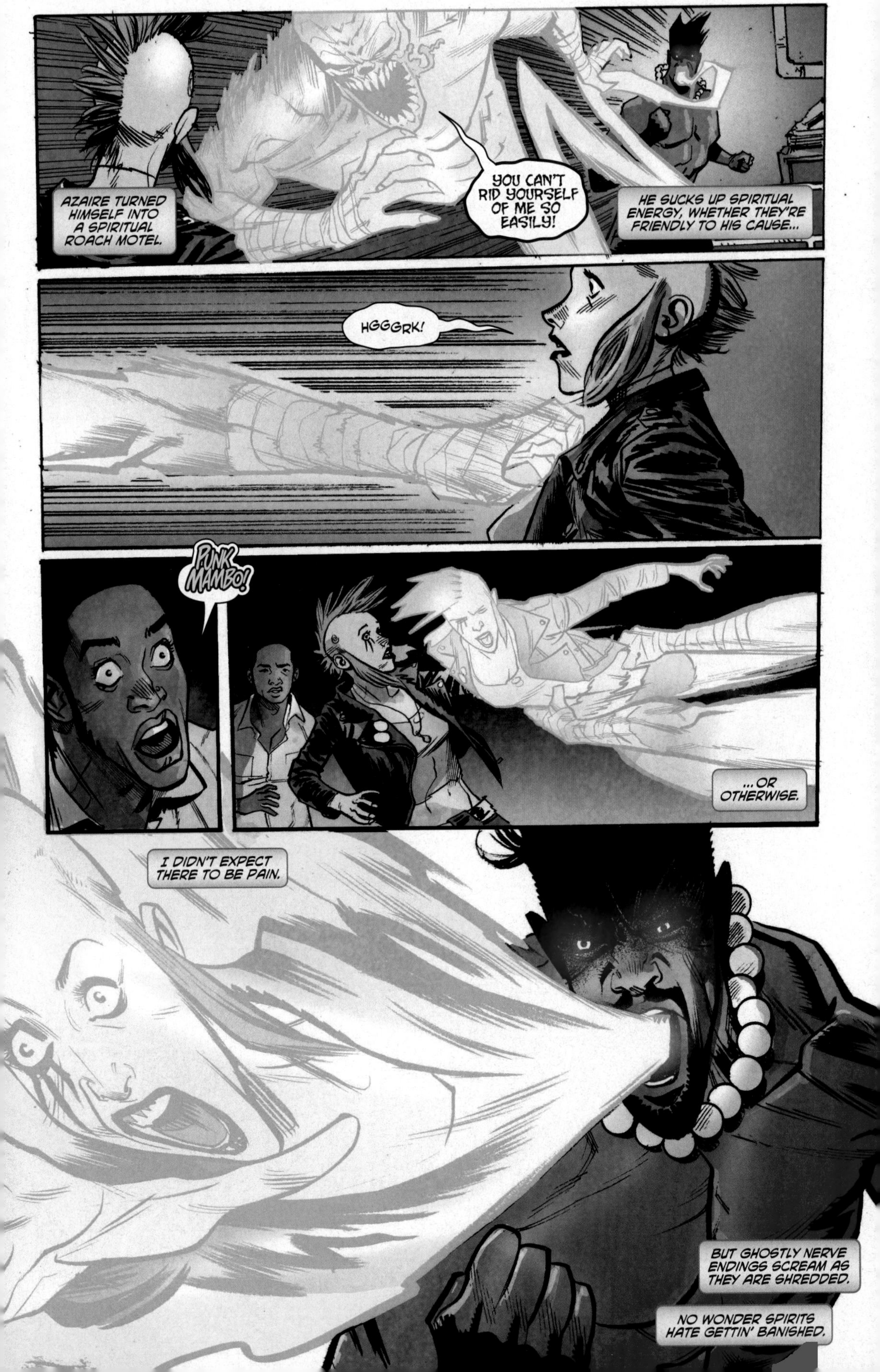
AZAIRE TURNED HIMSELF INTO A SPIRITUAL ROACH MOTEL.
YOU CAN'T RID YOURSELF OF ME SO EASILY!
HE SUCKS UP SPIRITUAL ENERGY, WHETHER THEY'RE FRIENDLY TO HIS CAUSE...
HGGGRK!
PUNK MAMBO!
...OR OTHERWISE.
I DIDN'T EXPECT THERE TO BE PAIN.
BUT GHOSTLY NERVE ENDINGS SCREAM AS THEY ARE SHREDDED.
NO WONDER SPIRITS HATE GETTIN' BANISHED.

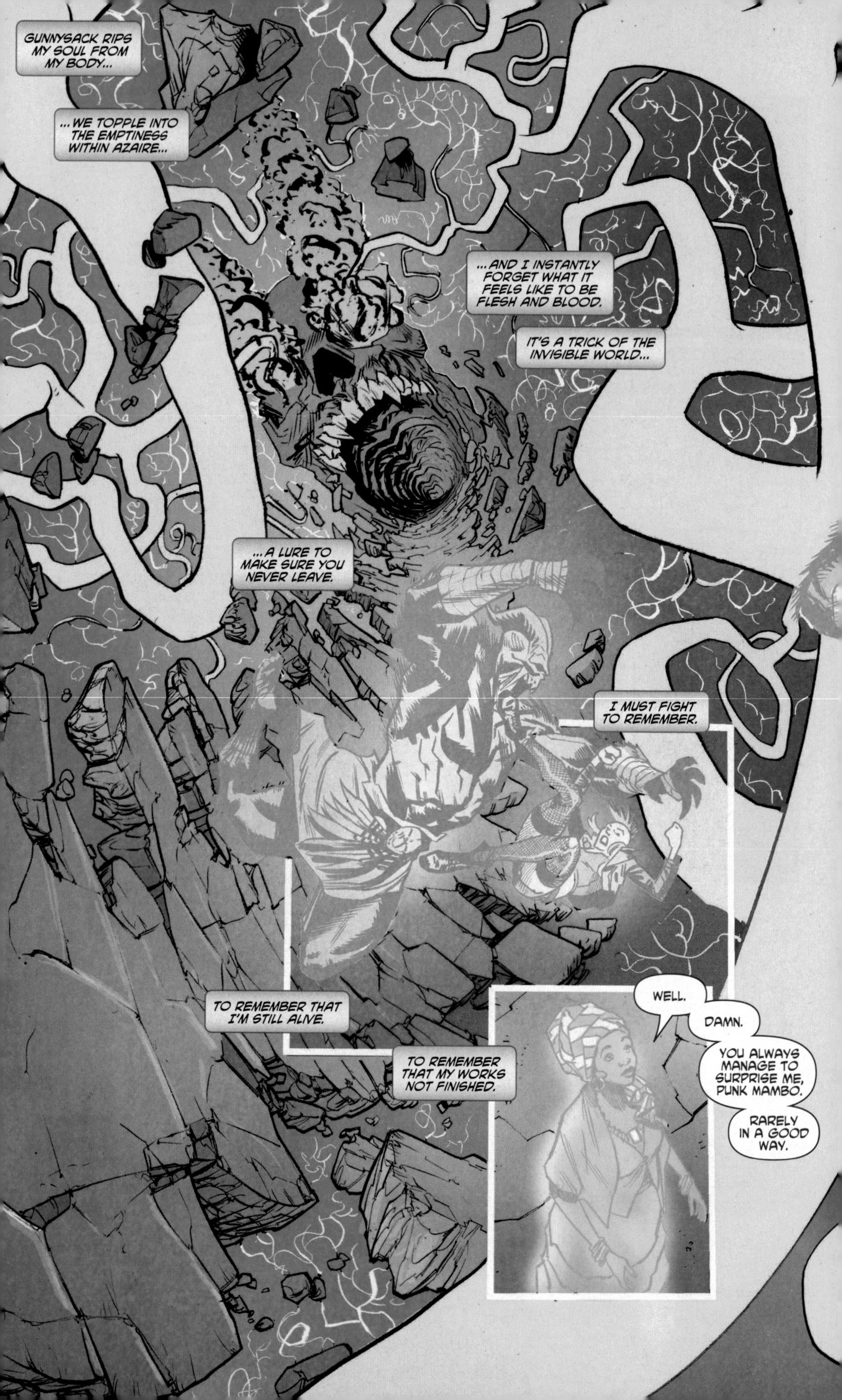
GUNNYSACK RIPS MY SOUL FROM MY BODY...
...WE TOPPLE INTO THE EMPTINESS WITHIN AZAIRE...
...AND I INSTANTLY FORGET WHAT IT FEELS LIKE TO BE FLESH AND BLOOD.
IT'S A TRICK OF THE INVISIBLE WORLD...
...A LURE TO MAKE SURE YOU NEVER LEAVE.
I MUST FIGHT TO REMEMBER.
TO REMEMBER THAT I'M STILL ALIVE.
TO REMEMBER THAT MY WORKS NOT FINISHED.
WELL.
DAMN.
YOU ALWAYS MANAGE TO SURPRISE ME, PUNK MAMBO.
RARELY IN A GOOD WAY.

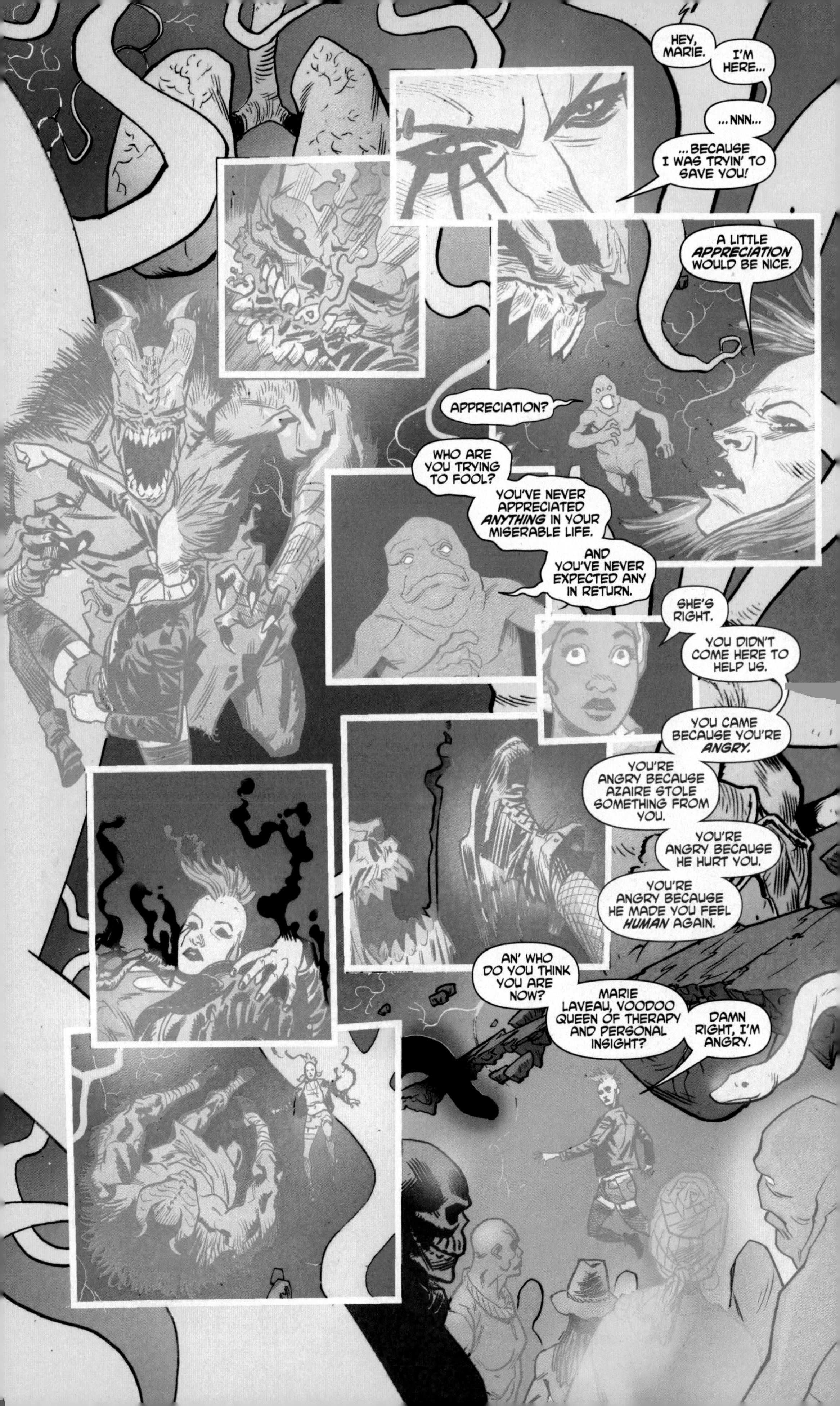
HEY, MARIE.
I'M HERE...
...NNN...
...BECAUSE I WAS TRYIN' TO SAVE YOU!
A LITTLE APPRECIATION WOULD BE NICE.
APPRECIATION?
WHO ARE YOU TRYING TO FOOL?
YOU'VE NEVER APPRECIATED ANYTHING IN YOUR MISERABLE LIFE.
AND YOU'VE NEVER EXPECTED ANY IN RETURN.
SHE'S RIGHT.
YOU DIDN'T COME HERE TO HELP US.
YOU CAME BECAUSE YOU'RE ANGRY.
YOU'RE ANGRY BECAUSE AZAIRE STOLE SOMETHING FROM YOU.
YOU'RE ANGRY BECAUSE HE HURT YOU.
YOU'RE ANGRY BECAUSE HE MADE YOU FEEL HUMAN AGAIN.
AN' WHO DO YOU THINK YOU ARE NOW?
MARIE LAVEAU, VOODOO QUEEN OF THERAPY AND PERSONAL INSIGHT?
DAMN RIGHT, I'M ANGRY.

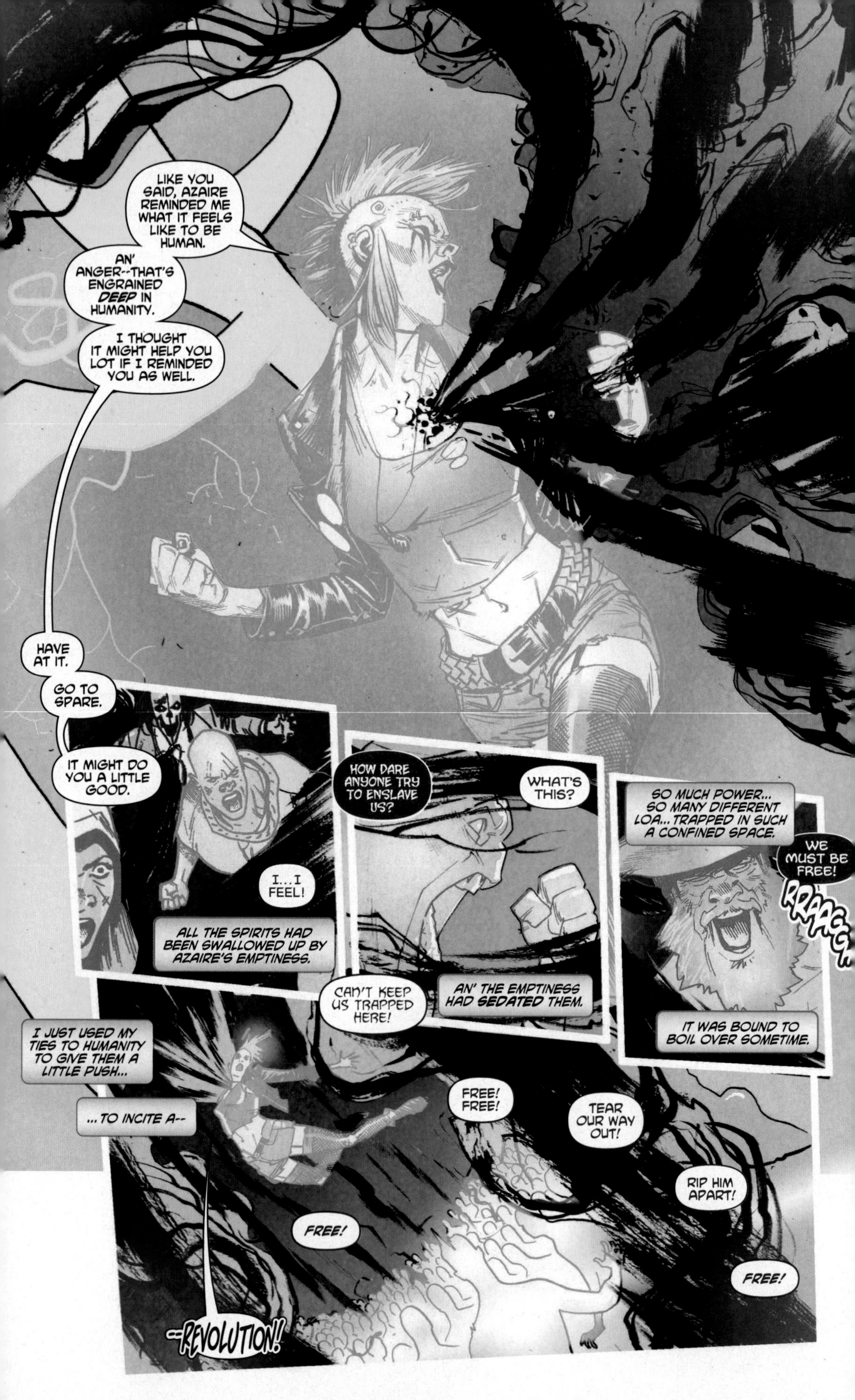
LIKE YOU SAID, AZAIRE REMINDED ME WHAT IT FEELS LIKE TO BE HUMAN.
AN' ANGER--THAT'S ENGRAINED *DEEP* IN HUMANITY.
I THOUGHT IT MIGHT HELP YOU LOT IF I REMINDED YOU AS WELL.
HAVE AT IT.
GO TO SPARE.
IT MIGHT DO YOU A LITTLE GOOD.
I...I FEEL!
ALL THE SPIRITS HAD BEEN SWALLOWED UP BY AZAIRE'S EMPTINESS.
HOW DARE ANYONE TRY TO ENSLAVE US?
WHAT'S THIS?
AN' THE EMPTINESS HAD *SEDATED* THEM.
CAN'T KEEP US TRAPPED HERE!
SO MUCH POWER... SO MANY DIFFERENT LOA... TRAPPED IN SUCH A CONFINED SPACE.
WE MUST BE FREE!
RRAAAGH
IT WAS BOUND TO BOIL OVER SOMETIME.
I JUST USED MY TIES TO HUMANITY TO GIVE THEM A LITTLE PUSH...
...TO INCITE A--
FREE! FREE!
TEAR OUR WAY OUT!
RIP HIM APART!
FREE!
FREE!
--REVOLUTION!

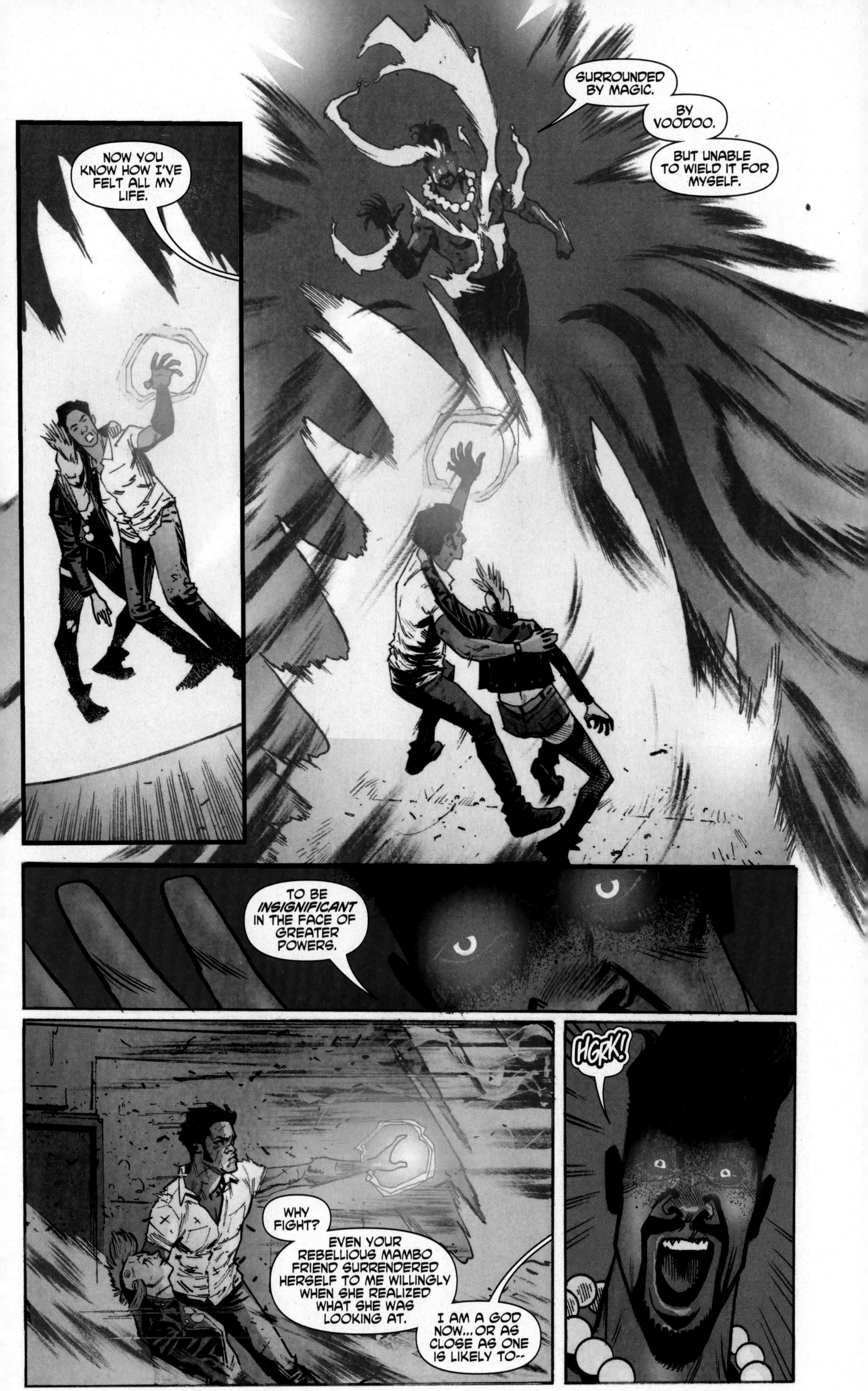
NOW YOU KNOW HOW I'VE FELT ALL MY LIFE.
SURROUNDED BY MAGIC.
BY VOODOO.
BUT UNABLE TO WIELD IT FOR MYSELF.
TO BE *INSIGNIFICANT* IN THE FACE OF GREATER POWERS.
WHY FIGHT?
EVEN YOUR REBELLIOUS MAMBO FRIEND SURRENDERED HERSELF TO ME WILLINGLY WHEN SHE REALIZED WHAT SHE WAS LOOKING AT.
I AM A GOD NOW...OR AS CLOSE AS ONE IS LIKELY TO--
HGRK!

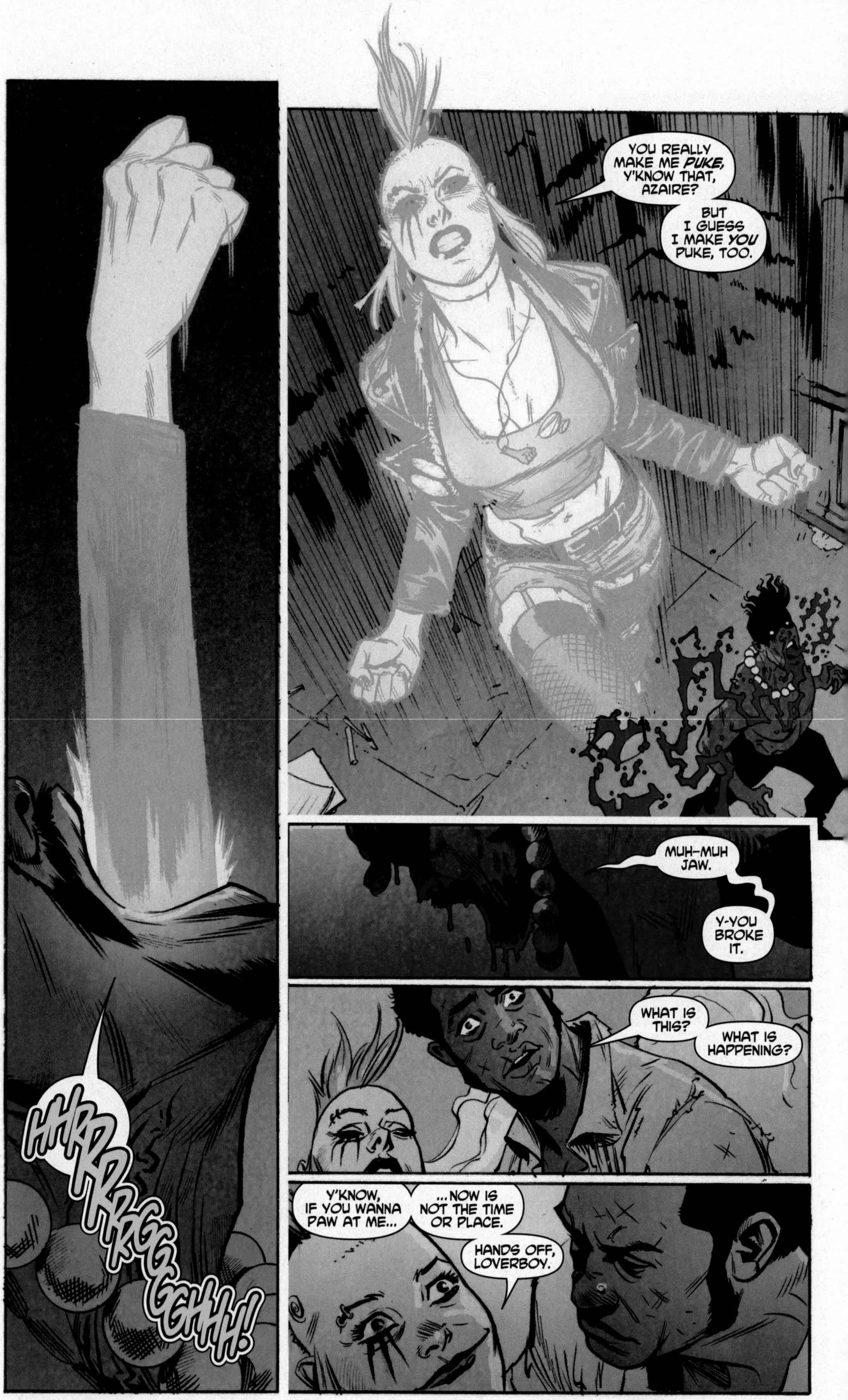
HHRRRRGGGGHHH!
YOU REALLY MAKE ME PUKE, Y'KNOW THAT, AZAIRE?
BUT I GUESS I MAKE YOU PUKE, TOO.
MUH-MUH JAW.
Y-YOU BROKE IT.
WHAT IS THIS?
WHAT IS HAPPENING?
Y'KNOW, IF YOU WANNA PAW AT ME...
...NOW IS NOT THE TIME OR PLACE.
HANDS OFF, LOVERBOY.

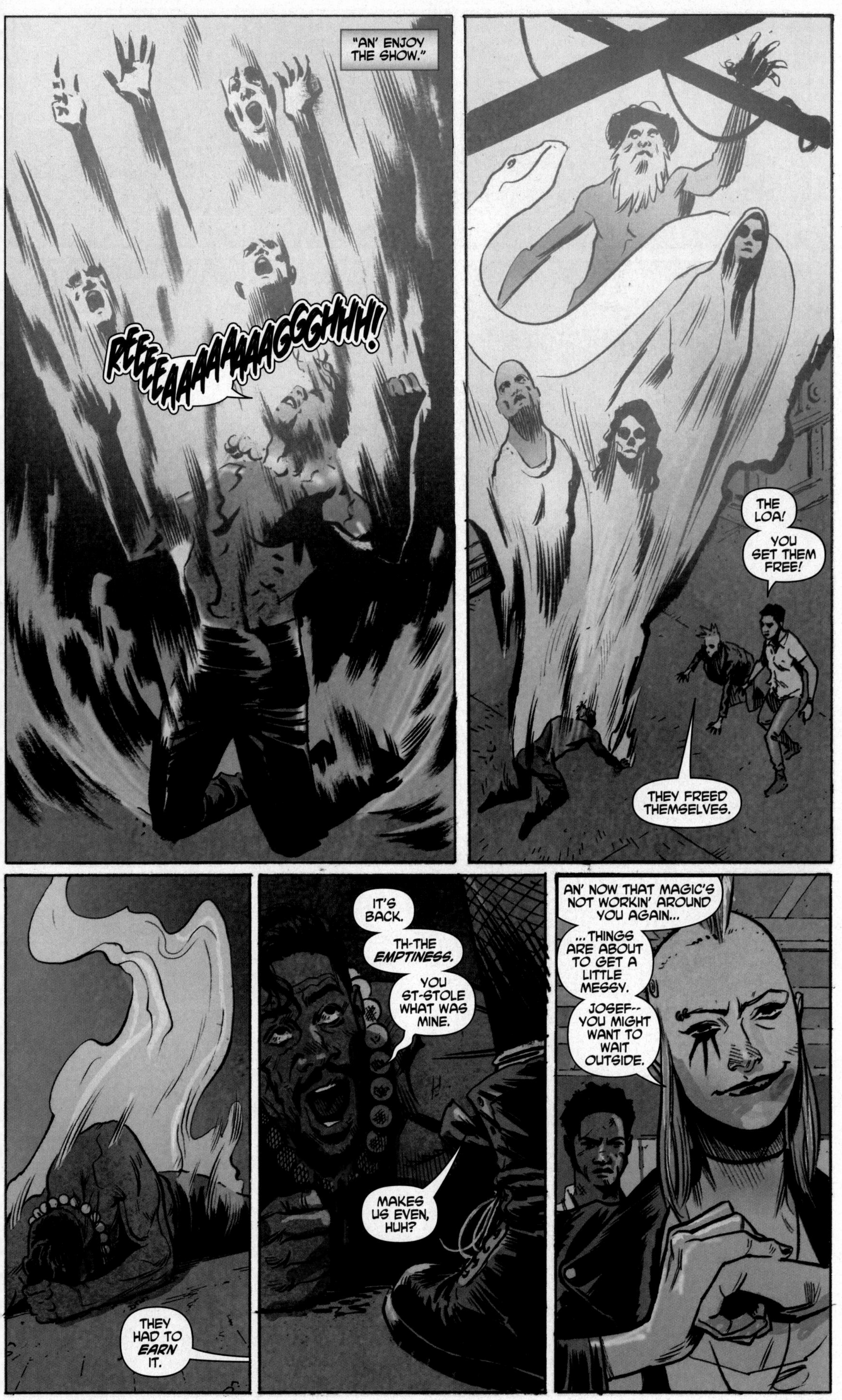
"AN' ENJOY THE SHOW."
REEEEAAAAAAAAAGGGHHH!
THE LOA!
YOU SET THEM FREE!
THEY FREED THEMSELVES.
THEY HAD TO *EARN* IT.
IT'S BACK.
TH-THE *EMPTINESS.*
YOU ST-STOLE WHAT WAS MINE.
MAKES US EVEN, HUH?
AN' NOW THAT MAGIC'S NOT WORKIN' AROUND YOU AGAIN...
...THINGS ARE ABOUT TO GET A LITTLE MESSY.
JOSEF-- YOU MIGHT WANT TO WAIT OUTSIDE.

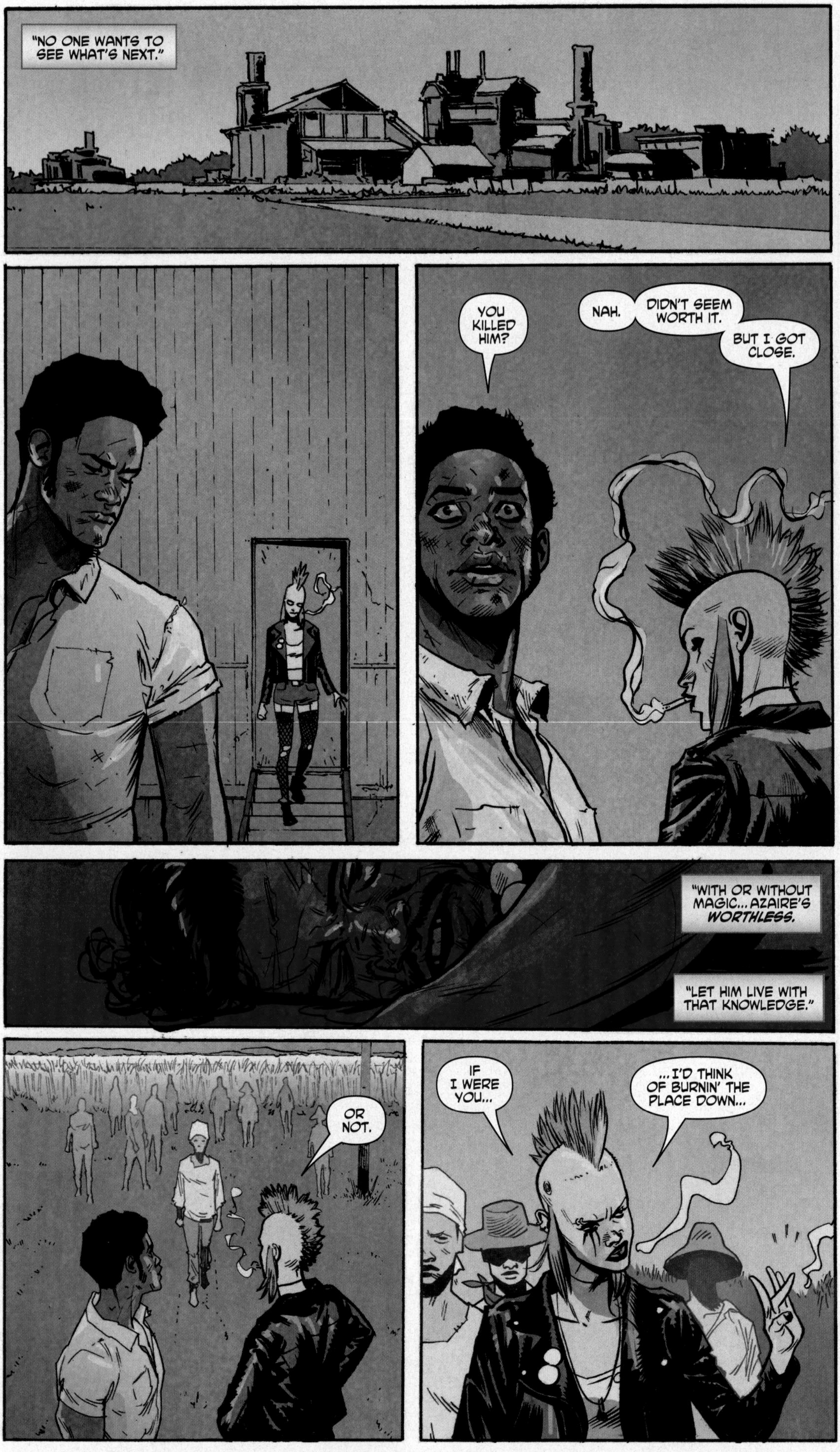
"NO ONE WANTS TO SEE WHAT'S NEXT."
YOU KILLED HIM?
NAH.
DIDN'T SEEM WORTH IT.
BUT I GOT CLOSE.
"WITH OR WITHOUT MAGIC... AZAIRE'S *WORTHLESS.*
"LET HIM LIVE WITH THAT KNOWLEDGE."
OR NOT.
IF I WERE YOU...
...I'D THINK OF BURNIN' THE PLACE DOWN...

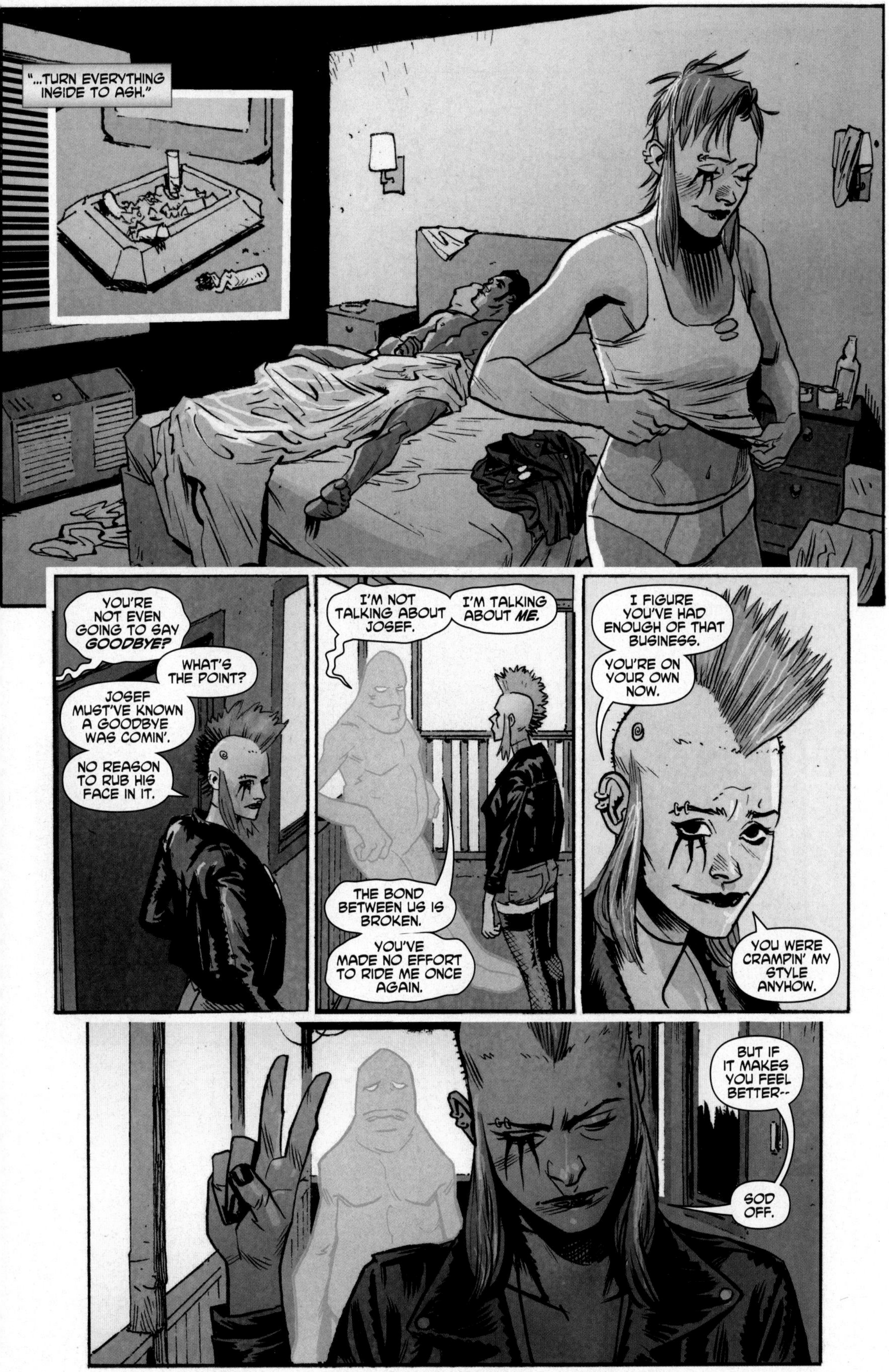
"...TURN EVERYTHING INSIDE TO ASH."
YOU'RE NOT EVEN GOING TO SAY *GOODBYE?*
WHAT'S THE POINT?
JOSEF MUST'VE KNOWN A GOODBYE WAS COMIN'.
NO REASON TO RUB HIS FACE IN IT.
I'M NOT TALKING ABOUT JOSEF.
I'M TALKING ABOUT *ME.*
THE BOND BETWEEN US IS BROKEN.
YOU'VE MADE NO EFFORT TO RIDE ME ONCE AGAIN.
I FIGURE YOU'VE HAD ENOUGH OF THAT BUSINESS.
YOU'RE ON YOUR OWN NOW.
YOU WERE CRAMPIN' MY STYLE ANYHOW.
BUT IF IT MAKES YOU FEEL BETTER--
SOD OFF.

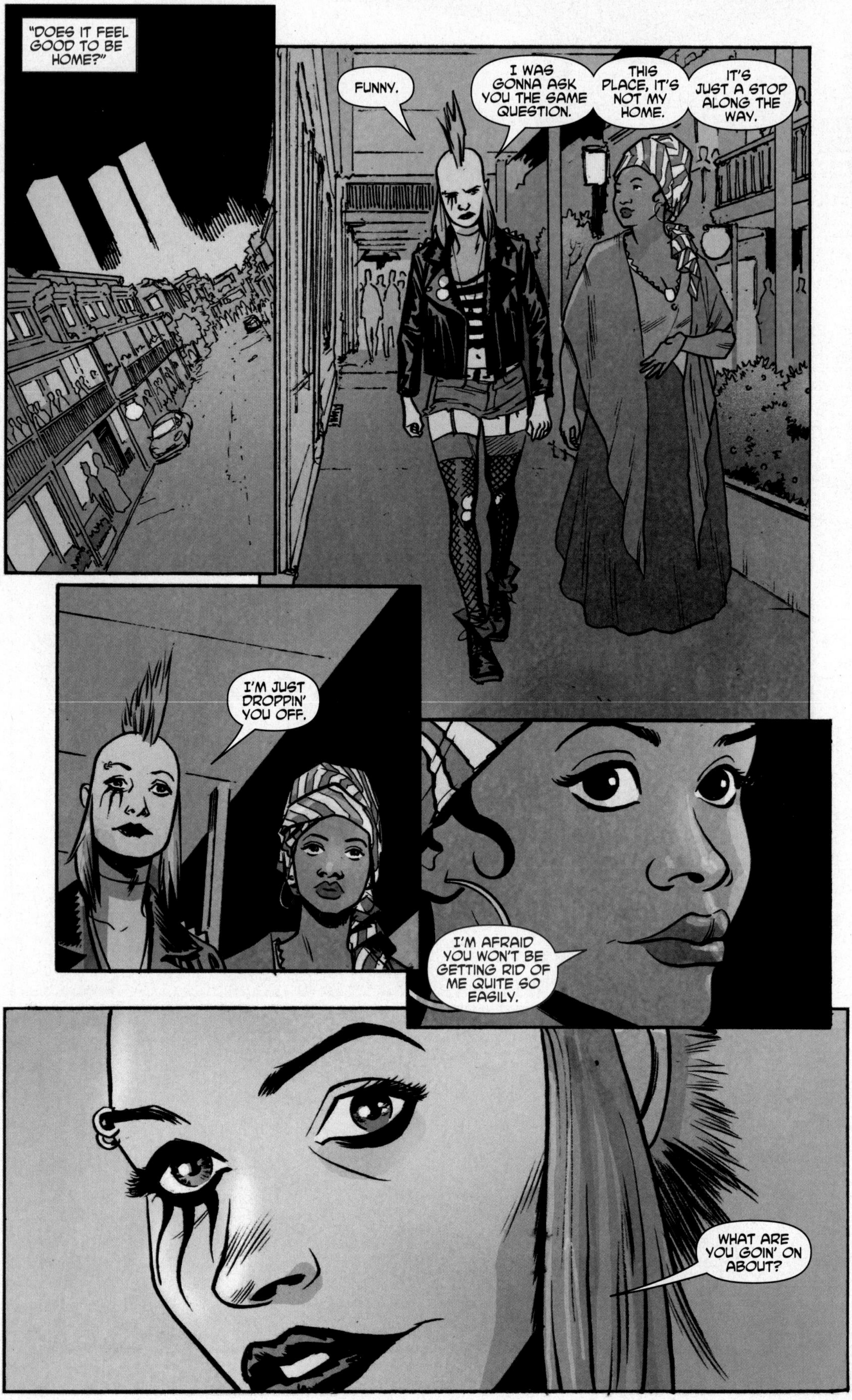
"DOES IT FEEL GOOD TO BE HOME?"
FUNNY.
I WAS GONNA ASK YOU THE SAME QUESTION.
THIS PLACE, IT'S NOT MY HOME.
IT'S JUST A STOP ALONG THE WAY.
I'M JUST DROPPIN' YOU OFF.
I'M AFRAID YOU WON'T BE GETTING RID OF ME QUITE SO EASILY.
WHAT ARE YOU GOIN' ON ABOUT?

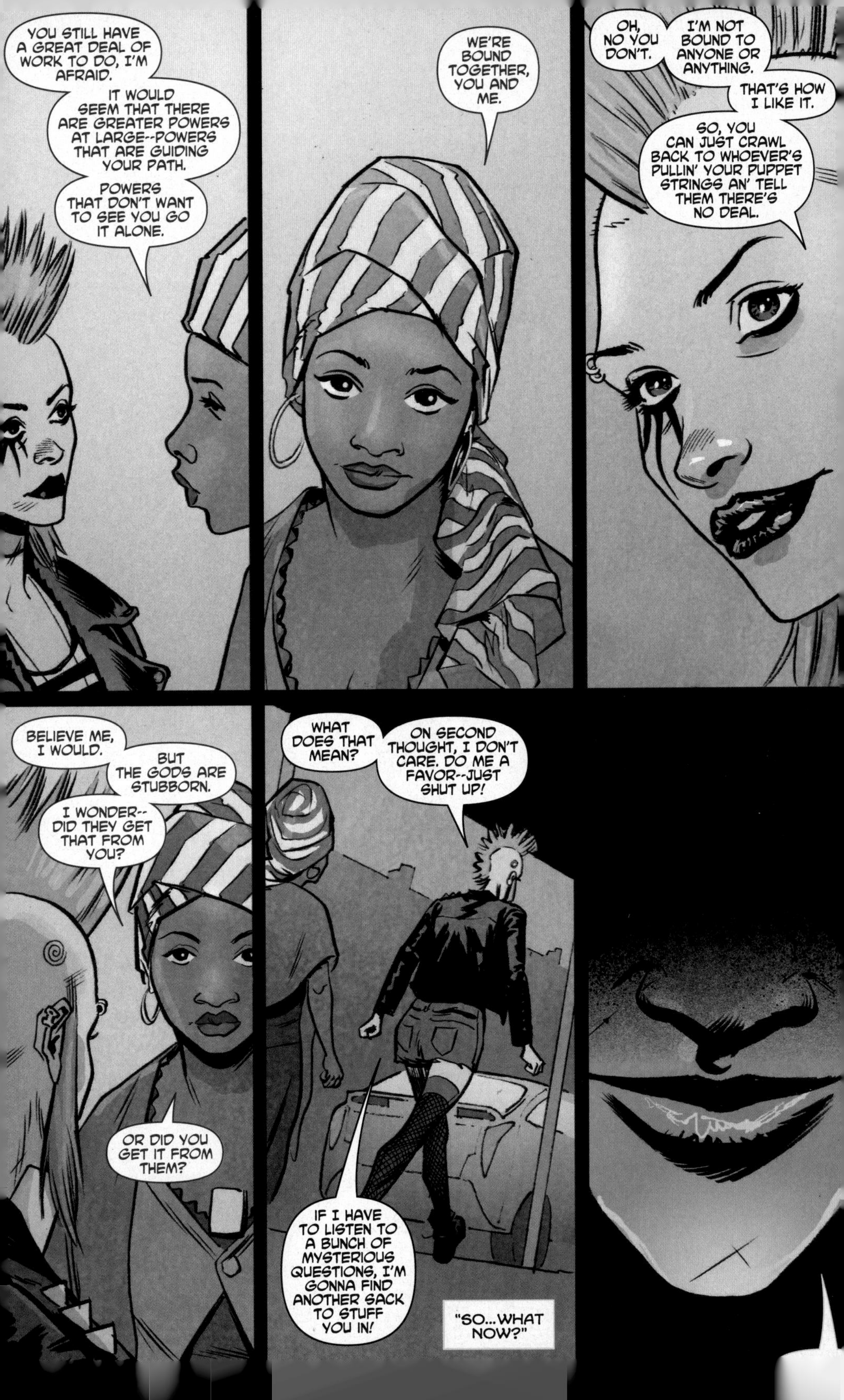
YOU STILL HAVE A GREAT DEAL OF WORK TO DO, I'M AFRAID.
IT WOULD SEEM THAT THERE ARE GREATER POWERS AT LARGE--POWERS THAT ARE GUIDING YOUR PATH.
POWERS THAT DON'T WANT TO SEE YOU GO IT ALONE.
WE'RE BOUND TOGETHER, YOU AND ME.
OH, NO YOU DON'T.
I'M NOT BOUND TO ANYONE OR ANYTHING.
THAT'S HOW I LIKE IT.
SO, YOU CAN JUST CRAWL BACK TO WHOEVER'S PULLIN' YOUR PUPPET STRINGS AN' TELL THEM THERE'S NO DEAL.
BELIEVE ME, I WOULD.
BUT THE GODS ARE STUBBORN.
I WONDER--DID THEY GET THAT FROM YOU?
OR DID YOU GET IT FROM THEM?
WHAT DOES THAT MEAN?
ON SECOND THOUGHT, I DON'T CARE. DO ME A FAVOR--JUST SHUT UP!
IF I HAVE TO LISTEN TO A BUNCH OF MYSTERIOUS QUESTIONS, I'M GONNA FIND ANOTHER SACK TO STUFF YOU IN!
"SO...WHAT NOW?"

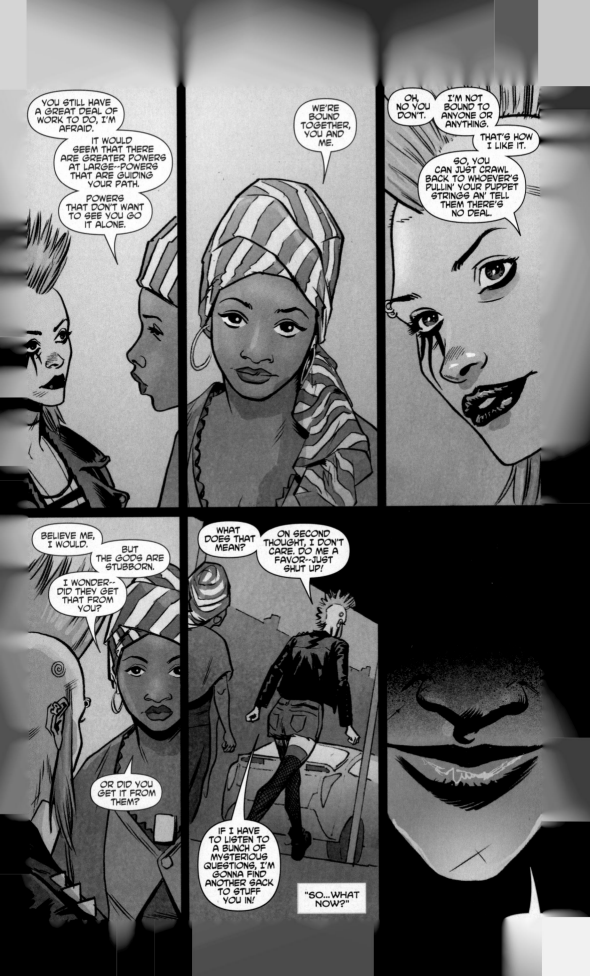

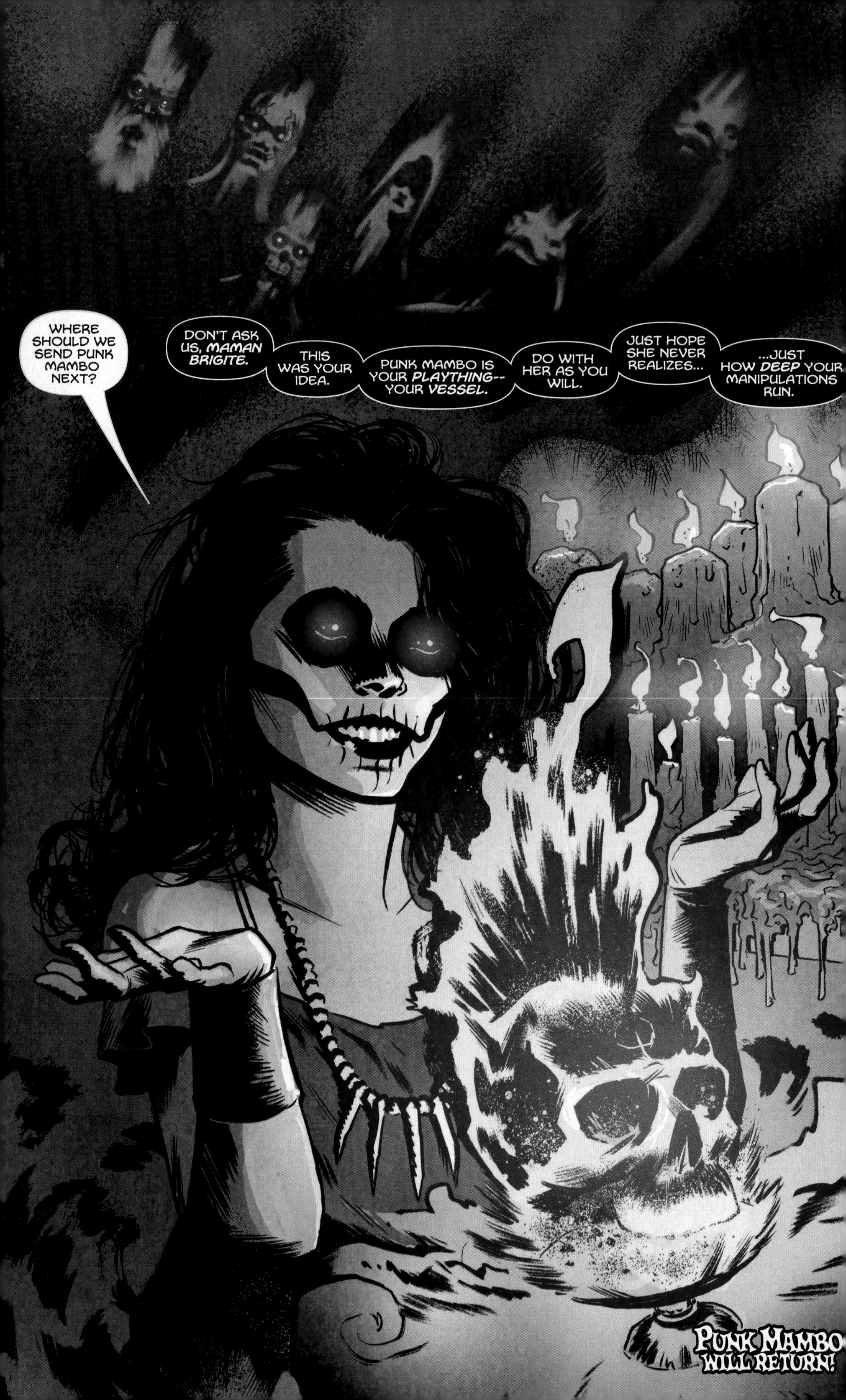
WHERE SHOULD WE SEND PUNK MAMBO NEXT?
DON'T ASK US, MAMAN BRIGITE.
THIS WAS YOUR IDEA.
PUNK MAMBO IS YOUR PLAYTHING-- YOUR VESSEL.
DO WITH HER AS YOU WILL.
JUST HOPE SHE NEVER REALIZES...
...JUST HOW DEEP YOUR MANIPULATIONS RUN.
PUNK MAMBO WILL RETURN!

THE ORIGIN OF PUNK MAMBO

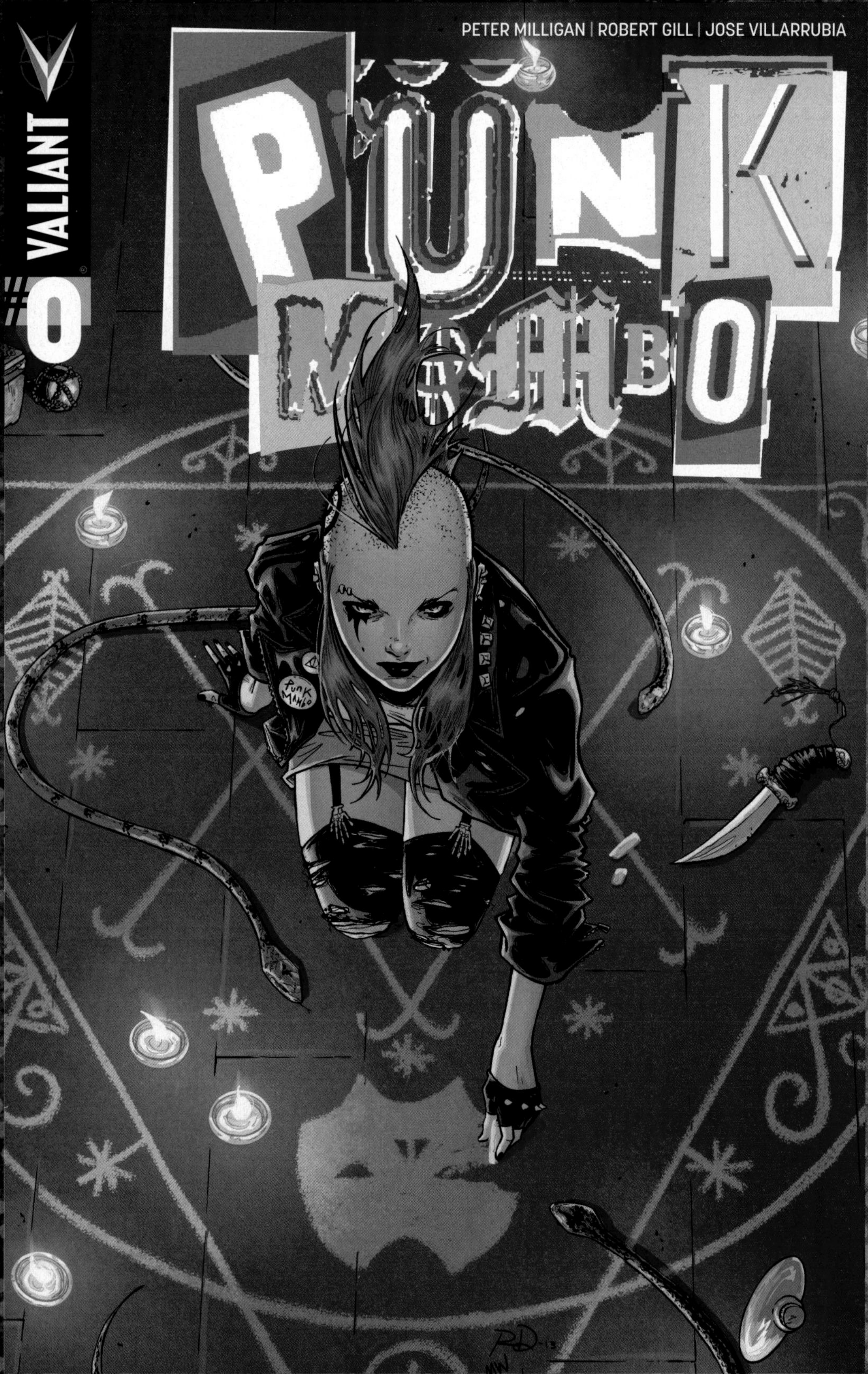

VALIANT
#0
PETER MILLIGAN | ROBERT GILL | JOSE VILLARRUBIA
PUNK MAMBO

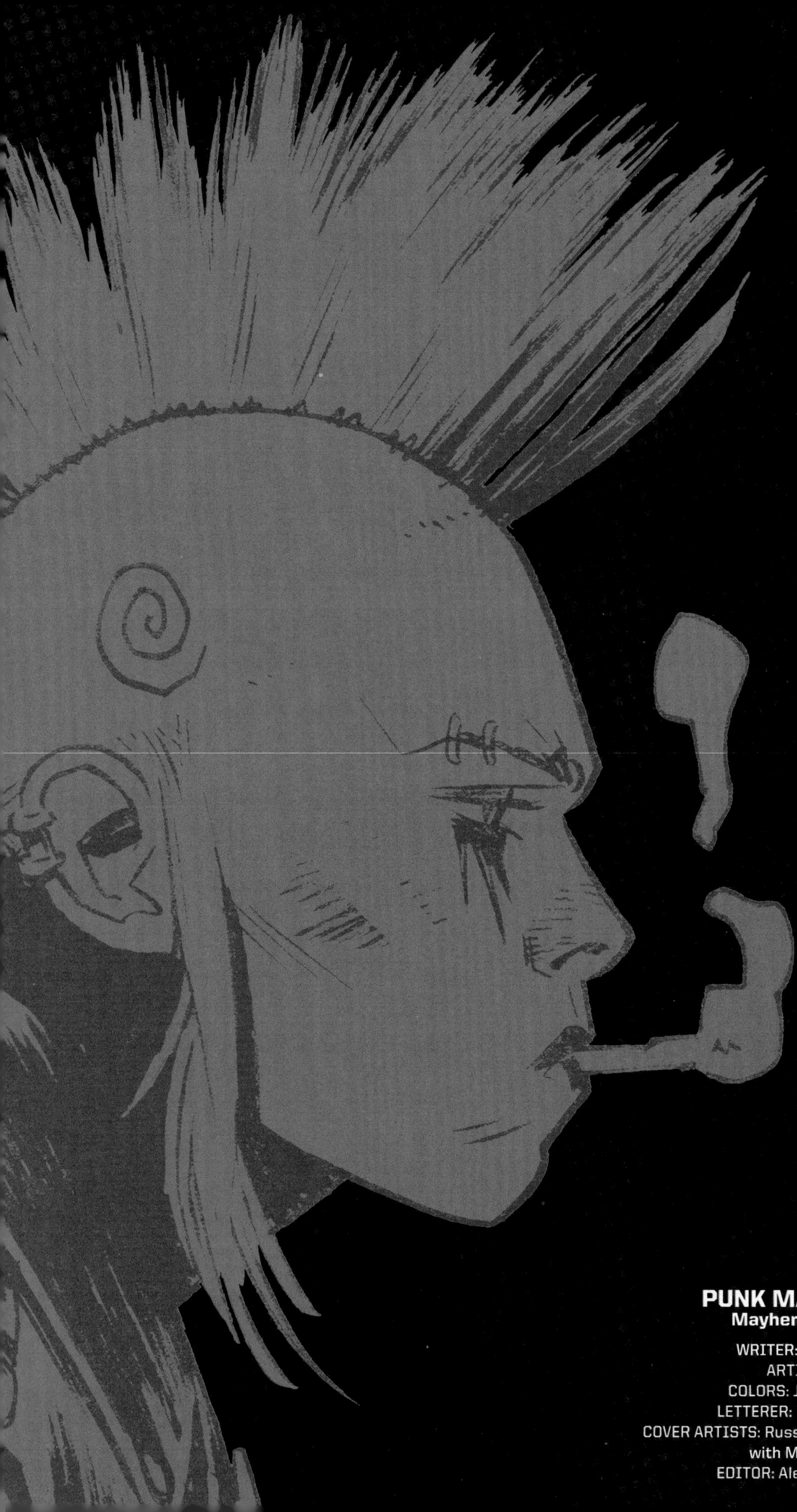

PUNK MAMBO #0
Mayhem & Revenge

WRITER: Peter Milligan
ARTIST: Robert Gill
COLORS: José Villarrubia
LETTERER: Dave Lanphear
COVER ARTISTS: Russell Dauterman
with Matthew Wilson
EDITOR: Alejandro Arbona

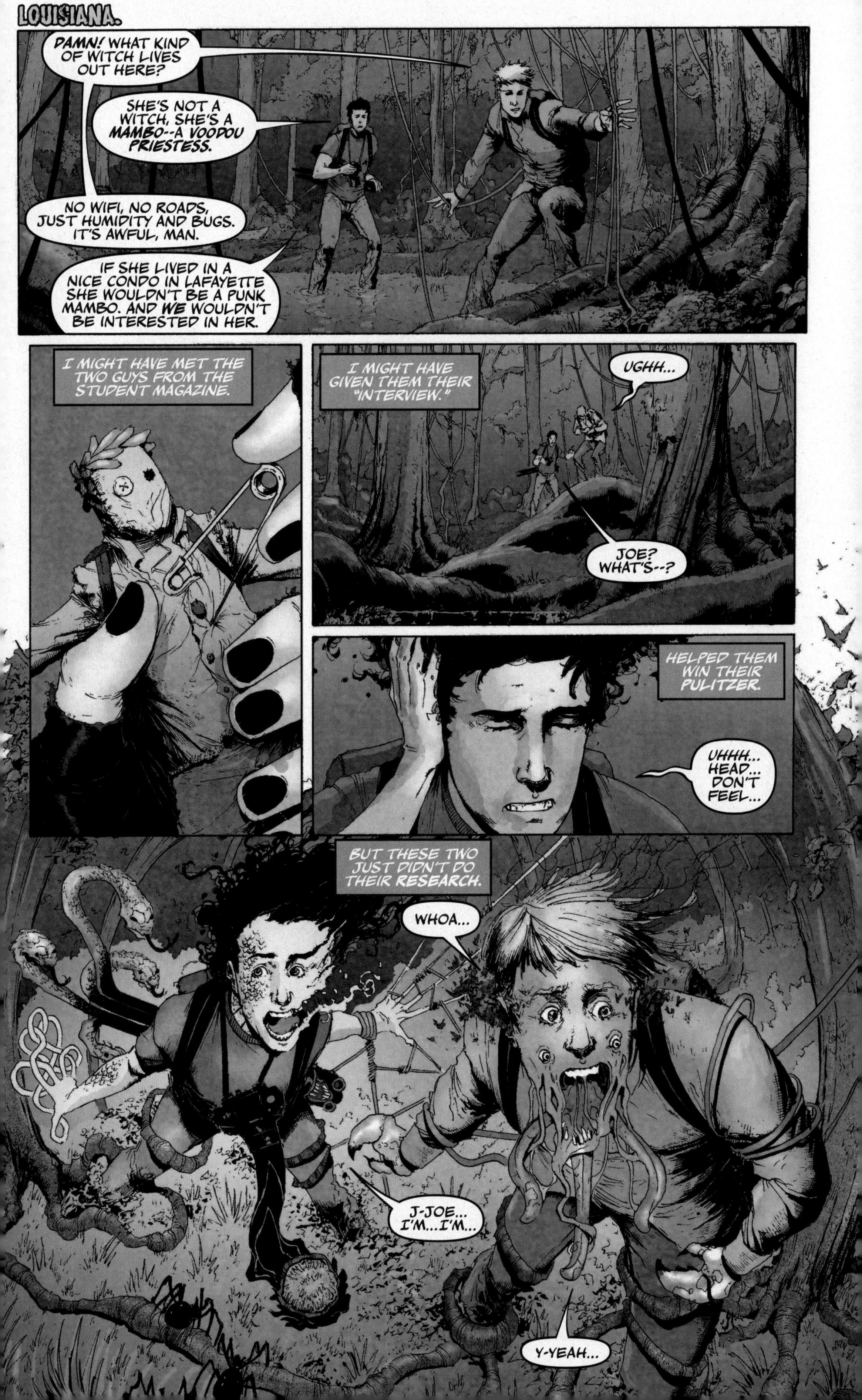
LOUISIANA.
DAMN! WHAT KIND OF WITCH LIVES OUT HERE?
SHE'S NOT A WITCH, SHE'S A MAMBO--A VOODOU PRIESTESS.
NO WIFI, NO ROADS, JUST HUMIDITY AND BUGS. IT'S AWFUL, MAN.
IF SHE LIVED IN A NICE CONDO IN LAFAYETTE SHE WOULDN'T BE A PUNK MAMBO. AND WE WOULDN'T BE INTERESTED IN HER.
I MIGHT HAVE MET THE TWO GUYS FROM THE STUDENT MAGAZINE.
I MIGHT HAVE GIVEN THEM THEIR "INTERVIEW."
UGHH...
JOE? WHAT'S--?
HELPED THEM WIN THEIR PULITZER.
UHHH... HEAD... DON'T FEEL...
BUT THESE TWO JUST DIDN'T DO THEIR RESEARCH.
WHOA...
J-JOE... I'M...I'M...
Y-YEAH...

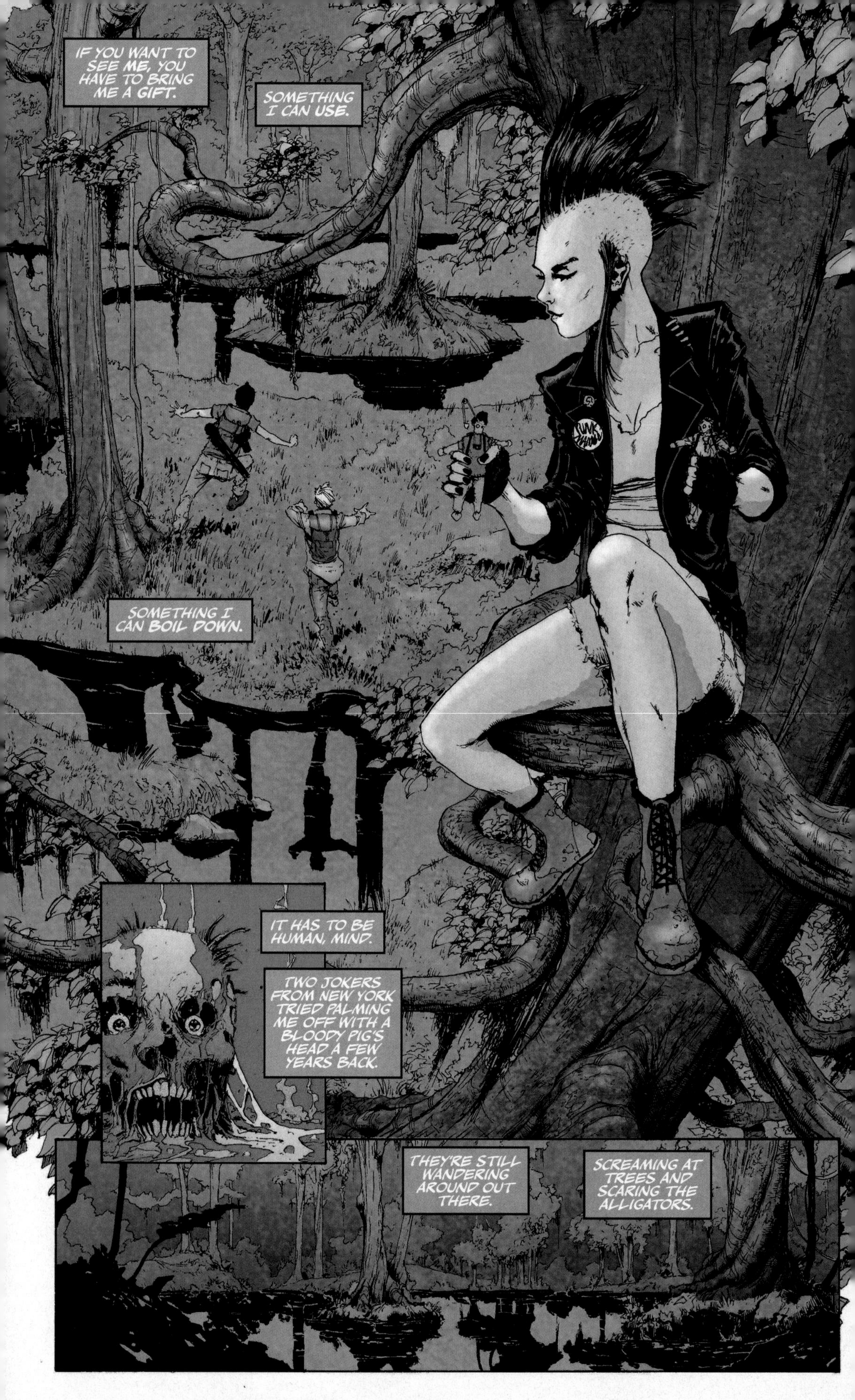

IF YOU WANT TO SEE ME, YOU HAVE TO BRING ME A GIFT.
SOMETHING I CAN USE.
SOMETHING I CAN BOIL DOWN.
IT HAS TO BE HUMAN, MIND.
TWO JOKERS FROM NEW YORK TRIED PALMING ME OFF WITH A BLOODY PIG'S HEAD A FEW YEARS BACK.
THEY'RE STILL WANDERING AROUND OUT THERE.
SCREAMING AT TREES AND SCARING THE ALLIGATORS.

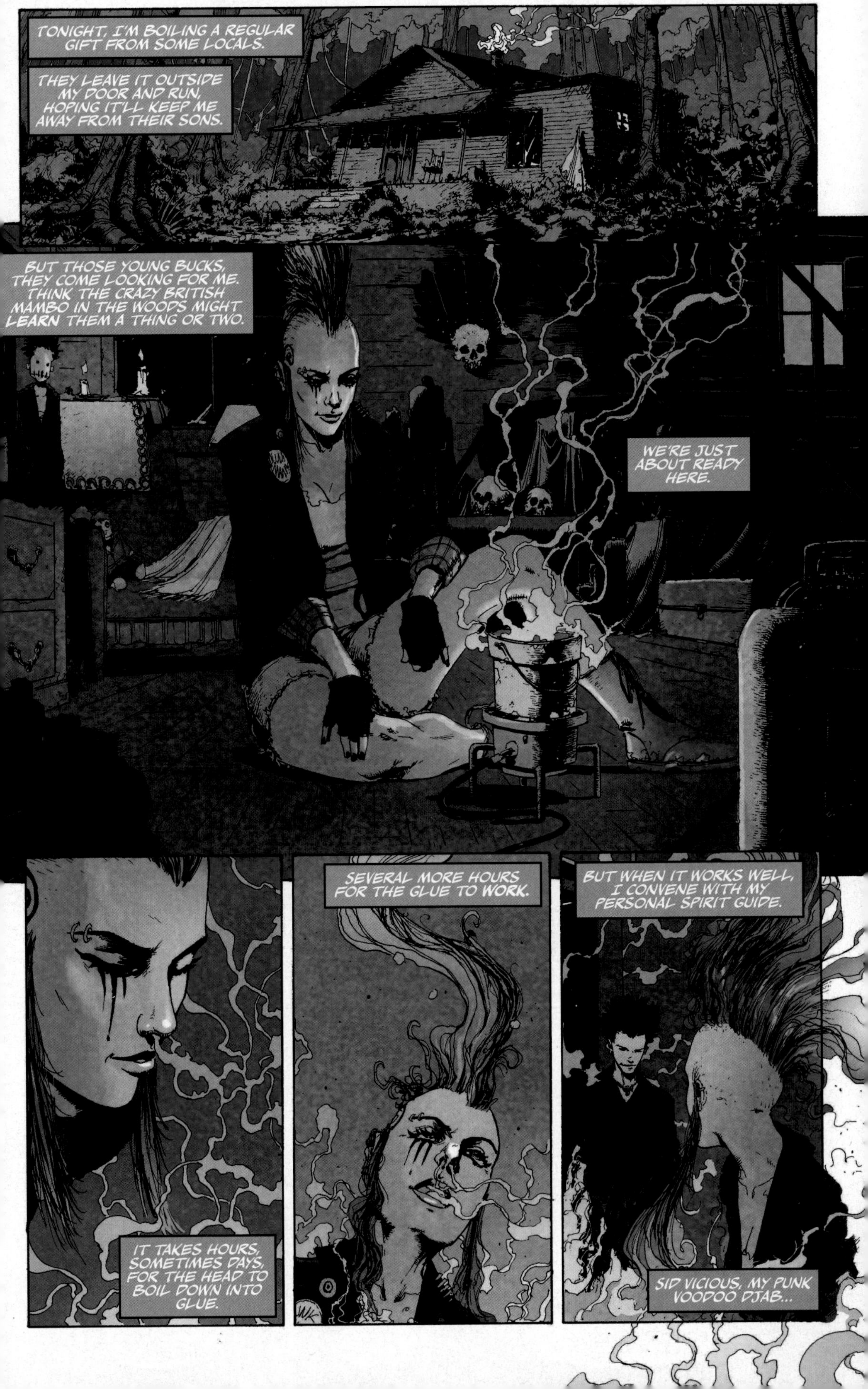
TONIGHT, I'M BOILING A REGULAR GIFT FROM SOME LOCALS.
THEY LEAVE IT OUTSIDE MY DOOR AND RUN, HOPING IT'LL KEEP ME AWAY FROM THEIR SONS.
BUT THOSE YOUNG BUCKS, THEY COME LOOKING FOR ME. THINK THE CRAZY BRITISH MAMBO IN THE WOODS MIGHT LEARN THEM A THING OR TWO.
WE'RE JUST ABOUT READY HERE.
IT TAKES HOURS, SOMETIMES DAYS, FOR THE HEAD TO BOIL DOWN INTO GLUE.
SEVERAL MORE HOURS FOR THE GLUE TO WORK.
BUT WHEN IT WORKS WELL, I CONVENE WITH MY PERSONAL SPIRIT GUIDE.
SID VICIOUS, MY PUNK VOODOO DJAB...

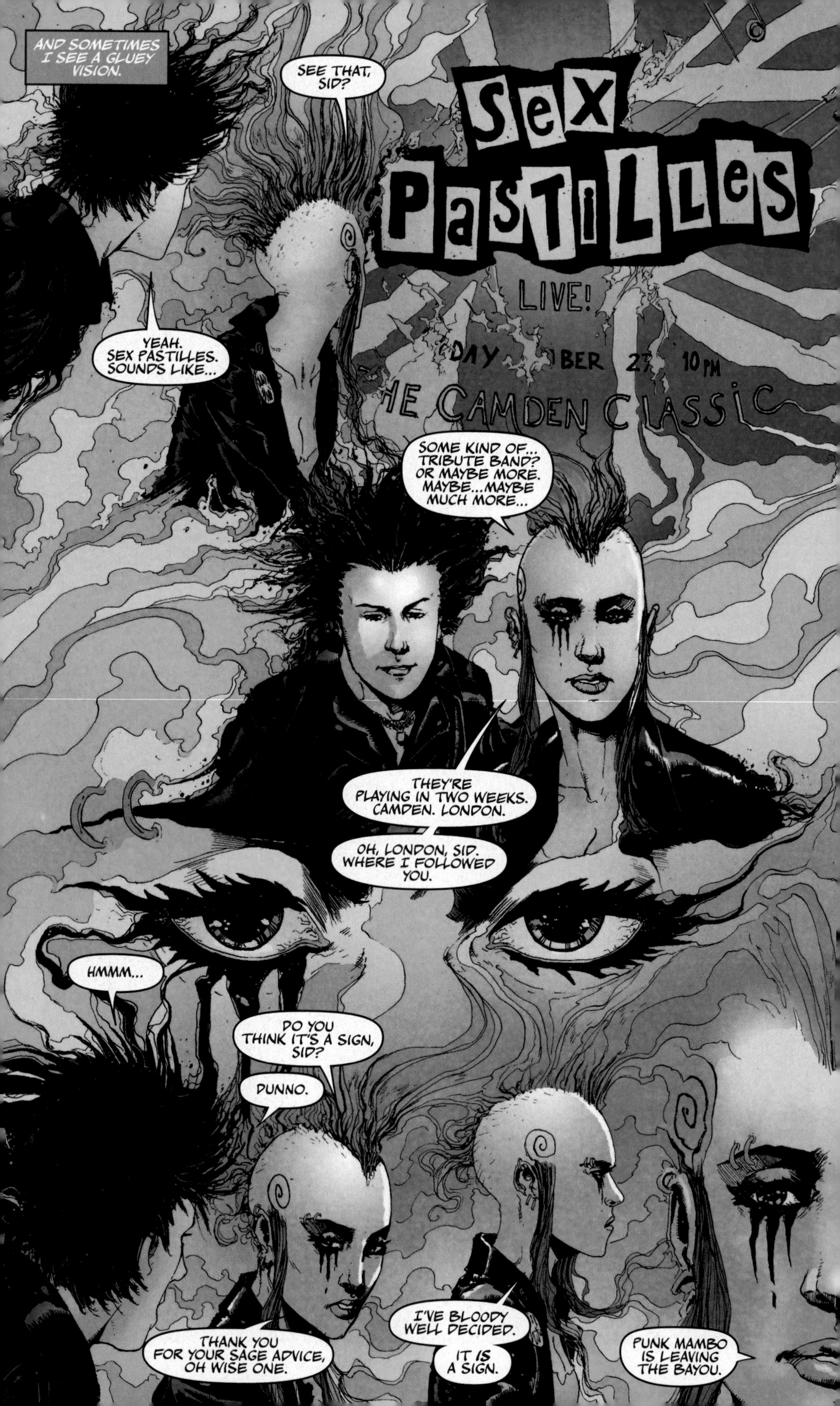

AND SOMETIMES I SEE A GLUEY VISION.
SEE THAT, SID?
Sex Pastilles
LIVE!
DAY BER 27 10 PM
HE CAMDEN CLASSIC
YEAH. SEX PASTILLES. SOUNDS LIKE...
SOME KIND OF... TRIBUTE BAND? OR MAYBE MORE. MAYBE...MAYBE MUCH MORE...
THEY'RE PLAYING IN TWO WEEKS. CAMDEN. LONDON.
OH, LONDON, SID. WHERE I FOLLOWED YOU.
HMMM...
DO YOU THINK IT'S A SIGN, SID?
DUNNO.
THANK YOU FOR YOUR SAGE ADVICE, OH WISE ONE.
I'VE BLOODY WELL DECIDED.
IT *IS* A SIGN.
PUNK MAMBO IS LEAVING THE BAYOU.

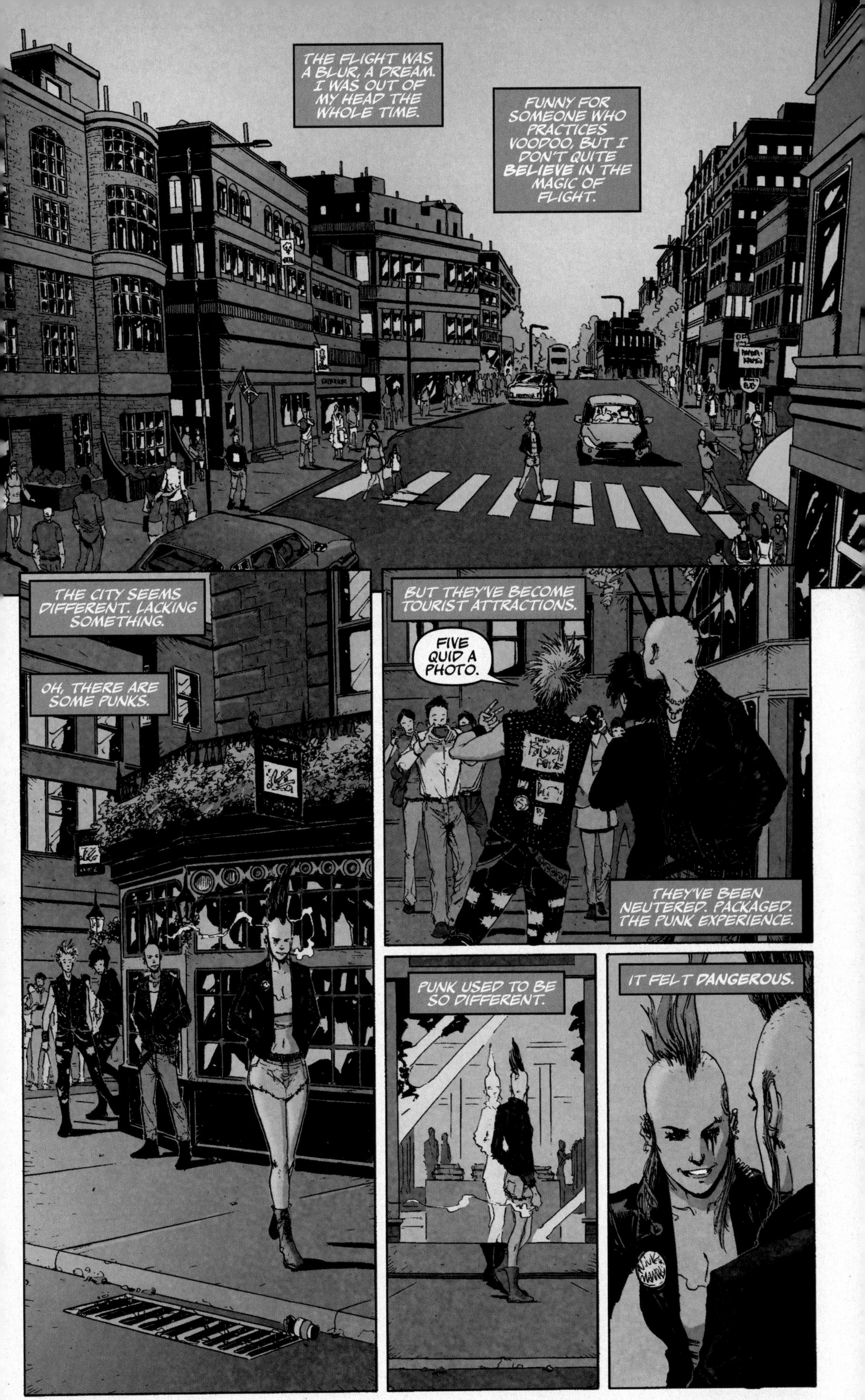
THE FLIGHT WAS A BLUR, A DREAM. I WAS OUT OF MY HEAD THE WHOLE TIME.
FUNNY FOR SOMEONE WHO PRACTICES VOODOO, BUT I DON'T QUITE BELIEVE IN THE MAGIC OF FLIGHT.
THE CITY SEEMS DIFFERENT. LACKING SOMETHING.
OH, THERE ARE SOME PUNKS.
BUT THEY'VE BECOME TOURIST ATTRACTIONS.
FIVE QUID A PHOTO.
THEY'VE BEEN NEUTERED. PACKAGED. THE PUNK EXPERIENCE.
PUNK USED TO BE SO DIFFERENT.
IT FELT DANGEROUS.

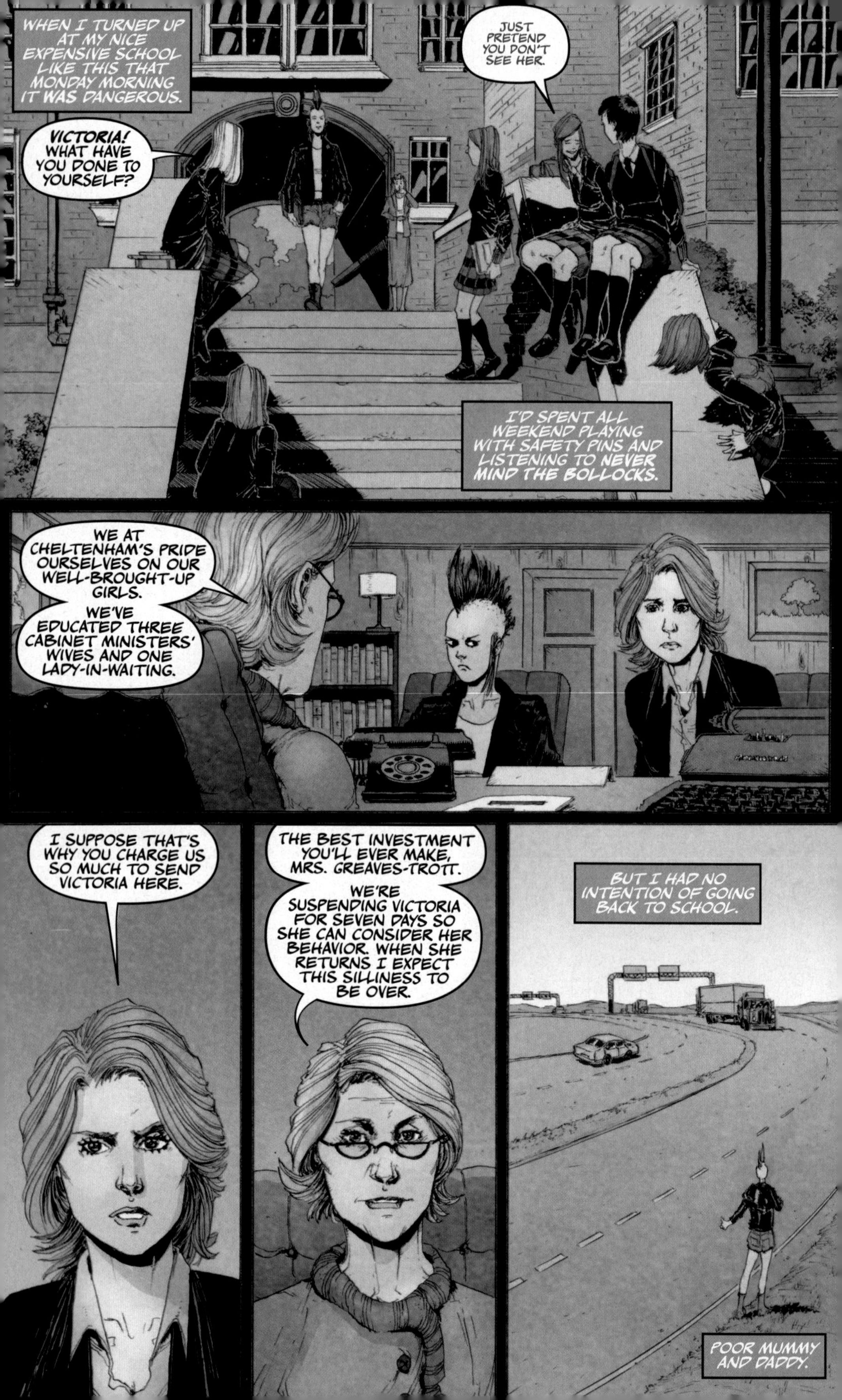
WHEN I TURNED UP AT MY NICE EXPENSIVE SCHOOL LIKE THIS THAT MONDAY MORNING IT WAS DANGEROUS.
VICTORIA! WHAT HAVE YOU DONE TO YOURSELF?
JUST PRETEND YOU DON'T SEE HER.
I'D SPENT ALL WEEKEND PLAYING WITH SAFETY PINS AND LISTENING TO NEVER MIND THE BOLLOCKS.
WE AT CHELTENHAM'S PRIDE OURSELVES ON OUR WELL-BROUGHT-UP GIRLS.
WE'VE EDUCATED THREE CABINET MINISTERS' WIVES AND ONE LADY-IN-WAITING.
I SUPPOSE THAT'S WHY YOU CHARGE US SO MUCH TO SEND VICTORIA HERE.
THE BEST INVESTMENT YOU'LL EVER MAKE, MRS. GREAVES-TROTT.
WE'RE SUSPENDING VICTORIA FOR SEVEN DAYS SO SHE CAN CONSIDER HER BEHAVIOR. WHEN SHE RETURNS I EXPECT THIS SILLINESS TO BE OVER.
BUT I HAD NO INTENTION OF GOING BACK TO SCHOOL.
POOR MUMMY AND DADDY.

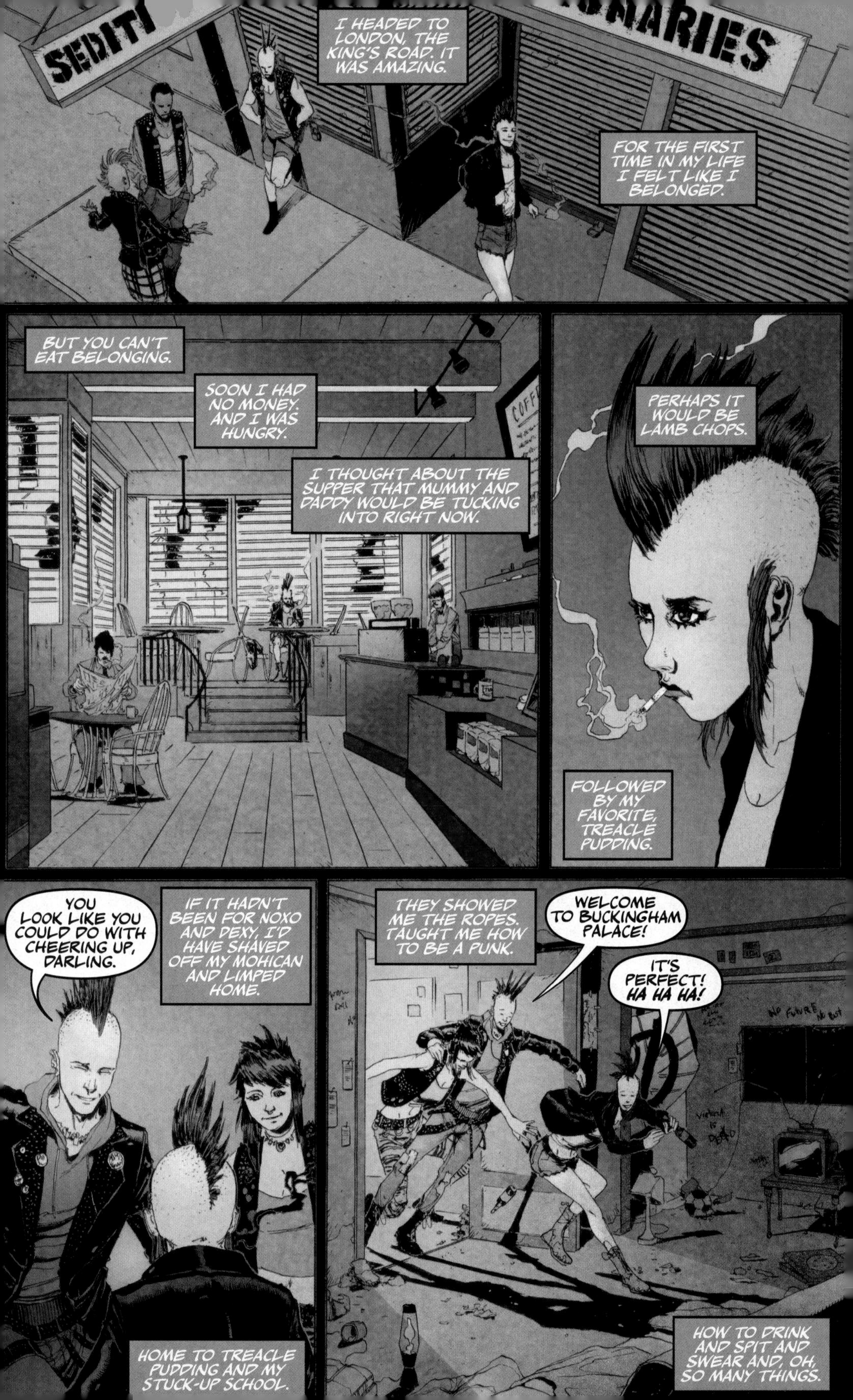
SEDITI
NARIES
I HEADED TO LONDON, THE KING'S ROAD. IT WAS AMAZING.
FOR THE FIRST TIME IN MY LIFE I FELT LIKE I BELONGED.
BUT YOU CAN'T EAT BELONGING.
SOON I HAD NO MONEY. AND I WAS HUNGRY.
I THOUGHT ABOUT THE SUPPER THAT MUMMY AND DADDY WOULD BE TUCKING INTO RIGHT NOW.
PERHAPS IT WOULD BE LAMB CHOPS.
FOLLOWED BY MY FAVORITE, TREACLE PUDDING.
YOU LOOK LIKE YOU COULD DO WITH CHEERING UP, DARLING.
IF IT HADN'T BEEN FOR NOXO AND DEXY, I'D HAVE SHAVED OFF MY MOHICAN AND LIMPED HOME.
HOME TO TREACLE PUDDING AND MY STUCK-UP SCHOOL.
THEY SHOWED ME THE ROPES, TAUGHT ME HOW TO BE A PUNK.
WELCOME TO BUCKINGHAM PALACE!
IT'S PERFECT! HA HA HA!
NO FUTURE
HOW TO DRINK AND SPIT AND SWEAR AND, OH, SO MANY THINGS.

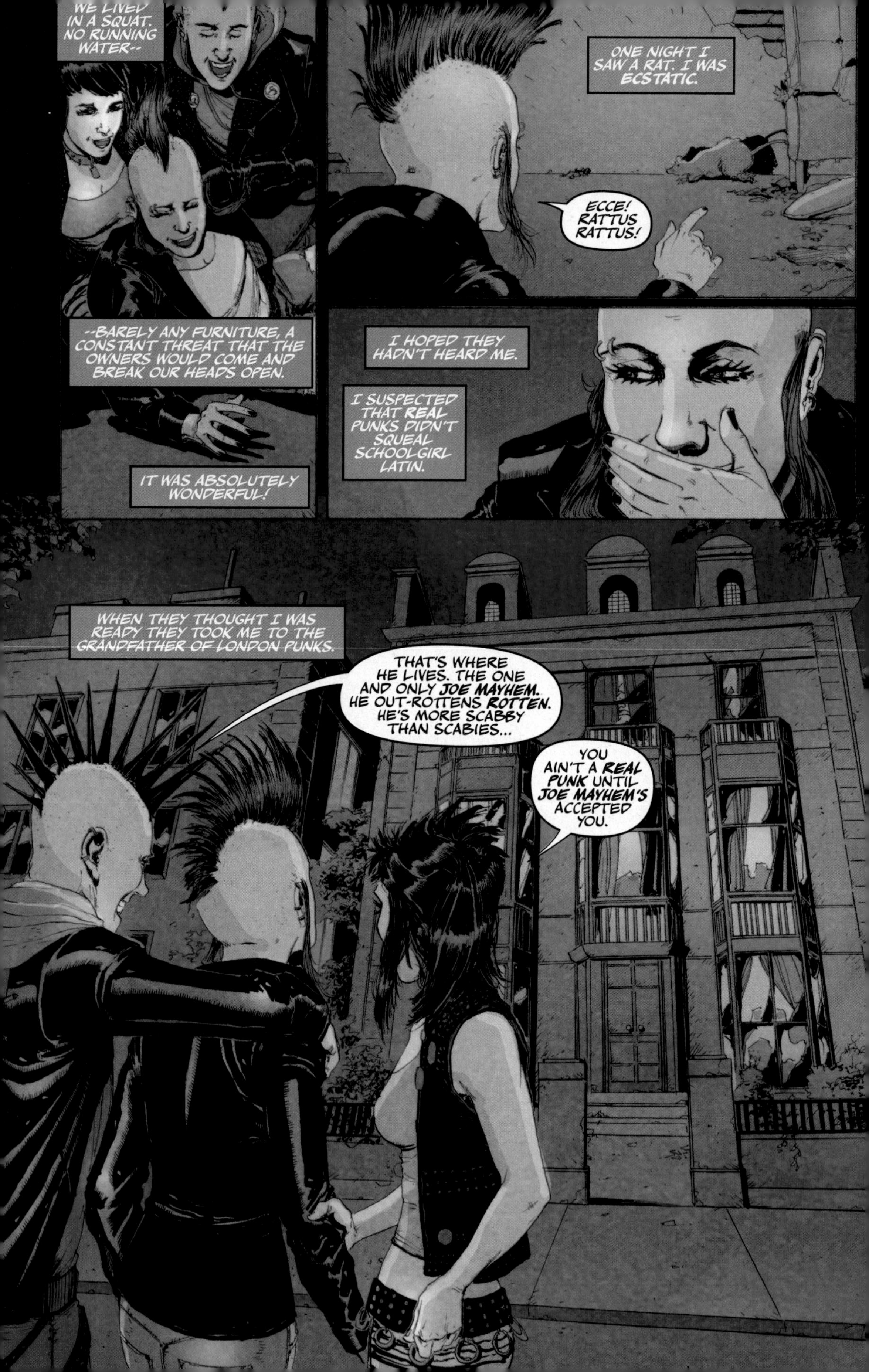
WE LIVED IN A SQUAT. NO RUNNING WATER--
ONE NIGHT I SAW A RAT. I WAS ECSTATIC.
ECCE! RATTUS RATTUS!
--BARELY ANY FURNITURE, A CONSTANT THREAT THAT THE OWNERS WOULD COME AND BREAK OUR HEADS OPEN.
IT WAS ABSOLUTELY WONDERFUL!
I HOPED THEY HADN'T HEARD ME.
I SUSPECTED THAT REAL PUNKS DIDN'T SQUEAL SCHOOLGIRL LATIN.
WHEN THEY THOUGHT I WAS READY THEY TOOK ME TO THE GRANDFATHER OF LONDON PUNKS.
THAT'S WHERE HE LIVES. THE ONE AND ONLY JOE MAYHEM. HE OUT-ROTTENS ROTTEN. HE'S MORE SCABBY THAN SCABIES...
YOU AIN'T A REAL PUNK UNTIL JOE MAYHEM'S ACCEPTED YOU.

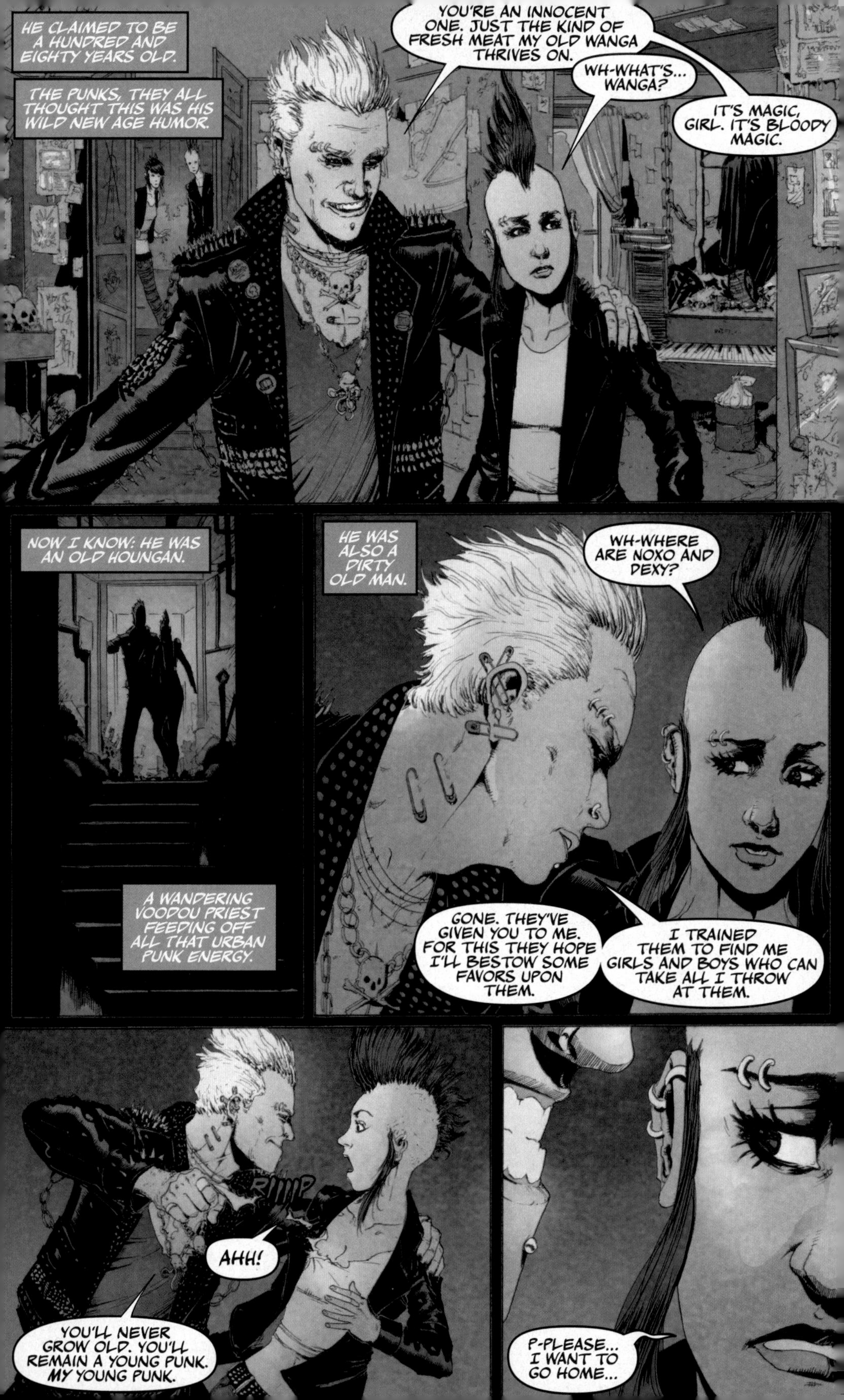
HE CLAIMED TO BE A HUNDRED AND EIGHTY YEARS OLD.
THE PUNKS, THEY ALL THOUGHT THIS WAS HIS WILD NEW AGE HUMOR.
YOU'RE AN INNOCENT ONE. JUST THE KIND OF FRESH MEAT MY OLD WANGA THRIVES ON.
WH-WHAT'S... WANGA?
IT'S MAGIC, GIRL. IT'S BLOODY MAGIC.
NOW I KNOW: HE WAS AN OLD HOUNGAN.
A WANDERING VOODOU PRIEST FEEDING OFF ALL THAT URBAN PUNK ENERGY.
HE WAS ALSO A DIRTY OLD MAN.
WH-WHERE ARE NOXO AND DEXY?
GONE. THEY'VE GIVEN YOU TO ME. FOR THIS THEY HOPE I'LL BESTOW SOME FAVORS UPON THEM.
I TRAINED THEM TO FIND ME GIRLS AND BOYS WHO CAN TAKE ALL I THROW AT THEM.
RIIIP
AHH!
YOU'LL NEVER GROW OLD. YOU'LL REMAIN A YOUNG PUNK. MY YOUNG PUNK.
P-PLEASE... I WANT TO GO HOME...

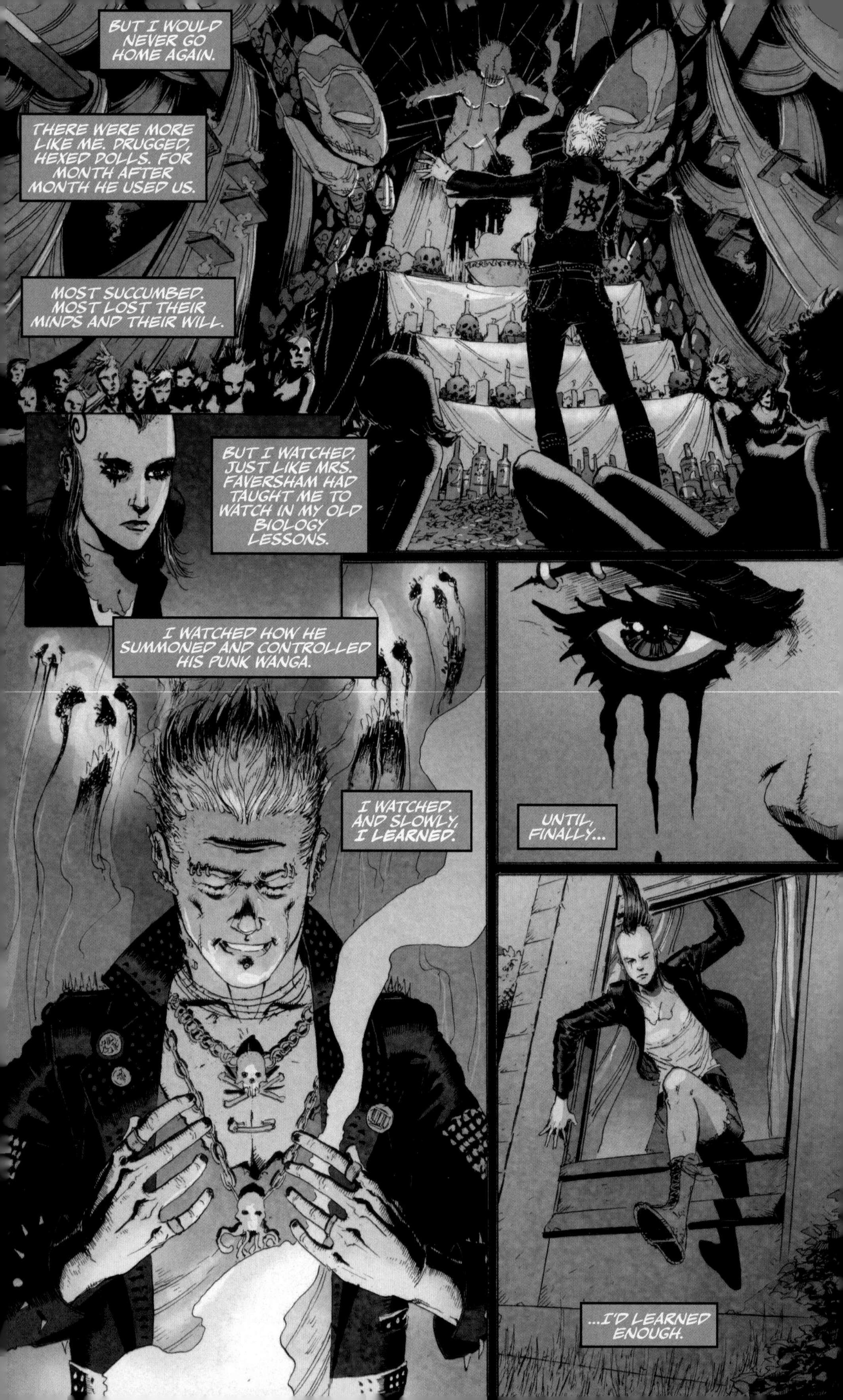
BUT I WOULD NEVER GO HOME AGAIN.
THERE WERE MORE LIKE ME. DRUGGED, HEXED DOLLS. FOR MONTH AFTER MONTH HE USED US.
MOST SUCCUMBED. MOST LOST THEIR MINDS AND THEIR WILL.
BUT I WATCHED, JUST LIKE MRS. FAVERSHAM HAD TAUGHT ME TO WATCH IN MY OLD BIOLOGY LESSONS.
I WATCHED HOW HE SUMMONED AND CONTROLLED HIS PUNK WANGA.
I WATCHED. AND SLOWLY, I LEARNED.
UNTIL, FINALLY...
...I'D LEARNED ENOUGH.

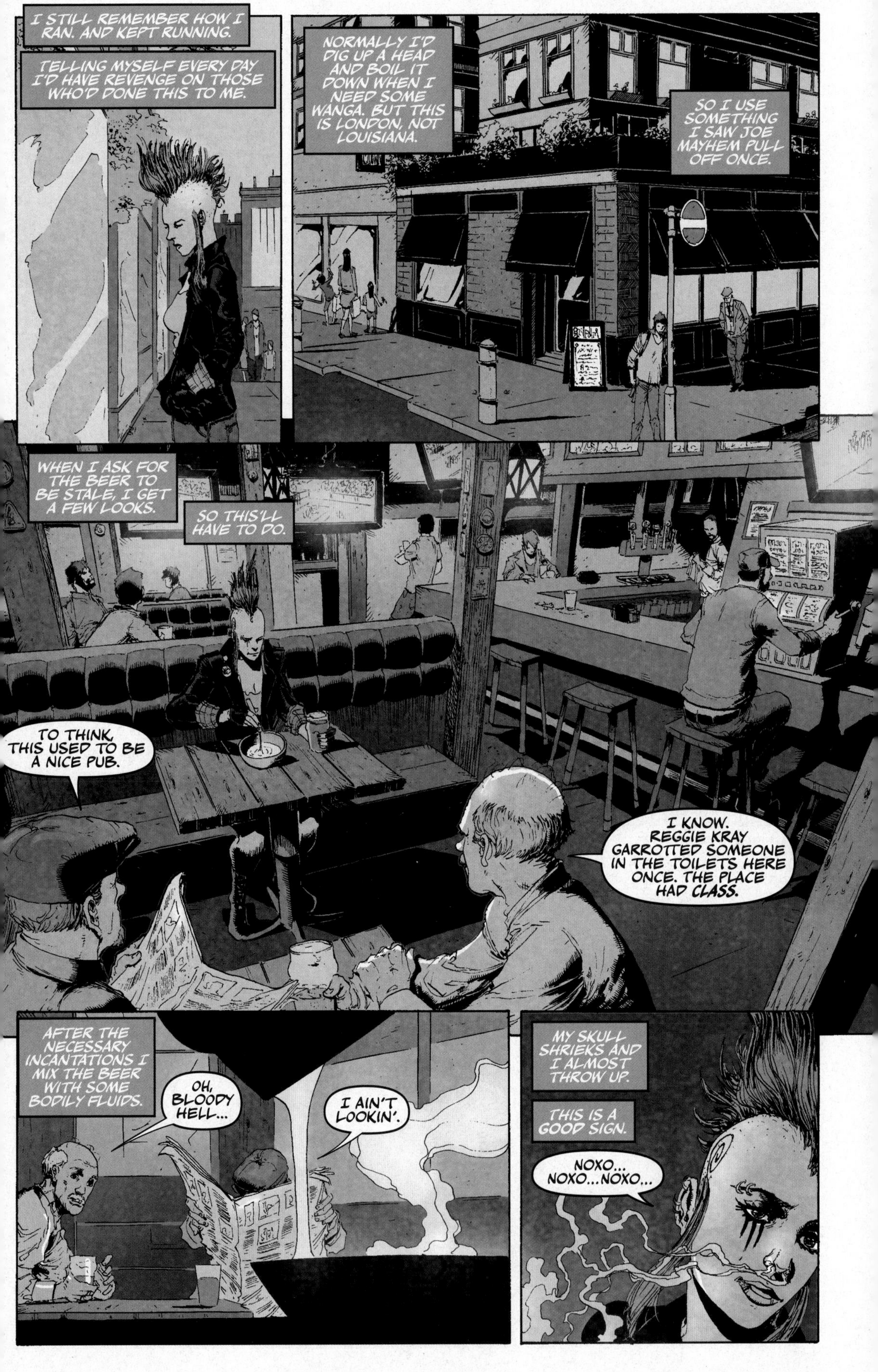
I STILL REMEMBER HOW I RAN. AND KEPT RUNNING.
TELLING MYSELF EVERY DAY I'D HAVE REVENGE ON THOSE WHO'D DONE THIS TO ME.
NORMALLY I'D DIG UP A HEAD AND BOIL IT DOWN WHEN I NEED SOME WANGA. BUT THIS IS LONDON, NOT LOUISIANA.
SO I USE SOMETHING I SAW JOE MAYHEM PULL OFF ONCE.
WHEN I ASK FOR THE BEER TO BE STALE, I GET A FEW LOOKS.
SO THIS'LL HAVE TO DO.
TO THINK, THIS USED TO BE A NICE PUB.
I KNOW. REGGIE KRAY GARROTTED SOMEONE IN THE TOILETS HERE ONCE. THE PLACE HAD CLASS.
AFTER THE NECESSARY INCANTATIONS I MIX THE BEER WITH SOME BODILY FLUIDS.
OH, BLOODY HELL...
I AIN'T LOOKIN'.
MY SKULL SHRIEKS AND I ALMOST THROW UP.
THIS IS A GOOD SIGN.
NOXO... NOXO...NOXO...

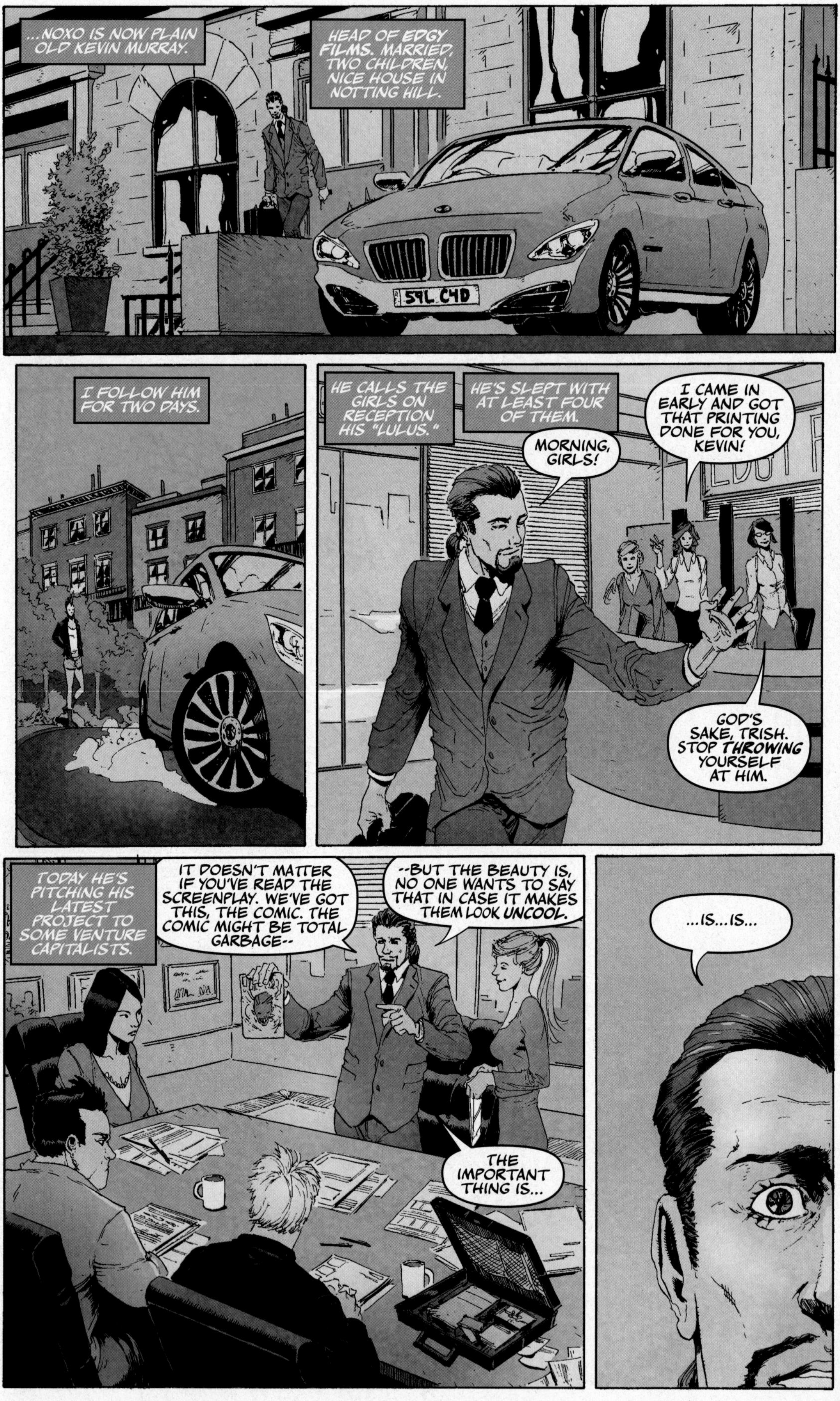
...NOXO IS NOW PLAIN OLD KEVIN MURRAY.
HEAD OF EDGY FILMS. MARRIED, TWO CHILDREN, NICE HOUSE IN NOTTING HILL.
59L C4D
I FOLLOW HIM FOR TWO DAYS.
HE CALLS THE GIRLS ON RECEPTION HIS "LULUS."
HE'S SLEPT WITH AT LEAST FOUR OF THEM.
MORNING, GIRLS!
I CAME IN EARLY AND GOT THAT PRINTING DONE FOR YOU, KEVIN!
GOD'S SAKE, TRISH. STOP THROWING YOURSELF AT HIM.
TODAY HE'S PITCHING HIS LATEST PROJECT TO SOME VENTURE CAPITALISTS.
IT DOESN'T MATTER IF YOU'VE READ THE SCREENPLAY. WE'VE GOT THIS, THE COMIC. THE COMIC MIGHT BE TOTAL GARBAGE--
--BUT THE BEAUTY IS, NO ONE WANTS TO SAY THAT IN CASE IT MAKES THEM LOOK UNCOOL.
THE IMPORTANT THING IS...
...IS...IS...

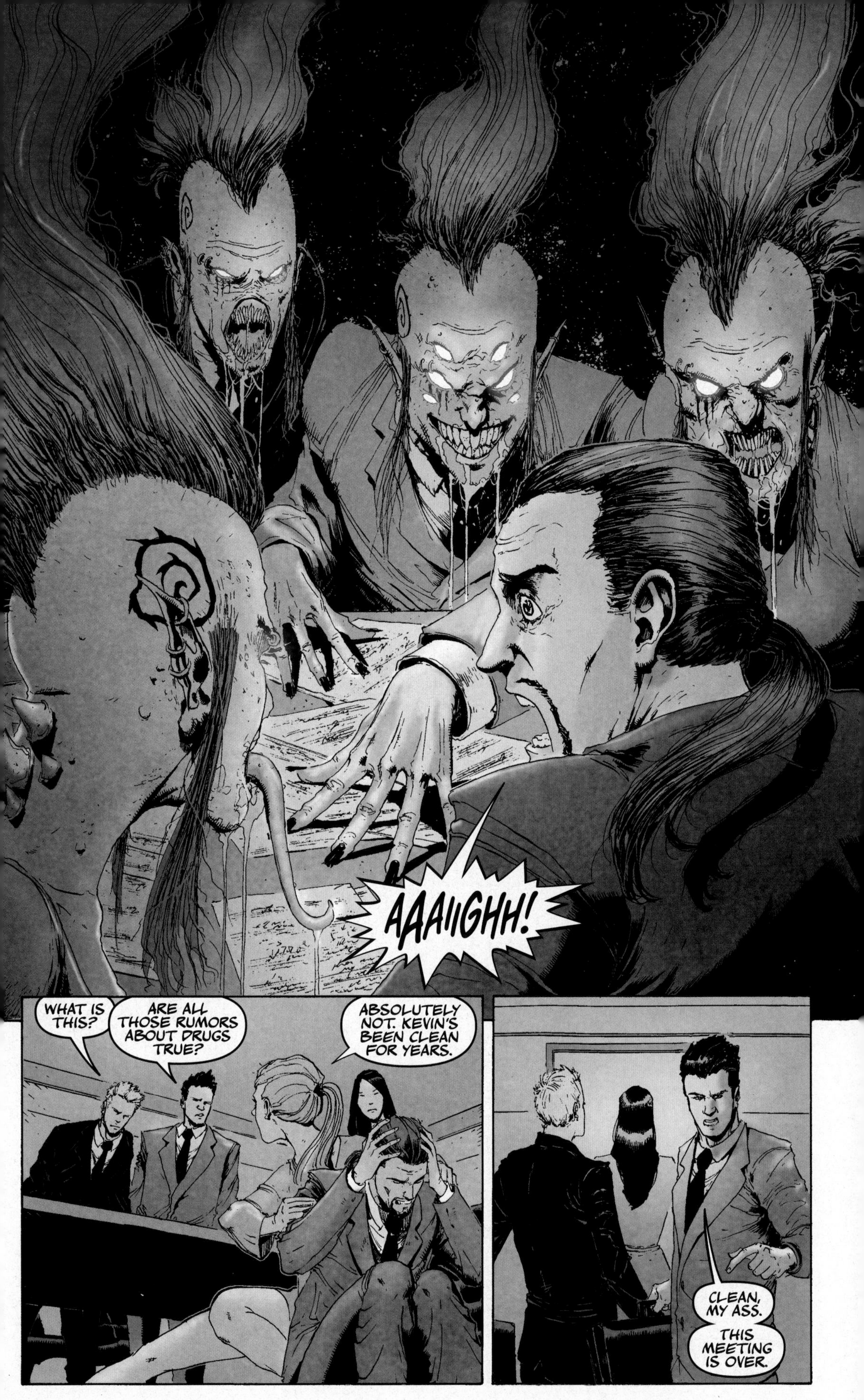
AAAIIGHH!
WHAT IS THIS?
ARE ALL THOSE RUMORS ABOUT DRUGS TRUE?
ABSOLUTELY NOT. KEVIN'S BEEN CLEAN FOR YEARS.
CLEAN, MY ASS.
THIS MEETING IS OVER.

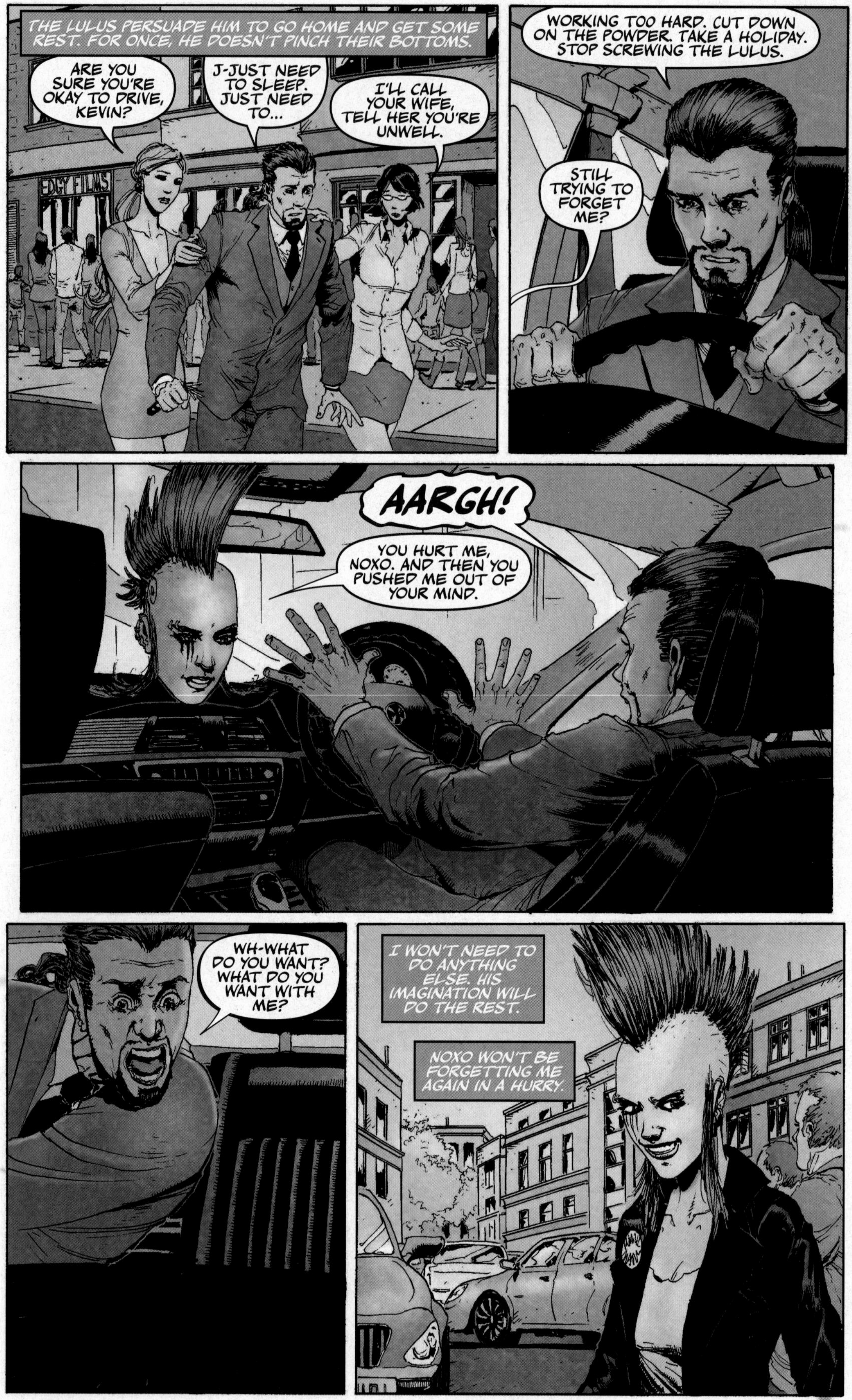

THE LULUS PERSUADE HIM TO GO HOME AND GET SOME REST. FOR ONCE, HE DOESN'T PINCH THEIR BOTTOMS.
ARE YOU SURE YOU'RE OKAY TO DRIVE, KEVIN?
J-JUST NEED TO SLEEP. JUST NEED TO...
I'LL CALL YOUR WIFE, TELL HER YOU'RE UNWELL.
EDGY FILMS
WORKING TOO HARD. CUT DOWN ON THE POWDER. TAKE A HOLIDAY. STOP SCREWING THE LULUS.
STILL TRYING TO FORGET ME?
AARGH!
YOU HURT ME, NOXO. AND THEN YOU PUSHED ME OUT OF YOUR MIND.
WH-WHAT DO YOU WANT? WHAT DO YOU WANT WITH ME?
I WON'T NEED TO DO ANYTHING ELSE. HIS IMAGINATION WILL DO THE REST.
NOXO WON'T BE FORGETTING ME AGAIN IN A HURRY.

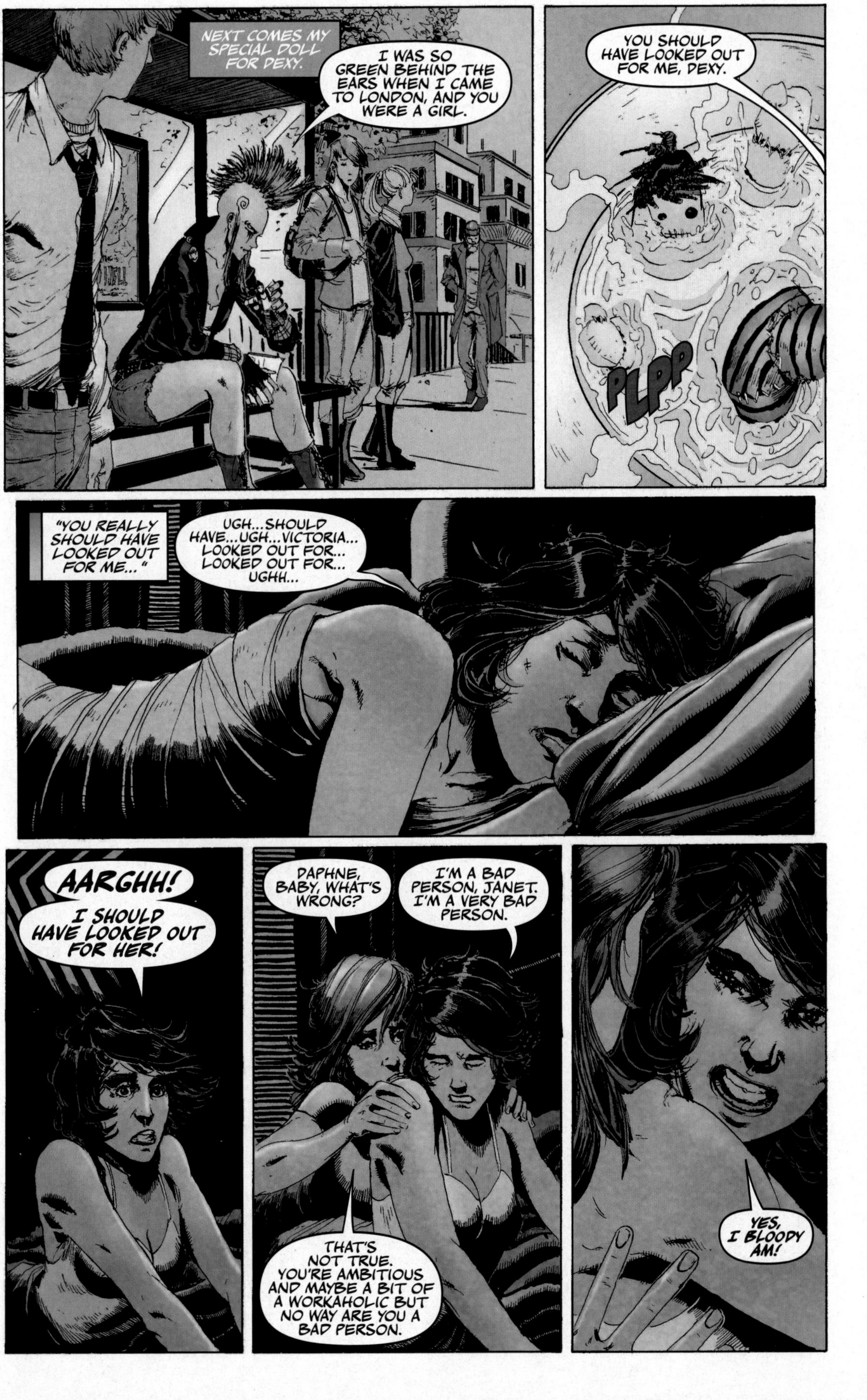
NEXT COMES MY SPECIAL DOLL FOR DEXY.
I WAS SO GREEN BEHIND THE EARS WHEN I CAME TO LONDON, AND YOU WERE A GIRL.
YOU SHOULD HAVE LOOKED OUT FOR ME, DEXY.
PLPP
"YOU REALLY SHOULD HAVE LOOKED OUT FOR ME..."
UGH...SHOULD HAVE...UGH...VICTORIA... LOOKED OUT FOR... LOOKED OUT FOR... UGHH...
AARGHH!
I SHOULD HAVE LOOKED OUT FOR HER!
DAPHNE, BABY, WHAT'S WRONG?
I'M A BAD PERSON, JANET. I'M A VERY BAD PERSON.
THAT'S NOT TRUE. YOU'RE AMBITIOUS AND MAYBE A BIT OF A WORKAHOLIC BUT NO WAY ARE YOU A BAD PERSON.
YES, I BLOODY AM!

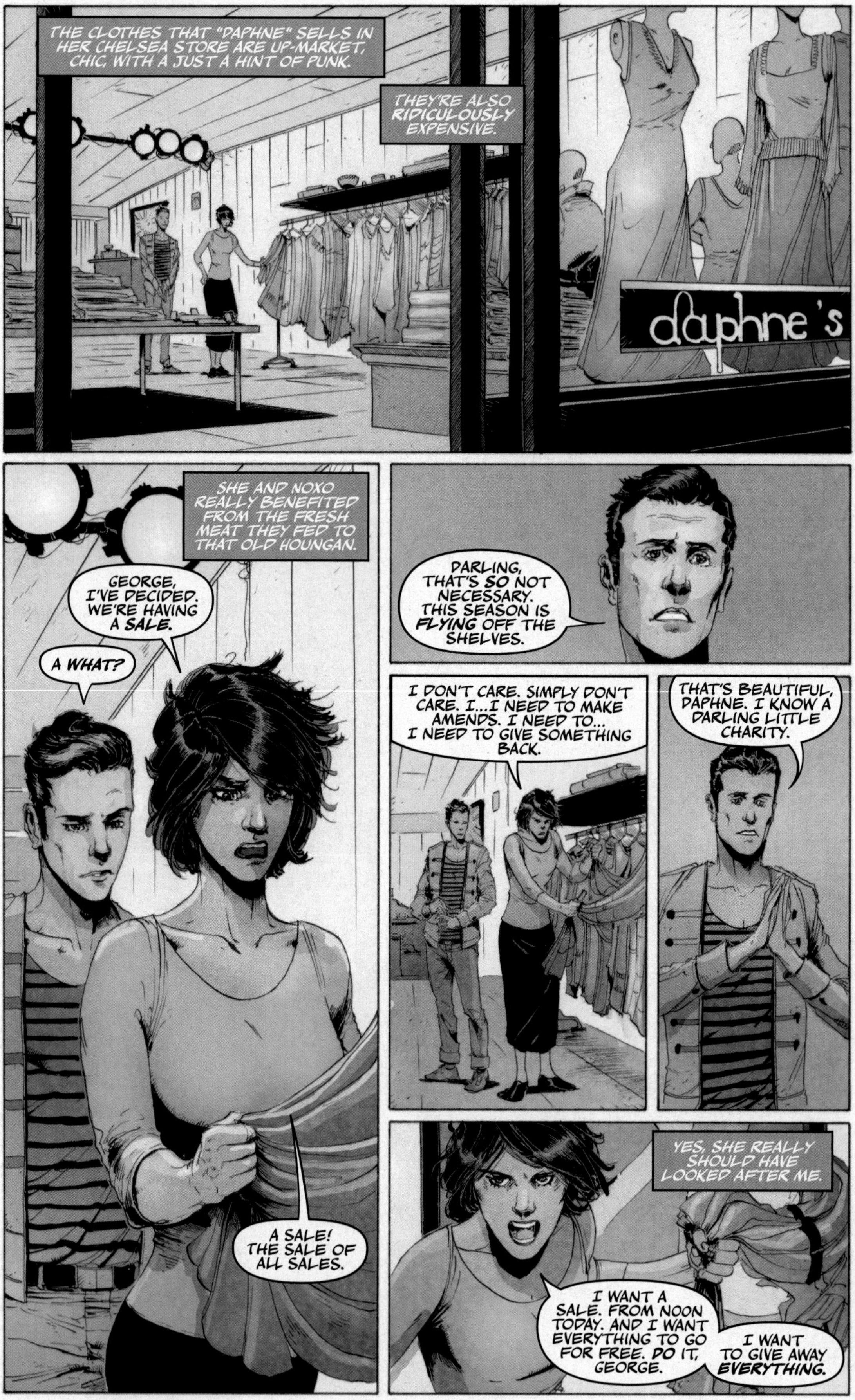
THE CLOTHES THAT "DAPHNE" SELLS IN HER CHELSEA STORE ARE UP-MARKET, CHIC, WITH A JUST A HINT OF PUNK.
THEY'RE ALSO RIDICULOUSLY EXPENSIVE.
daphne's
SHE AND NOXO REALLY BENEFITED FROM THE FRESH MEAT THEY FED TO THAT OLD HOUNGAN.
GEORGE, I'VE DECIDED. WE'RE HAVING A SALE.
A WHAT?
A SALE! THE SALE OF ALL SALES.
DARLING, THAT'S SO NOT NECESSARY. THIS SEASON IS FLYING OFF THE SHELVES.
I DON'T CARE. SIMPLY DON'T CARE. I...I NEED TO MAKE AMENDS. I NEED TO... I NEED TO GIVE SOMETHING BACK.
THAT'S BEAUTIFUL, DAPHNE. I KNOW A DARLING LITTLE CHARITY.
YES, SHE REALLY SHOULD HAVE LOOKED AFTER ME.
I WANT A SALE. FROM NOON TODAY. AND I WANT EVERYTHING TO GO FOR FREE. DO IT, GEORGE.
I WANT TO GIVE AWAY EVERYTHING.

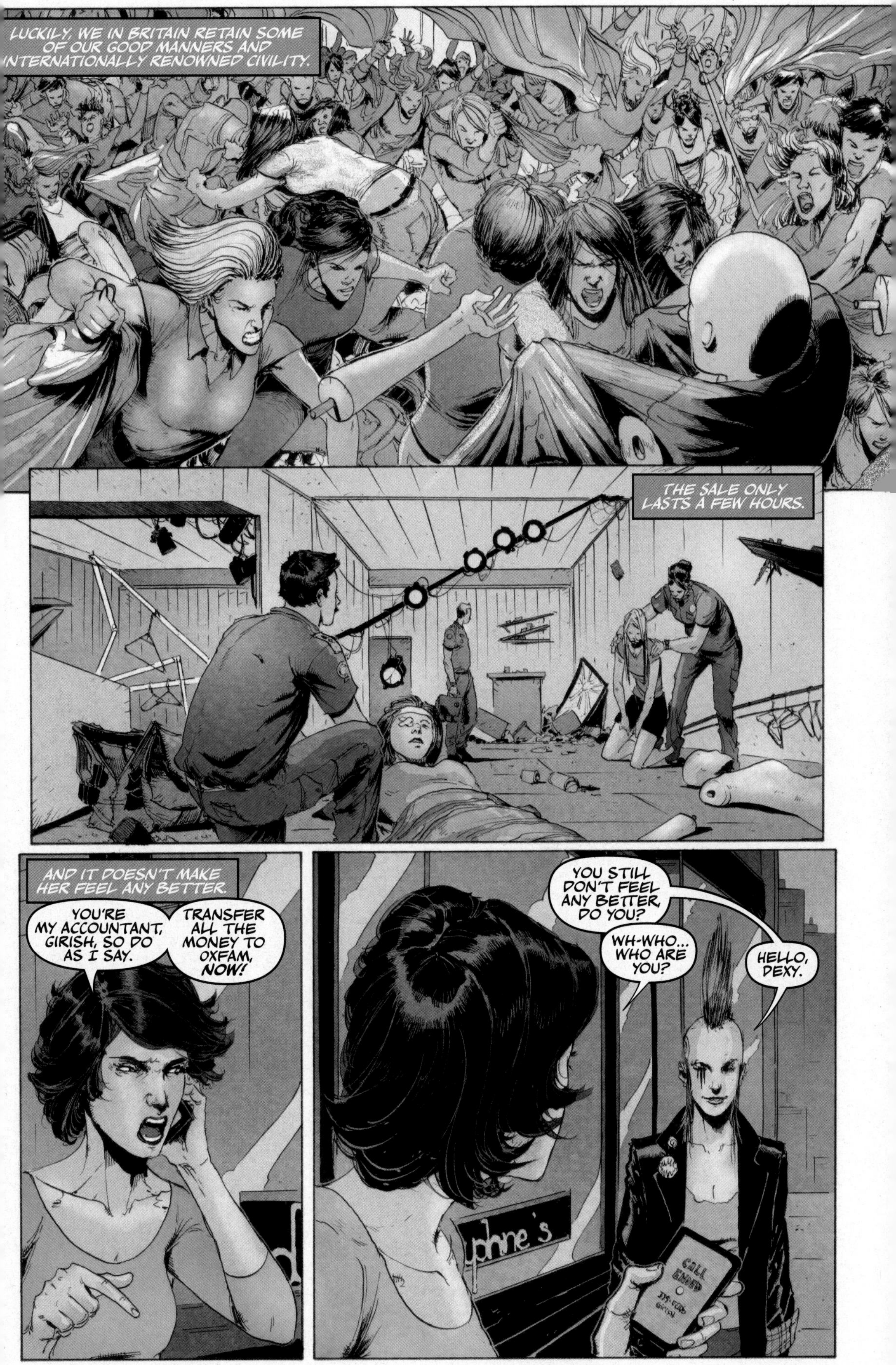
LUCKILY, WE IN BRITAIN RETAIN SOME OF OUR GOOD MANNERS AND INTERNATIONALLY RENOWNED CIVILITY.
THE SALE ONLY LASTS A FEW HOURS.
AND IT DOESN'T MAKE HER FEEL ANY BETTER.
YOU'RE MY ACCOUNTANT, GIRISH, SO DO AS I SAY.
TRANSFER ALL THE MONEY TO OXFAM, NOW!
YOU STILL DON'T FEEL ANY BETTER, DO YOU?
WH-WHO... WHO ARE YOU?
HELLO, DEXY.
CALL ENDED

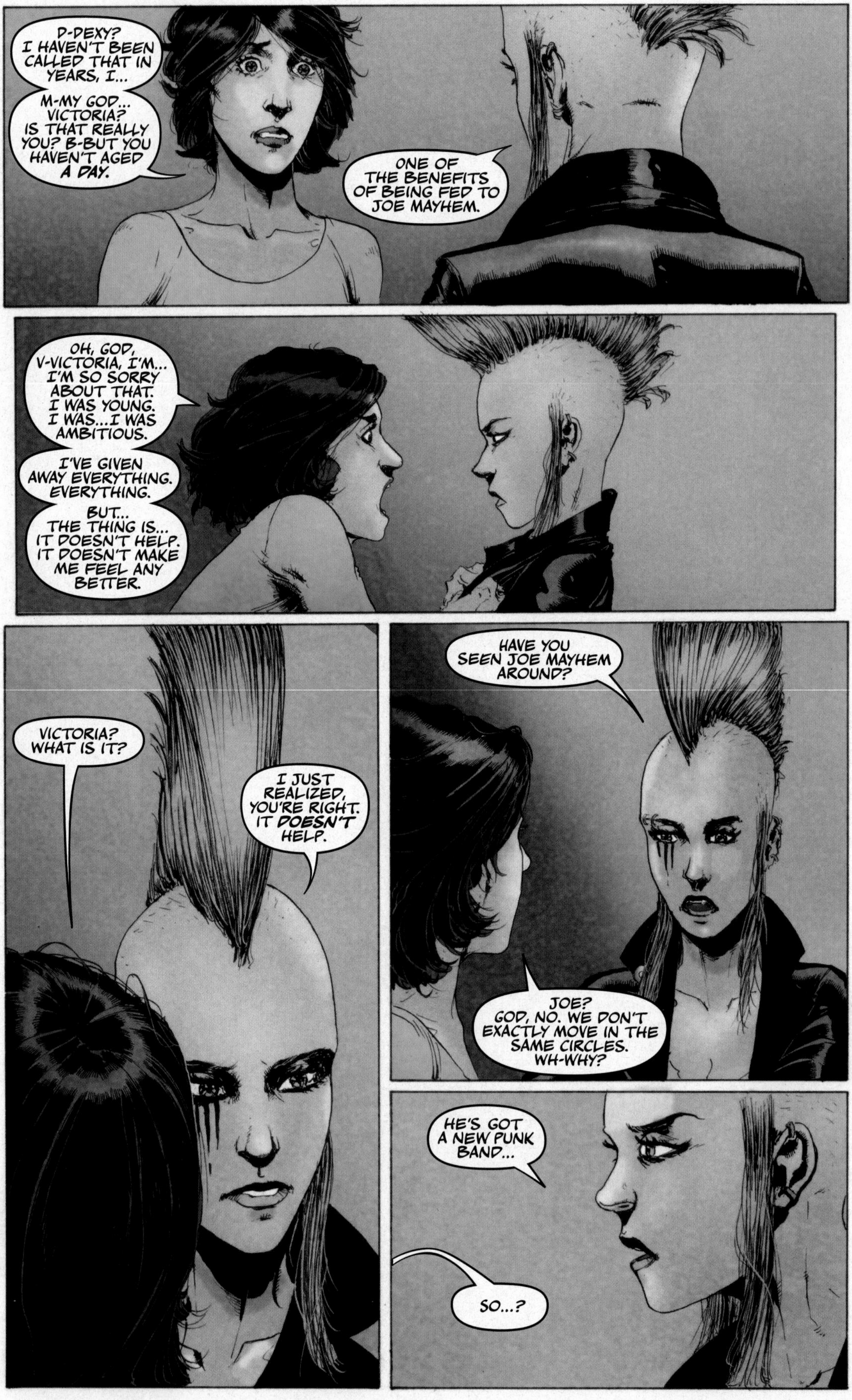
D-DEXY? I HAVEN'T BEEN CALLED THAT IN YEARS, I...
M-MY GOD... VICTORIA? IS THAT REALLY YOU? B-BUT YOU HAVEN'T AGED A DAY.
ONE OF THE BENEFITS OF BEING FED TO JOE MAYHEM.
OH, GOD, V-VICTORIA, I'M... I'M SO SORRY ABOUT THAT. I WAS YOUNG. I WAS...I WAS AMBITIOUS.
I'VE GIVEN AWAY EVERYTHING. EVERYTHING.
BUT... THE THING IS... IT DOESN'T HELP. IT DOESN'T MAKE ME FEEL ANY BETTER.
VICTORIA? WHAT IS IT?
I JUST REALIZED, YOU'RE RIGHT. IT DOESN'T HELP.
HAVE YOU SEEN JOE MAYHEM AROUND?
JOE? GOD, NO. WE DON'T EXACTLY MOVE IN THE SAME CIRCLES. WH-WHY?
HE'S GOT A NEW PUNK BAND...
SO...?

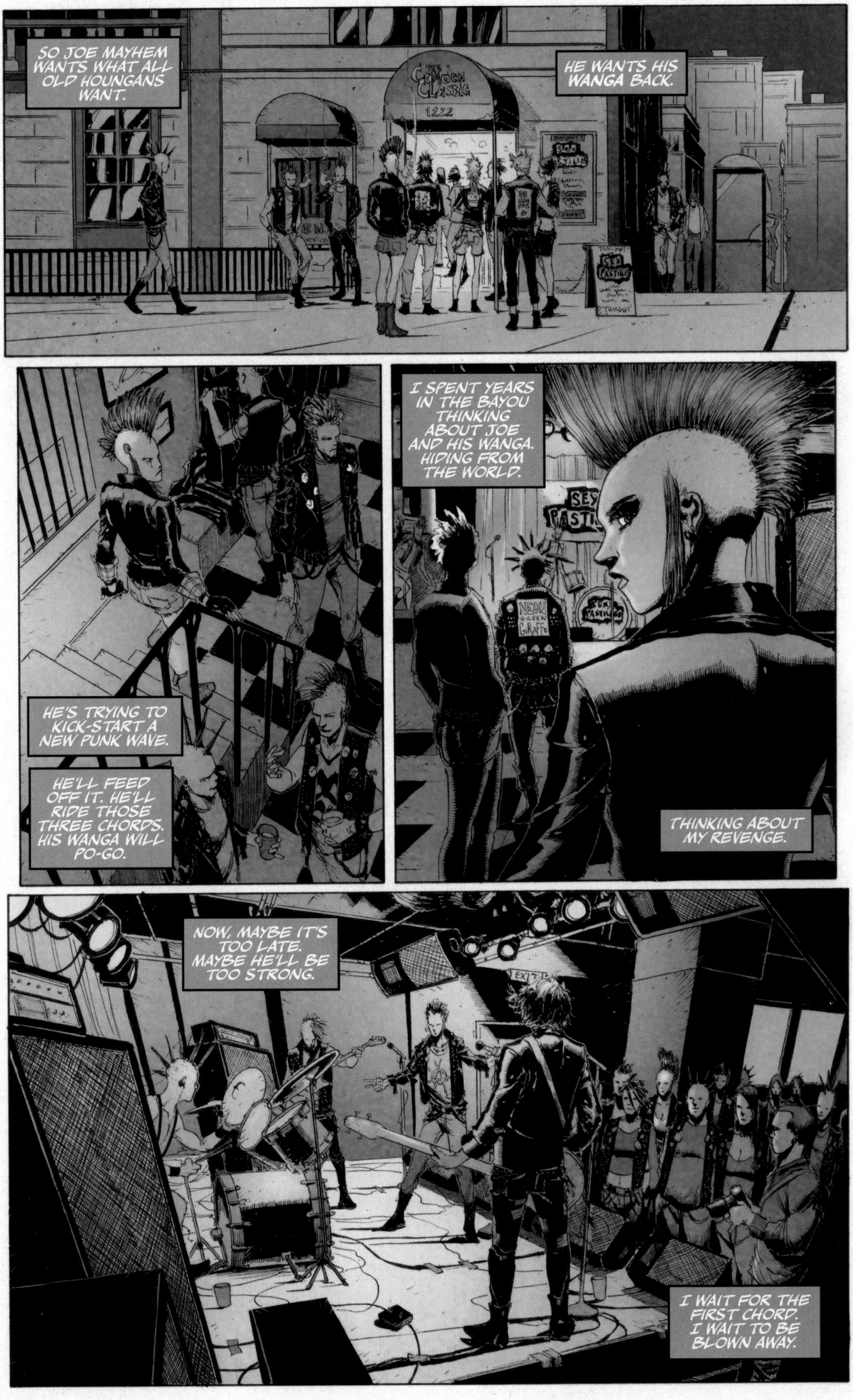
SO JOE MAYHEM WANTS WHAT ALL OLD HOUNGANS WANT.
Camden Classic
1222
HE WANTS HIS WANGA BACK.
HE'S TRYING TO KICK-START A NEW PUNK WAVE.
HE'LL FEED OFF IT. HE'LL RIDE THOSE THREE CHORDS. HIS WANGA WILL PO-GO.
I SPENT YEARS IN THE BAYOU THINKING ABOUT JOE AND HIS WANGA. HIDING FROM THE WORLD.
NEON GREEN GIRAFFE
THINKING ABOUT MY REVENGE.
NOW, MAYBE IT'S TOO LATE. MAYBE HE'LL BE TOO STRONG.
EXIT
I WAIT FOR THE FIRST CHORD. I WAIT TO BE BLOWN AWAY.

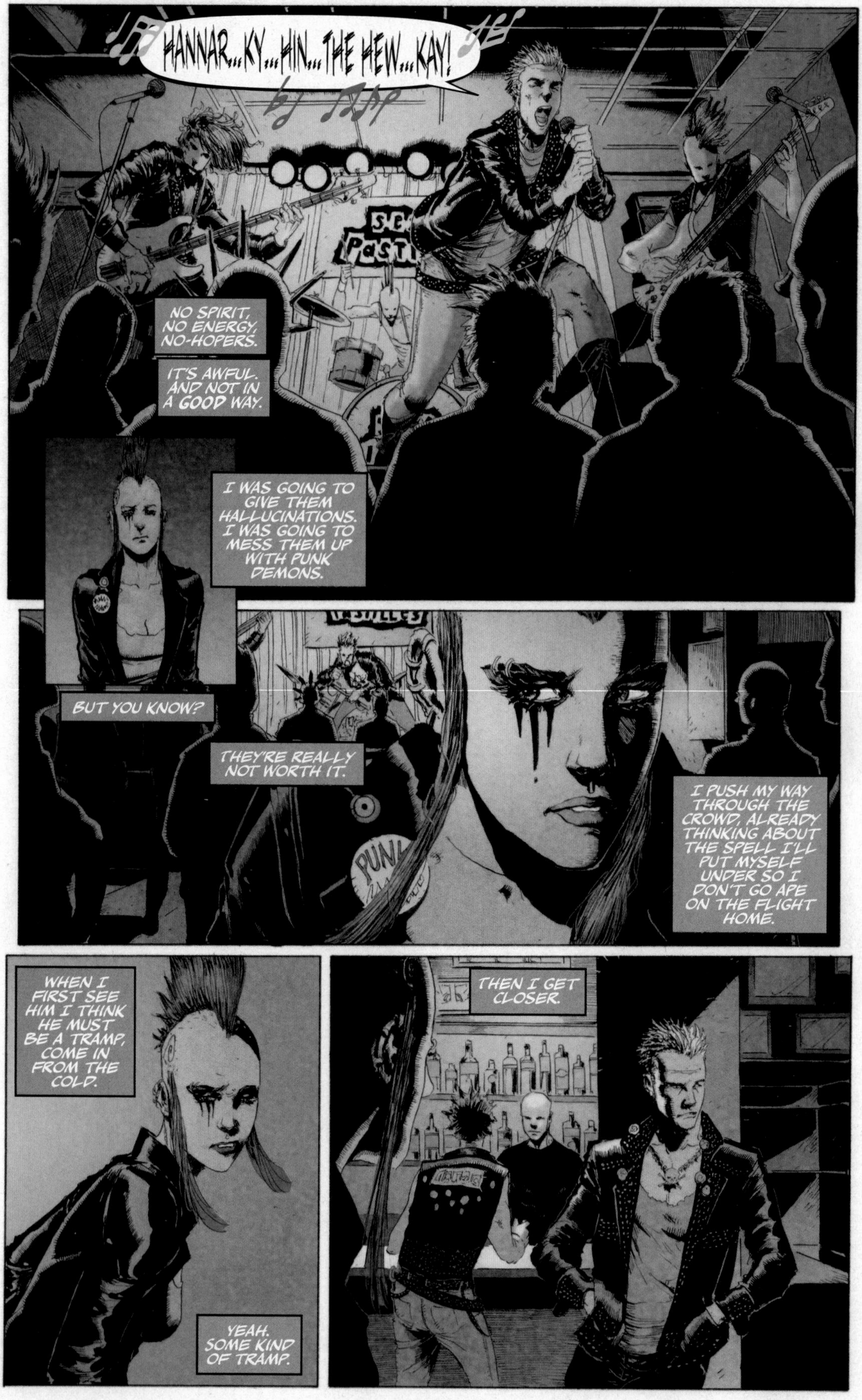
HANNAR...KY...HIN...THE HEW...KAY!
NO SPIRIT, NO ENERGY, NO-HOPERS.
IT'S AWFUL. AND NOT IN A GOOD WAY.
I WAS GOING TO GIVE THEM HALLUCINATIONS. I WAS GOING TO MESS THEM UP WITH PUNK DEMONS.
BUT YOU KNOW?
THEY'RE REALLY NOT WORTH IT.
I PUSH MY WAY THROUGH THE CROWD, ALREADY THINKING ABOUT THE SPELL I'LL PUT MYSELF UNDER SO I DON'T GO APE ON THE FLIGHT HOME.
WHEN I FIRST SEE HIM I THINK HE MUST BE A TRAMP, COME IN FROM THE COLD.
YEAH. SOME KIND OF TRAMP.
THEN I GET CLOSER.

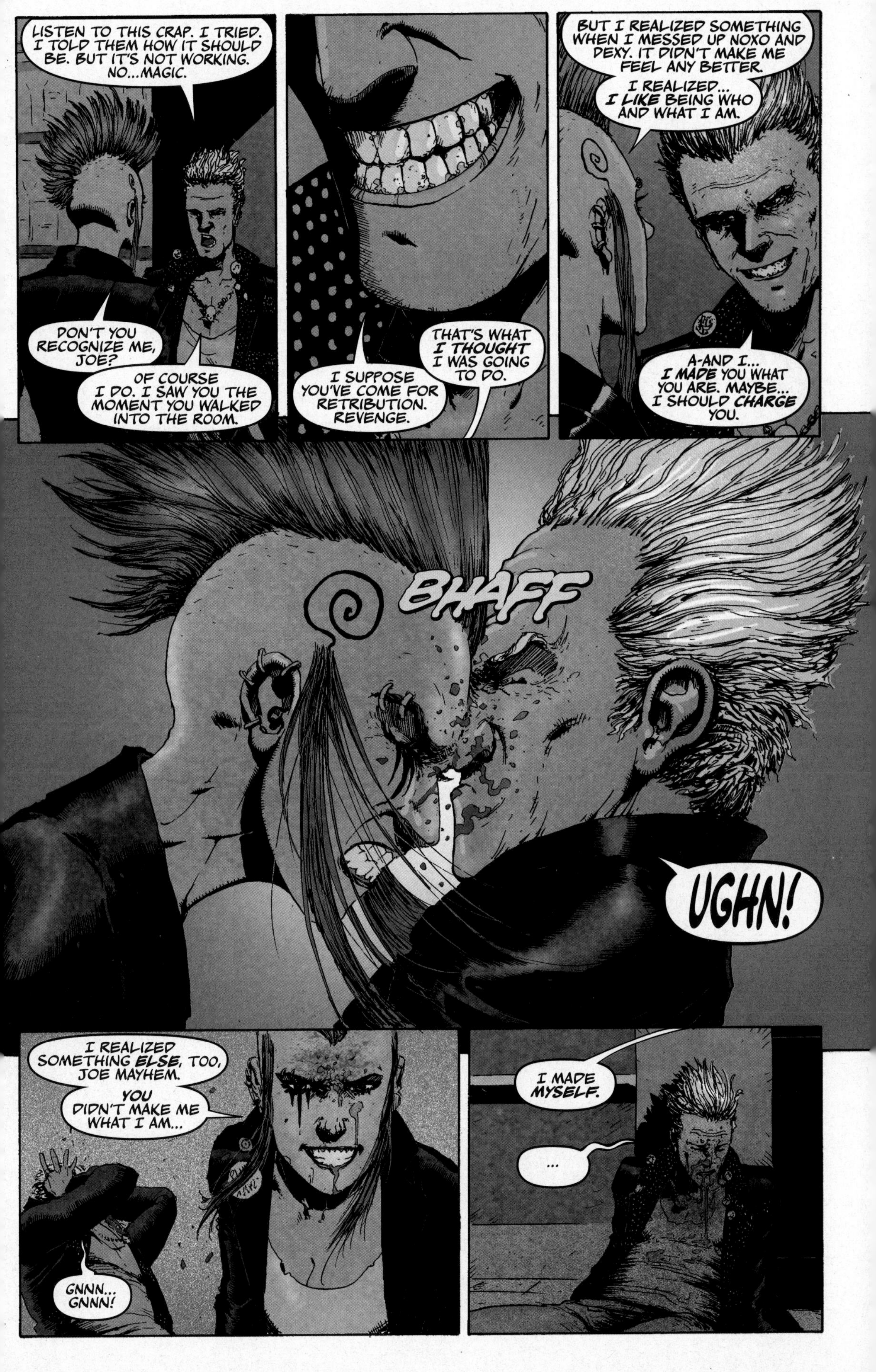
LISTEN TO THIS CRAP. I TRIED. I TOLD THEM HOW IT SHOULD BE. BUT IT'S NOT WORKING. NO...MAGIC.
DON'T YOU RECOGNIZE ME, JOE?
OF COURSE I DO. I SAW YOU THE MOMENT YOU WALKED INTO THE ROOM.
I SUPPOSE YOU'VE COME FOR RETRIBUTION. REVENGE.
THAT'S WHAT I THOUGHT I WAS GOING TO DO.
BUT I REALIZED SOMETHING WHEN I MESSED UP NOXO AND DEXY. IT DIDN'T MAKE ME FEEL ANY BETTER.
I REALIZED... I LIKE BEING WHO AND WHAT I AM.
A-AND I... I MADE YOU WHAT YOU ARE. MAYBE... I SHOULD CHARGE YOU.
BHAFF
UGHN!
I REALIZED SOMETHING ELSE, TOO, JOE MAYHEM.
YOU DIDN'T MAKE ME WHAT I AM...
GNNN... GNNN!
I MADE MYSELF.
...

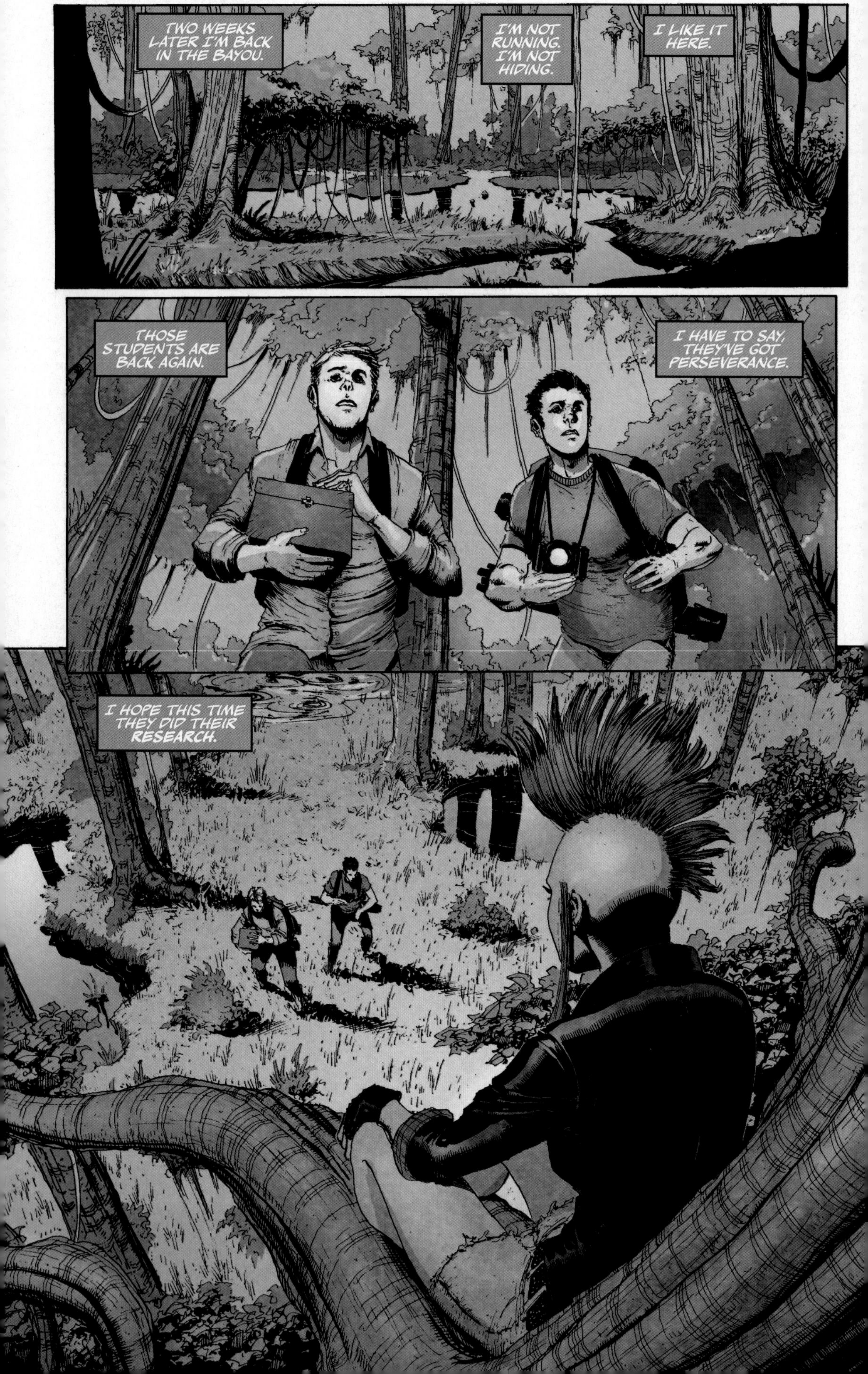

TWO WEEKS LATER I'M BACK IN THE BAYOU.
I'M NOT RUNNING. I'M NOT HIDING.
I LIKE IT HERE.
THOSE STUDENTS ARE BACK AGAIN.
I HAVE TO SAY, THEY'VE GOT PERSEVERANCE.
I HOPE THIS TIME THEY DID THEIR RESEARCH.

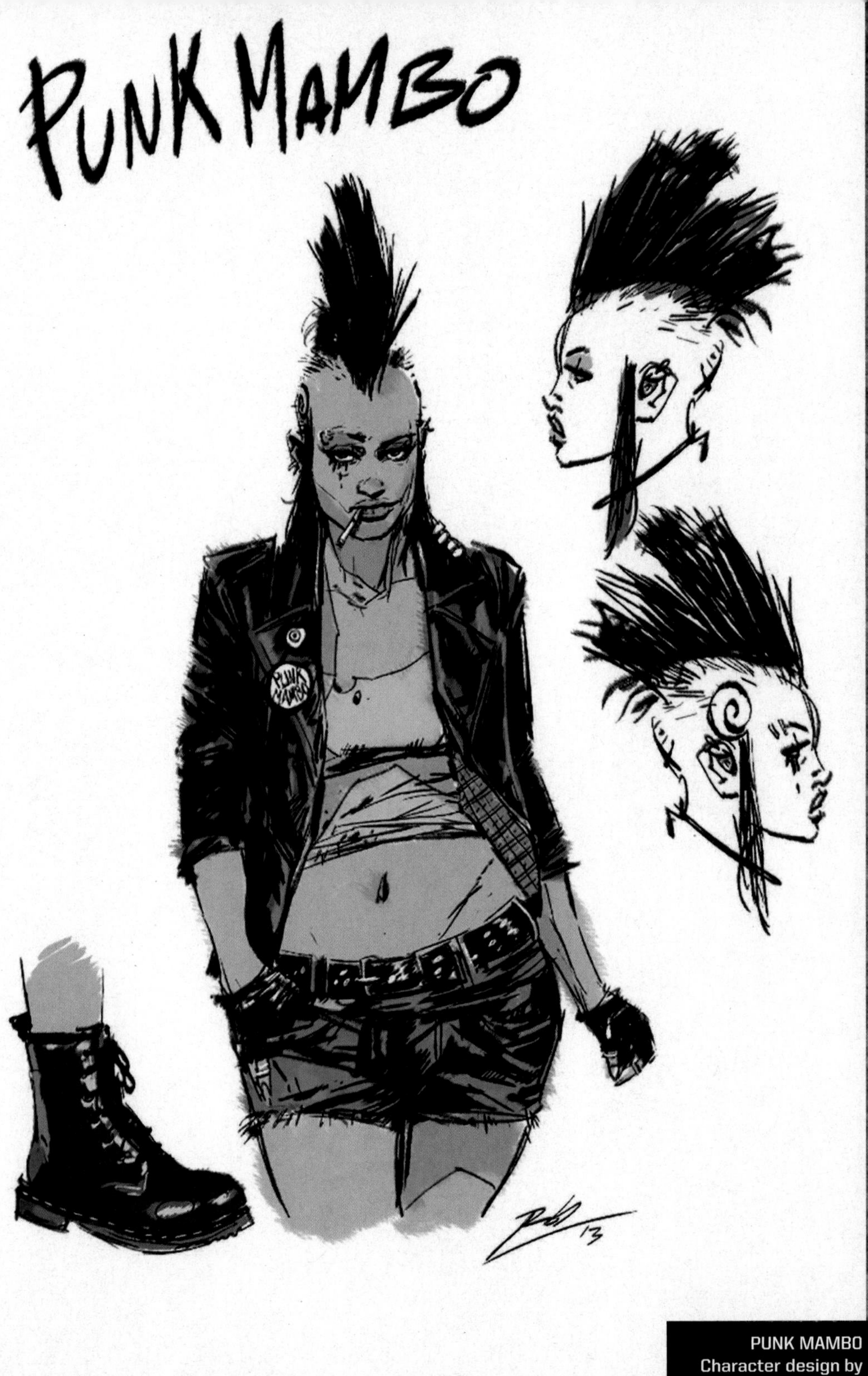
PUNK MAMBO
PUNK MAMBO

PUNK MAMBO
Character design by
ROBERTO DE LA TORRE

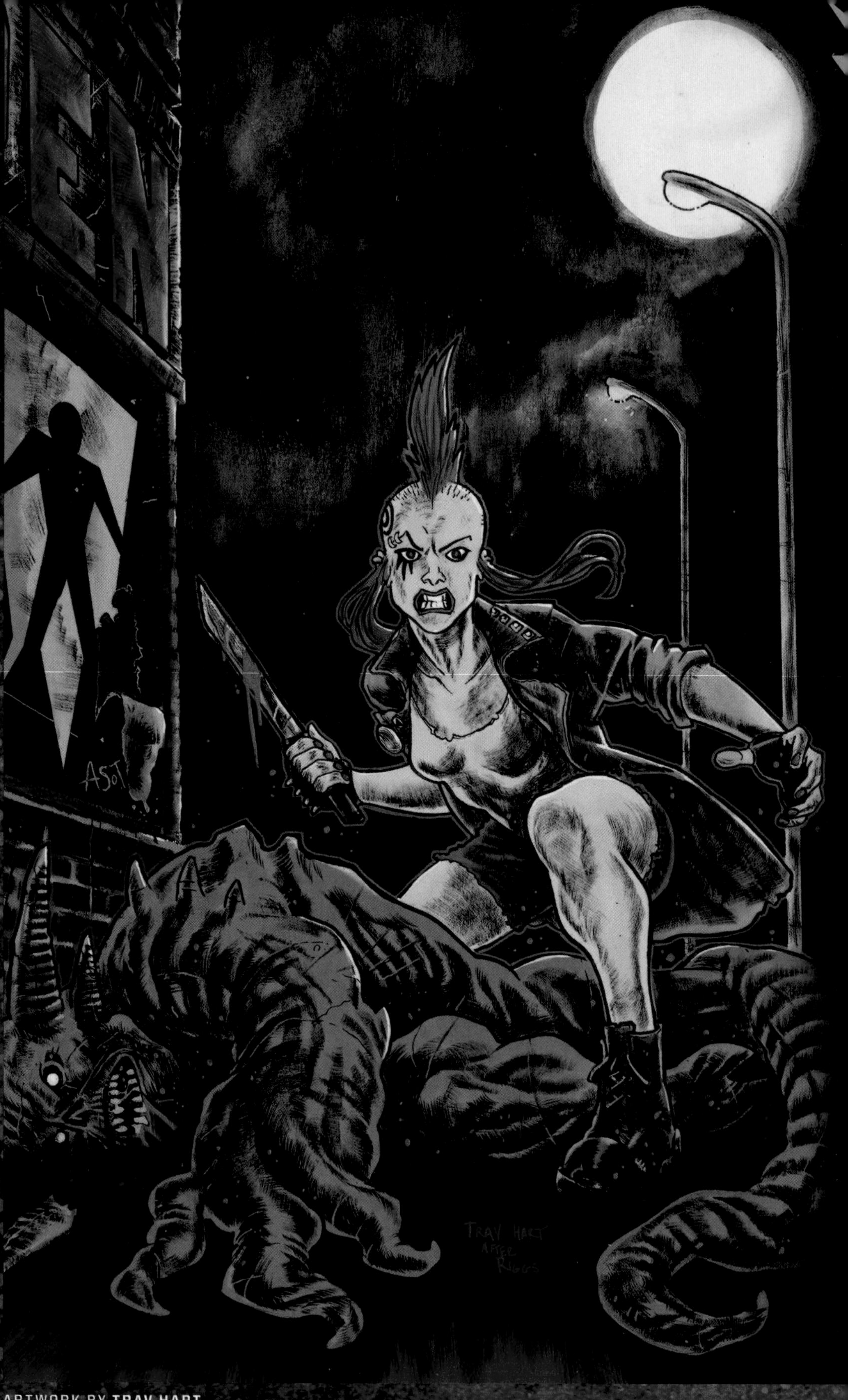
ASoT
TRAV HART
AFTER
RIGGS

ARTWORK BY **TRAV HART**

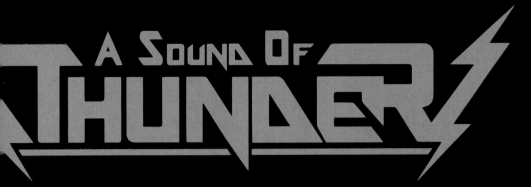

A SOUND OF THUNDER

FREE SONG DOWNLOAD, "PUNK MAMBO"

"Writing 'Punk Mambo' was a fun challenge for the band. From her first appearance it was clear she was going to be a breakout character for Valiant, and we wanted to do her justice. Attempting to pay homage to a punk was not necessarily an easy task for us as a metal band, but we embraced the character's spirit of fun and just went for it!

We knew we had to write something fast but not too complicated. Early Motörhead was a source of inspiration for the verses. To create an eerie, swampy mood, more suited to one of Punk Mambo's voodoo rituals, we veered from the punk sound into a murky, bluesy middle section. The saxophone represents Shadowman and is an homage to the original incarnation of that character. It also adds to the chaotic feel as the song races to its conclusion.

As a final touch we recorded Nina taking a very deep breath, added some heavy effects, and voilà, at the beginning of the song you have Punk Mambo herself inhaling the noxious, gluey fumes from a boiling skull!"

- JOSH SCHWARTZ, GUITARIST

"'That sounds terrible. It's a take.' So said our producer after recording my bass guitar parts for this song. Punk Mambo was written as an intentional piece of chaos on the otherwise fairly structured Tales from the Deadside album. It's gritty and a little obnoxious, just like Punk Mambo herself!"

- JESSE KEEN, BASSIST

"This was one of my favorite songs to write lyrics for and perform, and for that I thank the creators who made such a fun character! This song gave me the opportunity to use some of my more expressive vocals. I got to play around with grit and tone, so I had a great time in the studio recording it!"

- NINA OSEGUEDA, VOCALIST

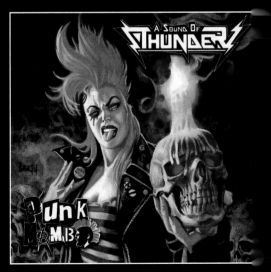

OWNLOAD LINK:
TPS://WWW.ASOUNDOFTHUNDERBAND.COM/VALIANT

A SOUND OF
THUNDER
PUNK
MAMBO

ARTWORK BY DAN BRERET

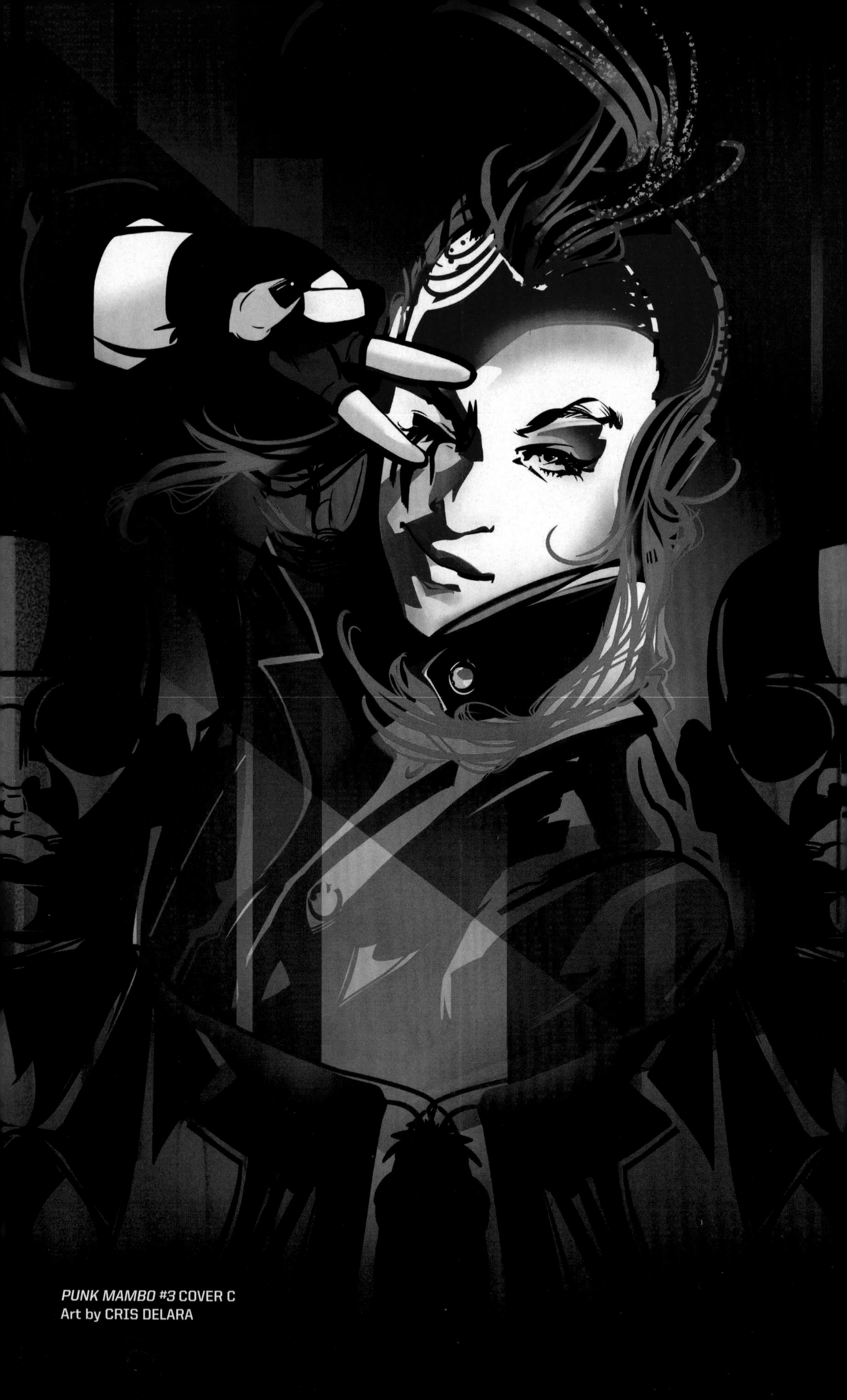

PUNK MAMBO #3 COVER C
Art by CRIS DELARA

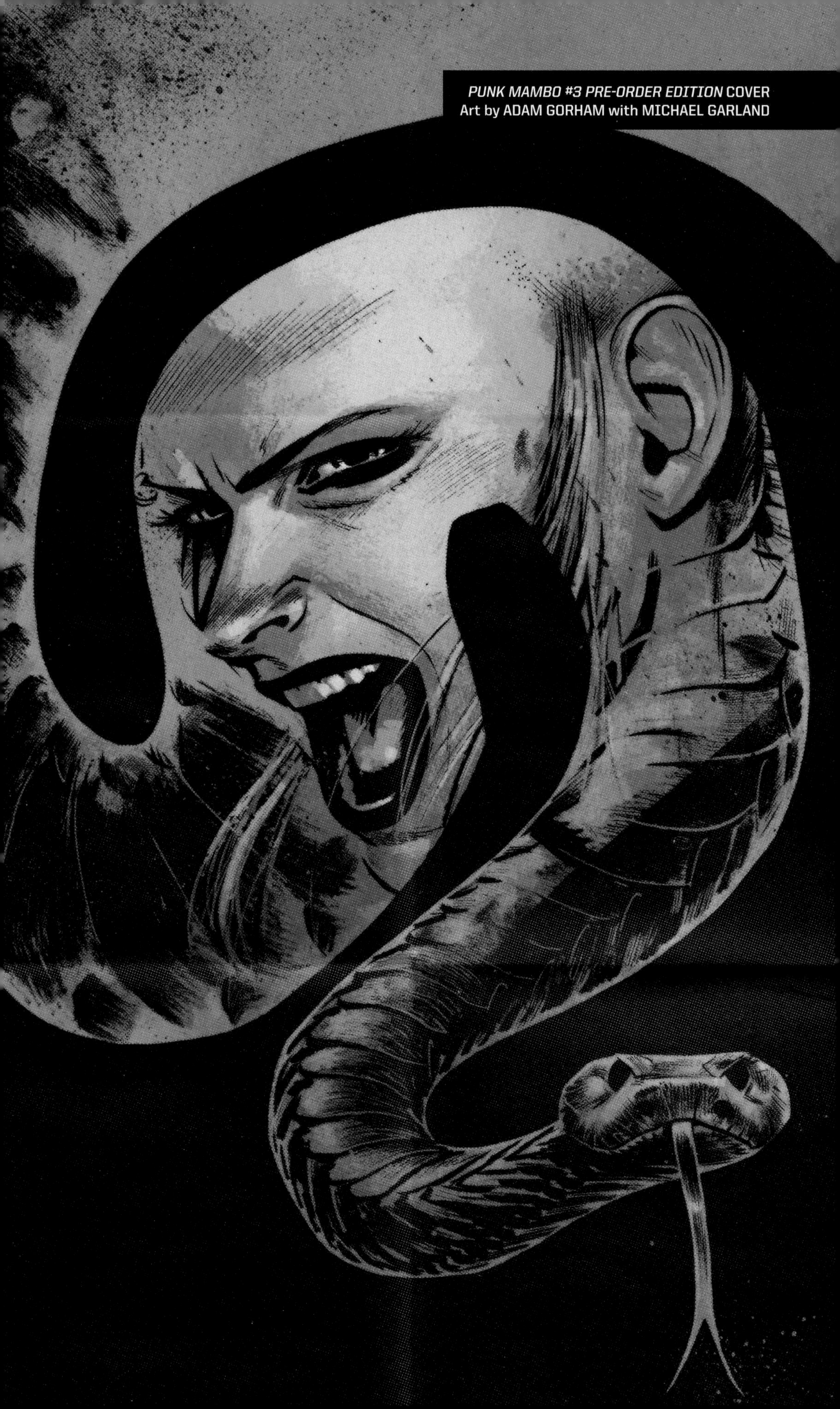

PUNK MAMBO #3 PRE-ORDER EDITION COVER
Art by ADAM GORHAM with MICHAEL GARLAND

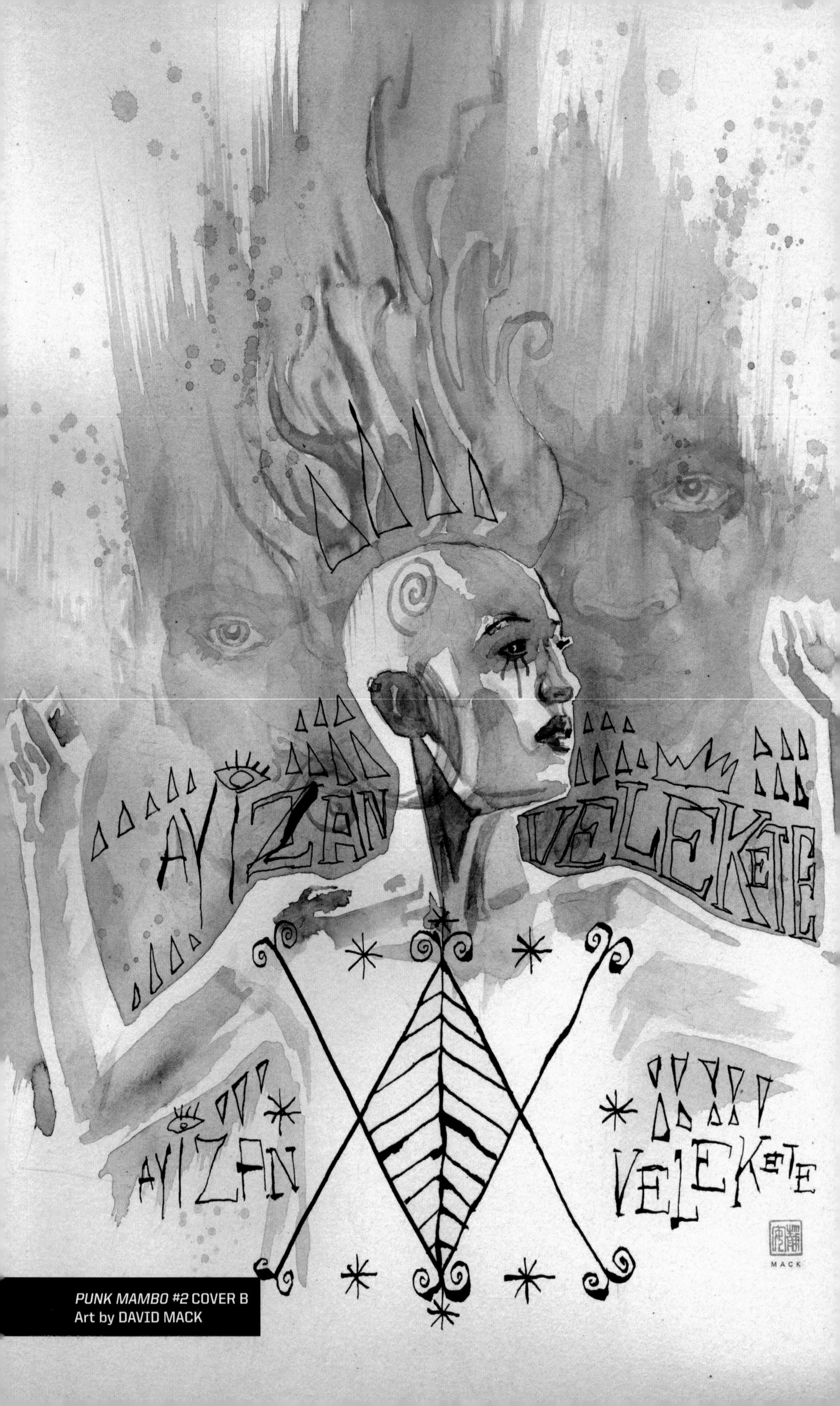
AYIZAN
VELEKETE
AYIZAN
VELEKETE
MACK

PUNK MAMBO #2 COVER B
Art by DAVID MACK

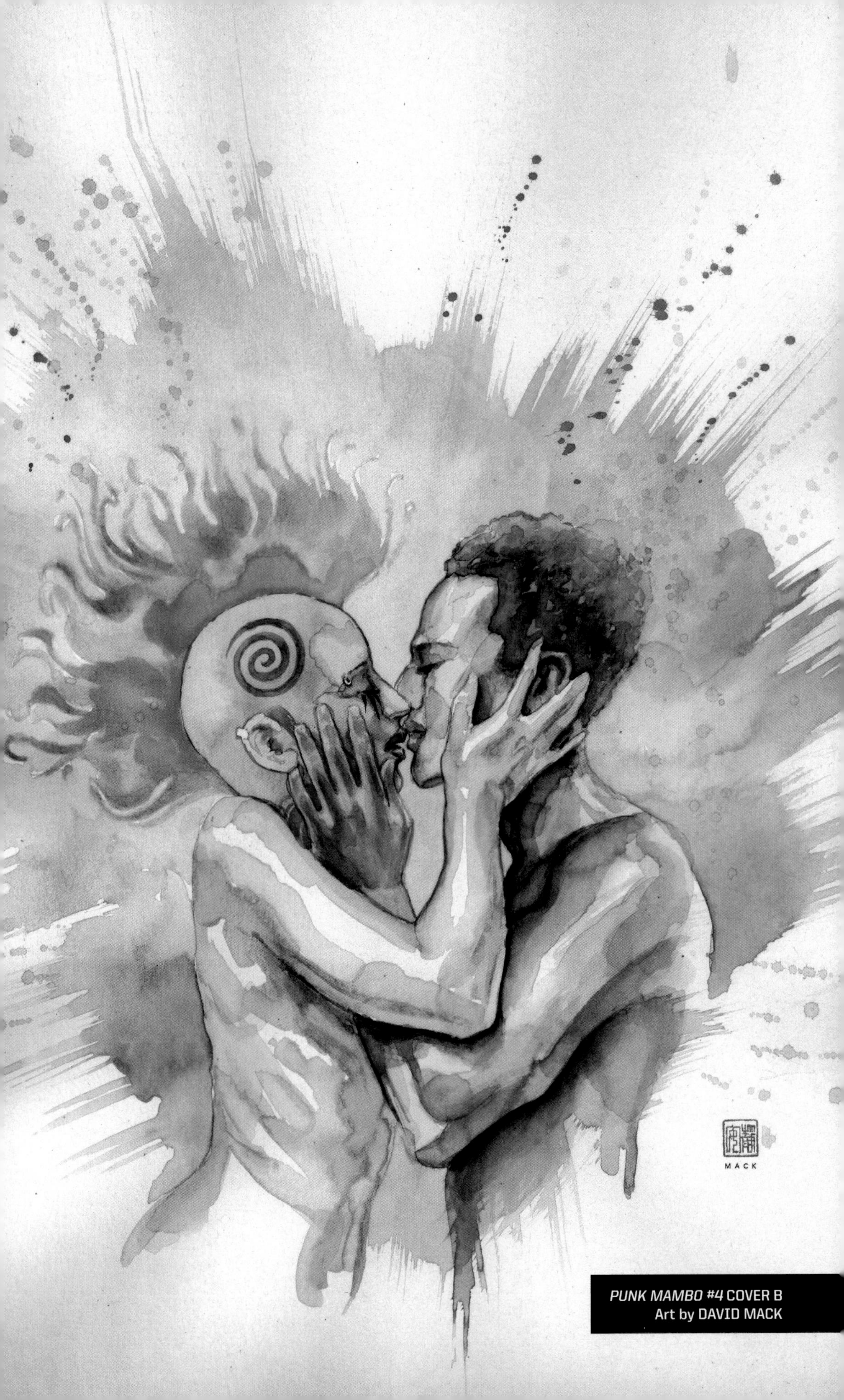
MACK

PUNK MAMBO #4 COVER B
Art by DAVID MACK

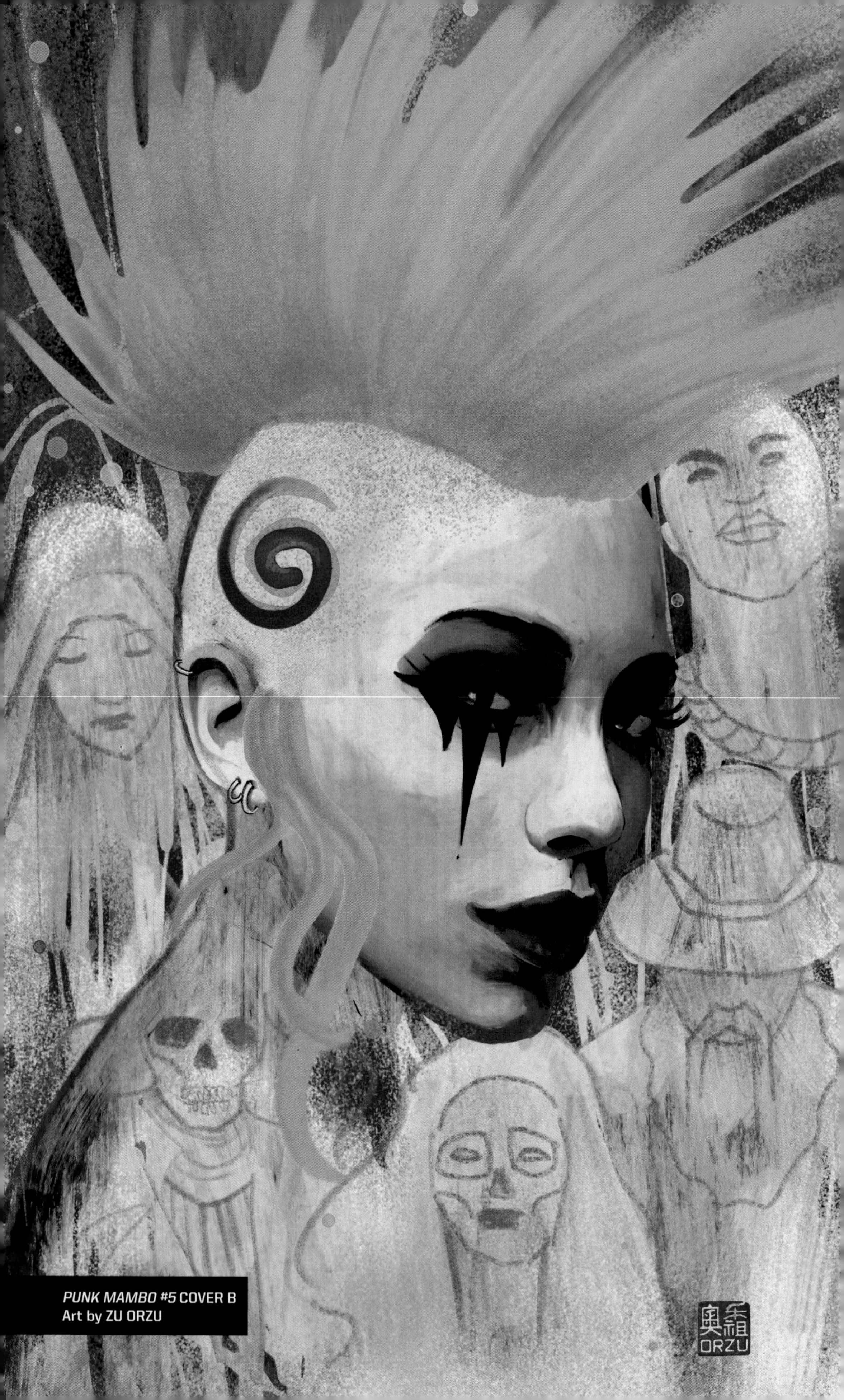
ORZU

PUNK MAMBO #5 COVER B
Art by ZU ORZU

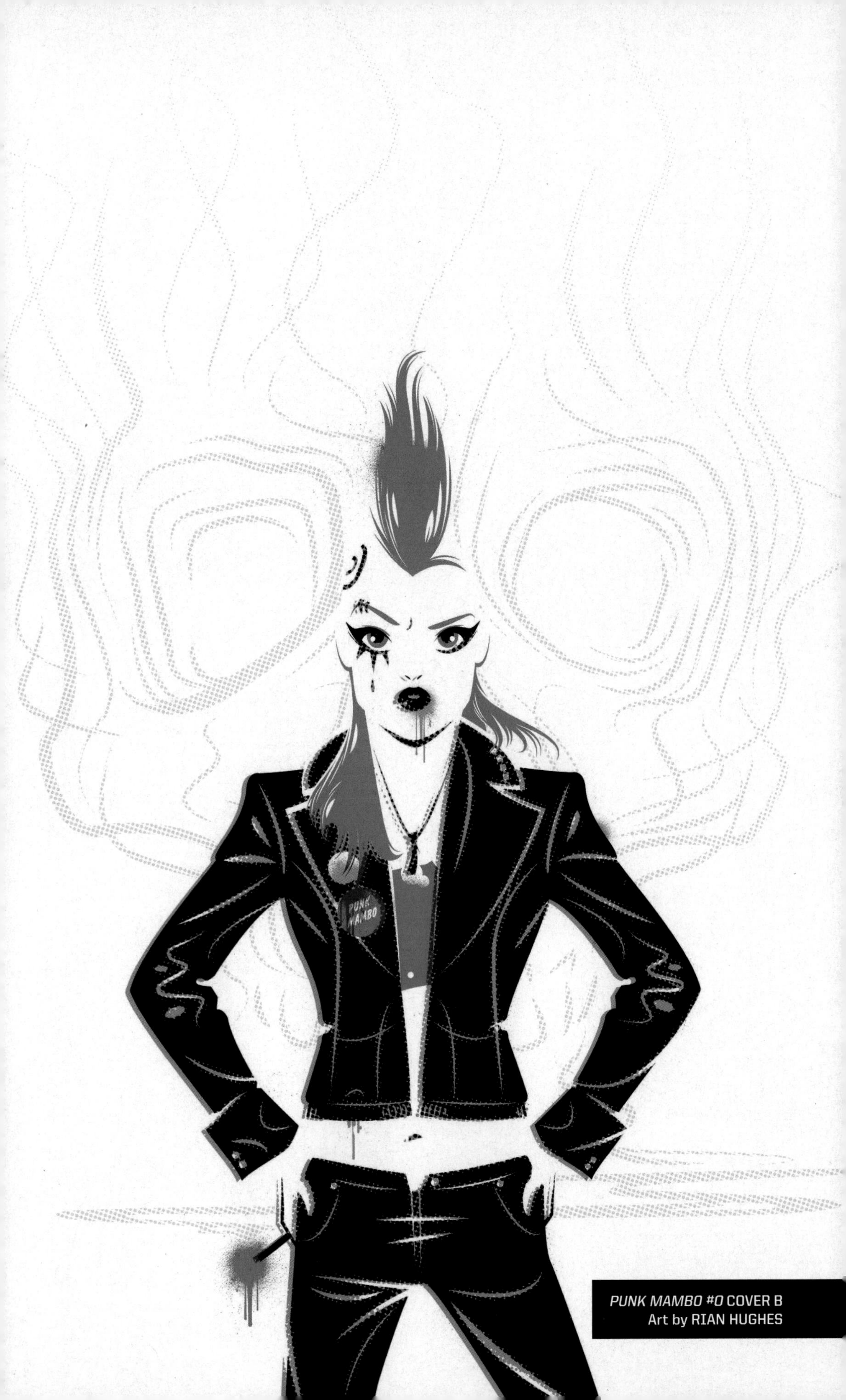
PUNK MAMBO

PUNK MAMBO #0 COVER B
Art by RIAN HUGHES

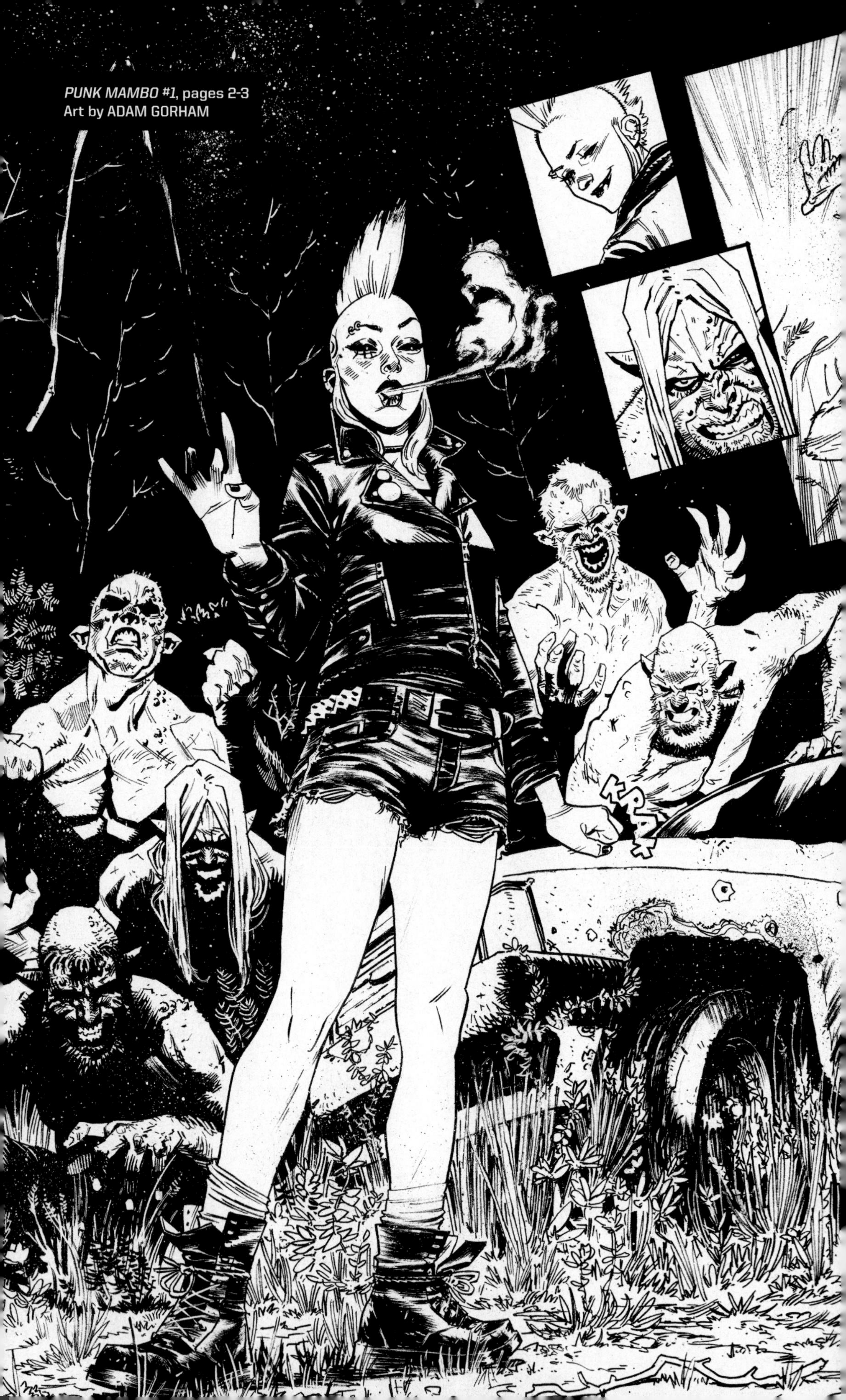
KRAK

PUNK MAMBO #1, pages 2-3
Art by ADAM GORHAM

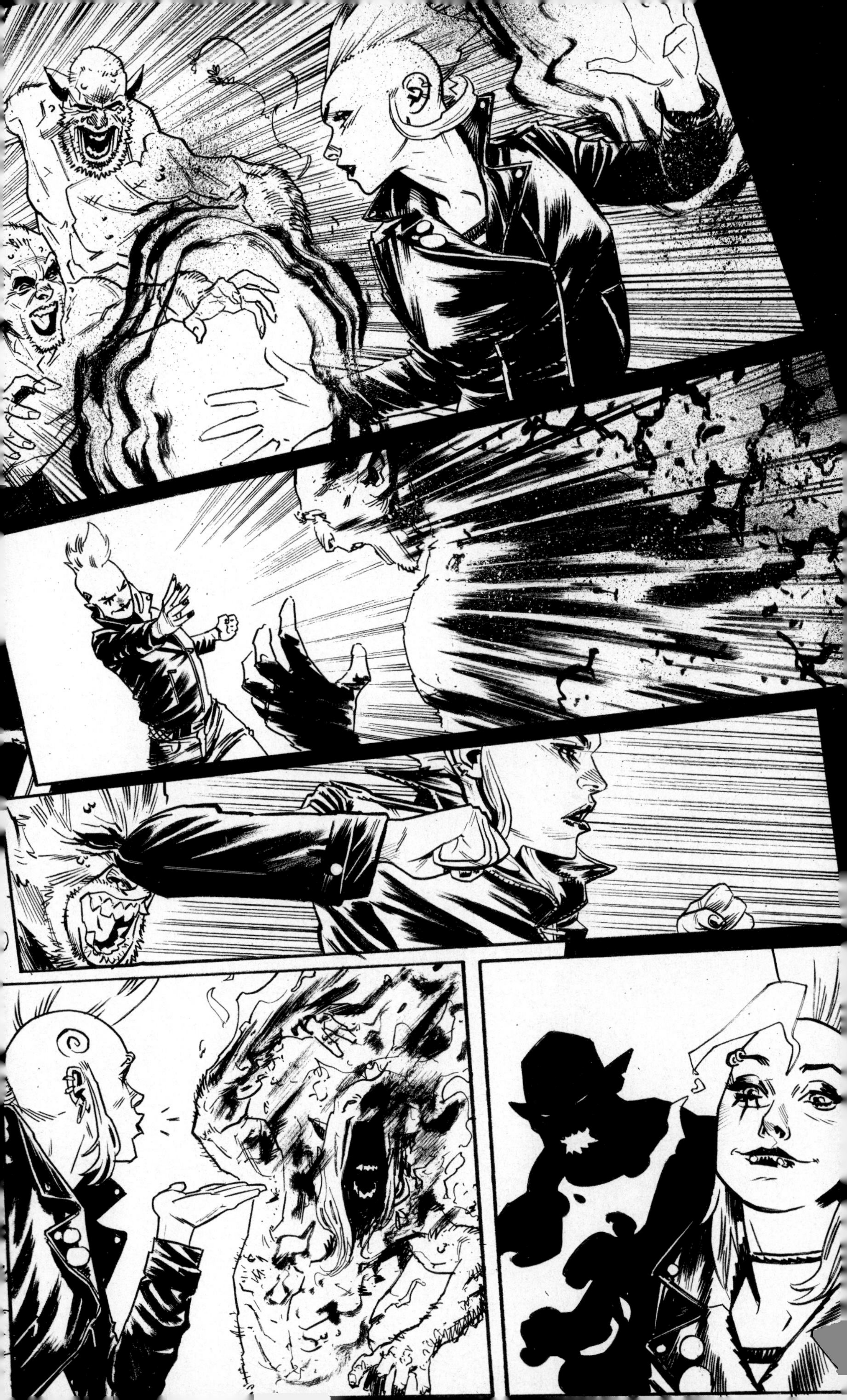

PUNK MAMBO #2, p. 16, 17, and (facing) 18
Art by ADAM GORHAM

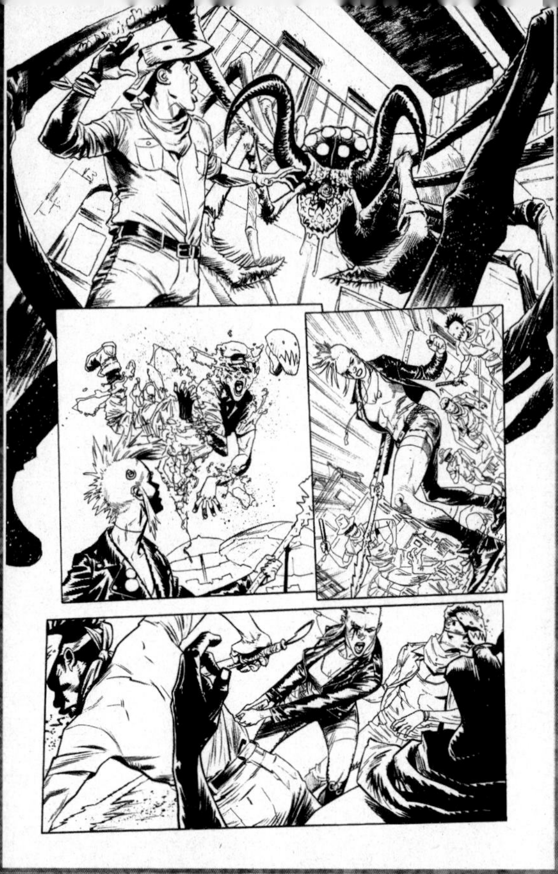

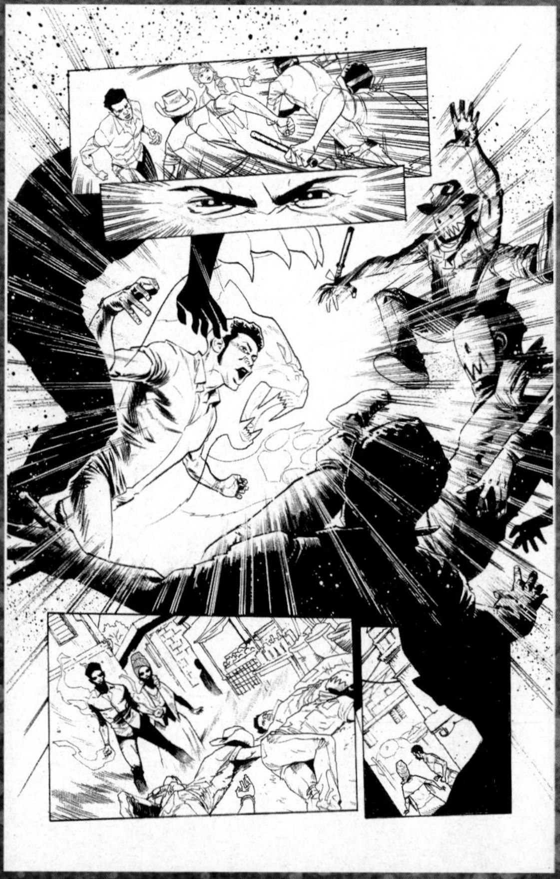

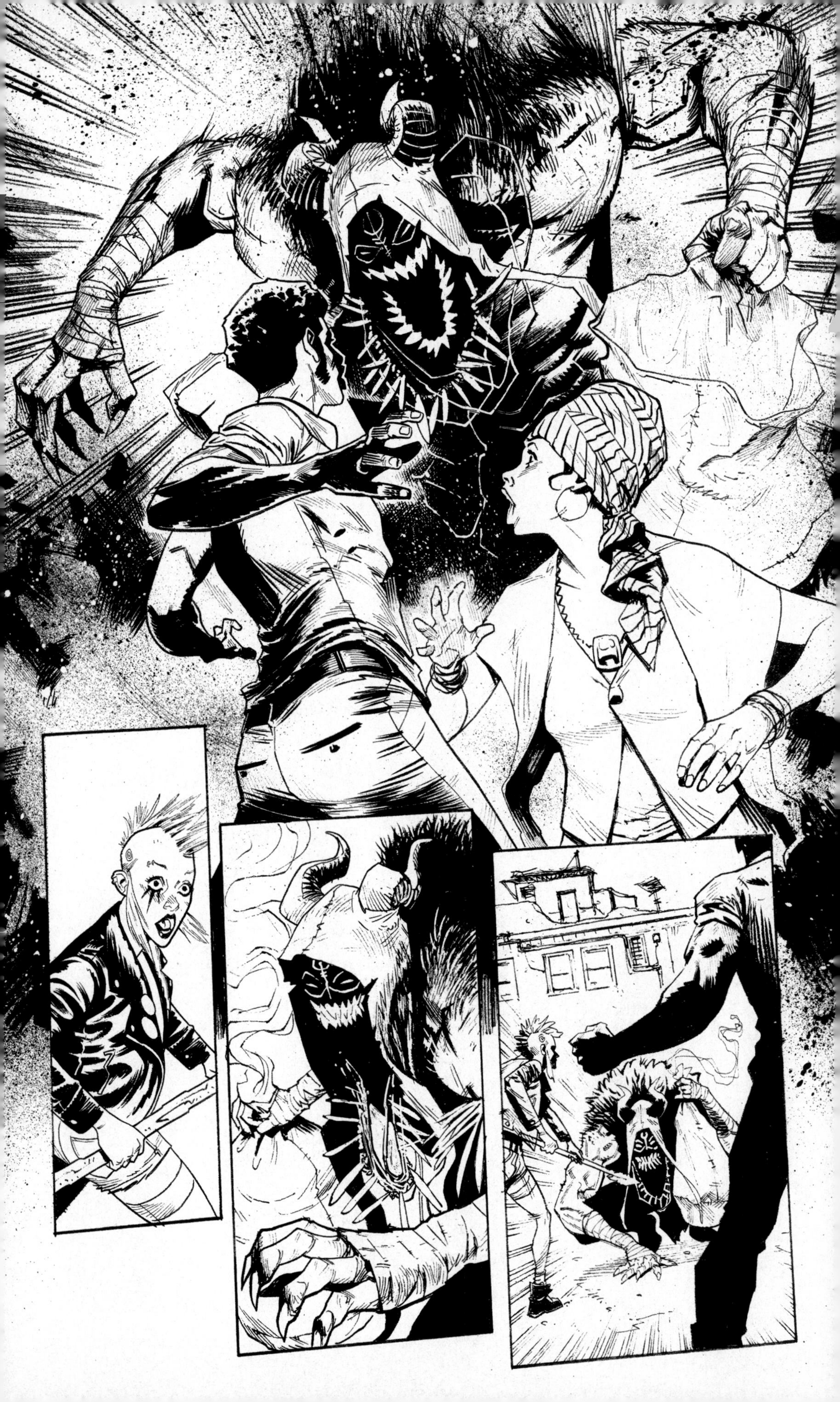

PUNK MAMBO #4, p. 8, 9, and (facing) 10
Art by ADAM GORHAM

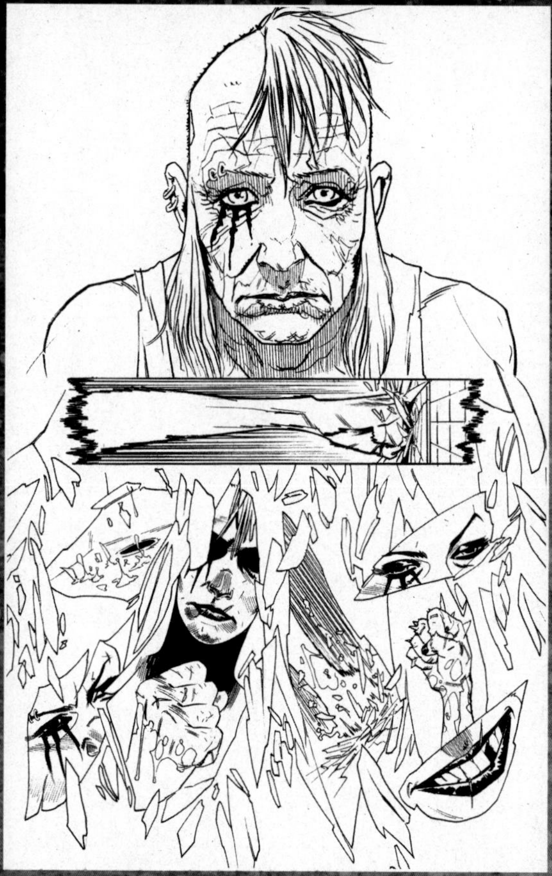

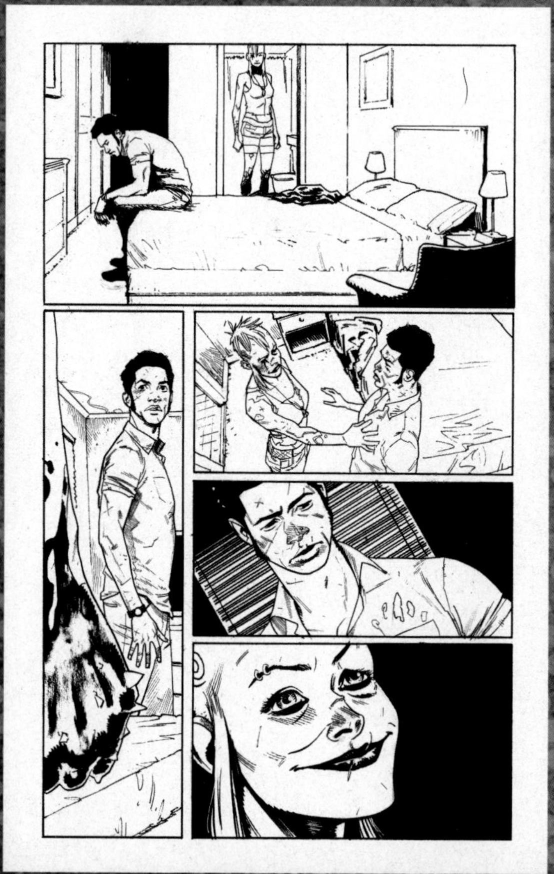

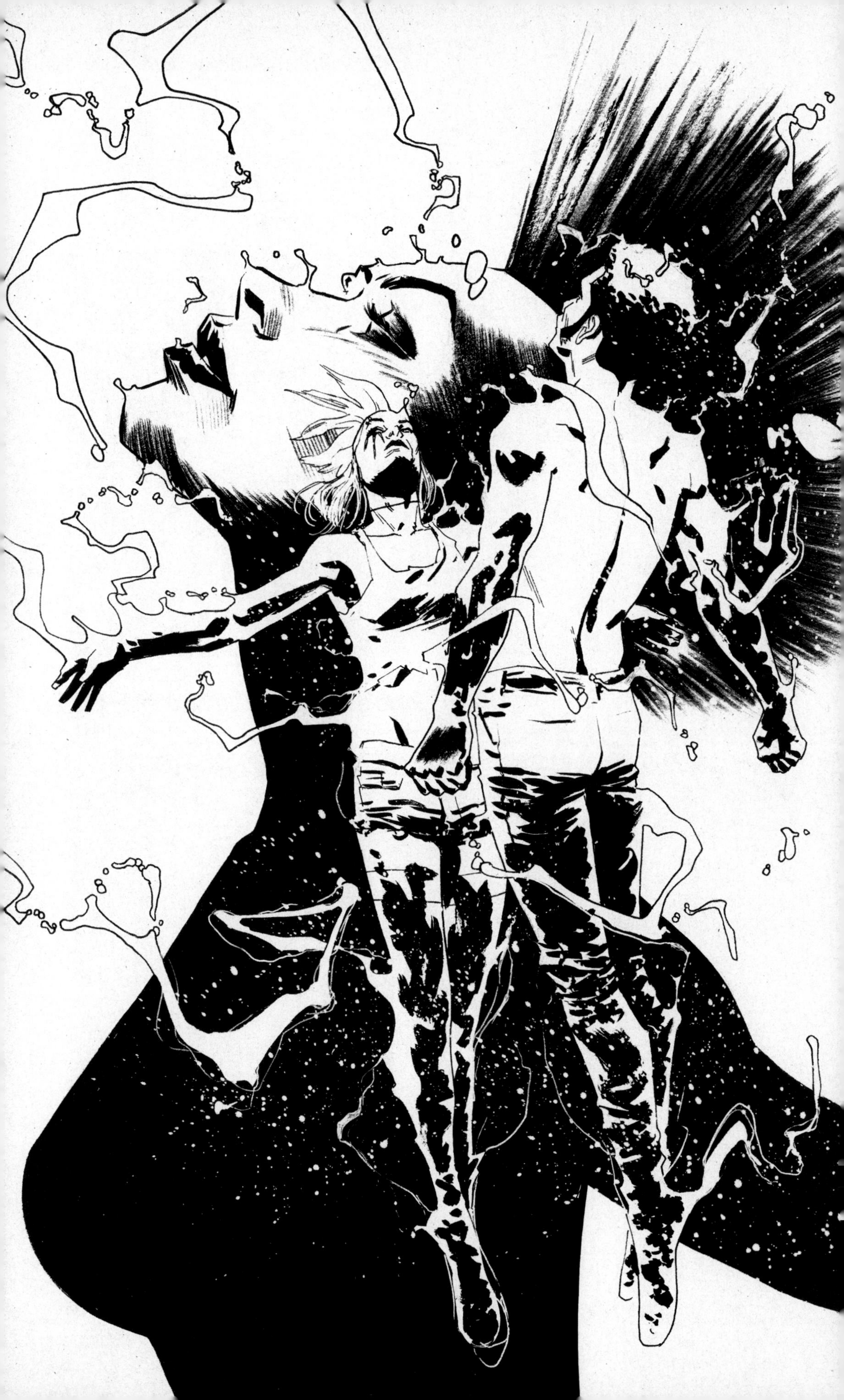

PUNK MAMBO #0, p. 19, 20, and (facing) 21
Art by ROBERT GILL

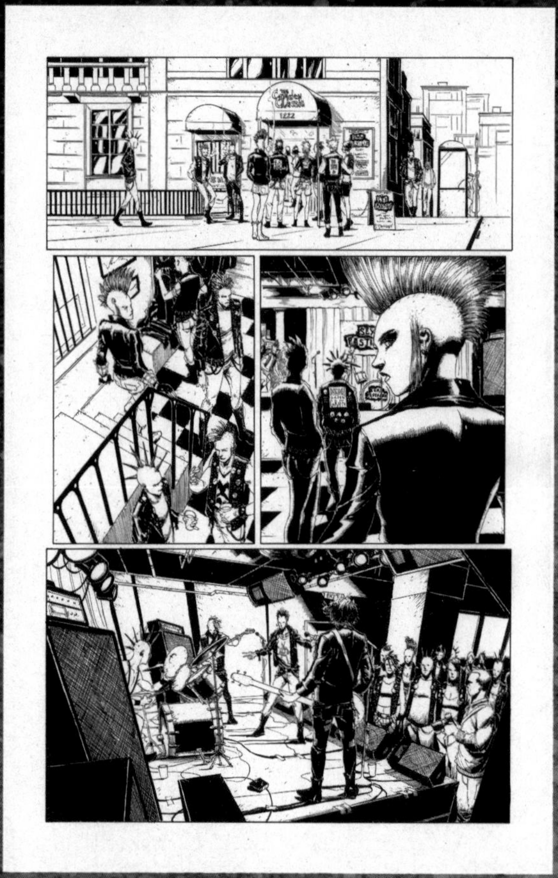

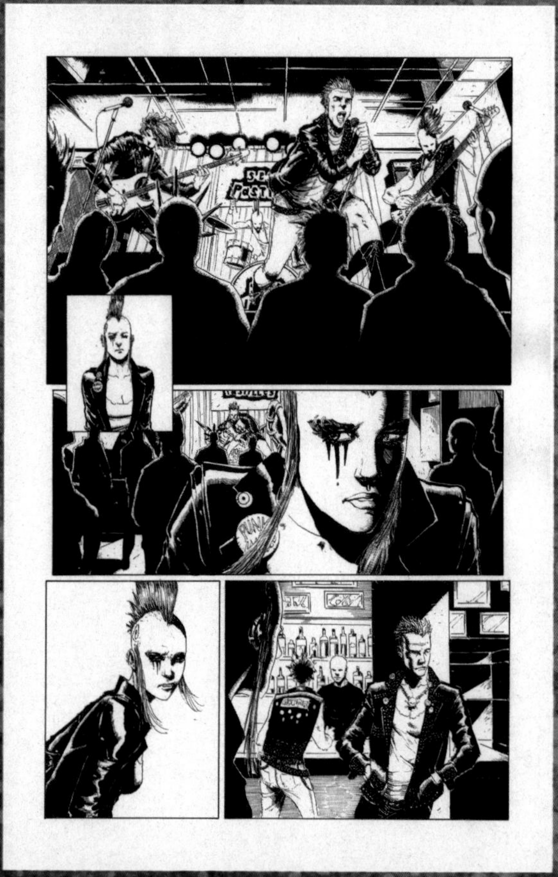

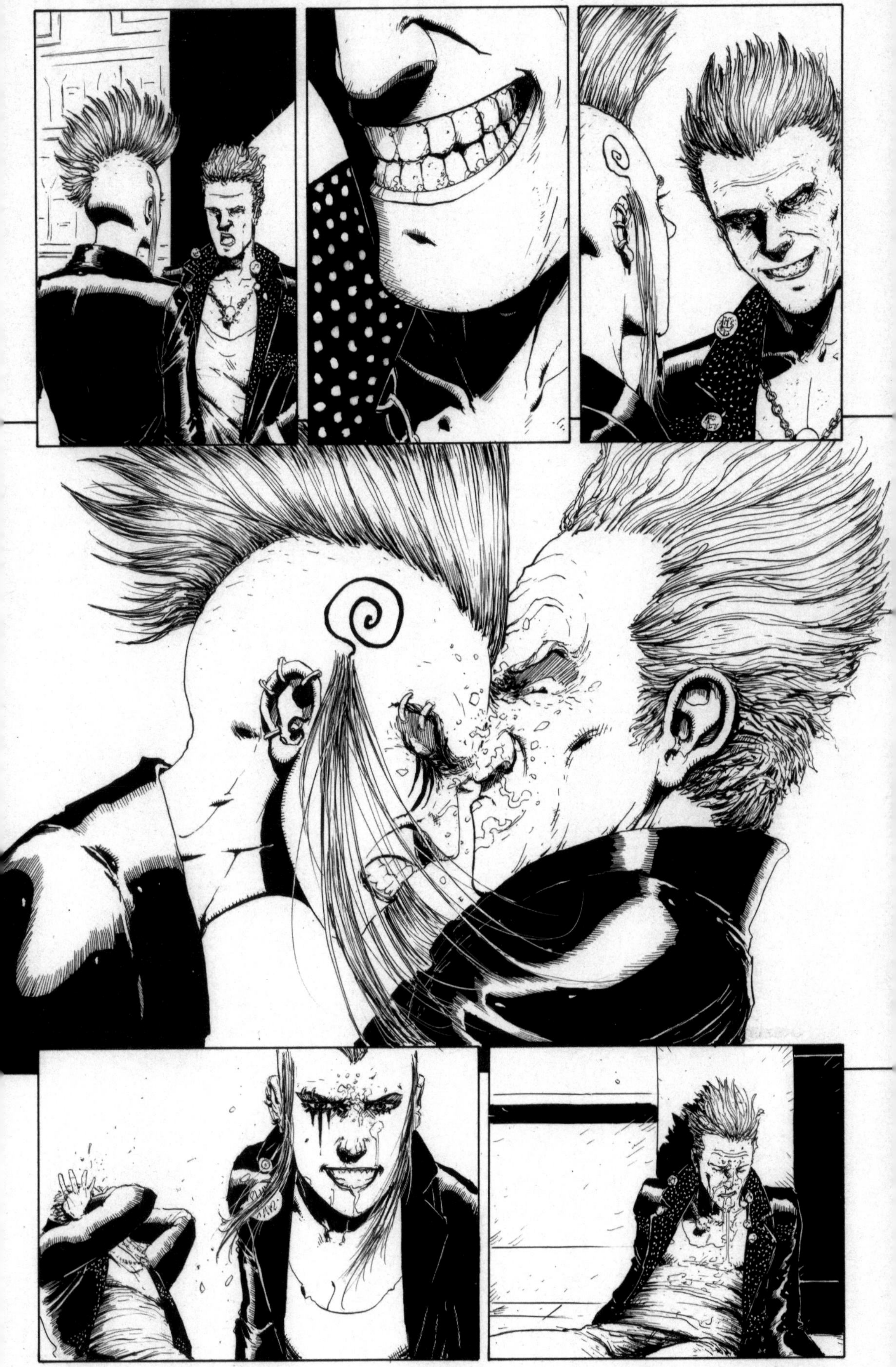

EXPLORE THE VALIANT

ACTION & ADVENTURE

BLOODSHOT SALVATION VOL. 1: THE BOOK
OF REVENGE
ISBN: 978-1-68215-255-3
NINJA-K VOL. 1: THE NINJA FILES
ISBN: 978-1-68215-259-1
SAVAGE
ISBN: 978-1-68215-189-1
WRATH OF THE ETERNAL WARRIOR VOL. 1:
RISEN
RISEN: 978-1-68215-123-5
X-O MANOWAR (2017) VOL. 1: SOLDIER
ISBN: 978-1-68215-205-8

BLOCKBUSTER ADVENTURE

4001 A.D.
ISBN: 978-1-68215-143-3
ARMOR HUNTERS
ISBN: 978-1-939346-45-2
BOOK OF DEATH
ISBN: 978-1-939346-97-1
HARBINGER WARS
ISBN: 978-1-939346-09-4
THE VALIANT
ISBN: 978-1-939346-60-5

COMEDY

A&A: THE ADVENTURES OF ARCHER &
ARMSTRONG VOL. 1: IN THE BAG
ISBN: 978-1-68215-149-5
THE DELINQUENTS
ISBN: 978-1-939346-51-3
QUANTUM AND WOODY! (2017) VOL. 1:
KISS KISS, KLANG KLANG
ISBN: 978-1-68215-269-0